NES

HIGH SCHOOL MATHEMATICS 304

By: Sharon Wynne, M.S.

XAMonline, INC.
Boston

To obtain permission(s) to use the material from this work for any purpose including workshops or seminars, please submit a written request to:

XAMonline, Inc.
21 Orient Avenue
Melrose, MA 02176
Toll Free 1-800-301-4647
Email: info@xamonline.com
Web: www.xamonline.com
Fax: 1-617-583-5552

Library of Congress Cataloging-in-Publication Data

Wynne, Sharon A.
    NES Highschool Mathematics 304 / Sharon A. Wynne. 2nd ed
    ISBN 978-1-60787-622-9
    1. Highschool Mathematics 304
    2. Study Guides
    3. NES
    4. Teachers' Certification & Licensure
    5. Careers

Disclaimer:
The opinions expressed in this publication are the sole works of XAMonline and were created independently from the National Education Association, Educational Testing Service, or any State Department of Education, National Evaluation Systems or other testing affiliates.

Between the time of publication and printing, state specific standards as well as testing formats and Web site information may change and therefore would not be included in part or in whole within this product. Sample test questions are developed by XAMonline and reflect content similar to that on real tests; however, they are not former test questions. XAMonline assembles content that aligns with state standards but makes no claims nor guarantees teacher candidates a passing score. Numerical scores are determined by testing companies such as NES or ETS and then are compared with individual state standards. A passing score varies from state to state.

Printed in the United States of America   œ-1

NES Highschool Mathematics 304
ISBN: 978-1-60787-622-9

Table of Contents

DOMAIN II

DOMAIN III
MEASUREMENT AND GEOMETRY

COMPETENCY 8
UNDERSTAND MEASUREMENT PRINCIPLES AND PROCEDURES

COMPETENCY 9
UNDERSTAND EUCLIDEAN GEOMETRY IN TWO AND THREE DIMENSIONS

COMPETENCY 10
UNDERSTAND COORDINATE AND TRANSFORMATIONAL GEOMETRY

DOMAIN IV
TRIGONOMETRY AND CALCULUS

COMPETENCY 11
UNDERSTAND TRIGONOMETRIC FUNCTIONS

COMPETENCY 16

SAMPLE TEST

NES

HIGH SCHOOL
MATHEMATICS 304

X

SECTION 1
ABOUT XAMONLINE

XAMonline—A Specialty Teacher Certification Company

Created in 1996, XAMonline was the first company to publish study guides for state-specific teacher certification examinations. Founder Sharon Wynne found it frustrating that materials were not available for teacher certification preparation and decided to create the first single, state-specific guide. XAMonline has grown into a company of over 1,800 contributors and writers and offers over 300 titles for the entire PRAXIS series and every state examination. No matter what state you plan on teaching in, XAMonline has a unique teacher certification study guide just for you.

XAMonline—Value and Innovation

We are committed to providing value and innovation. Our print-on-demand technology allows us to be the first in the market to reflect changes in test standards and user feedback as they occur. Our guides are written by experienced teachers who are experts in their fields. And our content reflects the highest standards of quality. Comprehensive practice tests with varied levels of rigor means that your study experience will closely match the actual in-test experience.

To date, XAMonline has helped nearly 600,000 teachers pass their certification or licensing exams. Our commitment to preparation exceeds simply providing the proper material for study—it extends to helping teachers **gain mastery** of the subject matter, giving them the **tools** to become the most effective classroom leaders possible, and ushering today's students toward a **successful future**.

SECTION 2
ABOUT THIS STUDY GUIDE

Purpose of This Guide

Is there a little voice inside of you saying, "Am I ready?" Our goal is to replace that little voice and remove all doubt with a new voice that says, "I AM READY. **Bring it on!**" by offering the highest quality of teacher certification study guides.

Organization of Content

You will see that while every test may start with overlapping general topics, each is very unique in the skills they wish to test. Only XAMonline presents custom content that analyzes deeper than a title, a subarea, or an objective. Only XAMonline presents content and sample test assessments along with **focus statements**, the deepest-level rationale and interpretation of the skills that are unique to the exam.

Title and field number of test

→Each exam has its own name and number. XAMonline's guides are written to give you the content you need to know for the specific exam you are taking. You can be confident when you buy our guide that it contains the information you need to study for the specific test you are taking.

Subareas

→These are the major content categories found on the exam. XAMonline's guides are written to cover all of the subareas found in the test frameworks developed for the exam.

Objectives

→These are standards that are unique to the exam and represent the main subcategories of the subareas/content categories. XAMonline's guides are written to address every specific objective required to pass the exam.

Focus statements

→These are examples and interpretations of the objectives. You find them in parenthesis directly following the objective. They provide detailed examples of the range, type, and level of content that appear on the test questions. **Only XAMonline's guides drill down to this level.**

How Do We Compare with Our Competitors?

XAMonline—drills down to the focus statement level.
CliffsNotes and REA—organized at the objective level
Kaplan—provides only links to content
MoMedia—content not specific to the state test

Each subarea is divided into manageable sections that cover the specific skill areas. Explanations are easy to understand and thorough. You'll find that every test answer contains a rejoinder so if you need a refresher or further review after taking the test, you'll know exactly to which section you must return.

How to Use This Book

Our informal polls show that most people begin studying up to eight weeks prior to the test date, so start early. Then ask yourself some questions: How much do you really know? Are you coming to the test straight from your teacher-education program or are you having to review subjects you haven't considered in ten years? Either way, take a **diagnostic or assessment test** first. Also, spend time on sample tests so that you become accustomed to the way the actual test will appear.

This guide comes with an online diagnostic test of 30 questions found online at *www.XAMonline.com*. It is a little boot camp to get you up for the task and reveal things about your compendium of knowledge in general. Although this guide is structured to follow the order of the test, you are not required to study in that order. By finding a time-management and study plan that fits your life you will be more effective. The results of your diagnostic or self-assessment test can be a guide for how to manage your time and point you toward an area that needs more attention.

After taking the diagnostic exam, fill out the **Personalized Study Plan** page at the beginning of each chapter. Review the competencies and skills covered in that chapter and check the boxes that apply to your study needs. If there are sections you already know you can skip, check the "skip it" box. Taking this step will give you a study plan for each chapter.

Week	Activity
8 weeks prior to test	Take a diagnostic test found at www.XAMonline.com
7 weeks prior to test	Build your Personalized Study Plan for each chapter. Check the "skip it" box for sections you feel you are already strong in. ✗ SKIP IT ☐
6-3 weeks prior to test	For each of these four weeks, choose a content area to study. You don't have to go in the order of the book. It may be that you start with the content that needs the most review. Alternately, you may want to ease yourself into plan by starting with the most familiar material.
2 weeks prior to test	Take the sample test, score it, and create a review plan for the final week before the test.
1 week prior to test	Following your plan (which will likely be aligned with the areas that need the most review) go back and study the sections that align with the questions you may have gotten wrong. Then go back and study the sections related to the questions you answered correctly. If need be, create flashcards and drill yourself on any area that you makes you anxious.

SECTION 3
ABOUT THE NES MATHEMATICS 304 EXAM

What Is the NES Mathematics 304 Exam?

The NES Mathematics 304 exam is meant to assess mastery of the basic skills required to teach high school students mathematics. It is administered by Pearson Education.

Often your own state's requirements determine whether or not you should take any particular test. The most reliable source of information regarding this is your state's Department of Education. This resource should have a complete list of testing centers and dates. Test dates vary by subject area and not all test dates necessarily include your particular test, so be sure to check carefully.

If you are in a teacher-education program, check with the Education Department or the Certification Officer for specific information for testing and testing time-lines. The Certification Office should have most of the information you need.

If you choose an alternative route to certification you can either rely on our website at *www.XAMonline.com* or on the resources provided by an alternative certification program. Many states now have specific agencies devoted to alternative certification and there are some national organizations as well, for example:

National Association for Alternative Certification
http://www.alt-teachercert.org/index.asp

Interpreting Test Results

Follow the guidelines provided by Pearson for interpreting your score. Scores are available two weeks after the test date for multiple choice tests and 4 weeks after the test date for tests with constructed response essays. Scores will be sent to you and your chosen institution(s).

What's on the Test?

The NES Mathematics 304 exam lasts up to 3 hours and 15 minutes and consists of 150 multiple-choice questions. The breakdown of the questions is as follows:

Category	Approximate Percentage of the Test
I: Mathematical Processes and Number Sense	19%
II: Patterns, Algebra, and Functions	24%
III: Measurement and Geometry	19%
IV: Trigonometry and Calculus	19%
V: Statistics, Probability, and Discrete Mathematics	19%

Question Types

You're probably thinking, enough already, I want to study! Indulge us a little longer while we explain that there is actually more than one type of multiple-choice question. You can thank us later after you realize how well prepared you are for your exam.

1. **Complete the Statement.** The name says it all. In this question type you'll be asked to choose the correct completion of a given statement. For example:

> The Dolch Basic Sight Words consist of a relatively short list of words that children should be able to:
>
> A. Sound out
>
> B. Know the meaning of
>
> C. Recognize on sight
>
> D. Use in a sentence

The correct answer is C. In order to check your answer, test out the statement by adding the choices to the end of it.

2. **Which of the Following.** One way to test your answer choice for this type of question is to replace the phrase "which of the following" with your selection. Use this example:

> **Which of the following words is one of the twelve most frequently used in children's reading texts:**
>
> A. There
>
> B. This
>
> C. The
>
> D. An

Don't look! Test your answer. _____ is one of the twelve most frequently used in children's reading texts. Did you guess C? Then you guessed correctly.

3. **Roman Numeral Choices.** This question type is used when there is more than one possible correct answer. For example:

> **Which of the following two arguments accurately supports the use of cooperative learning as an effective method of instruction?**
> I.   Cooperative learning groups facilitate healthy competition between individuals in the group.
> II. Cooperative learning groups allow academic achievers to carry or cover for academic underachievers.
> III. Cooperative learning groups make each student in the group accountable for the success of the group.
> IV. Cooperative learning groups make it possible for students to reward other group members for achieving.
>
> A. I and II
>
> B. II and III
>
> C. I and III
>
> D. III and IV

Notice that the question states there are **two** possible answers. It's best to read all the possibilities first before looking at the answer choices. In this case, the correct answer is D.

4. **Negative Questions.** This type of question contains words such as "not," "least," and "except." Each correct answer will be the statement that does **not** fit the situation described in the question. Such as:

> **Multicultural education is not**
>
> A. An idea or concept
>
> B. A "tack-on" to the school curriculum
>
> C. An educational reform movement
>
> D. A process

Think to yourself that the statement could be anything but the correct answer. This question form is more open to interpretation than other types, so read carefully and don't forget that you're answering a negative statement.

5. **Questions that Include Graphs, Tables, or Reading Passages.** As always, read the question carefully. It likely asks for a very specific answer and not a broad interpretation of the visual. Here is a simple (though not statistically accurate) example of a graph question:

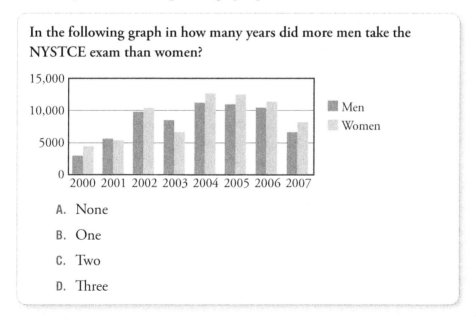

> **In the following graph in how many years did more men take the NYSTCE exam than women?**
>
> A. None
>
> B. One
>
> C. Two
>
> D. Three

It may help you to simply circle the two years that answer the question. Make sure you've read the question thoroughly and once you've made your determination, double check your work. The correct answer is C.

SECTION 4

HELPFUL HINTS

Study Tips

1. **You are what you eat.** Certain foods aid the learning process by releasing natural memory enhancers called CCKs (cholecystokinin) composed of tryptophan, choline, and phenylalanine. All of these chemicals enhance the neurotransmitters associated with memory and certain foods release memory enhancing chemicals. A light meal or snacks of one of the following foods fall into this category:

   • Milk   • Rice   • Eggs   • Fish

   • Nuts and seeds   • Oats   • Turkey

   The better the connections, the more you comprehend!

2. **See the forest for the trees.** In other words, get the concept before you look at the details. One way to do this is to take notes as you read, paraphrasing or summarizing in your own words. Putting the concept in terms that are comfortable and familiar may increase retention.

3. **Question authority.** Ask why, why, why? Pull apart written material paragraph by paragraph and don't forget the captions under the illustrations. For example, if a heading reads *Stream Erosion* put it in the form of a question (Why do streams erode? What is stream erosion?) then find the answer within the material. If you train your mind to think in this manner you will learn more and prepare yourself for answering test questions.

4. **Play mind games.** Using your brain for reading or puzzles keeps it flexible. Even with a limited amount of time your brain can take in data (much like a computer) and store it for later use. In ten minutes you can: read two paragraphs (at least), quiz yourself with flash cards, or review notes. Even if you don't fully understand something on the first pass, your mind stores it for recall, which is why frequent reading or review increases chances of retention and comprehension.

5. **The pen is mightier than the sword.** Learn to take great notes. A by-product of our modern culture is that we have grown accustomed to getting our information in short doses. We've subconsciously trained ourselves to assimilate information into neat little packages. Messy notes fragment the flow of information. Your notes can be much clearer with proper formatting. *The Cornell Method* is one such format. This method was popularized in *How to Study in College*, Ninth Edition, by Walter Pauk. You can benefit from the method without purchasing an additional book by simply looking up the method online. Below is a sample of how *The Cornell Method* can be adapted for use with this guide.

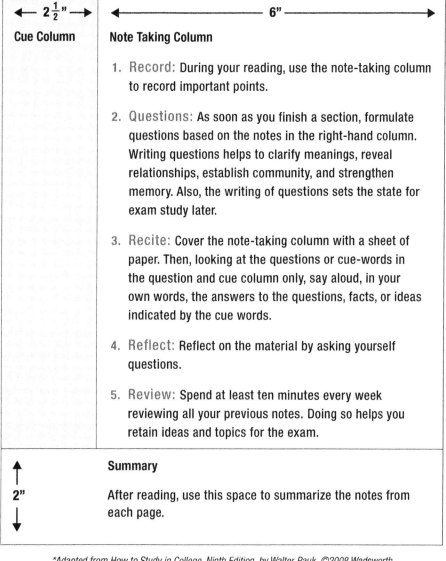

← $2\frac{1}{2}$" →	← 6" →
Cue Column	**Note Taking Column**
	1. Record: During your reading, use the note-taking column to record important points.
	2. Questions: As soon as you finish a section, formulate questions based on the notes in the right-hand column. Writing questions helps to clarify meanings, reveal relationships, establish community, and strengthen memory. Also, the writing of questions sets the state for exam study later.
	3. Recite: Cover the note-taking column with a sheet of paper. Then, looking at the questions or cue-words in the question and cue column only, say aloud, in your own words, the answers to the questions, facts, or ideas indicated by the cue words.
	4. Reflect: Reflect on the material by asking yourself questions.
	5. Review: Spend at least ten minutes every week reviewing all your previous notes. Doing so helps you retain ideas and topics for the exam.
↑ 2" ↓	**Summary** After reading, use this space to summarize the notes from each page.

Adapted from How to Study in College, Ninth Edition, by Walter Pauk, ©2008 Wadsworth

6. **Place yourself in exile and set the mood.** Set aside a particular place and time to study that best suits your personal needs and biorhythms. If you're a night person, burn the midnight oil. If you're a morning person set yourself up with some coffee and get to it. Make your study time and place as free from distraction as possible and surround yourself with what you need, be it silence or music. Studies have shown that music can aid in concentration, absorption, and retrieval of information. Not all music, though. Classical music is said to work best

7. **Get pointed in the right direction.** Use arrows to point to important passages or pieces of information. It's easier to read than a page full of yellow highlights. Highlighting can be used sparingly, but add an arrow to the margin to call attention to it.

8. **Check your budget.** You should at least review all the content material before your test, but allocate the most amount of time to the areas that need the most refreshing. It sounds obvious, but it's easy to forget. You can use the study rubric above to balance your study budget.

The proctor will write the start time where it can be seen and then, later, provide the time remaining, typically fifteen minutes before the end of the test.

Testing Tips

1. **Get smart, play dumb.** Sometimes a question is just a question. No one is out to trick you, so don't assume that the test writer is looking for something other than what was asked. Stick to the question as written and don't overanalyze.

2. **Do a double take.** Read test questions and answer choices at least twice because it's easy to miss something, to transpose a word or some letters. If you have no idea what the correct answer is, skip it and come back later if there's time. If you're still clueless, it's okay to guess. Remember, you're scored on the number of questions you answer correctly and you're not penalized for wrong answers. The worst case scenario is that you miss a point from a good guess.

3. **Turn it on its ear.** The syntax of a question can often provide a clue, so make things interesting and turn the question into a statement to see if it changes the meaning or relates better (or worse) to the answer choices.

4. **Get out your magnifying glass.** Look for hidden clues in the questions because it's difficult to write a multiple-choice question without giving away part of the answer in the options presented. In most questions you can readily eliminate one or two potential answers, increasing your chances of answering correctly to 50/50, which will help out if you've skipped a question and gone back to it (see tip #2).

5. **Call it intuition.** Often your first instinct is correct. If you've been studying the content you've likely absorbed something and have subconsciously retained the knowledge. On questions you're not sure about trust your instincts because a first impression is usually correct.

6. **Graffiti.** Sometimes it's a good idea to mark your answers directly on the test booklet and go back to fill in the optical scan sheet later. You don't get extra points for perfectly blackened ovals. If you choose to manage your test this way, be sure not to mismark your answers when you transcribe to the scan sheet.

7. **Become a clock-watcher.** You have a set amount of time to answer the questions. Don't get bogged down laboring over a question you're not sure about when there are ten others you could answer more readily. If you choose to follow the advice of tip #6, be sure you leave time near the end to go back and fill in the scan sheet.

Do the Drill

No matter how prepared you feel it's sometimes a good idea to apply Murphy's Law. So the following tips might seem silly, mundane, or obvious, but we're including them anyway.

1. **Remember, you are what you eat, so bring a snack.** Choose from the list of energizing foods that appear earlier in the introduction.

2. **You're not too sexy for your test.** Wear comfortable clothes. You'll be distracted if your belt is too tight or if you're too cold or too hot.

3. **Lie to yourself.** Even if you think you're a prompt person, pretend you're not and leave plenty of time to get to the testing center. Map it out ahead of time and do a dry run if you have to. There's no need to add road rage to your list of anxieties.

4. **Bring sharp number 2 pencils.** It may seem impossible to forget this need from your school days, but you might. And make sure the erasers are intact, too.

5. **No ticket, no test.** Bring your admission ticket as well as **two** forms of identification, including one with a picture and signature. You will not be admitted to the test without these things.

6. **You can't take it with you.** Leave any study aids, dictionaries, notebooks, computers, and the like at home. Certain tests **do** allow a scientific or four-function calculator, so check ahead of time to see if your test does.

7. **Prepare for the desert.** Any time spent on a bathroom break **cannot** be made up later, so use your judgment on the amount you eat or drink.

8. **Quiet, Please!** Keeping your own time is a good idea, but not with a timepiece that has a loud ticker. If you use a watch, take it off and place it nearby but not so that it distracts you. And **silence your cell phone**.

To the best of our ability, we have compiled the content you need to know in this book and in the accompanying online resources. The rest is up to you. You can use the study and testing tips or you can follow your own methods. Either way, you can be confident that there aren't any missing pieces of information and there shouldn't be any surprises in the content on the test.

If you have questions about test fees, registration, electronic testing, or other content verification issues please visit *www.education.pearsonassessments.com*.

Good luck!

Sharon Wynne
Founder, XAMonline

DOMAIN I

MATHEMATICAL PROCESSES AND NUMBER SENSE

COMPETENCY 1
UNDERSTAND MATHEMATICAL PROBLEM SOLVING

The process of problem solving in mathematics is similar to that in other disciplines. One of the first steps is to identify what is known about the problem. Each problem for which a solution can be found should provide enough information to form a starting point from which a valid sequence of reasoning leads to the desired conclusion: a solution to the problem. Between identification of known information and identification of a solution to the problem is a gray area that, depending on the problem, could potentially involve a myriad of different approaches. Two potential approaches that do not involve a "direct" solution method are discussed below.

> Each problem for which a solution can be found should provide enough information to form a starting point from which a valid sequence of reasoning leads to the desired conclusion: a solution to the problem.

Guess-and-Check

The guess-and-check strategy calls for making an initial guess of the solution, checking the answer, and using the outcome of this check to inform the next guess. With each successive guess, one should get closer to the correct answer. Constructing a table from the guesses can help organize the data.

Example: There are 100 coins in a jar: 10 are dimes, and the rest are pennies and nickels. If there are twice as many pennies as nickels, how many pennies and nickels are in the jar?

Based on the given information, there are 90 total nickels and pennies in the jar (100 coins − 10 dimes = 90 nickels and pennies). Also, there are twice as many pennies as nickels. Using this information, guess results that fulfill the criteria and then adjust the guess in accordance with the result. Continue this iterative process until the correct answer is found: 60 pennies and 30 nickels. The table below illustrates this process.

Number of Pennies	40	80	70	60
Number of Nickels	20	40	35	30
Total Number of Pennies and Nickels	60	120	105	90

Working Backward

Another non-direct approach to problem solving is working backwards. If the result of a problem is known (for example, in problems that involve proving a particular result), it is sometimes helpful to begin from the conclusion and attempt to work backwards to a particular known starting point. A slight variation of this approach involves both working backwards and working forwards until a common point is reached somewhere in the middle. The following example from trigonometry illustrates this process.

Example: Prove that $\frac{\sin x + \cos x}{\sec x + \csc x} = \frac{\sin x}{\sec x}$

If the method for proving this result is not clear, one approach is to work backwards and forwards simultaneously. The following two-column approach organizes the process.

$\dfrac{\sin x + \cos x}{\sec x + \csc x}$	$\dfrac{\sin x}{\sec x}$
$\dfrac{\sin x + \cos x}{\dfrac{1}{\cos x} + \dfrac{1}{\sin x}}$	$\dfrac{\sin x}{\dfrac{1}{\cos x}}$
$\dfrac{\sin x + \cos x}{\dfrac{\sin x + \cos x}{\sin x \cos x}}$	$\sin x \cos x$
$\dfrac{\sin x + \cos x}{1} \cdot \dfrac{\sin x \cos x}{\sin x + \cos x}$	
$\sin x \cos x$	

Thus, a proof is apparent based on the combination of the reasoning in these two columns.

Selection of an appropriate problem-solving strategy depends largely on the type of problem being solved and the particular area of mathematics with which the problem deals. For instance, problems that involve proving a specific result often require different approaches than do problems that involve finding a numerical result.

Reasonableness

When solving any problem, it is helpful to evaluate the reasonableness of the solution. Often, errors in the solution lead to final results that do not make any sense in the context of the problem. Thus, checking the reasonableness of the solution can be a fast way to help determine if an error was made at some point in the process. Although such checks help to raise confidence in a solution, they do not necessarily guarantee that a solution is correct.

For instance, an error can result in a relatively small deviation in a numerical result; although the answer might seem reasonable, it could still be incorrect.

Thus, the reasonableness of a solution is a necessary but not sufficient check of its correctness.

Two characteristics of a numerical answer that can be quickly evaluated are sign and magnitude. If a problem calls for determining the length of a side of some geometric figure, for example, then a negative number should indicate an error at some point in the solution. Similarly, a result that is magnitudes larger than would seem appropriate to the other aspects of the problem (such as the lengths of other measurements) could also indicate an error.

Additionally, the problem may provide information that limits the answer to a certain range. For example, if a problem asks for the average speed of an automobile over some distance and range of speeds, it is clear that the average speed should not exceed the maximum speed, nor should it be less than the minimum speed. Again, although this type of evaluation does not necessarily help to judge answers that fall within this range, it does help rule out results containing particularly egregious errors. On the other hand, if a speed distribution is shown that is weighted heavily toward faster speeds than slower speeds, it would then be reasonable to assume that the correct solution should be at the higher end of the speed range of the car. Similar types of qualitative evaluation or rough estimation for judging the reasonableness of a solution can be applied to other problems as well.

> *Two characteristics of a numerical answer that can be quickly evaluated are sign and magnitude.*

SKILL 1.2 **Analyze the use of estimation in a variety of situations** *(e.g., rounding, area, plausibility)*

There are several different ways of estimating. A common estimation strategy involves replacing numbers with simpler numbers that make for simpler computations. These methods include rounding, front-end digit estimation, and compensation.

> *Estimation and approximation can be used to check the reasonableness of answers or to speed up a calculation where exact answers are not required. Estimation can be particularly important when calculators are used. Estimation also requires good mental math skills.*

Front-End Estimation

Although rounding is done to a specific place value (e.g., the nearest ten or hundred), front-end estimation involves rounding or truncating to the place value of the first digit in the number. The following example uses front-end estimation.

Example: Estimate the result of the calculation $\frac{58 \times 810}{1989}$.

To simplify the calculation, round each number to the highest place value. Thus, the calculation becomes

$$\frac{58 \times 810}{1989} \approx \frac{60 \times 800}{2000} = \frac{48000}{2000} = 24.$$

A more precise result is 23.62. In this case, the estimated value is close to the exact result.

Compensation

Another estimation technique, compensation, involves replacing different numbers in different ways so that one change can more or less compensate for the other.

Example: Calculate 32 + 53.
Although this example is simple, it is noteworthy that compensation can make the numbers easier to handle mentally.

$$32 + 53 = 30 + 55 = 85$$

Here both numbers are replaced in a way that minimizes the change; one number is increased and the other is decreased. This technique can also be applied to algebraic expressions. In such cases, compensation or other similar forms of reorganization of numbers can drastically simplify certain operations.

Calculating a Range

A third estimation strategy calculates a range for the result.

Example: Estimate 458 + 873.
Again, this is a very simple example, but the principle can be applied to a range of different calculations. A simple range containing the answer can be found as follows.

$$458 + 873 > 400 + 800 = 1200$$
$$458 + 873 < 500 + 900 = 1400$$

Thus, the correct answer is in the following range:

$$1200 < 458 + 873 < 1400.$$

Various other estimation techniques can be applied as well, depending on the problem being solved.

Reasonableness

The reasonableness of an estimate can be judged in various ways, depending on the context of the problem. For instance, if the exact result of a calculation or the exact solution to a problem is known, then the estimated value can be considered reasonable if it varies from the exact value by a sufficiently small percentage.

The reasonableness of an estimate can be judged in various ways, depending on the context of the problem. For instance, if the exact result of a calculation or the exact solution to a problem is known, then the estimated value can be considered reasonable if it varies from the exact value by a sufficiently small percentage.

Often, a variation of a few percentage points is acceptable; in some contexts, up to 10% variation is likewise acceptable. Large variations, however, may indicate that the estimate is not reasonable.

If the exact result or solution is not known, the reasonableness of an estimate can be judged to some extent by the expected effect of the procedure used in the estimate. For example, if a number is rounded in a calculation and the process of rounding has a small effect on the value of the number (only a percentage point or two, for instance), it may be likely that the estimate is reasonable.

The particular operations involved in a calculation are important to making a good judgment, however. Consider the calculation $10.4929 - 10.5103$. If these numbers are rounded to the nearest one, or even to the nearest tenth, then the estimated result is zero instead of -0.0174. In some contexts, this difference may be negligible, but in other contexts, it may be very important. Thus, estimating the reasonableness of an estimate requires consideration of not only the numbers and the operations involved in the problem but also the context of the problem.

SKILL 1.3 **Solve mathematical and real-world problems involving integers, fractions, decimals, and percents**

Real numbers can be represented in a variety of formats. Some of these formats are more amenable to certain problems than others, and it is important to be able to select the proper representation of a real number for a given situation.

For instance, if exact calculations are required, **decimal representations** (or, similarly, **percent representations**—which are simply the decimal representation multiplied by 100) of irrational numbers are not appropriate. The use of a decimal necessarily requires use of a finite representation; thus, the decimal form of an irrational number must be rounded to some digit, leading to inaccuracies in calculations. Thus, irrational numbers such as the number π and square roots of certain integers should often be left in their symbolic or square root forms. If inexact calculations are acceptable, then a decimal or approximate fractional representation may be suitable.

If the decimal is repeating (such as $0.1111111\ldots$), a **fractional representation** may be the best approach. A fraction can be manipulated easily, and it is sometimes more conducive to exact calculations than are repeating decimals (or even long non-repeating decimals in some cases).

In other instances, an **exponential form** is useful. Exponentials (or their

MATHEMATICAL PROCESSES AND NUMBER SENSE

inverses, logarithms) may be a preferred representation of real numbers in various cases. In addition to considering whether exact or inexact calculations are needed for a particular problem, the simplicity of the calculation is also important when selecting an appropriate representation of a number. For hand/mental calculations, simplicity may be paramount, for instance.

SCIENTIFIC NOTATION is a convenient method for writing very large and very small numbers. It employs two factors: the first factor is a number between −10 and 10, and the second factor is a power of 10. This notation is a shorthand way to express large numbers (like the weight in kilograms of 100 freight cars) or small numbers (like the weight in grams of an atom).

> **SCIENTIFIC NOTATION:** a convenient method for writing very large and very small numbers

For example, 356.73 can be written in various forms.

$$
\begin{aligned}
356.73 &= 3567.3 \times 10^{-1} & (1) \\
&= 356.73 \times 10^{-0} & (2) \\
&= 35.673 \times 10^{1} & (3) \\
&= 3.5673 \times 10^{2} & (4) \\
&= 0.35673 \times 10^{3} & (5)
\end{aligned}
$$

Only (4) is written in proper scientific notation format.

Example: Write 46,368,000 in scientific notation.

1. Introduce a decimal point. $46{,}368{,}000 = 46{,}368{,}000.0$

2. Move the decimal place to **left** until only one nonzero digit is in front of it, in this case, between the 4 and 6.

3. Count the number of digits the decimal point moved, in this case, seven. This is the nth the power of 10 and is **positive** because the decimal point moved **left**.

Therefore, $46{,}368{,}000 = 4.6368 \times 10^{7}$.

Thus, there are a number of possible representations for a given real number depending on the problem or situation under consideration. The following examples illustrate some problems where certain representations of given real numbers are better than others.

Example: A particular material has a mass of 0.01 grams in one liter. What is the material's density in grams per milliliter?

A cursory examination of this problem shows that it will be necessary to divide a small number (0.01 grams) by a large number (1000 milliliters = 1 liter) to get the density. Thus, scientific notation is a helpful representation of the numbers in the problem. The density d is then the following:

8

NES HIGHSCHOOL MATHEMATICS 304

$$d = \frac{1 \times 10^{-2}\,\text{g}}{1 \times 10^{3}\,\text{mL}} = 1 \times 10^{-5}\,\frac{\text{g}}{\text{mL}}$$

The calculation and the result in this case are simplified considerably through the use of scientific notation. The solution is in a much neater form than 0.00001.

Example: Express the repeating decimal $0.\overline{254}$ as a number in closed form.

This problem calls for selecting an appropriate closed-form representation in the real number system for a repeating decimal. First, note that because the decimal repeats, the three repeating digits can be isolated as follows. Let d be equal to the repeating decimal $0.\overline{254}$.

$$1000d = 254.\overline{254} = 254 + d$$
$$999d = 254$$
$$d = \frac{254}{999}$$

Thus, this repeating decimal can be expressed in closed form using a fractional representation.

Example: The total snowfall was 27.3 inches in January, 31.5 inches in February, and 18.2 inches in March. What was the average monthly snowfall during these three months?

By definition, to find the average we add all three numbers and divide by 3.

$$\begin{array}{r} 27.3 \\ 31.5 \\ +\ 18.2 \\ \hline 77.0 \end{array}$$

Dividing 77 by 3 we get 25.666... ≈ 25.67

Therefore, the average monthly snowfall from January through March was 25.67 inches.

See Skill 1.4 for more examples and for problems involving percents.

SKILL 1.4 Solve mathematical and real-world problems involving ratios, proportions, and average rates of change

Consumer Applications

The **UNIT RATE** when purchasing an item is its price divided by the number of units of measure (pounds, ounces, etc.) in the item. The item with the lower unit rate has the lower price.

> **UNIT RATE:** the price of an item divided by the number of units of measure

Example: Find the item with the best unit price:
$1.79 for 10 ounces
$1.89 for 12 ounces
$5.49 for 32 ounces

$\frac{1.79}{10} = 0.179$ per ounce $\qquad \frac{1.89}{12} = 0.1575$ per ounce $\qquad \frac{5.49}{32} = 0.172$ per ounce

$1.89 for 12 ounces is the best price.

A second way to find the better buy is to make a proportion with the price over the number of ounces (or whatever). Cross-multiply the proportion, writing the products above the numerator that is used. The better price will have the smaller product.

Example: Find the better buy: $8.19 for forty pounds or $4.89 for twenty-two pounds. Find the unit costs.

$$\frac{40}{8.19} = \frac{1}{x}$$
$$40x = 8.19$$
$$x = 0.20475$$

$$\frac{22}{4.89} = \frac{1}{x}$$
$$22x = 4.89$$
$$x = 0.222\overline{27}$$

Since $0.20475 < 0.222\overline{27}$, $8.19 is the lower price and a better buy.

To find the amount of sales tax on an item, change the percent of sales tax into an equivalent decimal number. Then multiply the decimal number times the price of the object to find the sales tax. The total cost of an item will be the price of the item plus the sales tax.

Example: A guitar costs $120.00 plus 7% sales tax. How much are the sales tax and the total cost?

$7\% = .07$ as a decimal
$(.07)(120) = \$8.40$ sales tax
$\$120.00 + \$8.40 = \$128.40 \leftarrow$ total price

An alternative method to find the total cost is to multiply the price times the factor 1.07:

$1.07 = 1 + 0.07$
$\$120.00 \times 1.07 = \$128.40$

This gives you the total cost in fewer steps.

Example: A suit costs $450.00 plus $6\frac{1}{2}\%$ sales tax. How much are the sales tax and the total cost?

$6\frac{1}{2}\% = .065$ as a decimal
$(.065)(450) = \$29.25$ sales tax

$450.00 + $29.25 = $479.25 \leftarrow$ total price

An alternative method to find the total cost is to multiply the price times the factor 1.065:

$450.00 \times 1.065 = $479.25

This gives you the total cost in fewer steps.

Ratios

A RATIO is a comparison of two numbers. If a class has 11 boys and 14 girls, the ratio of boys to girls could be written one of three ways:

11:14   or   11 to 14   or $\frac{11}{14}$

The ratio of girls to boys is

14:11   or   14 to 11   or $\frac{14}{11}$

Ratios can be reduced when possible. A ratio of 12 cats to 18 dogs would reduce to 2:3, 2 to 3, or $\frac{2}{3}$.

Note: Read ratio questions carefully. Given a group of 6 adults and 5 children, the ratio of children to the entire group would be 5:11.

> **RATIO:** a comparison of two numbers

Proportions

A PROPORTION is an equation in which a fraction is set equal to another. To solve the proportion, multiply each numerator by the other fraction's denominator. Set these two products equal to each other and solve the resulting equation. This is called CROSS-MULTIPLYING the proportion.

Example: $\frac{4}{15} = \frac{x}{60}$ *is a proportion.*
To solve this, cross-multiply:

$(4)(60) = (15)(x)$
$240 = 15x$
$16 = x$

Example: $\frac{x+3}{3x+4} = \frac{2}{5}$ *is a proportion.*

$5(x + 3) = 2(3x + 4)$
$5x + 15 = 6x + 8$
$7 = x$

> **PROPORTION:** an equation in which a fraction is set equal to another

> **CROSS-MULTIPLYING:** multiplying one fraction's numerator by another fraction's denominator

Example: $\dfrac{x+2}{8} = \dfrac{2}{x-4}$ *is another proportion.*

To solve, cross-multiply:

$(x+2)(x-4) = 8(2)$

$x^2 - 2x - 8 = 16$

$x^2 - 2x - 24 = 0$

$(x-6)(x+4) = 0$

$x = 6$ or $x = -4$

Both answers work.

Fractions, decimals, and percents can be used interchangeably in problems.

- To change a percent into a decimal, move the decimal point two places to the left and drop the percent sign.

- To change a decimal into a percent, move the decimal point two places to the right and add a percent sign.

- To change a fraction into a decimal, divide the numerator by the denominator.

- To change a decimal number into an equivalent fraction, write the decimal part of the number as the fraction's numerator. As the fraction's denominator, use the place value of the last column of the decimal. Reduce the resulting fraction as far as possible.

Example: J.C. Nickels has Hunch jeans for sale at $\frac{1}{4}$ off the usual price of $36.00. Shears and Roadster have the same jeans for sale at 30% off their regular price of $40. Find the cheaper price.

$\frac{1}{4} = .25$ so $.25(36) = \$9.00$ off; $\$36 - 9 = \$27$ sale price

$30\% = .30$ so $.30(40) = \$12$ off; $\$40 - 12 = \$28$ sale price

The price at J.C Nickels is actually $1 lower.

See Skill 5.1 for a discussion of rates of change.

COMPETENCY 2
UNDERSTAND MATHEMATICAL COMMUNICATION, CONNECTIONS, AND REASONING

SKILL 2.1   **Translate between representations** *(e.g., graphic, verbal, symbolic)*

Throughout this guide, mathematical operations and situations are represented through words, algebraic symbols, geometric diagrams, and graphs. A few commonly used representations are discussed below.

The basic mathematical operations include addition, subtraction, multiplication and division. In word problems, these are represented by the following typical expressions.

Operation	Descriptive Words
Addition	plus, combine, sum, total, put together
Subtraction	minus, less, take away, difference
Multiplication	product, times, groups of
Division	quotient, into, split into equal groups

Symbolic representation is the basic language of mathematics. Converting data to symbols allows for easy manipulation and problem solving. Students should have the ability to recognize what the symbolic notation represents and to convert verbal information into symbolic form. For example, from the graph of a line, students should have the ability to determine the slope and intercepts and derive the line's equation from the observed data. Another possible application of symbolic representation is the formulation of algebraic expressions and relations from data presented in word-problem form.

Some verbal and symbolic representations of basic mathematical operations include the following:

Verbal	Symbolic
7 added to a number	$n + 7$
a number decreased by 8	$n - 8$
12 times a number divided by 7	$12n \div 7$
28 less than a number	$n - 28$
the ratio of a number to 55	$\dfrac{n}{55}$
4 times the sum of a number and 21	$4(n + 21)$

Multiplication can be shown using arrays. For instance, 3×4 can be expressed as 3 rows of 4 each.

□ □ □ □
□ □ □ □
□ □ □ □

In a similar manner, addition and subtraction can be demonstrated with symbols.

ψψψζζζ
$3 + 4 = 7$
$7 - 3 = 4$

Fractions can be represented using pattern blocks, fraction bars, or paper folding.

Diagrams of arithmetic operations can present mathematical data in visual form. For example, a number line can be used to add and subtract, as illustrated below.

Five added to negative four on the number line, or $-4 + 5 = 1$.

Pictorial representations can also be used to explain the arithmetic processes.

The diagram above shows that two groups of four equal eight, or $2 \times 4 = 8$. The next diagram illustrates the addition of two objects to three objects, resulting in five objects.

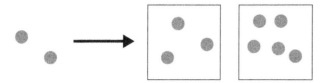

Concrete examples are real-world applications of mathematical concepts. For example, measuring the shadow produced by a tree or a building is a real-world application of trigonometric functions, the acceleration or velocity of a car is an application of derivatives, and finding the volume or the area of a swimming pool is a real-world application of geometric principles.

Pictorial illustrations of mathematic concepts help clarify difficult ideas and simplify problem solving. The following example illustrates the use of pictures.

Rectangle R represents the 300 students in School A. Circle P represents the 150 students that participate in band. Circle Q represents the 170 students that participate in a sport. 70 students participate in both band and a sport. $P + Q - P \cap Q$.

$150 + 170 - 70 = 250$ represents the number of students in band or orchestra. If the school population is 300, then $300 - 250$ or 50 students are not enrolled in either.

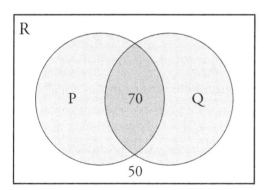

SKILL 2.2 Recognize connections between mathematical concepts

Recognition and understanding of the relationships between concepts and topics is important to mathematical problem solving and the explanation of more complex processes. It becomes much easier for a student to retain information when it is presented from different viewpoints and linked to other familiar concepts. Ideally, a teacher will not present the information outright but will let students think for themselves and discover the connections on their own with guidance from the teacher. Some examples of connections between familiar mathematical concepts are discussed below.

Multiplication is simply repeated addition. This relationship explains the concept of variable addition.

We can show that the expression $4x + 3x = 7x$ is true by rewriting 4 times x and 3 times x as repeated addition, yielding the expression $(x + x + x + x) + (x + x + x)$. Thus, because of the relationship between multiplication and addition, variable addition is accomplished by coefficient addition.

Addition and subtraction are really the same operation acting in opposite directions on the number line. Understanding this concept helps students in working with negative numbers which are difficult for many middle-school children to grasp.

The concept of **rate** appears in many different guises in mathematics, such as in the speed of a vehicle, interest rate, or the price per unit of an item. The concept of rate is also directly connected to the concept of slope of a straight line.

Commonly used formulae such as $a^2 - b^2 = (a + b)(a - b)$ or $(a + b)^2 = a^2 + 2ab + b^2$ are not magical relationships that need to be memorized. They can simply be calculated by performing the familiar **FOIL** operation.

Example: $(a + b)(a - b) = a^2 - ab + ba - b^2 = a^2 - b^2$
In geometry, the perimeters, areas and volumes of different figures are usually presented as separate formulae. It is useful to point out that every area contains the product of two dimensions (e.g., lw or πr^2) and every volume contains the product of three dimensions (e.g., l^3, $\pi r^2 h$). This helps students understand the meaning of square and cubic units.

The relationships between points, lines and planes become easier to visualize if one understands that **a point is to a line as a line is to a plane.** Just as two lines intersect in a point, two planes intersect in a line.

Students can discover many more connections in the classroom with the teacher's help. This will not only enhance the quality of their learning but will also make them better and more eager learners.

SKILL 2.3 Analyze inductive and deductive reasoning

The two forms of reasoning are inductive and deductive. INDUCTIVE REASONING involves making inferences from specific facts to general principles; DEDUCTIVE REASONING involves making inferences from general principles to specific facts. As such, inductive reasoning is generally weaker than deductive reasoning. (Inductive reasoning—or induction—should not be confused with mathematical induction, which is not an example of inductive reasoning, strictly speaking.)

Inductive Reasoning

Inductive reasoning generally involves finding a representative set of examples that support the general application of a broader principle. In a common context, an example of inductive reasoning would be inferring from the fact that only black crows have ever been spotted to the general statement that all crows are black. This inference has a foundation in numerous observations, and it thereby gains significant weight. Nevertheless, it is feasible that somewhere a white (or other-colored) crow does exist but hasn't yet been spotted. Thus, inductive inferences can never acquire 100% certainty, regardless of the amount of information in support of them.

Example:

Suppose:
On Monday Mr. Peterson eats breakfast at McDonald's.
On Tuesday Mr. Peterson eats breakfast at McDonald's.
On Wednesday Mr. Peterson eats breakfast at McDonald's.
On Thursday Mr. Peterson eats breakfast at McDonald's.

Conclusion:
On Friday Mr. Peterson will eat breakfast at McDonald's again.

This is a conclusion based on inductive reasoning. Based on several days' observations, you conclude that Mr. Peterson will eat at McDonald's. This may or may not be true, but it is a valid inductive conclusion.

Regardless of the uncertainty associated with induction, inductive inferences can be helpful for building a theory or for making a conjecture about some aspect of life, mathematics, or any other area. The physical sciences are a particular example where induction is commonly used to develop theories about the universe. Although these theories may be founded on a large body of empirical and mathematical evidence, a single counterexample could topple their status.

> **INDUCTIVE REASONING:** makes inferences from specific facts to general principles

> **DEDUCTIVE REASONING:** makes inferences from general principles to specific facts

> *Inductive inferences can be helpful for building a theory or for making a conjecture about some aspect of life, mathematics, or any other area.*

Thus, inductive reasoning can be helpful, but it is much weaker than deductive reasoning.

Inductive reasoning, because it is weaker than deduction, is also less rigorous in its application of specific rules for the process of arriving at conclusions. For instance, there is no rule concerning how much evidence constitutes a sufficient reason to inductively accept a particular hypothesis. (Thus, there is no minimum number of sightings of black crows that is required prior to making an inference that all crows are black.) The particular area in which inductive reasoning is applied and the amount of potential evidence that could reasonably be gathered are factors that help determine what constitutes an acceptable inductive inference.

In a mathematical context, induction can serve to make conjectures for which a proof (or a proof of the contrary) can then be sought. For instance, Fermat's Last Theorem states that there are no integer solutions x, y, and z to the expression $x^n + y^n = z^n$ for $n > 2$. Although this theorem was suspected to be true (largely by induction from numerous test cases) for hundreds of years, only recently was a deductive proof discovered. Thus, induction can serve as a less rigorous method of making tentative conclusions pending a formal proof.

Deductive Reasoning

Deductive reasoning is a method of reasoning that is stronger and more rigorous than inductive reasoning. Deductive arguments reason from a set of premises to a conclusion and are classified as invalid, valid, or sound. An **INVALID ARGUMENT** is one in which the conclusion does not necessarily follow from the premises. A **VALID ARGUMENT** is one in which the conclusion necessarily follows from the premises. A **SOUND ARGUMENT** is a valid argument for which all the premises are true. Thus, the following argument is valid but not sound:

> Premise 1:   All dogs are black.
> Premise 2:   Rover is a dog.
> Conclusion: Rover is black.

Were premises 1 and 2 both true, the conclusion would necessarily be true as well. Premise 1 is false, however, so the argument is valid but not sound. On the other hand, the following argument is both valid *and* sound.

> Premise 1:   All integers are real numbers.
> Premise 2:   1 is an integer.
> Conclusion: 1 is a real number.

Both premises 1 and 2 are true, and the conclusion follows from the premises. Specific examples of deductive logical steps that can be taken in developing or evaluating an argument include *modus ponens* ("if A, then B" and "A is true" necessarily implies "B is true") and *modus tollens* ("if A, then B" and "B is false" necessarily implies "A is false").

INVALID ARGUMENT: one in which the conclusion does not necessarily follow from the premises

VALID ARGUMENT: one in which the conclusion necessarily follows from the premises

SOUND ARGUMENT: a valid argument for which all the premises are true

Because deductive reasoning is more rigorous and the rules clearer, the process of arriving at an acceptable conclusion from a given set of premises (or the process of evaluating a deductive argument) is likewise clearer. Demonstrating the truth of the premises, however, may still be a complicated process. The premises may even require inductive reasoning to demonstrate their truth (at least tentatively). Thus, whether a deductive argument is sound can still be a matter that rests on the strength of a particular instance of inductive reasoning.

SKILL 2.4 **Apply principles of logic to solve problems**

Logical Connectives and Conditional Statements

A **SIMPLE STATEMENT** represents a simple idea that can be described either as *true* or *false*, but not both. A small letter of the alphabet represents a simple statement.

Example: "Today is Monday."
This is a simple statement, since we can determine that this statement is either true or false. We can write p = "Today is Monday."

Example: "Justin, please be quiet!"
We do not consider this a simple statement in our study of logic, since we cannot assign a truth value to it.

Simple statements joined by connectives (*and, or, not, if–then,* and *if and only if*) result in compound statements. Note that we can also form compound statements using *but, however,* or *nevertheless.* We can assign a truth value to a compound statement.

We frequently write conditional statements in *if–then* form. The *if* clause of the conditional is known as the **HYPOTHESIS**, and the *then* clause is called the **CONCLUSION**. In a proof, the hypothesis is the information that is assumed to be true, while the conclusion is what is to be proven true. We consider a conditional to be of the form "if p, then q," where p is the hypothesis and q is the conclusion.

$p \rightarrow q$ is read, "if p, then q."
$\sim$ (statement) is read, "It is not true that (statement)."

Example: If an angle has a measure of 90 degrees, then it is a right angle.
In this statement, "an angle has a measure of 90 degrees" is the hypothesis, and "it is a right angle" is the conclusion.

> **SIMPLE STATEMENT:** represents a simple idea that can be described either as true or false, but not both

> **HYPOTHESIS:** known as the *if* clause of the conditional statement

> **CONCLUSION:** called the *then* clause of a conditional statement

Example: If you are in Pittsburgh, then you are in Pennsylvania.

In this statement, "you are in Pittsburgh" is the hypothesis, and "you are in Pennsylvania" is the conclusion.

Logical Quantifiers and Negations

QUANTIFIERS are words that describe a quantity under discussion. These include words such as *all, none* (or *no*), and *some*.

QUANTIFIERS: words that describe a quantity under discussion

NEGATION of a statement: If a statement is true, then its negation must be false (and vice versa).

NEGATION: if a statement is true, then its negation must be false (and vice versa)

NEGATION RULES	
Statement	**Negation**
q	not q
not q	q
π and s	(not π) or (not s)
π or s	(not π) and (not s)
if p, then q	(p) and (not q)

Example: Select the statement that is the negation of "Some winter nights are not cold."

    A. All winter nights are not cold.

    B. Some winter nights are cold.

    C. All winter nights are cold.

    D. None of the winter nights is cold.

The negation of "some are" is "none is." Therefore, the negation statement is "None of the winter nights is cold." Therefore, the answer is D.

Example: Select the statement that is the negation of "If it rains, then the beach party will be called off."

    A. If it does not rain, then the beach party will not be called off.

    B. If the beach party is called off, then it will not rain.

    C. It does not rain, and the beach party will not be called off.

    D. It rains, and the beach party will not be called off.

The negation of "If p, then q" is "p and (not q)." The negation of the given statement is "It rains, and the beach party will not be called off." Select D.

Example: Select the negation of the statement "If they are elected, then all politicians go back on election promises."
   A. If they are elected, then many politicians go back on election promises.

   B. They are elected and some politicians go back on election promises.

   C. If they are not elected, some politicians do not go back on election promises.

   D. None of the above statements is the negation of the given statement.

   E. Identify the key words of "if ... then" and "all ... go back." The negation of the given statement is "They are elected and none of the politicians goes back on election promises." So select response D, since statements A, B, and C are not the negations.

Example: Select the statement that is the negation of "The sun is shining bright, and I feel great."
   A. If the sun is not shining bright, I do not feel great.

   B. The sun is not shining bright, and I do not feel great.

   C. The sun is not shining bright, or I do not feel great.

   D. The sun is shining bright, and I do not feel great.

The negation of "r and s" is "(not r) or (not s)." Therefore, the negation of the given statement is "The sun is *not* shining bright, *or* I do not feel great." We select response C.

Inverse, Converse, and Contrapositive

LOGICAL COMPARISONS	
Conditional: If p, then q	p is the hypothesis, and q is the conclusion.
Inverse: If ~ p, then ~ q	Negate both the hypothesis and the conclusion from the original conditional. (If not p, then not q.)
Converse: If q, then p	Reverse the two clauses. The original hypothesis becomes the conclusion. The original conclusion then becomes the new hypothesis.
Contrapositive: If ~ q, then ~ p	Reverse the two clauses. The "If not q, then not p" original hpothesis becomes the conclusion. The original conclusion then becomes the new hypothesis. Then negate both the new hypothesis and the new conclusion.

*Example: Given the **conditional**:*
> If an angle has 60°, then it is an acute angle.

Its **inverse**, in the form "If ~ p, then ~ q," would be:
> If an angle doesn't have 60°, then it is not an acute angle.

Notice that the inverse is false, even though the conditional statement was true.

Its **converse**, in the form "If q, then p," would be:
> If an angle is an acute angle, then it has 60°.

Notice that the converse is false, even though the conditional statement was true.

Its **contrapositive**, in the form "If q, then p," would be:
> If an angle isn't an acute angle, then it doesn't have 60°.

Notice that the contrapositive is true, assuming the original conditional statement was true.

Example: Find the inverse, converse, and contrapositive of the following conditional statements. Also determine whether each of the four statements is true or false.

Conditional: If $x = 5$ then $x^2 - 25 = 0$.	True
Inverse: If $x \neq 5$, then $x^2 - 25 \neq 0$.	False, x could be -5
Converse: If $x^2 - 25 = 0$, then $x = 5$	False, x could be -5
Contrapositive: If $x^2 - 25 \neq 0$, then $x \neq 5$.	True
Conditional: If $x = 5$, then $6x = 30$.	True
Inverse: If $x \neq 5$, then $6x \neq 30$.	True
Converse: If $6x = 30$, then $x = 5$.	True
Contrapositive: If $6x \neq 30$, then $x \neq 5$	True

Sometimes, as in this example, all four statements can be logically equivalent, but the only statement that will always be logically equivalent to the original conditional is the contrapositive.

Tip: *If you are asked to pick a statement that is logically equivalent to a given conditional, look for the contrapositive. The inverse and converse are not always logically equivalent to every conditional. The contrapositive is always logically equivalent.*

Venn Diagrams

VENN DIAGRAM: a diagram using conditional statements

We can diagram conditional statements using a **VENN DIAGRAM**. We can draw a diagram with one figure inside another figure. The inner figure represents the hypothesis, and the outer figure represents the conclusion. If we take the hypothesis to be true, then you are located inside the inner figure. If you are located in the inner figure, then you are also inside the outer figure, so that proves that the conclusion is true.

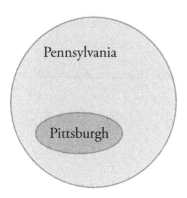

Sometimes that conclusion can then be used as the hypothesis for another conditional, which can result in a second conclusion.

Suppose the following statements were given to you, and you were asked to try to reach a conclusion:

A. All swimmers are athletes.
    All athletes are scholars.

    In "if-then" form, these would be:
    If you are a swimmer, then you are an athlete.
    If you are an athlete, then you are a scholar.

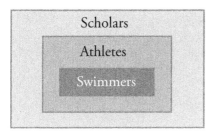

    Clearly, if you are a swimmer, then you are also an athlete. This includes you in the group of scholars.

B. All swimmers are athletes.
    All wrestlers are athletes.

    In "if-then" form, these would be:
    If you are a swimmer, then you are an athlete.
    If you are a wrestler, then you are an athlete.

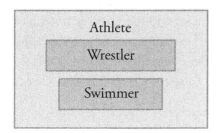

Clearly, if you are a swimmer or a wrestler, then you are also an athlete. This does NOT allow you to come to any other conclusions.

A swimmer may or may NOT also be a wrestler. Therefore, NO CONCLUSION IS POSSIBLE.

C. All rectangles are parallelograms.
Quadrilateral ABCD is not a parallelogram.

In "if–then" form, the first statement would be:
If a figure is a rectangle, then it is also a parallelogram.

Note that the second statement is the negation of the conclusion of statement one. Remember also that the contrapositive is logically equivalent to a given conditional—that is, "*If* ~ *q, then* ~ *p*." Since "ABCD is not a parallelogram" is like saying "*If* ~ *q*," you can come to the conclusion "*then* ~ *p*." Therefore, the conclusion is ABCD is not a rectangle.

Looking at the following Venn diagram, if all rectangles are parallelograms, then rectangles are included as part of the parallelograms. Since quadrilateral ABCD is not a parallelogram, that it is excluded from anywhere inside the parallelogram box. This allows you to conclude that ABCD cannot be a rectangle either.

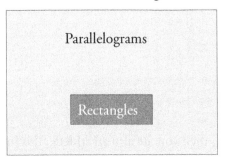

Counterexamples

A **COUNTEREXAMPLE** is an exception to a proposed rule or conjecture that disproves the conjecture. For example, the existence of a single non-brown dog disproves the conjecture "All dogs are brown." Thus, any non-brown dog is a counterexample.

In searching for mathematic counterexamples, one should consider extreme cases near the ends of the domain of an experiment and special cases where an additional property is introduced. Examples of extreme cases are numbers near zero and obtuse triangles that are nearly flat. An example of a special case for a problem involving rectangles is a square because a square is a rectangle with the additional property of symmetry.

Example: Identify a counterexample for the following conjectures.

1. If n is an even number, then $n + 1$ is divisible by 3.

   $n = 4$

   $n + 1 = 4 + 1 = 5$

   5 is not divisible by 3.

2. If n is divisible by 3, then $n^2 - 1$ is divisible by 4.

   $n = 6$

   $n^2 - 1 = 6^2 - 1 = 35$

   35 is not divisible by 4.

SKILL 2.5 Demonstrate knowledge of the historical development of major mathematical concepts, including contributions from diverse cultures

Mathematics predates recorded history. Prehistoric cave paintings have been dated prior to 20,000 BCE in Africa and France which use geometrical figures and slash counting. Some of the earliest uses of mathematics were in the fields of astronomy, architecture, trading and taxation.

The early history of mathematics is found in Mesopotamia (Sumeria and Babylon), Egypt, Greece, and Rome. Noted mathematicians from these times include Euclid, Pythagoras, Apollonius, Ptolemy, and Archimedes.

Islamic culture from the sixth through the twelfth centuries drew its math knowledge from areas of the globe ranging from Africa and Spain to India. This mixture of cultures and ideas brought about many developments, including the concept of algebra, our current numbering system, and additional major developments such as the concept of zero. India was the primary source of many of these developments. Notable scholars of this era include Omar Khayyam and Muhammad al-Khwarizmi.

In Babylonia and Greece, archeological digs have located counting boards. These include the abacus, whose current form dates from approximately 1200 CE. Prior to the development of the zero, a counting board or abacus was the common method used for all types of calculations.

Abelard and Fibonacci brought Islamic texts to Europe in the twelfth century. By the seventeenth century, major works appeared from Galileo and Copernicus (astronomy), Newton and Leibniz (calculus), and Napier and Briggs (logarithms). Other significant mathematicians of this era include René Descartes, Carl Gauss, Pierre de Fermat, Leonhard Euler, and Blaise Pascal.

The growth of mathematics since 1800 has been enormous and has affected nearly every aspect of life. Some names significant in the history of mathematics since 1800 and the work they are most known for include:

1. Joseph-Louis Lagrange (theory of functions and of mechanics)

2. Pierre-Simon LaPlace (celestial mechanics, probability theory)

3. Joseph Fourier (number theory)

4. Lobachevsky and Bolyai (non-Euclidean geometry)

5. Charles Babbage (calculating machines, origin of the computer)

6. Lady Ada Lovelace (first known program)

7. Florence Nightingale (nursing, statistics of populations)

8. Bernard Russel (logic)

9. James Maxwell (differential calculus and analysis)

10. John von Neumann (economics, quantum mechanics and game theory)

11. Alan Turing (theoretical foundations of computer science)

12. Albert Einstein (theory of relativity)

13. Gustav Roch (topology)

COMPETENCY 3
UNDERSTAND NUMBER THEORY

SKILL 3.1 Analyze the group structure of the real numbers

Real Numbers

The following chart shows the relationships among the subsets of the real numbers.

Real Numbers

REAL NUMBERS are denoted by $\mathbb{R}$ and are numbers that can be shown by an infinite decimal representation such as 3.286275347 . . . . Real numbers include rational numbers, such as 242 and $\frac{-23}{129}$, and irrational numbers, such as $\sqrt{2}$ and π, and can be represented as points along an infinite number line. Real numbers are also known as "the unique complete Archimedean *ordered field*." Real numbers are to be distinguished from imaginary numbers, which involve a factor of $\sqrt{-1}$.

> **REAL NUMBERS:** numbers that can be represented by an infinite decimal representation

Real numbers are classified as follows:

CLASSIFICATIONS OF REAL NUMBERS	
Natural Numbers, Denoted by $\mathbb{N}$	The counting numbers. 1, 2, 3, . . .
Whole Numbers	The counting numbers along with zero. 0, 1, 2, 3, . . .
Integers, Denoted by $\mathbb{Z}$	The counting numbers, their opposites, and zero. . . . , –2, –1, 0, 1, 2, . . .
Rationals, Denoted by $\mathbb{Q}$	All of the fractions that can be formed using whole numbers. Zero cannot be the denominator. In decimal form, these numbers will be either terminating or repeating decimals. Simplify square roots to determine if the number can be written as a fraction.
Irrationals	Real numbers that cannot be written as a fraction. The decimal forms of these numbers neither terminate nor repeat. Examples include π, e and $\sqrt{2}$.

The set of complex numbers is denoted by $\mathbb{C}$. The set $\mathbb{C}$ is defined as $\{a + bi : a, b \in \mathbb{R}\}$ ($\in$ means "element of"). In other words, complex numbers are an extension of real numbers made by attaching an imaginary number i, which satisfies the equality $i^2 = -1$. **COMPLEX NUMBERS** are of the form $a + bi$, where a and b are real numbers and $i = \sqrt{-1}$. Thus, a is the real part of the number and b is the imaginary part of the number. When i appears in a fraction, the fraction is usually simplified so that i is not in the denominator. The set of complex numbers includes the set of real numbers, where any real number n can be written in its equivalent complex form as $n + 0i$. In other words, it can be said that $\mathbb{R} \subseteq \mathbb{C}$ (or $\mathbb{R}$ is a subset of $\mathbb{C}$).

> **COMPLEX NUMBERS:**
> numbers of the form $a + bi$, where a and b are real numbers and $i = \sqrt{-1}$

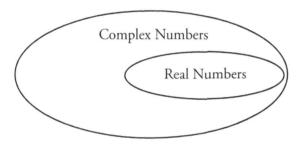

The number $3i$ has a real part 0 and imaginary part 3; the number 4 has a real part 4 and an imaginary part 0. As another way of writing complex numbers, we can express them as ordered pairs:

Complex Number	Ordered Pair
$3 + 2i$	$(3, 2)$
$\sqrt{3} + \sqrt{3}i$	$(\sqrt{3}, \sqrt{3})$
$7i$	$(0, 7)$
$\dfrac{6 + 2i}{7}$	$\left(\dfrac{6}{7}, \dfrac{2}{7}\right)$

The basic operations for complex numbers can be summarized as follows, where $z_1 = a_1 + b_1 i$ and $z_2 = a_2 + b_2 i$. Note that the operations are performed in the standard manner, where i is treated as a standard radical value. The result of each operation is written in the standard form for complex numbers. Also note that the **COMPLEX CONJUGATE** of a complex number $z = a + bi$ is denoted as $z^* = a - bi$.

> **COMPLEX CONJUGATE:**
> for a complex number $z = a + bi$, this is denoted as $z^* = a - bi$

$$z_1 + z_2 = (a_1 + a_2) + (b_1 + b_2)i$$
$$z_1 - z_2 = (a_1 - a_2) + (b_1 - b_2)i$$

$$z_1 z_2 = (a_1 a_2 - b_1 b_2) + (a_1 b_2 - a_2 b_1)i$$

$$\frac{z_1}{z_2} = \frac{z_1}{z_2} \frac{z_2^*}{z_2^*} = \frac{a_1 a_2 + b_1 b_2}{a_2^2 + b_2^2} + \frac{a_2 b_1 - a_1 b_2}{a_2^2 + b_2^2} i$$

Note that, because the division operation above is defined, the multiplicative inverse of any complex number $z \neq 0$ is also defined (where z_1 is 1 and z_2 is z) in the set of complex numbers.

In addition to these operations, the absolute value of a complex number, $z = a + bi$ (written $|z|$ or $|a + bi|$), is also defined. (The absolute value may also be termed the "magnitude" or the "modulus" of the number.)

$$|z| = \sqrt{zz^*} = \sqrt{a^2 + b^2}$$

When i appears in an answer, it is acceptable unless it is in a denominator. When i^2 appears in a problem, it is always replaced by -1. Remember: $i^2 = -1$.

Adding Complex Numbers

To add complex numbers, add the real parts together and add the imaginary parts together.

Example: Add (3 + 4i) and (5 − 2i).

$$(3 + 4i) + (5 - 2i) = (3 + 5) + (4i - 2i)$$
$$= 8 + 2i$$

Example: Find the sum of (3 + 6i), (-5 + i), (9 − 4i), and (5i).

$$(3 + 6i) + (-5 + i) + (9 - 4i) + (5i) = (3 - 5 + 9) + (6i + i - 4i + 5i)$$
$$= 7 + 8i$$

Example: Simplify (-1 − i) + (4 − 2i) + (3i) + (10) + (7 + 6i).

$$(-1 - i) + (4 - 2i) + (3i) + (10) + (7 + 6i) =$$
$$(-1 + 4 + 0 + 10 + 7) + (-i + -2i + 3i + 6i) =$$
$$20 + 6i$$

Subtracting Complex Numbers

To subtract a complex number, change the sign of the real and imaginary parts and add.

Example 1: Simplify (2 + 3i) − (1 + 3i).

$$(2 + 3i) - (1 + 3i) = (2 + 3i) + (-1 - 3i)$$
$$= (2 - 1) + (3i - 3i)$$
$$= 1$$

Example 2: Subtract (5 − 3i) from (3 + 2i).

$$(3 + 2i) − (5 − 3i) = (3 + 2i) + (\text{-}5 + 3i)$$
$$= (3 − 5) + (2i + 3i)$$
$$= \text{-}2 + 5i$$

Example 3: Subtract (7i) + (2 − 2i) − (4 + 3i) − (12 − 3i).

$$= (2 − 4 − 12) + (7i − 2i − 3i + 3i)$$
$$= \text{-}14 + 5i$$

Multiplying Complex Numbers

Multiplication of complex numbers is just like multiplication of binomials. Note that $i^2 = \text{-}1$.

To multiply two complex numbers, FOIL the two numbers together. Replace i^2 with -1 and finish combining like terms. Answers should have the form $a + bi$.

Example: Multiply (8 + 3i)(6 − 2i). FOIL this.

$$48 − 16i + 18i − 6i^2 \qquad \text{Let } i^2 = \text{-}1$$
$$48 − 16i + 18i − 6(\text{-}1)$$
$$48 − 16i + 18i + 6$$
$$54 + 2i \qquad \text{This is the answer.}$$

Example: Multiply (5 + 8i)². ← Write this out twice.

$$(5 + 8i)(5 + 8i) \qquad \text{FOIL this.}$$
$$25 + 40i + 40i + 64i^2 \qquad \text{Let } i^2 = \text{-}1$$
$$25 + 40i + 40i + 64(\text{-}1)$$
$$25 + 40i + 40i − 64$$
$$\text{-}39 + 80i \qquad \text{This is the answer.}$$

Example: Simplify (2 + i) (3 + 2i).

$$(2 + i)(3 + 2i) = 2 \times 3 + 2 \times 2i + i \times 3 + i \times 2i$$
$$= 6 + 4i + 3i − 2$$
$$= 4 + 7i$$

Example: Find the product of (1 − i), (3 + 4i) and (2 − 3i).

$$(1 − i)(3 + 4i)(2 − 3i) = (1 \times 3 + 1 \times 4i − i \times 3 − i \times 4i)(2 − 3i)$$
$$(3 + 4i − 3i + 4)(2 − 3i)$$
$$= (7 + i)(2 − 3i)$$
$$= 7 \times 2 − 7 \times 3i + 2i − i \times 3i$$
$$= 14 − 21i + 2i + 3$$
$$= 17 − 19i$$

Dividing Complex Numbers

When dividing two complex numbers, you must eliminate the complex number in the denominator. If the complex number in the denominator is of the form $b\,i$, multiply both the numerator and the denominator by i. Remember to replace i^2 with -1 and then continue simplifying the fraction.

Example: $\dfrac{2+3i}{5i}$

Mulitply this by $\dfrac{i}{i}$

$$\frac{2+3i}{5i} \times \frac{i}{i} = \frac{(2+3i)i}{5i \times i} = \frac{2i+3i^2}{5i^2} = \frac{2i+3(-1)}{-5} = \frac{-3+2i}{-5} = \frac{3-2i}{5}$$

If the complex number in the denominator is of the form $a+bi$, multiply both the numerator and the denominator by the conjugate of the denominator. The **CONJUGATE** of the denominator of a complex number is the same two terms with the opposite sign between the two terms (the real term does not change signs). The conjugate of $2-3i$ is $2+3i$. The conjugate of $-6+11i$ is $-6-11i$. Multiply the factors on the top and bottom of the fraction. Remember to replace i^2 with -1, combine like terms, and then continue simplifying the fraction.

> **CONJUGATE:** the conjugate of the denominator of a complex number is the same two terms with the opposite sign between the two terms (the real term does not change signs)

Example: $\dfrac{4+7i}{6-5i}$

Mulitply by $\dfrac{6+5i}{6+5i}$, the conjugate.

$$\frac{(4+7i)}{(6-5i)} \times \frac{(6+5i)}{(6+5i)} = \frac{24+20i+42i+35i^2}{36+30i-30-25i^2} = \frac{24+62i+35i(-1)}{36-25(-1)} = \frac{-11+62i}{61}$$

Example: $\dfrac{24}{-3-5i}$

Multiply by $\dfrac{-3+5i}{-3+5i}$, the conjugate.

$$\frac{24}{(-3-5i)} \times \frac{-3+5i}{-3+5i} = \frac{-72+120i}{9-25i^2} = \frac{-72+120i}{9+25} = \frac{-72+120i}{34} = \frac{-36+60i}{17}$$

Divide everything by 2 to reduce the fraction.

SKILL 3.3 Analyze the properties of numbers and operations

Fields and Rings

Any set that includes at least two nonzero elements that satisfies the field axioms for addition and multiplication is a **FIELD**. The real numbers, $\mathbb{R}$, as well as the complex numbers, $\mathbb{C}$, are each a field, with the real numbers being a subset of the complex numbers. The field axioms are summarized below.

> **FIELD:** any set that includes at least two nonzero elements that satisfies the field axioms for addition and multiplication

FIELD AXIOMS	
ADDITION	
Commutativity	$a + b = b + a$
Associativity	$a + (b + c) = (a + b) + c$
Identity	$a + 0 = a$
Inverse	$a + (-a) = 0$

MULTIPLICATION	
Commutativity	$ab = ba$
Associativity	$a(bc) = (ab)c$
Identity	$a \times 1 = a$
Inverse	$a \times \frac{1}{a} = 1 \qquad (a \neq 0)$
ADDITION AND MULTIPLICATION	
Distributivity	$a(b + c) = (b + c)a = ab + ac$

Note that both the real numbers and the complex numbers satisfy the axioms summarized above.

> **RING:** an integral domain with two binary operations (addition and multiplication) where, for every nonzero element a and b in the domain, the product ab is nonzero

A **RING** is an integral domain with two binary operations (addition and multiplication) where, for every nonzero element a and b in the domain, the product ab is nonzero. A field is a ring in which multiplication is commutative, or $a \times b = b \times a$, and all nonzero elements have a multiplicative inverse. The set $\mathbb{Z}$ (integers) is a ring that is not a field in that it does not have the multiplicative inverse; therefore, integers are not a field. A polynomial ring is also not a field, as it also has no multiplicative inverse. Furthermore, matrix rings do not constitute fields because matrix multiplication is not generally commutative.

> **Note:** Multiplication is implied when there is no symbol between two variables. Thus, $a \times b$ can be written ab. Multiplication can also be indicated by a raised dot ($\cdot$).

Real numbers are an ordered field and can be ordered

As such, an ordered field F must contain a subset P (such as the positive numbers) such that if a and b are elements of P, then both $a + b$ and ab are also elements of P. (In other words, the set P is closed under addition and multiplication.) Furthermore, it must be the case that for any element c contained in F, exactly one of the following conditions is true: c is an element of P, $-c$ is an element of P, or $c = 0$.

The rational numbers also constitute an ordered field

The set P can be defined as the positive rational numbers. For each a and b that are elements of the set $\mathbb{Q}$ (the rational numbers), $a + b$ is also an element of P, as is ab. (The sum $a + b$ and the product ab are both rational if a and b are rational.) Since P is closed under addition and multiplication, $\mathbb{Q}$ constitutes an ordered field.

Complex numbers, unlike real numbers, cannot be ordered

Consider the number $i = \sqrt{-1}$ contained in the set $\mathbb{C}$ of complex numbers. Assume that $\mathbb{C}$ has a subset P (positive numbers) that is closed under both addition and multiplication. Assume that $i > 0$. A difficulty arises in that $i^2 = -1 < 0$, so i cannot be included in the set P. Likewise, assume $i < 0$. The problem once again arises that $i^4 = 1 > 0$, so i cannot be included in P. It is clearly the case that $i \neq 0$, so there is no place for i in an ordered field. Thus, the complex numbers cannot be ordered.

Example: Prove that for every integer y, if y is an even number, then y² is even.
The definition of *even* implies that for each integer y there is at least one integer x such that $y = 2x$.

$$y = 2x$$
$$y^2 = 4x^2$$

Since $4x^2$ is always evenly divisible by two ($2x^2$ is an integer), y^2 is even for all values of y.

Example: If a, b, and c are positive real numbers, prove that
c(a + b) = (b + a)c.
Use the properties of the set of real numbers.

$$
\begin{aligned}
c(a + b) &= c(b + a) \qquad \text{Additive commutativity} \\
&= cb + ca \qquad \text{Distributivity} \\
&= bc + ac \qquad \text{Multiplicative commutativity} \\
&= (b + a)c \qquad \text{Distributivity}
\end{aligned}
$$

Example: Given real numbers a, b, c, and d, where ad = -bc, prove that
(a + bi)(c + di) is real.
Expand the product of the complex numbers.

$$(a + bi)(c + di) = ac + bci + adi + bdi^2$$

Use the definition of i^2.

$$(a + bi)(c + di) = ac - bd + bci + adi$$

Apply the fact that $ad = -bc$.

$$(a + bi)(c + di) = ac - bd + bci - bci = ac - bd$$

Since a, b, c and d are all real, $ac - bd$ must also be real.

Closure

Another useful property that can describe arbitrary sets of numbers (including fields and rings) is CLOSURE. A set is closed under an operation if the operation performed on any given elements of the set always yields a result that is likewise an element of the set. For instance, the set of real numbers is closed under multiplication, because for any two real numbers a and b, the product ab is also a real number.

> CLOSURE: a set is closed under an operation if the operation performed on any given elements of the set always yield a result that is likewise an element of the set

Example: Determine if the set of integers is closed under division.

For the set of integers to be closed under division, it must be the case that $\frac{a}{b}$ is an integer for any integers a and b. Consider $a = 2$ and $b = 3$.

$$\frac{a}{b} = \frac{2}{3}$$

This result is not an integer. Therefore, the set of integers is not closed under division.

SKILL 3.4 **Apply the principles of basic number theory** *(e.g., prime factorization, greatest common factor, least common multiple)*

Prime factorization is the process of breaking a number down into factors, or multiplied pieces, where each factor is a prime number. For instance, 50 factors into 5×10, but 10 is not a prime number. Break 10 into 5×2 and combine all factors to present the prime factorization.

$$50 = 5 \times 5 \times 2 = 2 \times 5^2$$

Example: Find the prime factorization of 54 two ways.

1) $54 = 9 \times 6$
$= 3 \times 3 \times 3 \times 2 = 2 \times 3^3$

2) $54 = 2 \times 27$
$= 2 \times 9 \times 3$
$= 2 \times 3 \times 3 \times 3 = 2 \times 3^3$

It should be noted that every integer has a unique prime factorization. Even though the steps show "two ways" to get the answer, the answers are the same.

Greatest Common Factor

GCF is the abbreviation for Greatest Common Factor. The GCF is the largest number that is a factor of all the numbers given in a problem. The GCF can be no larger than the smallest number given in the problem. If no other number is a common factor, then the GCF will be the number 1.

To find the GCF, list all possible factors of the smallest number (include the number itself). Starting with the largest factor (which is the number itself), determine if that factor is also a factor of all the other given numbers. If so, that factor is the GCF. If that factor doesn't divide evenly into the other given numbers, try the same method on the next smaller factor. Continue until a common factor is found. That factor is the GCF.

Example: Find the GCF of 12, 20, and 36.

The smallest number in the problem is 12. The factors of 12 are 1, 2, 3, 4, 6 and 12. 12 is the largest of these factors, but it does not divide evenly into 20.

Neither does 6. However, 4 will divide into both 20 and 36 evenly. Therefore, 4 is the GCF.

Example: Find the GCF of 14 and 15.

The factors of 14 are 1, 2, 7 and 14. 14 is the largest factor, but it does not divide evenly into 15. Neither does 7 or 2. Therefore, the only factor common to both 14 and 15 is the number 1, the GCF.

Least Common Multiple

LCM is the abbreviation for Least Common Multiple. The least common multiple of a group of numbers is the smallest number that all of the given numbers will divide into. The LCM will always be the largest of the given numbers or a multiple of the largest number.

Example: Find the LCM of 20, 30, and 40.

The largest number given is 40, but 30 will not divide evenly into 40. The next multiple of 40 is 80 (2 3 40), but 30 will not divide evenly into 80 either. The next multiple of 40 is 120. 120 is divisible by both 20 and 30, so 120 is the LCM.

Example: Find the LCM of 96, 16, and 24.

The largest number is 96. 96 is divisible by both 16 and 24, so 96 is the LCM.

DOMAIN II
PATTERNS, ALGEBRA, AND FUNCTIONS

COMPETENCY 4
UNDERSTAND RELATIONS AND FUNCTIONS

**SKILL Demonstrate knowledge of relations and functions and their
4.1 applications**

A RELATION is any set of ordered pairs. The DOMAIN OF A RELATION is the set containing all the first coordinates of the ordered pairs, and the RANGE OF A RELATION is the set containing all the second coordinates of the ordered pairs.

A FUNCTION is a relation in which each value in the domain corresponds to only one value in the range. It is notable, however, that a value in the range may correspond to any number of values in the domain. Thus, although a function is necessarily a relation, not all relations are functions, since a relation is not bound by this rule.

Example: Which set illustrates a function?

A. { (0,1) (0,2) (0,3) (0,4) }

B. { (3,9) (−3,9) (4,16) (−4,16) }

C. { (1,2) (2,3) (3,4) (1,4) }

D. { (2,4) (3,6) (4,8) (4,16) }

For a relation to be a function, each number in the domain can be matched with only one number in the range. Choice A is not a function because 0 is mapped to 4 different numbers in the range. In choice C, 1 is mapped to two different numbers. In choice D, 4 is also mapped to two different numbers. So the answer is choice B.

A relation can also be described algebraically. An equation such as $y = 3x + 5$ describes a relation between the independent variable x and the dependent variable y. Thus, y is written as $f(x)$ or a "function of x."

On a graph, use the **vertical line test** to check whether a relation is a function. If any vertical line intersects the graph of a relation in more than one point, then the relation is not a function.

> **RELATION:** any set of ordered pairs

> **DOMAIN OF A RELATION:** the set containing all the first coordinates of the ordered pairs

> **RANGE OF A RELATION:** the set containing all the second coordinates of the ordered pairs

> **FUNCTION:** a relation in which each value in the domain corresponds to only one value in the range

Example: Determine whether the following graph depicts a function.

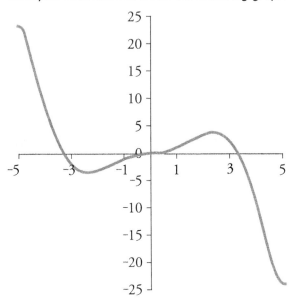

Use the vertical line test on the graph, as shown below. Every vertical line crosses the plotted curve only once. Therefore, the graph depicts a function.

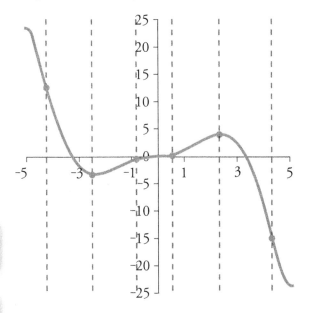

MAPPING: essentially the same as a function

A mapping is essentially the same as a function. Mappings (or maps) can be depicted using diagrams with arrows drawn from each element of the domain to the corresponding element (or elements) of the range.

A **MAPPING** is essentially the same as a relation. Mappings (or maps) can be depicted using diagrams with arrows drawn from each element of the domain to the corresponding element (or elements) of the range. If two arrows originate from any single element in the domain, then the mapping is not a function. Likewise, for a function, if each arrow is drawn to a unique value in the range (that is, there are no cases where more than one arrow is drawn to a given value in the range), then the function is one-to-one.

Example: Are the mappings shown below true functions?

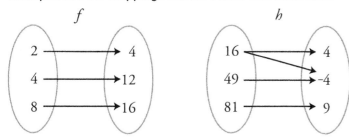

The mapping *f* is a function, but *h* is not.

The domain and the range of a function may be determined by inspecting the graph of the function or by analyzing the algebraic formula for the function.

Example: Determine the domain and the range of the following graph:

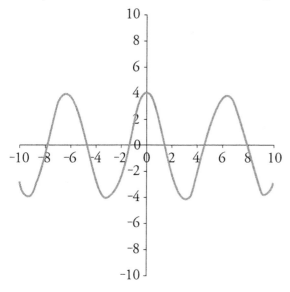

The domain of the function shown in the graph is infinite in both directions. Since the function is periodic and the *y* values vary between +4 and -4, the range of the function is -4 to +4.

Example: Determine the domain of the function depicted in the following graph.

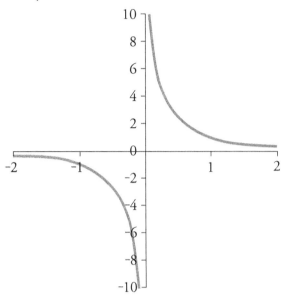

Note that this function is not continuous. It has two asymptotes: one for $y = 0$ and one for $x = 0$. It is apparent that the function is not defined for $x = 0$, but that it has finite values everywhere else. Thus, the domain of the function is all real numbers except 0.

The function plotted here is $y = \frac{1}{x}$; thus, by way of the function, it is clear that the range includes all real values except 0, for which the function goes to either positive or negative infinity in the limit (depending on the direction).

Example: Give the domain for the function over the set of real numbers:
$$y = \frac{3x + 2}{2x^2 - 3}$$
Find the values of x for which the denominator is 0. These values are excluded from the domain.

$$2x^2 - 3 = 0$$
$$2x^2 = 3$$
$$x^2 = \frac{3}{2}$$
$$x = \pm \sqrt{\frac{3}{2}} = \pm \sqrt{\frac{3}{2}} \times \sqrt{\frac{2}{2}} = \pm \frac{\sqrt{6}}{2}$$

Therefore the domain of the function is all real numbers except $\pm \dfrac{\sqrt{6}}{2}$

Example: Determine the domain and the range of this mapping.

4   6   domain: {4, -5}

-5   8   range: {8}

11

Evaluation of Functions

A function can be evaluated for a given input. For instance, let $h(x) = 7x - 3$ and evaluate the function for $x = -2$

Substitute -2 for x.

$h(-2) = 7(-2) - 3 = -14 - 3 = -17$

$h(-2) = -17$ reads as "h of negative 2 equals -17" and represents the given function evaluated for $x = -2$

Addition of Functions

$(f + g)(x) = f(x) + g(x)$

To add two functions, add together their solutions.

For example, if $f(x) = x^2 + 1$ and $g(x) = 6x - 1$,

$(f + g)(1) = f(1) + g(1) = 2 + 5 = 7$

$(f + g)(x) = f(x) + g(x) = (x^2 + 1) + (6x - 1) = x^2 + 6x.$

Subtraction of Functions

$(f - g)(x) = f(x) - g(x)$

To subtract two functions, subtract the solution of one from the solution of the other. For example, if $f(x) = 3x - 4$ and $g(x) = 5x + 2$,

$(f - g)(2) = f(2) - g(2) = 2 - 12 = -10.$

$(f - g)(x) = f(x) - g(x) = (3x - 4) - (5x + 2) = -2x - 6.$

Example: Given $f(x) = 3x + 1$ and $g(x) = 4 + 3x$, find $(f + g)(x)$, $(f - g)(x)$, $(f \times g)(x)$, and $\left(\frac{f}{g}\right)(x)$.

To find the answers, just apply the indicated operations (addition, subtraction, multiplication, and division).

$$(f + g)(x) = f(x) + g(x) = [3x + 1] + [4 + 3x]$$
$$= 3x + 3x + 1 + 4$$
$$= 6x + 5$$
$$(f - g)(x) = f(x) - g(x) = [3x + 1] - [4 + 3x]$$
$$= 3x - 3x + 1 - 4$$
$$= -3$$
$$(f \times g)(x) = [f(x)][g(x)] = (3x + 1)(4 + 3x)$$
$$= 12x + 4 + 9x^2 + 3x$$

$$= 9x^2 + 15x + 4$$

$$\left(\frac{f}{g}\right)x = \frac{f(x)}{g(x)} = \frac{3x + 1}{4 + 3x}$$

Example: Given f(x) = 2x, g(x) = x + 4, and h(x) = 5 − x³, find (f + g)(2), (h − g)(2), (f × h)(2), and ($\frac{h}{g}$)(2).

$f(2) = 2(2) = 4$

$g(2) = (2) + 4 = 6$

$h(2) = 5 - (2)^3 = 5 - 8 = \text{-}3$

Evaluate the following:

$(f + g)(2) = f(2) + g(2) = 4 + 6 = 10$

$(h - g)(2) = h(2) - g(2) = \text{-}3 - 6 = \text{-}9$

$(f \times h)(2) = f(2) \times h(2) = (4)(\text{-}3) = \text{-}12$

$(\frac{h}{g})(2) = h(2) \div g(2) = \text{-}3 \div 6 = \text{-}0.5$

The addition of functions is commutative and associative:

$f + g = g + f$ and $(f + g) + h = f + (g + h)$.

Composition of Functions

Composition of functions is way of combining functions such that the range of one function is the domain of another. For instance, the composition of functions f and g can be either $f \circ g$ (the composite of f with g) or $g \circ f$ (the composite of g with f). Another way of writing these compositions is $f(g(x))$ and $g(f(x))$. The domain of includes all values x such that $g(x)$ is in the domain of $f(x)$.

Example: What is the composition f ∘ g for functions f(x) = ax and g(x) = bx²?

The correct answer can be found by substituting the function $g(x)$ into $g \circ f$.

$f(g(x)) = ag(x) = abx^2$

On the other hand, the composition $g \circ f$ would yield a different answer.

$g(f(x)) = b(f(x))^2 = b(ax)^2 = a^2bx^2$

Example: If f(x) = √(x) and g(x) = x + 2, find the composition functions f ∘ g and g ∘ f and state their domains.

$(f \circ g)(x) = f(g(x)) = f(x + 2) = \sqrt{x + 2}$

$(g \circ f)(x) = g(f(x)) = g(\text{sqrt}(x)) = \sqrt{x} + 2$

The domain of $f(g(x))$ is $x \geq \text{-}2$ because $x + 2$ must be nonnegative in order to take the square root.

The domain of $g(f(x))$ is $x \geq 0$ because x must be nonnegative in order to take the square root.

Note that defining the domain of composite functions is important when square roots are involved.

Inverses of Functions

The **inverse** of a function $f(x)$ is typically labeled $f^{-1}(x)$ and satisfies the following two relations:

$$f(f^{-1}(x)) = x$$
$$f^{-1}(f(x)) = x$$

For a function $f(x)$ to have an inverse, it must be one-to-one. This fact is easily seen, since both $f(x)$ and $f^{-1}(x)$ must satisfy the vertical line test (that is, both must be functions). A function takes each value in a domain and relates it to only one value in the range. Logically, then, the inverse must do the same, only backwards: relate each value in the range to a single value in the domain.

Finding inverses of functions

Finding the inverse of a function can be a difficult or impossible task, but there are some simple approaches that can be followed in many cases. The simplest method for finding the inverse of a function is to interchange the variable and the function symbols and then solve to find the inverse. The approach is summarized in the outline below, given a one-to-one function $f(x)$.

1. Replace the symbol $f(x)$ with x

2. Replace all instances of x in the function definition with $f^{-1}(x)$ (or y or some other symbol)

3. Solve for $f^{-1}(x)$

4. Check the result using $f(f^{-1}(x)) = x$ or $f^{-1}(f(x)) = x$

Example: Determine if the function f(x) = x² has an inverse. If so, find the inverse.
First, determine if $f(x)$ is one-to-one. Note that $f(1) = f(-1) = 1$, so $f(x)$ is not one-to-one, and it therefore has no inverse function.

Example: Determine if the function f(x) = x³ + 1 has an inverse. If so, find the inverse.
The function $f(x) = x^3 + 1$ has an inverse because it increases monotonically for $x > 0$ and decreases monotonically for $x < 0$. As a result, it is one-to-one, and

the inverse exists. To calculate the inverse, let y be $f^{-1}(x)$. Replace $f(x)$ with x and replace x with y.

$$f(x) = x^3 + 1 \rightarrow x = y^3 + 1$$

Solve for y.

$$x - 1 = y^3$$
$$y = \sqrt[3]{x - 1}$$
$$f^{-1}(x) = \sqrt[3]{x - 1}$$

Test the result.

$$f^{-1}(f(x)) = \sqrt[3]{(x^3 + 1) - 1}$$
$$f^{-1}(f(x)) = \sqrt[3]{x^3 + 1 - 1} = \sqrt[3]{(x^3)} = x$$

The result is thus correct.

SKILL 4.3 Analyze characteristics of functions

*A function is symmetric about the y-axis if, for every point (**x, y**) that is included on the graph of the function, the point (-**x, y**) is also included on the graph.*

Symmetries in a function can also be described in terms of reflections or "mirror images." A function can be symmetric about the the y-axis (but not about the x-axis, except for the function $f(x) = 0$, since every function must pass the vertical line test). A function is symmetric about the y-axis if, for every point (x, y) that is included on the graph of the function, the point $(-x, y)$ is also included on the graph. Consider the function $f(x) = x^2$. Note that for each point (x, x^2) on the graph, the point $(-x, x^2)$ is also on the graph. The symmetry of the function about the y-axis can also be seen in the graph below.

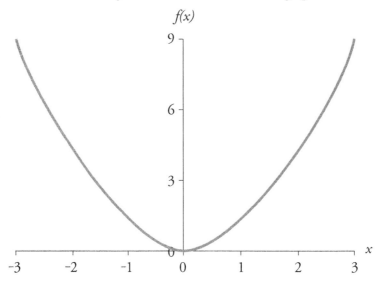

A function that is symmetric about the *y*-axis is also called an **EVEN FUNCTION**.

Although functions cannot be symmetric about the *x*-axis, relations that do not obey the vertical line test can be symmetric in this way. A relation is symmetric about the *x*-axis if, for every point (*x, y*) in the graph of the relation, the point (*x, −y*) is also in the graph.

Consider, for instance, the relation $g(x) = \pm\sqrt{x}$. For every value of *x* in the domain, the points $(x, \sqrt{x})$ and $(x, -\sqrt{x})$ are both in the graph, as shown below.

> **EVEN FUNCTION:** a function that is symmetric with respect to the *y*-axis

> *A relation is symmetric about the **x**-axis if for every point (**x, y**) in the graph of the relation, the point (**x, −y**) is also in the graph.*

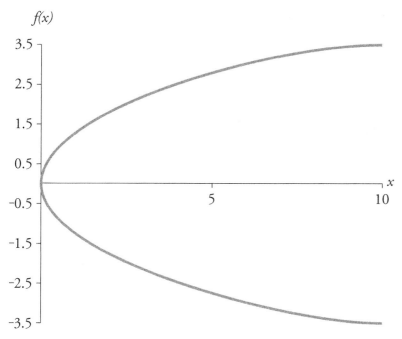

Functions may also be symmetric with respect to the origin. Such functions are called **ODD (OR ANTISYMMETRIC) FUNCTIONS** and are defined by the property that for any point (*x, y*) on the graph of the function, the point (−*x*, −*y*) is also on the graph of the function. The function $f(x) = x^3$, for instance, is symmetric with respect to the origin, as shown in the graph below.

> **ODD (OR ANTISYMMETRIC) FUNCTION:** a function that is symmetric with respect to the origin

> *A function is symmetric with respect to the origin if for any point (**x, y**) on the graph of the function, the point (−**x**, −**y**) is also on the graph of the function.*

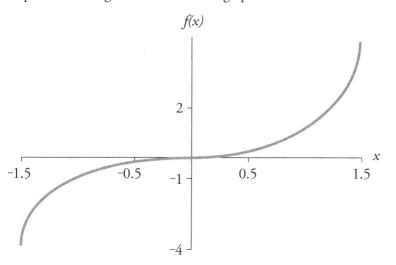

Example: Determine if the given function is even, odd, or neither even nor odd.

> A function f is even if
> f(-x) = f(x) and odd if
> f(-x) = -f(x) for all x in the
> domain of f.

1. $f(x) = x^4 - 2x^2 + 7$

    $f(-x) = (-x)^4 - 2(-x)^2 + 7$

    $f(-x) = x^4 - 2x^2 + 7$

    1. Find $f(-x)$.

    2. Replace x with $-x$.

    3. Since $f(-x) = f(x)$, $f(x)$ is an even function.

2. $f(x) = 3x^3 + 2x$

    $f(-x) = 3(-x)^3 + 2(-x)$

    $f(-x) = -3x^3 - 2x$

    $f(-x) = -(3x^3 + 2x)$

    $f(-x) = -f(x)$

    1. Find $f(-x)$.

    2. Replace x with $-x$.

    3. Factor out a (-1).

    4. Notice that $-(3x^3 + 2x) = -(f(x))$.

    5. Since $f(-x) = -f(x)$, $f(x)$ is an odd function.

3. $g(x) = 2x^2 - x + 4$

    $g(-x) = 2(-x)^2 - (-x) + 4$

    $g(-x) = 2x^2 + x + 4$

    $g(x) = -2x^2 + x - 4$

    1. First find $g(-x)$.

    2. Replace x with $-x$.

    3. Since $g(-x)$ does not equal $g(x)$, $g(x)$ is not an even function

    4. Note that $-g(x) = -2x^2 + 2x - 4$ which does not match $g(-x)$.

    5. Since $-g(x)$ does not equal $g(-x)$, $g(x)$ is not an odd function.

Thus, $g(x)$ is neither an even nor an odd function.

> A relation is considered
> one-to-one if each value in
> the domain corresponds to
> only one value in the range
> and if each value in the
> range corresponds to only
> one value in the domain.
> Thus, a one-to-one relation
> is also a function, but it adds
> an additional condition.

A relation is considered one-to-one if each value in the domain corresponds to only one value in the range and if each value in the range corresponds to only one value in the domain. Thus, a one-to-one relation is also a function, but it adds an additional condition.

In the same way that the graph of a relation can be examined using the vertical line test to determine whether it is a function, the horizontal line test can be used to determine if a function is a one-to-one relation. If no horizontal lines superimposed on the plot intersect the graph of the relation in more than one place, then the relation is one-to-one (assuming it also passes the vertical line test and, therefore, is a function).

SKILL 4.4 Interpret different representations of functions

A relationship between two quantities can be represented in a variety of ways, including as a symbolic expression (for instance, $f(x) = 3x^2 + \sin x$), a graph, a table of values, and a common-language expression (for example, "The speed of the car increases linearly from zero to 100 miles per hour in twelve seconds."). In the following example, the rule $y = 9x$ describes the relationship between the total amount earned, y, and the total number of pairs of $9 sunglasses sold, x. In a relationship of this type, one of the quantities (e.g., total amount earned) is dependent on the other (e.g., number of glasses sold). They are known as the **dependent** and **independent** variables, respectively.

A table using these data would appear as:

Number of Sunglasses Sold	1	5	10	15
Total Dollars Earned	9	45	90	135

Each (x, y) relationship between a pair of values is called the **COORDINATE PAIR** that can be plotted on a graph. The coordinate pairs (1, 9), (5, 45), (10, 90), and (15, 135) are plotted on the graph below.

COORDINATE PAIR: the (x, y) relationship between a pair of values

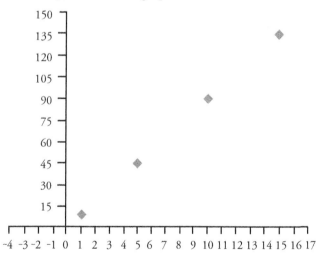

This graph shows a linear relationship. A linear relationship is one in which two quantities are proportional to each other. Doubling x also doubles y. On a graph, a straight line depicts a linear relationship.

The function or relationship between two quantities may be analyzed to determine how one quantity depends on the other.

For example, the function above shows a relationship between y and x where every y is 9 times the input, x. Therefore the rule can be written as $y = 9x$:

Consider another function: $y = 2x + 1$.

The relationship between two or more variables can be analyzed using a table, graph, written description, or symbolic rule. The function $y = 2x + 1$ is written as a symbolic rule. The same relationship is also shown in the table below:

x	0	2	3	6	9
y	1	5	7	13	19

This relationship could be written in words by saying that the value of y is equal to two times the value of x, plus one. This relationship could be shown on a graph by plotting given points such as the ones shown in the table above.

The ability to convert among various representations of a function depends on how much information is provided. For instance, although a graph of a function can provide some clues as to its symbolic representation, it is often difficult or impossible to obtain an exact symbolic form based only on a graph. The same difficulty applies to tables.

Converting from a symbolic form to a graph or table, however, is relatively simple, especially if a computer is available. The symbolic expression need simply be evaluated for a representative set of points that can be used to produce a sufficiently detailed graph or table. In other words, the equation $y = 2x + 1$ has been evaluated for $x = 0, 2, 3, 6, 9$ to generate the table of values shown.

COMPETENCY 5

UNDERSTAND LINEAR, QUADRATIC, AND HIGHER-ORDER POLYNOMIAL FUNCTIONS

SKILL 5.1 **Analyze the relationship between a linear, quadratic, or higher-order polynomial function and its graph**

A **LINEAR FUNCTION** is a function defined by the equation $f(x) = mx + b$ where m is the slope of the line representing the function and b is the y-intercept, or the y-coordinate where the line crosses the y-axis. In a linear function, the rate of change is constant.

Many real-world situations involve linear relationships. One example is the relationship between the elapsed time and the distance traveled when a car is moving at a constant speed. The relationship between the price and the quantity of a bulk item bought at a store is also linear, assuming that the unit price remains constant. These relationships can be expressed using the equation of a straight line and the slope is often used to describe a constant or average rate of change expressed in miles per hour or dollars per year, for instance. Where the line intercepts an axis indicates a starting point or a point at which values change from positive to negative or negative to positive.

Example: A man drives a car at a speed of 30 mph along a straight road. Express the distance d *traveled as a function of the time* t *assuming the man's initial position is* d_0.

The equation relating d and t in this case is

$d = 30t + d_0$.

Notice that this equation is in the familiar slope-intercept form $y = mx + b$. In this case, time t (in hours) is the independent variable, the distance d (in miles) is the dependent variable. The slope is the rate of change of distance in relation to time, i.e., the speed (in mph). The y-intercept, or intercept on the distance axis d_0, represents the initial position of the car at the start time $t = 0$.

The above equation is plotted below with $d_0 = 15$ miles (the point on the graph where the line crosses the y-axis).

$d = 30t + d_0$

> **LINEAR FUNCTION:** a function defined by the equation $f(x) = mx + b$ where m is the slope of the line representing the function and b is the y-intercept, or the y-coordinate where the line crosses the y-axis

> *Many real-world situations involve linear relationships. One example is the relationship between the elapsed time and the distance traveled when a car is moving at a constant speed. The relationship between the price and the quantity of a bulk item bought at a store is also linear, assuming that the unit price remains constant.*

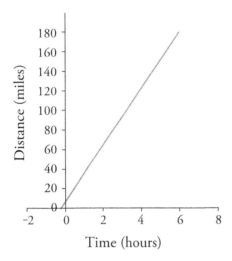

The x-intercept, or intercept on the time axis, represents the time at which the car would have been at $d = 0$ assuming it was traveling with the same speed before $t = 0$. This value can be found by setting d equal to 0 in the equation.

$$0 = 30t + 15$$
$$30t = -15$$
$$t = \frac{-15}{30} = -\frac{1}{2} \text{ hr.}$$

This simply means that if the car was at $d = 15$ miles when we started measuring the time ($t = 0$), it was at $d = 0$ miles half an hour before that.

Example: A model for the distance traveled by a migrating monarch butterfly is f(t) = 80t , *where* t *represents time in days.*

We interpret this to mean that the average speed of the butterfly is 80 miles per day and distance traveled may be computed by substituting the number of days traveled for t.

Example: The town of Verdant Slopes has been experiencing a boom in population growth. By the year 2000, the population had grown to 45,000, and by 2005, the population had reached 60,000.

Using the formula for slope as a model, find the average rate of change in population growth, expressing your answer in people per year. Then using the average rate of change determined, predict the population of Verdant Slopes in the year 2010.

Let t represent the time and p represent population growth. The two observances are represented by (t_1, p_1) and (t_2, p_2).

1st observance = (t_1, p_1) = (2000, 45000)
2nd observance = (t_2, p_2) = (2005, 60000)

Use the formula for slope to find the average rate of change.

$$\text{Rate of change} = \frac{p_2 - p_1}{t_2 - t_1}$$
$$= \frac{60000 - 45000}{2005 - 2000}$$
$$= \frac{15000}{5} = 3000 \text{ people/year}$$

The average rate of change in population growth for Verdant Slopes between the years 2000 and 2005 was 3,000 people per year. The population of Verdant Slopes can be predicted using the following:

3,000 people per year $\times$ 5 years $=$ 15,000 people,
60,000 people $+$ 15,000 people $=$ 75,000 people.

At a continuing average rate of growth of 3,000 people per year, the population of Verdant Slopes could be expected to reach 75,000 by the year 2010.

Graphing

Any function can be graphed by choosing reasonable input values, using them to evaluate the function, graphing the ordered pairs, and looking for a pattern to sketch in the complete graph. This process is often referred to as making a table and plotting points. It helps, however, to be able to predict the expected graph pattern of the function being graphed. A first degree function is linear and will create a line. A second degree equation is classified as quadratic, and will graph as a parabola.

A first degree function is linear and will create a line. A second degree equation is classified as quadratic, and will graph as a parabola.

The general form of a quadratic function is $y = ax^2 + bx + c$. Once a function is identified as quadratic, it is helpful to recognize several features that can indicate the form of the graph. The parabola has an axis of symmetry along $x = -\frac{b}{2a}$ which is the x-coordinate of the vertex (turning point) of the graph.

This can be understood more clearly if we consider an alternate form of a quadratic equation, the standard form for a parabola

$$y = a(x - h)^2 + k,$$

where point (h, k) denotes the coordinates of the vertex of the parabola.

By transforming the general form $y = ax^2 + bx + c$ into the above form, we get

$$y = a\left(x^2 + \frac{b}{a}x\right) + c$$
$$y = a\left(x^2 + 2\frac{b}{2a}x + \left(\frac{b}{2a}\right)^2\right) - \frac{b^2}{4a} + c$$
$$y = a\left(x + \frac{b}{2a}\right)^2 - \frac{b^2}{4a} + c$$

The coordinates of the vertex are given as $\left(-\frac{b}{2a}, -\frac{b^2}{4a} + c\right)$.

Example: Graph $y = 3x^2 + x - 2$.

Expressing this function in standard form we get
$$y = 3\left(x + \tfrac{1}{6}\right)^2 - \tfrac{25}{12}.$$

The graph is a parabola with an axis of symmetry $x = -\tfrac{1}{6}$, and the vertex is located at the point $\left(-\tfrac{1}{6}, -\tfrac{25}{12}\right)$.

Choose x values on either side of the vertex to create a table of ordered pairs to represent the parabola. Note that the original version of the function is used to evaluate x inputs here. Calculations are easier with this form.

x	$y = 3x^2 + x - 2$
-2	8
-1	0
0	-2
1	2
2	12

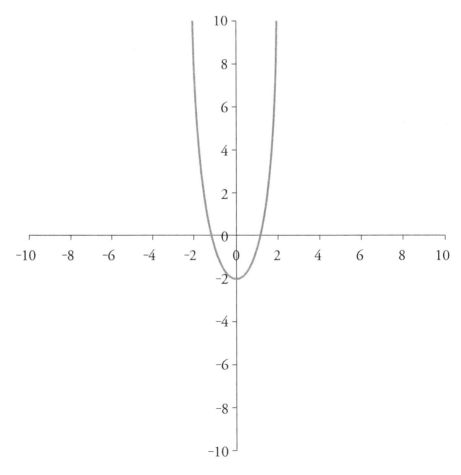

If the quadratic term is positive, the parabola is concave up; if the quadratic term is negative, the parabola is concave down. The function $-x^2 - 2x - 3$ is one such example and is shown below.

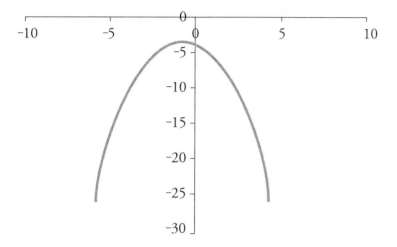

A quadratic function with two real roots (such as $y = 3x^2 + x - 2$ graphed previously) will have two crossings of the *x*-axis. A quadratic function with one real root will graph as a parabola that is tangent to the *x*-axis. An example of such a quadratic function is shown in the example below for the function $x^2 + 2x + 1$. The function has a single real root at $x = -1$.

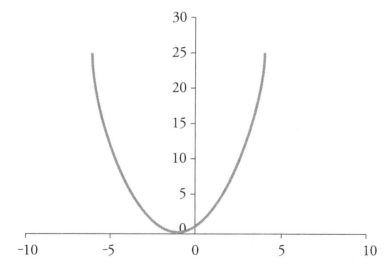

A quadratic function with no real roots will not cross the axis at any point. An example is the function $x^2 + 2x + 2$, which is plotted below.

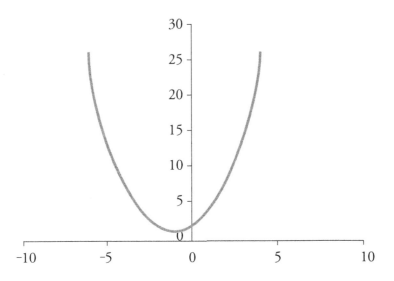

Example: Solve by graphing: $x^2 - 8x + 15 = 0$.

The roots of the polynomial $x^2 - 8x + 15$ are the x values for which the graph intersects the x-axis.

x	$y = x^2 - 8x + 15$
-2	35
-1	24
0	15
1	8
2	3

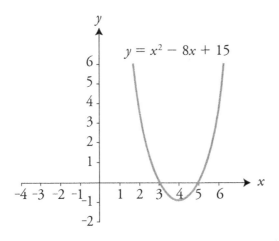

From the above graph, the x-intercepts, or zeros, are 3 and 5. So the solutions of the given quadratic equation are 3 and 5.

To graph a quadratic inequality, graph the quadratic as if it were an equation; however, if the inequality sign is $>$ or $<$, the curved line is dotted; if the inequality sign is $\geq$ or $\leq$, the curved line is solid. Shade above the curve for $>$ or $\geq$. Shade below the curve for $<$ or $\leq$.

Example: Graph the inequality $y < -x^2 + x - 2$.
The quadratic function $-x^2 + x - 2$ is plotted with a dotted line since the inequality sign is $<$ and not $\leq$. Since y is "less than" this function, the shading is done below the curve.

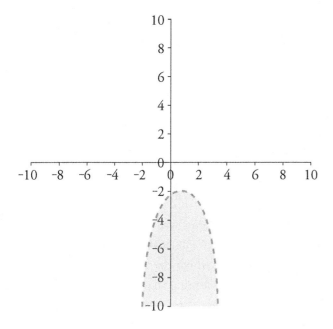

Example: Graph the inequality $y \geq x^2 - 2x - 9$.
The quadratic function $x^2 - 2x - 9$ is plotted with a solid line since the inequality sign is $\geq$. Since y is "greater than or equal to" this function, the shading is done above the curve.

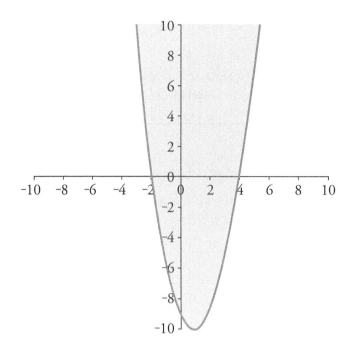

Polynomial Functions

A polynomial is a sum of terms where each term is a constant multiplied by a variable raised to a positive integer power. The general form of a polynomial $P(x)$ is

$$P(x) = a_n x^n + a_{n-1} x^{n-1} + \ldots + a_2 x^2 + a_1 x + a_0$$

Polynomials written in standard form have the terms written in decreasing exponent value, as shown above. The **DEGREE OF A POLYNOMIAL FUNCTION IN ONE VARIABLE** is the value of the largest exponent to which the variable is raised. The above expression is a polynomial of degree n (assuming that $a_n \neq 0$). Any function that represents a line is a polynomial function of degree one. Quadratic functions are polynomials of degree two. For instance, $5x^2 - 4x - 6$ is a second degree polynomial whereas $2x^3 - 5x^2 + x$ is a polynomial of degree three. If a term has more than one variable (e.g., $2xy$) it is necessary to add the exponents of the variables within the term to get the degree of the polynomial. Since $1 + 1 = 2$, $2xy$ is a polynomial of the second degree.

A polynomial may also be represented in tabular or graphical form as shown in the example below.

DEGREE OF A POLYNOMIAL FUNCTION IN ONE VARIABLE: the value of the largest exponent to which the variable is raised

Any function that represents a line is a polynomial function of degree one. Quadratic functions are polynomials of degree two. For instance, $5x^2 - 4x - 6$ is a second degree polynomial whereas $2x^3 - 5x^2 + x$ is a polynomial of degree three.

Example: Express the polynomial $x^3 - 6x + 4$ in tabular and graphical form.

x	y
-3	-5
-2	8
-1	9
0	4
1	-1
2	0
3	13

Note the change in sign of the y value between $x = -3$ and $x = -2$. This indicates there is a zero between $x = -3$ and $x = -2$. Since there is another change in sign of the y value between $x = 0$ and $x = 1$, there is a second root there. When $x = 2$, $y = 0$ so $x = 2$ is an exact root of this polynomial.

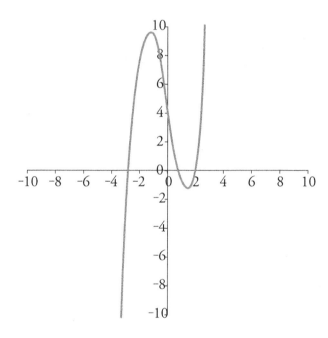

SKILL 5.2 Solve linear and quadratic equations and inequalities using a variety of methods

Solving Equations and Inequalities

To solve an equation or inequality, follow these steps:

Step 1	If there are parentheses, use the distributive property to eliminate them.
Step 2	If there are fractions, determine their LCD (least common denominator). Multiply every term of the equation by the LCD. This will cancel out all of the fractions, making it easier to solve the equation or inequality.
Step 3	If there are decimals, find the largest decimal. Multiply each term by a power of 10 (10, 100, 1,000, etc.) with the same number of zeros as the length of the decimal. This will eliminate all decimals while solving the equation or inequality.
Step 4	Combine the like terms on each side of the equation or inequality.
Step 5	If there are variables on both sides of the equation, add or subtract one of those variable terms to move it to the other side. Combine like terms.
Step 6	If there are constants on both sides, add or subtract one or more of those constants on both sides. Combine like terms.
Step 7	If there is a coefficient in front of the variable, divide both sides by this number to get the answer to the equation. Remember: *Dividing or multiplying an inequality by a negative number will reverse the direction of the inequality sign.*
Step 8	The solution of a linear equation is a single number. The solution of an inequality is a range of values shown using an inequality sign.

Example: Solve $3(2x + 5) - 4x = 5(x + 9)$.

$$6x + 15 - 4x = 5x + 45 \qquad \text{Step 1}$$
$$2x + 15 = 5x + 45 \qquad \text{Step 4}$$
$$-3x + 15 = 45 \qquad \text{Step 5}$$
$$-3x = 30 \qquad \text{Step 6}$$
$$x = -10 \qquad \text{Step 7}$$

Example: Solve $\frac{1}{2}(5x + 34) = \frac{1}{4}(3x - 5)$.

$$\frac{5}{2x} + 17 = \frac{3}{4x} - \frac{5}{4} \qquad \text{Step 1}$$

The LCD of $\frac{5}{2}$, $\frac{3}{4}$, and $\frac{5}{4}$ is 4.
Multiply by the LCD of 4.

$$4(\frac{5}{2x} + 17) = (\frac{3}{4x} - \frac{5}{4})4 \qquad \text{Step 2}$$
$$10x + 68 = 3x - 5$$
$$7x + 68 = -5 \qquad \text{Step 5}$$

$7x = -73$ Step 6

$x = \frac{-73}{7}$ or $-10\frac{3}{7}$ Step 7

Check:

$$\frac{1}{2}[5\frac{-73}{7} + 34] = \frac{1}{4}[3(\frac{-73}{7}) - 5]$$

$$\frac{-73(5)}{14} + 17 = \frac{3(-73)}{28} - \frac{5}{4}$$

$$\frac{-73(5) + 17(14)}{14} = \frac{3(-73)}{28} - \frac{5}{4}$$

$$\frac{-73(5) + 17(14)}{14} = \frac{3(-73) - 35}{28}$$

$$(\frac{-365 + 238}{28}) \times 2 = \frac{-219 - 35}{28}$$

$$\frac{-254}{28} = \frac{-254}{28}$$

Example: Solve 6x + 21 < 8x + 31.

$-2x + 21 < 31$ Step 5

$-2x < 10$ Step 6

$x > -5$ Step 7

Note that the inequality sign has changed direction.

Solving Quadratic Equations

A quadratic equation is expressed in the form $ax^2 + bx + c = 0$, where a, b, and c are real numbers and $a \neq 0$. The degree of a quadratic equation (i.e., the highest exponent of the variable x) is 2. Examples of quadratic equations are $5x^2 + 6x + 7 = 0$, $9x^2 - 4 = 0$, and $2x^7 - 3x = 0$.

If $p(x) = 0$ is a quadratic equation, then the zeros of the polynomial $p(x)$ are called the roots or solutions of equation $p(x) = 0$. Finding the roots of a quadratic equation is known as "solving for x." There are several different methods for solving quadratic equations:

- Factoring

- Completing the Square

- Quadratic Formula

- Graphing

Factoring

This method is applicable only for quadratic equations where the polynomial can be expressed as a product of linear factors. If a quadratic polynomial $ax^2 + bx + c = 0$ can be expressed as a product of two linear factors, say $(px + q)$ and $(rx + s)$, where p, q, r, s are real numbers, $ax^2 + bx + c = 0$ can be rewritten as

$(px + q)(rx + s) = 0$.

This implies that either of the two factors must be equal to zero.
$$(px + q) = 0 \text{ or } (rx + s) = 0$$

By solving these linear equations, we get the possible roots of the given quadratic equation.
$$x = -\frac{q}{p} \text{ and } x = -\frac{s}{r}$$

Example: Solve the following equation.

$x^2 + 10x - 24 = 0$	
$(x + 12)(x - 2) = 0$	Factor.
$x + 12 = 0 \quad \text{or} \quad x - 2 = 0$	Set each factor equal to 0.
$x = -12 \qquad x = 2$	Solve.

Check:

$$x^2 + 10x - 24 = 0$$

$(-12)^2 + 10(-12) - 24 = 0$	$(2)^2 + 10(2) - 24 = 0$
$144 - 120 - 24 = 0$	$4 + 20 - 24 = 0$
$0 = 0$	$0 = 0$

Completing the Square

A quadratic equation can be solved by completing the square. To complete the square, the coefficient of the x^2 term must be 1.

To solve a quadratic equation using this method:

1. Isolate the x^2 and x terms.

2. Add half of the coefficient of the x term, squared, to both sides of the equation.

3. Finally, take the square root of both sides and solve for x.

Example: Solve the following equation: $x^2 - 6x + 8 = 0$.

$x^2 - 6x = -8$	Move the constant to the right side.
$x^2 - 6x + 9 = -8 + 9$	Add the square of half the coefficient of x to both sides.
$(x - 3)^2 = 1$	Write the left side as a perfect square.
$x - 3 = \pm\sqrt{1}$	Take the square root of both sides.
$x - 3 = 1 \quad x - 3 = -1$	Solve.
$x = 4 \qquad x = 2$	

Check:

$$x^2 - 6x + 8 = 0$$

$4^2 - 6(4) + 8 = 0$	$2^2 - 6(2) + 8 = 0$
$16 - 24 + 8 = 0$	$4 - 12 + 8 = 0$
$0 = 0$	$0 = 0$

Quadratic Formula

To solve a quadratic equation using the quadratic formula, make sure that your equation is in the form $ax^2 + bx + c = 0$. Substitute these values into the formula:

$$x = \frac{-b \pm \sqrt{b^2 - 4ac}}{2a}.$$

Simplify the result to find the answers. (Remember, there could be two real answers, one real answer, or two complex answers that include i. See the preceding skill sections.)

> *To solve a quadratic equation using the quadratic formula, be sure that your equation is in the form $ax^2 + bx + c = 0$.*

Example: Solve the following equation using the quadratic formula:
$3x^2 = 7 + 2x$.

Rearrange the equation and use the quadratic formula as follows.

$$3x^2 = 7 + 2x \rightarrow 3x^2 - 2x - 7 = 0$$

$$a = 3 \quad b = -2 \quad c = -7$$

$$x = \frac{-(-2) \pm \sqrt{(-2)^2 - 4(3)(-7)}}{2(3)}$$

$$x = \frac{2 \pm \sqrt{4 + 84}}{6}$$

$$x = \frac{2 \pm \sqrt{88}}{6}$$

$$x = \frac{2 \pm 2\sqrt{22}}{6}$$

$$x = \frac{1 \pm \sqrt{22}}{3}$$

SKILL 5.3 **Solve systems of linear equations or inequalities using a variety of methods**

Linear Models

Many word problems may be modeled and solved using systems of linear equations and inequalities. Some examples are given below.

> *Many word problems may be modeled and solved using systems of linear equations and inequalities.*

Example: Farmer Greenjeans bought 4 cows and 6 sheep for $1,700. Mr. Ziffel bought 3 cows and 12 sheep for $2,400. If all the cows were the same price and all the sheep were another fixed price, find the price charged for a cow and the price charged for a sheep.

Let x = price of a cow

Let y = price of a sheep

Then Farmer Greenjeans's equation would be: $\qquad 4x + 6y = 1700$

Mr. Ziffel's equation would be: $\qquad 3x + 12y = 2400$

To solve by addition-subtraction:

Multiply the first equation by -2: $\qquad -2(4x + 6y = 1700)$

Keep the other equation the same: $\qquad (3x + 12y = 2400)$

Now the equations can be added to each other to eliminate one variable, and you can solve for the other variable.

$$-8x - 12y = -3400$$
$$\underline{3x + 12y = 2400} \qquad \text{Add these equations.}$$
$$-5x \qquad\quad = -1000$$

$x = 200 \leftarrow$ the price of a cow was $200.

Solving for y, $y = 150 \leftarrow$ the price of a sheep was $150. (This problem can also be solved by substitution or determinants.)

Example: Mrs. Allison bought 1 pound of potato chips, a 2-pound beef roast, and 3 pounds of apples for a total of $8.19. Mr. Bromberg bought a 3-pound beef roast and 2 pounds of apples for $9.05. Kathleen Kaufman bought 2 pounds of potato chips, a 3-pound beef roast, and 5 pounds of apples for $13.25. Find the per pound price of each item.

To solve by substitution:

Let x = price of a pound of potato chips.

Let y = price of a pound of roast beef.

Let z = price of a pound of apples.

Mrs. Allison's equation is $\qquad 1x + 2y + 3z = 8.19.$

Mr. Bromberg's equation is $\qquad 3y + 2z = 9.05.$

K. Kaufman's equation is $\qquad 2x + 3y + 5z = 13.25.$

Solve the first equation for x. (This equation was chosen because x is the easiest variable to isolate in this set of equations.) This equation becomes

$$x = 8.19 - 2y - 3z.$$

Substitute this expression into the other equations in place of x.

Equation 2: $3y + 2z = 9.05$

Equation 3: $2(8.19 - 2y - 3z) + 3y + 5z = 13.25$

Simplify the equation by combining like terms.

Equation 2: $3y + 2z = 9.05$

Equation 3: $-1y - 1z = -3.13$

Solve equation 3 for either y or z.

$y = 3.13 - z$ (*)

Substitute this into equation 2 for y.

Equation 2: $3(3.13 - z) + 2z = 9.05$

Equation 3: $-1y - 1z = -3.13$

Combine like terms in equation 2.

$9.39 - 3z + 2z = 9.05$

$z = \$0.34$ per pound (price of apples)

Substitute .34 for z in the above equation marked with an asterisk (*) and solve for y.

$y = 3.13 - z$

$y = 3.13 - .34$

$y = \$2.79 = $ per pound price of roast beef

Substitute .34 for z and 2.79 for y in one of the original equations and solve for x.

$1x + 2y + 3z = 8.19$

$1x + 2(2.79) + 3(.34) = 8.19$

$x + 5.58 + 1.02 = 8.19$

$x + 6.60 = 8.19$

$x = \$1.59 = $ per pound of potato chips

$(x, y, z) = (\$1.59, \$2.79, \$0.34)$

Example: Aardvark Taxi charges $4.00 initially, plus $1.00 for every mile traveled. Baboon Taxi charges $6.00 initially, plus $.75 for every mile traveled. Determine when it is cheaper to ride with Aardvark Taxi and when it is cheaper to ride with Baboon Taxi.

Aardvark Taxi's equation:	$y = 1x + 4$
Baboon Taxi's equation:	$y = .75x + 6$
Using substitution:	$.75y + 6 = 1x + 4$
Multiplying by 4:	$3y + 24 = 4x + 16$
Solving for x:	$8 = x$

This tells you that at eight miles, the total charge for the two companies is the same. If you compare the charge for one mile, Aardvark charges $5.00 and Baboon charges $6.75. Therefore, Aardvark is cheaper for distances up to eight miles, but Baboon Taxi is cheaper for distances greater than eight miles.

This problem can also be solved by graphing the two equations.

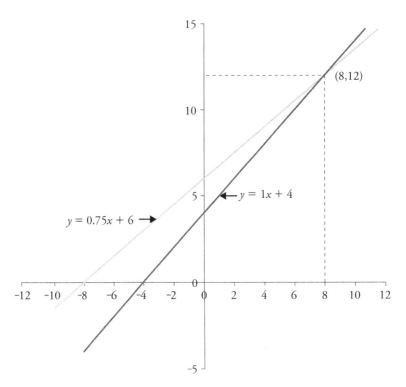

The lines intersect at (8,12); therefore at eight miles, both companies charge $12.00. At values of less than eight miles, Aardvark Taxi charges less (the graph is below Baboon). At values greater than eight miles, Aardvark charges more (the graph is above Baboon).

<table>
<tr><td>

LINEAR PROGRAMMING: the optimization of a linear quantity that is subject to constraints expressed as linear equations or inequalities

</td></tr>
</table>

LINEAR PROGRAMMING is the optimization of a linear quantity that is subject to constraints expressed as linear equations or inequalities. It is often used in various industries, ecological sciences, and governmental organizations to determine or project production costs, the amount of pollutants dispersed into the air, etc. The key to most linear programming problems is to organize the information in the word problem into a chart or graph of some type.

Example: The YMCA wants to sell raffle tickets to raise at least $32,000. If they must pay $7,250 in expenses and prizes out of the money collected from the tickets, how many $25 tickets must they sell?

Since they want to raise *at least* $32,000, that means they would be happy to get 32,000 *or more*. This requires an inequality.

Let x = number of tickets sold.

Then $25x$ = total amount of money collected for x tickets.

The total amount of money minus expenses is greater than $32,000.

$$25x - 7,250 \geq 32,000$$
$$25x \geq 39,250$$
$$x \geq 1,570$$

If they sell 1,570 tickets or more, they will raise at least $32,000.

Example: A printing manufacturer makes two types of printers, a Printmaster and a Speedmaster. The Printmaster requires 10 cubic feet of space and weighs 5,000 pounds; the Speedmaster takes up 5 cubic feet of space and weighs 600 pounds. The total available space for storage before shipping is 2,000 cubic feet and the weight limit for the space is 300,000 pounds. The profit on the Printmaster is $125,000 and the profit on the Speedmaster is $30,000. How many of each machine should be stored to maximize profitability and what is the maximum possible profit?

Let x represent the number of Printmaster units sold and let y represent the number of Speedmaster units sold. The equation for the space required to store the units is

$10x + 5y \leq 2000$

$2x + y \leq 400.$ Divide each term by 5 to make smaller numbers and easier calculations.

Since the number of units for both models cannot be less than 0, also impose the restrictions that $x \geq 0$ and $y \geq 0$. The restriction on the total weight can be expressed as

$5000x + 600y \leq 300000$

$25x + 3y \leq 1500.$

The expression for the profit P from sales of the printer units is

$P = \$125{,}000x + \$30{,}000y$

The solution to this problem is found by maximizing P subject to the constraints given in the preceding inequalities, along with the constraints that $x \geq 0$ and $y \geq 0$ since no negative amounts of printers will be sold. The equations are grouped below for clarity.

$x \geq 0$

$y \geq 0$

$2x + y \leq 400$

$25x + 3y \leq 1500$

$P = \$125{,}000x + \$30{,}000y$

The two inequalities in two variables are plotted in the graph below. The shaded region represents the set of solutions that obey both inequalities. (Note that when selecting ordered pairs from the shaded region, consider only points where both x and y are whole numbers.)

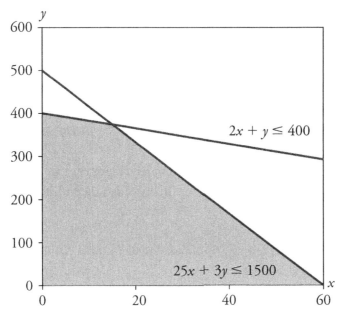

Note that the border of the shaded region that is formed by the two inequalities includes the solutions that constitute the maximum value of y for a given value of x. Note also that x cannot exceed 60 (since it would violate the second inequality). The solution to the problem must lie on the border of the shaded region since the border spans all the possible solutions that maximize the use of space and weight for a given number x.

To visualize the solution, plot the profit as a function of the solutions to the inequalities that lie along the border of the shaded area.

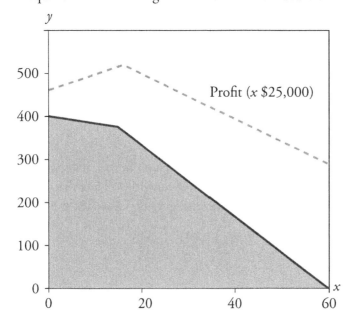

The profit curve shows a maximum at about $x = 16$. Verify this result by using a table to test several values.

x	y	P (x$25,000)
15	370	519
16	366	519.2
17	358	514.6

Also double check to be sure that the result obeys the two inequalities.

$2(16) + (366) = 398 \leq 400$

$25(16) + 3(366) = 1498 \leq 1500$

The optimum result is storage of 16 Printmaster and 366 Speedmaster printer units.

Example: Sharon's Bike Shoppe can assemble a 3-speed bike in 30 minutes and a 10-speed bike in 60 minutes. The profit on each bike sold is $60 for a 3-speed or $75 for a 10-speed bike. How many of each type of bike should be assembled during an 8-hour day (480 minutes) to maximize the possible profit? Total daily profit must be at least $300.

Let x be the number of 3-speed bikes and y be the number of 10-speed bikes. Since there are only 480 minutes to use each day, the first inequality is

$30x + 60y \leq 480$

$x + 2y \leq 16.$

Since the total daily profit must be at least $300, the second inequality can be written as follows, where P is the profit for the day:

$P = \$60x + \$75y \geq \$300$

$4x + 5y \geq 20.$

To visualize the problem, plot the two inequalities and show the potential solutions as a shaded region.

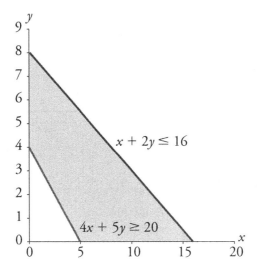

The number of bikes assembled must always be an integer value, so points within the shaded area of the graph must have integer values. The maximum profit will occur at or near a corner of the shaded portion of this graph. Those points occur at (0,4), (0,8), (16,0), and (5,0).

Since profits are $60/three-speed and $75/ten-speed, the profits for these four points would be:

$$
\begin{array}{ll}
(0, 4) & 60(0) + 75(4) = 300 \\
(0, 8) & 60(0) + 75(8) = 600 \\
(16, 0) & 60(16) + 75(0) = 960 \leftarrow \text{Maximum profit} \\
(5, 0) & 60(5) + 75(0) = 300
\end{array}
$$

The maximum profit will occur if 16 three-speed bikes are made daily.

Quadratic Models

Other word problems may be modeled using quadratic equations or inequalities. Examples of this type of problem follow.

Example: A family is planning to add a new room to their house. They would like the room to have a length that is 10 feet more than the width and a total area of 375 square feet. Find the length and width of the room.

Let x be the width of the room. The length of the room is then $x + 10$. The quadratic equation is

$$
x(x + 10) = 375
$$
$$
x^2 + 10x - 375 = 0.
$$

Factor the quadratic expression to solve the equation.

$$x^2 + 25x - 15x - 375 = 0 \qquad \text{Break up the middle}$$
$$x(x + 25) - 15(x + 25) = 0 \qquad \text{term using factors of 375}$$
$$(x + 25)(x - 15) = 0$$
$$x = -25 \text{ or } x = 15$$

Since the dimensions of a room cannot be negative, we choose the positive solution, $x = 15$. The width of the room is 15 feet and the length of the room is 25 feet.

Example: The formula for the maximum height of a projectile fired upward at a velocity of v meters per second from an original height of h meters is $y = h + vx - 4.9x^2$. If a rocket is fired from an original height of 250 meters with an original velocity of 4800 meters per second, find the approximate time the rocket would drop to sea level (a height of 0).

Substituting the height and velocity into the equation yields the equation $y = 250 + 4800x - 4.9x^2$. If the height at sea level is 0, then $y = 0$, so $0 = 250 + 4800x - 4.9x^2$. Use the quadratic formula to solve for x.

$$x = \frac{-4800 \pm \sqrt{4800^2 - 4(-4.9)(250)}}{2(-4.9)}$$
$$x \approx 979.53 \text{ or } x \approx -0.05 \text{ seconds}$$

Since the time has to be positive, it will be approximately 980 seconds until the rocket reaches sea level.

Example: A family wants to enclose 3 sides of a rectangular garden, at least 4800 square feet in area, with 200 feet of fence. A wall borders the fourth side of the garden. How long can the garden be?

In order to have a garden with an area of at least 4800 square feet, find the dimensions the garden should have.

Solution:

Let x = distance from the wall

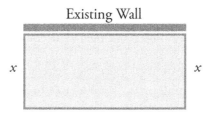

Existing Wall

Then amount of fence needed for these 2 sides is $2x$ feet. The side opposite the existing wall would use the remainder of the 200 feet of fence, that is, $200 - 2x$ feet of fence. Therefore the width (w) of the garden is x feet and the length (l) is $(200 - 2x)$ feet.

The area is calculated using the formula $A = lw = x(200 - 2x) = 200x - 2x^2$, and the area needs to be greater than or equal to 4800 square feet. The expression for this inequality is $4800 \leq 200x - 2x^2$. Subtract 4800 from each side and the inequality becomes

$$2(-x^2 + 100x - 2400) \geq 0$$
$$-x^2 + 100x - 2400 \geq 0$$
$$(-x + 60)(x - 40) \geq 0$$
$$-x + 60 \geq 0$$
$$-x \geq -60$$
$$x \leq 60$$
$$x - 40 \geq 0$$
$$x \geq 40.$$

The area will be at least 4800 square feet if the width of the garden is from 40 up to 60 feet. (The length of the rectangle would vary from 120 feet to 80 feet depending on the width of the garden.)

SKILL 5.4 Solve higher-order polynomial equations and inequalities in one and two variables

The Fundamental Theorem of Algebra

The **FUNDAMENTAL THEOREM OF ALGEBRA** states that a polynomial expression of degree n must have n roots (which may be real or complex and which may not be distinct). It follows from the theorem that if the degree of a polynomial is odd, then it must have at least one real root.

> **FUNDAMENTAL THEOREM OF ALGEBRA:** a polynomial expression of degree n must have n roots (which may be real or complex and which may not be distinct)

Polynomial equations are in the form of $P(x)$ given below, where n is the degree of the polynomial and the constant a_n is non-zero.

$$P(x) = a_n x^n + a_{n-1} x^{n-1} + \ldots + a_2 x^2 + a_1 x + a_0$$

If $P(c) = 0$ for some number c, then c is said to be a *zero* (or *root*) of the function. A zero is also called a *solution* to the equation.

The existence of n solutions can be seen by looking at a factorization of $P(x)$. For instance, consider $P(x) = x^2 - x - 6$. This second-degree polynomial can be factored into

$$P(x) = (x + 2)(x - 3).$$

Note that $P(x)$ has two roots in this case: $x = -2$ and $x = 3$. This corresponds to the degree of the polynomial, $n = 2$. In some cases, however, there may be non-distinct roots. Consider $P(x) = x^2$.

$$P(x) = (x)(x)$$

Note that the polynomial is factored in the same way as the previous example, but, in this case, the roots are identical: $x = 0$. Thus, although there are two roots for this second-degree polynomial, the roots are not distinct.

Likewise, roots of a polynomial may be complex. Consider $P(x) = x^2 + 1$. The range of this function is $P(x) \geq 1$, so there is no root in the sense that the function crosses the real x-axis. Nevertheless, if complex values of x are permitted, there are cases where $P(x)$ is zero. Factor $P(x)$ as before, but this time use complex numbers.

$$P(x) = (x + i)(x - i)$$

The solutions are $x = i$ and $x = -i$. Thus, this second-degree polynomial still has two roots.

For a general n^{th} degree polynomial, the function $P(x)$ can be factored in a similar manner.

$$P(x) = (x - c_n)(x - c_{n-1}) \dots (x - c_2)(x - c_1)$$

If a factor $(x - c)$ occurs k times in the factorization of a polynomial, the root c is said to have a **multiplicity** of k. For the polynomial $P(x) = x^2$, for instance, the root $x = 0$ has a multiplicity of 2.

The zeros of a rational function $\frac{p(x)}{q(x)}$ are the zeros of the numerator, $p(x)$, provided they are not also zeros of the denominatoar, $q(x)$.

Consider the functions $a(x) = \frac{x-2}{x+2}$ and $b(x) = \frac{x-2}{x^2-4} = \frac{x-2}{(x+2)(x-2)}$.

The function $a(x)$ has a zero at $x = 2$, but the function $b(x)$ does not. This is because $x = 2$ makes the denominator of $b(x)$ zero and, therefore, lies outside the domain of that function.

Polynomial

A range of methods can be used to solve polynomial equations. Several theorems, including the Fundamental Theorem of Algebra discussed previously, are useful in this regard.

As mentioned previously in this competency, a polynomial of degree n may be factored as follows:

$$P(x) = (x - c_n)(x - c_{n-1}) \dots (x - c_2)(x - c_1)$$

The Factor Theorem states that a polynomial $P(x)$ has a factor $(x - a)$ if and only if $P(a) = 0$. Thus, the constants $C_n, C_{n-1} \dots C_1$ in the expression given above are the roots of the polynomial equation $P(x) = 0$.

The Factor Theorem states that a polynomial $P(x)$ has a factor $(x - a)$ if and only if $P(a) = 0$.

If a single root c is known, then the polynomial can be simplified (that is, it can be reduced by one degree) using division.

$$Q(x) = \frac{P(x)}{x - c}$$

Here, if $P(x)$ has degree n, then $Q(x)$ has degree $n - 1$. If some roots are known, the task of finding the other roots can be simplified by performing the division represented above. As each successive root is found, the degree of the polynomial can be reduced again to further simplify finding the remaining roots.

In some cases, dividing a polynomial by $(x - c)$ is simple, but generally speaking it is a complicated process. The process can be simplified using synthetic division, however.

To perform synthetic division of a polynomial $P(x)$ by $(x - c)$ to get a new polynomial $Q(x)$, first draw an upside-down division symbol as shown below, using the coefficients of $P(x)$ and the root c.

$$P(x) = a_n x^n + a_{n-1} x^{n-1} + \ldots + a_2 x^2 + a_1 x + a_0$$
$$Q(x) = \frac{P(x)}{x - c}$$

$$c \ \big|\ a_n \quad a_{n-1} \quad a_{n-2} \quad \ldots$$

The first step of synthetic division is to carry the first term, a_{n-1}.

$$c \ \big|\ a_n \quad a_{n-1} \quad a_{n-2} \quad \ldots$$
$$a_n$$

Each successive step involves multiplying c by the previously carried term and then placing the result under the next term. Then add the two results to get the next carry value.

$$c \ \big|\ a_n \quad a_{n-1} \quad a_{n-2} \quad \ldots$$
$$ca_n$$
$$a_n$$

$$c \ \big|\ a_n \quad a_{n-1} \quad a_{n-2} \quad \ldots$$
$$ca_n$$
$$(ca_{n-1} - ca_n)$$

Repeat the process until the last carry term is found. The result should be zero. (If the final carry value is not zero, c is not a root. This can be a useful test of whether a particular value is a root, especially for polynomials of high degrees.) The result of the division is the set of new coefficients for the quotient.

$$Q(x) = a_n x^{n-1} + (a_{n-1} - ca_n) x^{n-2} + \ldots$$

Example: Divide x⁴ − 7x² − 6x by (x + 2). Find the roots of the polynomial.

Use synthetic division. Notice that even the terms with coefficient zero must be included. (In other words, first write the polynomial as $x^4 + 0x^3 - 7x^2 - 6x + 0$.)

$$-2 \;\big|\; \begin{array}{ccccc} 1 & 0 & -7 & -6 & 0 \end{array}$$

Perform the division.

$$-2 \;\big|\; \begin{array}{ccccc} 1 & 0 & -7 & -6 & 0 \\ \\ 1 & & & & \end{array}$$

$$-2 \;\big|\; \begin{array}{ccccc} 1 & 0 & -7 & -6 & 0 \\ & -2 & & & \\ 1 & -2 & & & \end{array}$$

$$-2 \;\big|\; \begin{array}{ccccc} 1 & 0 & -7 & -6 & 0 \\ & -2 & 4 & & \\ 1 & -2 & -3 & & \end{array}$$

$$-2 \;\big|\; \begin{array}{ccccc} 1 & 0 & -7 & -6 & 0 \\ & -2 & 4 & 6 & \\ 1 & -2 & -3 & 0 & \end{array}$$

$$-2 \;\big|\; \begin{array}{ccccc} 1 & 0 & -7 & -6 & 0 \\ & -2 & 4 & 6 & 0 \\ 1 & -2 & -3 & 0 & 0 \end{array}$$

These numbers represent the coefficients of the polynomial answer to the division problem. Exclude the value on the right, as it is the remainder. Then work from right to left building a polynomial with increasing powers of *x*.

$$0x^0 - 3x^1 - 2x^2 + 1x^3$$

Thus, −2 is indeed a root of the polynomial. The result is

$$\frac{x^4 - 7x^2 - 6x}{x + 2} = x^3 - 2x^2 - 3x$$

Note that the remaining roots of this polynomial can be found much more easily than if the original polynomial were analyzed as is. Factor the result further.

$$x^3 - 2x^2 - 3x = x(x^2 - 2x - 3) = x(x - 3)(x + 1)$$

The roots are −2, −1, 0, and 3.

According to the **Complex Conjugate Root Theorem**, for a polynomial $P(x)$ with real coefficients, if $P(x)$ has a complex root z, then it must also have a complex root $\bar{z}$. (The bar notation indicates complex conjugate. Thus, if $z = a + bi$, then $\bar{z} = a - bi$.)

The **Rational Root Theorem**, also known as the Rational Zero Theorem, allows determination of all possible rational roots (or zeros) of a polynomial equation with integer coefficients. (A root is a value of x such that $P(x) = 0$.) Every rational root of $P(x)$ can be written as $x = \frac{p}{q}$, where p is an integer factor of the constant term a_0 and q is an integer factor of the leading coefficient a_n.

Example: Find the rational roots of $P(x) = 3x^3 - 7x^2 + 3x - 2$.
By the Rational Root Theorem, the roots must be of the form
$$x = \pm\frac{1.2}{1.3}.$$

The candidates are then
$$x = \pm 1, \pm\frac{1}{3}, \pm\frac{2}{3}, \pm 2.$$

Test each possibility. The only result that works is $x = 2$.
$$3(2)^3 - 7(2)^2 + 3(2) - 2$$
$$3(8) - 7(4) + 6 - 2$$
$$24 - 28 + 4$$
$$0$$

(Note that the Rational Root Theorem does not guarantee that each potential rational number that includes factors of the leading and constant terms is a root. The theorem only states that roots will include these factors.)

In cases where a polynomial is highly complicated or involves constants that do not permit methods such as factoring, a numerical approach may be appropriate. Newton's method is one possible approach to solving a polynomial equation numerically. At other times it may require a graphical approach whereby the behavior of the function is examined on a visual plot. When using Newton's method, graphing the function can be helpful for estimating the locations of the real roots (if any).

SKILL 5.5 Analyze the characteristics of linear, quadratic, and higher-order polynomial equations

For a quadratic function of the form $ax^2 + bx + c$, the **discriminant** is the portion of the quadratic formula which is found under the square root sign, $b^2 - 4ac$.

According to the quadratic formula, the zeros of the function are given by

$$x = \frac{-b \pm \sqrt{b^2 - 4ac}}{2a}.$$

Note that the radical sign is not part of the discriminant. Determine the value of the discriminant by substituting the values of a, b, and c from the equation $ax^2 + bx + c = 0$.

The discriminant can be used to determine the nature of the solution of a quadratic equation.

1. If $b^2 - 4ac < 0$, there are no real roots and two complex roots that include the imaginary number i (square root of -1).

2. If $b^2 - 4ac = 0$, there is only one real rational root.

3. If $b^2 - 4ac > 0$ and also a perfect square, there are two real rational roots. (There are no longer any radical signs.)

4. If $b^2 - 4ac > 0$ and not a perfect square, there are two real irrational roots. (There are still unsimplified radical signs.)

Example: Find the value of the discriminant for the equation
$2x^2 - 5x + 6 = 0$. Then determine the number and nature of the solutions of that quadratic equation.
The discriminant is
$$b^2 - 4ac = (-5)^2 - 4\,(2)(6) = 25 - 48 = -23.$$

Since -23 is a negative number, there are no real roots and two complex roots, which are given below.
$$x = \frac{5}{4} \pm \frac{i\sqrt{23}}{4}$$

Example: Find the value of the discriminant for the equation
$3x^2 - 12x + 12 = 0$. Then determine the number and nature of the solutions of the quadratic equation.
The discriminant is
$$b^2 - 4ac = (-12)^2 - 4\,(3)(12) = 144 - 144 = 0.$$

Since the value of the discriminant is 0, there is only one real rational root: $x = 2$.

Also see Skills 5.1 and 5.4

SKILL 5.6 Analyze real-world problems involving linear, quadratic, and higher-order polynomial functions

See Skill 5.3 for problems involving linear and quadratic functions. An example involving a polynomial function is given below.

Example: A cubic container is modified so that its length is increased by 4 inches and its width is shortened by 2 inches. The height of the container remains unchanged. If the volume of the container is 16 cubic inches, what is it height?

Let the side of the original cube be x inches.

The volume of the modified container is given by

$$x(x + 4)(x - 2) = 16.$$

Distributing and rearranging we get

$$x(x^2 + 2x - 8) = 16$$
$$\rightarrow x^3 + 2x^2 - 8x - 16 = 0.$$

The third order polynomial equation above can be grouped and factored as follows:

$$x^2(x + 2) - 8(x + 2) = 0$$
$$\rightarrow (x + 2)(x^2 - 8) = 0.$$

The solutions to the equation are, therefore, $x = -2, -2\sqrt{2}, 2\sqrt{2}$.

Since the height of the box must be a positive number, we choose the positive solution. The height is $2\sqrt{2}$ inches.

COMPETENCY 6

UNDERSTAND EXPONENTIAL AND LOGARITHMIC FUNCTIONS

SKILL Apply the laws of exponents and logarithms
6.1

Exponentials and logarithms are complementary. The general relationship for logarithmic and exponential functions is

$y = \log_b x$ if and only if $x = b^y$.

For the exponential base e and the natural logarithm (ln) the relationship is

$y = \ln x$ if and only if $e^y = x$.

When changing common logarithms to exponential form,

$y = \log_b x$ if and only if $x = b^y$.

Natural logarithms can be changed to exponential form by using

$\log_e x = \ln x$, or $\ln x = y$ can be written as $e^y = x$.

Logarithms

Example: Express in exponential form.

$\log_3 81 = 4$

$x = 81$ $b = 3$ $y = 4$ Identify values.

$81 = 3^4$ Rewrite in exponential form.

Example: Solve by writing in exponential form.

$\log_x 125 = 3$

$x^3 = 125$ Write in exponential form.

$x^3 = 5^3$ Write 125 in exponential form.

$x = 5$ Bases must be equal if exponents are equal.

Use a scientific calculator to solve.

Example: Find ln 72.

$\ln 72 = 4.2767$

Use the "ln x" key to find natural logs.

The next example "checks" the previous problem through use of the inverse operation.

Example: Find ln x = 4.2767

Write in exponential form to find x.

$e^{4.2767} = x$ Use the "e^x" key (or "2nd" "ln x").

$x = 72.002439$ The small difference is due to rounding.

The following properties of logarithms are helpful in solving equations.

PROPERTIES OF LOGARITHMS	
Multiplication Property	$\log_b mn = \log_b m + \log_b n$
Quotient Property	$\log_b \frac{m}{n} = \log_b m - \log_b n$
Powers Property	$\log_b n^r = r\log_b n$
Equality Property	$\log_b n = \log_b m$ if and only if $n = m$
Change of Base Formula	$\log_b n = \frac{\log n}{\log b}$
	$\log_b b^x = x$ and $b^{\log_b x} = x$

Exponentials

The following properties can be used to simplify expressions involving exponents.

KEY EXPONENT RULES: FOR 'a' NONZERO AND 'm' AND 'n' REAL NUMBERS		
Product Rule	$a^m \times a^n = a^{(m+n)}$	$(3^4)(3^5) = 3^9$
	$a^m \times b^m = (ab)^m$	$(4^2)(5^2) = 20^2$
	$(a^m)^n = a^{mn}$	$(2^3)^2 = 2^6$
Quotient Rule	$\frac{a^m}{a^n} = a^{(m-n)}$	$2^5 \div 2^3 = 2^2$
Rule of Negative Exponents	$a^{-m} = \frac{1}{a^m}$	$2^{-2} = \frac{1}{2^2}$

Example: Simplify $\dfrac{3^5(3^{-2} + 3^{-3})}{9}$.

$$\frac{3^5(3^{-2} + 3^{-3})}{9} = \frac{3^5(3^{-2} + 3^{-3})}{3^2} = 3^3(3^{-2} + 3^{-3})$$

$$= 3^3 3^{-2} + 3^3 3^{-3} = 3^{3-2} + 3^{3-3} = 3 + 1 = 4$$

Example: Simplify $\frac{3^2 \times 5^{-2} \times 2^5}{6^2 \times 5}$.

$$\frac{3^2 \times 5^{-2} \times 2^5}{6^2 \times 5} = \frac{3^2 \times 5^{-2} \times 2^5}{3^2 \times 2^2 \times 5} = 5^{-2-1} \times 2^{5-2} = \frac{2^3}{5^3} = \frac{8}{125}$$

Unless the negative sign is inside the parentheses and the exponent is outside the parentheses, the sign is not affected by the exponent.

Example:

$$(-2)^4 = (-2) \times (-2) \times (-2) \times (-2) = 16$$

In this case, -2 is multiplied by itself 4 times.

$$-2^4 = -(2 \times 2 \times 2 \times 2) = -16$$

In this case, 2 is multiplied by itself 4 times and the answer is negated.

A radical may also be expressed using a rational exponent.

$$\sqrt[n]{a} = a^{\frac{1}{n}}$$

Example:

$$\sqrt{5} = 5^{\frac{1}{2}}; \ \sqrt[5]{7} = 7^{\frac{1}{5}}$$

All the exponent laws discussed above also apply to rational exponents.

Example:

$$(\sqrt[5]{6})^3 = (6^{\frac{1}{5}})^3 = 6^{(\frac{1}{5}) \times 3} = 6^{\frac{3}{5}}$$

Example: Simplify $(-32)^{\frac{3}{5}} + 16^{\frac{3}{4}}$.

$$(-32)^{\frac{3}{5}} + 16^{\frac{3}{4}} = (\sqrt[5]{-32})^3 + (\sqrt[4]{16})^3 = (-2)^3 + 2^3 = -8 + 8 = 0$$

Example: Solve $\log_6 (x - 5) + \log_5 x = 2$.

$\log_6 x(x - 5) = 2$	Use product property.
$\log_6 x^2 - 5x = 2$	Distribute.
$x^2 - 5x = 6^2$	Write in exponential form.
$x^2 - 5x - 36 = 0$	Solve quadratic equation.
$(x + 4)(x - 9) = 0$	
$x = -4 \quad x = 9$	

***Be sure to check results. Remember, x must be greater than zero in $\log x = y$.

$\log_6(x - 5) + \log_6 x = 2$	
$\log_6(-4 - 5) + \log_6 (-4) = 2$	Substitute the first answer.
$\log_6(-9) + \log_6 (-4) = 2$	This is undefined (the argument is less than zero).
$\log_6(9 - 5) + \log_6 9 = 2$	Substitute the second answer.
$\log_6 4 + \log_6 9 = 2$	
$\log_6 (4)(9) = 2$	Multiplication property.

$$\log_6 36 = 2$$
$$6^2 = 36 \qquad \text{Write in exponential form.}$$
$$36 = 36$$

Therefore the only solution to the problem is $x = 9$

SKILL 6.2 **Analyze the relationship between exponential and logarithmic functions**

An **exponential function** is defined by the equation $y = ab^x$, where a is the starting value, b is the growth factor, and x is the exponent of the growth factor. For exponential functions, the ratio between successive ys, or outputs, are constant. In other words, each y, or output, is a constant multiple of the previous y.

If $a > 0$ and b is between 0 and 1, the graph of the exponential function will be decreasing or decaying.

If $a > 0$ and b is greater than 1, the graph will be increasing or growing.

An exponential function is defined by the equation $y = ab^x$, where a is the starting value, b is the growth factor, and x is the exponent of the growth factor. For exponential functions, the ratio between successive ys or outputs are constant. In other words, each y or output, is a constant multiple of the previous y.

Example: Identify the pattern represented by $y = 100(1.5)^x$

x	y	Ratio of change is a constant 50% increase indicated by multiplying by 1.5:
0	100	
1	150	1.5(100) = 150
2	225	1.5(150) = 225
3	337.5	1.5(225) = 337.5
4	506.25	1.5(337.51) = 506.25

With $b > 1$, the equation represents exponential growth. The increasing values in the table indicate growth as well.

Logarithmic functions of base a are of the basic form
$$f(x) = \log_a x, \text{ where } a > 0 \text{ and not equal to 1.}$$

Expressed verbally, the logarithm $f(x)$ of a number x is the exponent or power to which the base must be raised to equal x. For example, 10 raised to the power 3 is 1000. Therefore, the base 10 logarithm of 1000 is 3.

The logarithmic function essentially transforms a geometrical progression into an arithmetic one. This is clear if one considers that the base 10 logarithm of 10, 10^2, 10^3, ... is 1, 2, 3, and so on.

Graphing exponential and logarithmic functions involves finding a set of representative points, plotting these points on a graph, and then connecting the points with appropriate curves. The domain of an exponential function includes all real numbers; the domain of a logarithmic function includes only the positive real numbers. The basic shapes of the exponential and logarithmic functions are illustrated below.

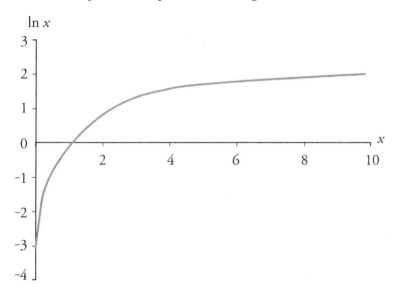

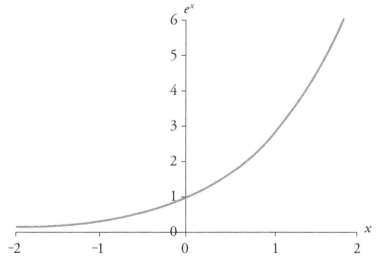

Note that the function e^x has an asymptote at $y = 0$ (the limit of the exponential function as x goes to negative infinity is zero), and the function $\ln x$ has an asymptote at $x = 0$. (The limit of the natural logarithmic function as x goes to zero from the right is negative infinity.) The x-intercept of the logarithmic function, irrespective of base, is always $(1, 0)$ since any number raised to the power of 0 is equal to one. The y-intercept of e^x is $(0, 1)$ because any base raised to the power of 0 equals 1.

See also Skill 6.1

**SKILL
6.3** **Analyze exponential and logarithmic functions and their graphs**

In order to understand the relationship between the graphical characteristics of an exponential or logarithmic function and its symbolic representation, we will look at several examples to see how a change in the algebraic expression is reflected on the graph.

We will also see how knowing the intercepts and asymptotes aids the process of drawing a graph.

Example: Graph the function $f(x) = \log_2 (x + 1)$.
The domain of the function is all values of x such that $x + 1 > 0$.

Thus, the domain of $f(x)$ is $x > $ -1. The range of $f(x)$ is infinite in both directions.

The vertical asymptote of $f(x)$ is the value of x that satisfies the equation $x + 1 = 0$. Thus, the vertical asymptote is $x = $ -1.

The x-intercept of $f(x)$ is the value of x that satisfies the equation $x + 1 = 1$ because $2^0 = 1$. Thus, the x-intercept of $f(x)$ is $(0, 0)$.

Finally, we find two additional values of $f(x)$, one between the vertical asymptote and the x-intercept and the other to the right of the x-intercept. $f(-0.5) = $ -1 and $f(3) = 2$.

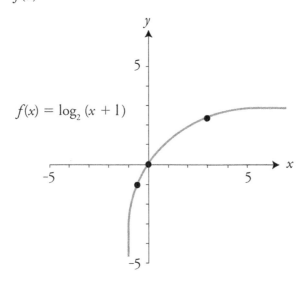

$f(x) = \log_2 (x + 1)$

Example: Graph the function f(x) = 2^x − 4.

The domain of the function is the set of all real numbers and the range is $y > -4$. Because the base is greater than 1, the function is increasing. The y-intercept of $f(x)$ is $(0, -3)$. The x-intercept of $f(x)$ is $(2, 0)$. The horizontal asymptote of $f(x)$ is $y = -4$.

Finally, to construct the graph of $f(x)$ we find two additional values for the function. For example, $f(-2) = -3.75$ and $f(3) = 4$.

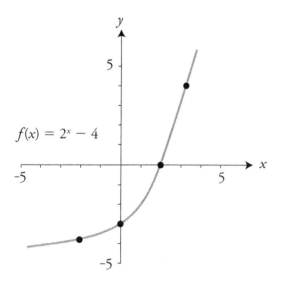

Note that the horizontal asymptote of any exponential function of the form $g(x) = a^x + b$ is $y = b$. Note also that the graph of such exponential functions is the graph of $h(x) = a^x$ shifted b units up or down. Finally, the graph of exponential functions of the form $g(x) = a^{(x + b)}$ is the graph of $h(x) = a^x$ shifted b units left or right.

Example: Sketch the graph of the function f(x) = ln(x^2 − 2).

In this case, the domain of the function is the set of values for which $x^2 - 2 > 0$, which requires that $x > \sqrt{2}$ or $x < -\sqrt{2}$. Note that the asymptotes are located at the x value for which the argument of the natural logarithm is zero.

$$x^2 - 2 = 0$$
$$x^2 = 2$$
$$x = \pm \sqrt{2}$$

Also note that the function is symmetric about the y-axis. Some values for the function for $x > \sqrt{2}$ are shown in the table below.

x	f(x)
1.5	-1.39
1.75	0.06
2	0.69
3	1.95
4	2.64
5	3.14
6	3.53

The plot of the function is shown below, with the asymptotes displayed as dashed lines.

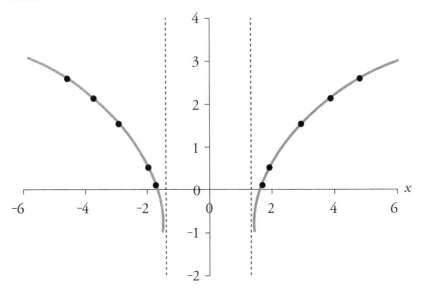

Example: Sketch the graph of the function $f(x) = e^{2x-1} + 1$.
The function $f(x)$ has an asymptote at $y = 1$, since
$$\lim_{x \to -\infty} e^{2x-1} + 1 = e^{-2\infty - 1} + 1 = 0 + 1 = 1$$

The y-intercept of the function is
$$f(0) = e^{2(0)-1} + 1 = e^{-1} + 1 = \frac{1}{e} + 1 \approx 1.368$$

The following table of values can be used to plot the function.

x	f(x)
-5	1.00
-4	1.00
-3	1.00
-2	1.01
-1	1.05
0	1.37
1	3.72
2	21.1

The graph of the function is shown below with the asymptote displayed as a dashed line.

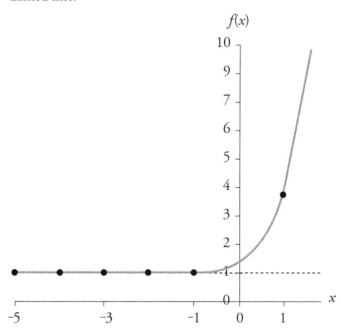

Analyze real-world problems involving exponential and logarithmic functions

Exponential Growth

A quantity which grows by a fixed percent at regular intervals (i.e., in proportion to the existing amount) demonstrates exponential growth. If a population has a constant birth rate through the years and is not affected by famine or disease, it has exponential growth. The birth rate alone controls how fast the population grows exponentially.

> *A quantity which grows by a fixed percent at regular intervals (i.e., in proportion to the existing amount) demonstrates exponential growth.*

Example: A population of a city is 20,000 and it increases at an annual rate of 20%. What will be the population of the city after 10 years?

The formula for the growth is $y = a(1 + r)^t$, where a is the initial amount, r is the growth rate, and t is the number of time intervals.

In this case,

$a = 20000$

$r = 20\% = 0.2$

$t = 10$

Substituting the values,

$$\text{population growth} = y = 20000(1 + 0.2)^{10}$$
$$= 20000(1 + 0.2)^{10}$$
$$= 20000(1.2)^{10}$$
$$= 20000(6.19)$$
$$= 123800$$

The population of the city after 10 years is 123,800.

What will be the population of the city after 50 years?

In 50 years,

$$\text{population} = 20000(1 + 0.2)^{50}$$
$$= 20000(1 + 0.2)^{50}$$
$$= 20000(1.2)^{50}$$
$$= 20000(9100.44)$$
$$= 182008800$$

The population after 50 years will be 182,008,800.

Another example of exponential growth is the growth of money through compound interest. See later in this competency for examples.

Exponential Decay

Exponential decay is decrease by a fixed percent at regular intervals of time. Radioactive decay is an example of this.

Example: If 40 grams of radioactive iodine has reduced to 20 grams in 6 days, what is the rate of decay?

The formula for exponential decay is $Q = ae^{rt}$, where Q is the amount of material at time t, a is the initial amount, r is the decay rate and t is the time period in days.

$$Q = ae^{rt}$$
$$20 = 40e^{r(6)} \qquad \text{Isolate e}$$
$$0.5 = e^{6r} \qquad \text{Take ln of both sides}$$
$$\ln 0.5 = 6r \qquad \text{Solve for } r$$
$$\frac{\ln 0.5}{6} = r$$
$$r = -0.1155$$

Note: r is negative because it is decay.
The rate of decay is 0.1155, or 11.55%.

Example: A 10-gram sample of Einsteinium-254 decays radioactively with a half-life of about 276 days. What is the remaining mass of Einsteinium-254 after 5 years (assume each year is 365 days).

Use the exponential decay formula derived above, where $m(t)$ is the mass (m) of Einsteinium in the sample at time t.

$$m(t) = Ce^{kt}$$

The initial mass of Einsteinium-254 is 10 grams. Use this to find the value of C.

$$m(0) = 10g = Ce^{k(0)} = C$$

Thus, C is 10 grams. To find k, note that, after 276 days, the amount of remaining Einsteinium-254 must be half the initial amount.

$$m(276d) = (10g)e^{k(276d)} = 5g$$
$$e^{k(276d)} = \frac{1}{2}$$

Solve for k. Note that, to make the argument of the exponential dimensionless, the units of k should be inverse days.

$$\ln[e^{k(276d)}] = \ln \frac{1}{2}$$
$$(276d)k = \ln \frac{1}{2}$$
$$k = \frac{1}{276d} \ln \frac{1}{2}$$
$$k \approx -0.00251 \frac{1}{2}$$

The complete expression for m is the following, where t is in days:

$$m(t) \approx (10g)e^{-0.00251t}$$

Finally, calculate the amount of Einsteinium remaining after 5 years (1,825 days).
$$m(1825) \approx (10g)e^{-0.00251(1825)}$$
$$m(1825) \approx 0.102g$$

After 5 years, only about 0.102 grams of the initial sample remain.

Logarithmic Scales

A logarithmic scale transforms a wide range into a linear scale that is limited to a smaller range of numbers.

Many familiar measurement scales, including the Richter scale that measures the magnitude of an earthquake and the decibel scale used to measure the loudness of sound, are logarithmic; they transform a nonlinear scale that spans a wide range into a linear scale that is limited to a smaller range of numbers. Thus, phenomena that span a wide range of magnitudes can be conveniently represented and graphed using a narrow range of variable values. Values on the Richter or decibel scale do not have absolute units but are expressed in terms of a reference value.

The Richter Scale

On the Richter scale, the magnitude of an earthquake of intensity I is given by
$$R = \log_{10}\left(\frac{I}{I_0}\right)$$

where I_0 is the intensity of an earthquake of reference magnitude zero.

Example: What is the ratio of the intensities of two earthquakes of magnitudes 6.0 and 8.0 on the Richter scale?

The intensity of the earthquake of magnitude 6.0 is given by
$$I_1 = I_0 10^6$$

The intensity of the earthquake of magnitude 8.0 is given by $I_2 = I_0 10^8$

Thus, the ratio of their intensities $= \frac{I_2}{I_1} = \frac{I_0 10^8}{I_0 10^6} = 100$.

Each unit on the Richter scale represents a factor of 10. Thus, an earthquake that is 2 points higher on the scale is 100 times more powerful.

The Decibel Scale

The decibel scale used to measure the loudness of sound is a similar relative logarithmic scale that uses the typical human hearing threshold intensity as the reference level.
$$\text{Loudness (dB)} = 10\log_{10}\left(\frac{I}{I_0}\right)$$

The factor of 10 transforms the original unit, bel, into decibel, a unit 10 times smaller and of a more convenient size, since the ear can detect a change of 1 decibel.

Example: The threshold of human hearing has been measured at 10^{-12} Watts/m². Using this as the reference level, what is the loudness of a voice with a power of 6.4×10^{-6} Watts/m² in decibels?

$$\text{Loudness} = 10\log\left(\frac{6.4 \times 10^{-6}}{10^{-12}}\right) dB = 10\log(6.4 \times 10^{6}) \, dB = 68 \, dB$$

Mathematics of Finance

We use an exponential function to determine the growth of an investment accumulating compounded interest. The formula for calculating the value of an investment after a given compounding period is

$$A(t) = A_0(1 + \tfrac{i}{n})^{nt}.$$

In finance, the value of a sum of money with compounded interest increases at a rate proportional to the original value.

A_0 is the principal, the original value of the investment. The rate of interest is i, the time in years is t, and the number of times the interest is compounded per year is n.

We can solve the compound interest formula for any of the variables by utilizing the properties of exponents and logarithms.

Example: Determine how long it will take \$100 to increase to \$1000 at 8% interest compounded 4 times annually.

In this problem we are given the principal ($A_0 = 100$), the final value ($A(t) = 1000$), the interest rate ($i = .08$), and the number of compounding periods per year ($n = 4$). Thus, we solve the compound interest formula for t. Solving for t involves the use of logarithms, the inverse function of exponents. To simplify calculations, we use the natural logarithm, ln.

$$A(t) = A_0(1 + \tfrac{i}{n})^{nt}$$
$$\frac{A(t)}{A_0} = (1 + \tfrac{i}{n})^{nt}$$
$$\ln\frac{A(t)}{A_0} = \ln(1 + \tfrac{i}{n})^{nt} \qquad \text{Take the ln of both sides.}$$
$$\ln\frac{A(t)}{A_0} = (nt)\ln(1 + \tfrac{i}{n})$$

Use the properties of logarithms with exponents.

$$\ln\frac{1000}{100} = (4t)\ln(1 + \tfrac{0.08}{4}) \qquad \text{Substitute and solve for time } (t).$$
$$t = \frac{\ln 10}{4(\ln 1.02)} = 29.07 \text{ years}$$

Example: Find the principal (A_0) that yields \$500 with an interest rate of 7.5% compounded semiannually for 20 years.

In this problem $A(t) = 500$, the interest rate (i) is 0.075, $n = 2$, and $t = 20$. To find the principal, we solve for A_0.

$$A(t) = A_0(1 + \tfrac{i}{n})^{nt}$$
$$500 = A_0(1 + \tfrac{0.075}{2})^{2(20)} \qquad \text{Substitute and solve for } A_0.$$
$$A_0 = \frac{500}{1.0375^{40}} = \$114.67$$

Example: How long will it take $2,000 to triple if it is invested at 15% compounded continuously?

The exponential growth formula for continuously compounding interest is

$$A = Pe^{rt},$$

where A is the amount of money in the account, P is the principal amount invested, r stands for rate of interest, t is the period in years, and e is the base of the natural log (an irrational number with value 2.71828…).

Substituting the given values in the formula:

$$A = Pe^{rt}$$
$$6000 = 2000e^{0.15t}$$
$$3 = e^{0.15t}$$
$$\ln 3 = \ln e^{0.15t}$$
$$\ln 3 = 0.15t \,(\ln e)$$
$$\ln 3 = 0.15t$$
$$1.098 = 0.15t$$
$$t = \frac{1.098}{0.15} = 7.3$$

The original amount of $2,000 triples in 7.3 years.

Example: Calculate the balance after 20 years for a savings account with an initial balance of $1,000 and an annual interest rate of 3%. Assume that the interest is compounded continuously.

In this case, the exponential growth formula can be used, where $A(t)$ is the amount of money in the account after t years. The equation is expressed using the standard "Pert" form.

$$A(t) = Pe^{rt}$$

The initial balance ($t = 0$) is $1,000.

$$A(0) = \$1,000 = Pe^{r(0)} = P$$
$$A(0) = \$1,000e^{rt}$$

The annual interest rate is 3%, or 0.03. Thus, after 1 year, the balance in the account must be 3% higher than the initial balance, or $1,030. But the final calculation for this problem requires knowing the continuous interest rate, which is different than the annual interest rate.

$$A(1) = \$1,030 = \$1,000e^{r(1)}$$
$$e^r = \frac{1030}{1000} = 1.03$$
$$\ln(e^r) = \ln 1.03$$
$$r = \ln 1.03 \approx 0.0296 \text{ so the continuous interest rate is 2.96\%}$$
$$A(t) = \$1,000e^{0.0296t}$$
$$A(20) = \$1,000e^{0.0296(20)} = \$1,807.60$$

The balance in the account after 20 years is $1,807.60.

COMPETENCY 7

UNDERSTAND RATIONAL, RADICAL, ABSOLUTE VALUE, AND PIECEWISE DEFINED FUNCTIONS

SKILL 7.1 Manipulate rational, radical, and absolute value expressions, equations, and inequalities

Finding the LCD

Find the LCD for $x^2 - 4$, $x^2 + 5x + 6$, and $x^2 + x - 6$.

$x^2 - 4$	factors into $(x - 2)(x + 2)$
$x^2 + 5x + 6$	factors into $(x + 3)(x + 2)$
$x^2 + x - 6$	factors into $(x + 3)(x - 2)$

The LCD is $(x + 3)(x + 2)(x - 2)$.

Adding Algebraic Fractions

To **add** algebraic fractions, first express the fractions in terms of their lowest common denominator (LCD), and then add their numerators to obtain the numerator that is divided by the LCD to arrive at the answer.

Example: Add $\left(\frac{3a}{2}\right)$ and $\left(\frac{5a}{3}\right)$.

$$\left(\tfrac{3a}{2}\right) + \left(\tfrac{5a}{3}\right) = \left(\tfrac{3a \times 3}{6}\right) + \left(\tfrac{5a \times 2}{6}\right)$$
$$= \tfrac{9a}{6} + \tfrac{10a}{6}$$
$$= \tfrac{19a}{6}$$

Example: Find the sum of $\left(\frac{5}{x + y}\right)$ and $\left(\frac{4}{x - y}\right)$.

$$\left(\tfrac{5}{x + y}\right) + \left(\tfrac{4}{x - y}\right) = \left[\tfrac{5(x - y)}{(x + y)(x - y)}\right] + \left[\tfrac{4(x + y)}{(x + y)(x - y)}\right]$$
$$= \tfrac{5(x - y) + 4(x + y)}{(x + y)(x - y)}$$
$$= \tfrac{5x - 5y + 4x + 4y}{x^2 - y^2}$$
$$= \tfrac{9x - y}{x^2 - y^2}$$

Example: Find the value of $\left(\frac{7x}{8}\right) + 4$.

$$\left(\tfrac{7x}{8}\right) + 4 = \left(\tfrac{7x \times 1}{8}\right) + \left(\tfrac{4 \times 8}{8}\right)$$
$$= \frac{7x + 32}{8}$$

Example:

$$\frac{5}{6a^3b^2} + \frac{1}{4ab^3} = \frac{5(2b)}{6a^3b^2(2b)} + \frac{1(3a^2)}{4ab^3(3a^2)} = \frac{10b}{12a^3b^3} + \frac{3a^2}{12a^3b^3} = \frac{10b + 3a^2}{12a^3b^3}$$

This will not reduce, since all three terms are not divisible by a common factor.

Subtracting Algebraic Fractions

To **subtract** algebraic fractions, first express the fractions in terms of their LCD and then subtract their numerators to obtain the numerator that is divided by the LCD to arrive at the answer.

Example:

$$\frac{2}{x^2 - 4} - \frac{3}{x^2 + 5x + 6} + \frac{7}{x^2 + x - 6} =$$

$$\frac{2}{(x - 2)(x + 2)} - \frac{3}{(x + 3)(x + 2)} + \frac{7}{(x + 3)(x - 2)} =$$

$$\frac{2(x + 3)}{(x - 2)(x + 2)(x + 3)} - \frac{3(x - 2)}{(x + 3)(x + 2)(x - 2)} + \frac{7(x + 2)}{(x + 3)(x - 2)(x + 2)} =$$

$$\frac{2x + 6}{(x - 2)(x + 2)(x + 3)} - \frac{3x - 6}{(x + 3)(x + 2)(x - 2)} + \frac{7x + 14}{(x + 3)(x - 2)(x + 2)} =$$

$$\frac{2x + 6 - (3x - 6) + 7x + 14}{(x + 3)(x - 2)(x + 2)} = \frac{6x + 26}{(x + 3)(x - 2)(x + 2)}$$

This will not reduce.

Multiplying Algebraic Fractions

Factor the numerators and denominators. Then cancel the factors that are common to the numerator and denominator before applying multiplication to obtain the answer.

Example: Find the product of $\left(\frac{a}{3}\right)$ and $\left(\frac{b}{4}\right)$.

$$\left(\tfrac{a}{3}\right) \times \left(\tfrac{b}{4}\right) = \frac{a \times b}{3 \times 4} = \frac{ab}{12}$$

Example: Simplify $\left(\frac{5x^2}{2x^2 - 2x}\right)\left(\frac{x^2 - 1}{x^2 + x}\right)$.

$\left(\frac{5x^2}{2x^2 - 2x}\right)\left(\frac{x^2 - 1}{x^2 + x}\right) = \left[\frac{5x^2}{2x(x - 1)}\right]\left[\frac{(x + 1)(x - 1)}{x(x + 1)}\right] = \frac{5}{2}$, since all of the common factors from the numerator and the denominator are canceled.

Example: Multiply $\left(\frac{4x^2}{x - 2}\right)\left(\frac{x^2 - 4}{12}\right)$.

$$\left(\tfrac{4x^2}{x - 2}\right)\left(\tfrac{x^2 - 4}{12}\right) = \left(\tfrac{4x^2}{x - 2}\right)\left[\frac{(x - 2)(x + 2)}{(4 \times 3)}\right]$$
$$= \frac{x^2(x + 2)}{3}$$

Dividing Algebraic Fractions

To divide the algebraic fractions, invert the second fraction and multiply it by the first fraction. In other words, you must multiply both fractions after taking the reciprocal of the divisor. Then factor the numerator and denominator and cancel all the common factors.

Example: Simplify $(\frac{x-3}{4}) \div (\frac{x+3}{8})$.

$$(\frac{x-3}{4}) \div (\frac{x+3}{8}) = (\frac{x-3}{4})(\frac{8}{x+3})$$
$$= \frac{2(x-3)}{x+3}$$

Example: Simplify $(\frac{m^2+2m}{3m^3}) \div (\frac{5m+10}{6})$.

$$(\frac{m^2+2m}{3m^3}) \div (\frac{5m+10}{6}) = [\frac{m(m+2)}{3m^3}] \div [\frac{5(m+2)}{6}]$$
$$= [\frac{m(m+2)}{3m^3}][\frac{6}{5(m+2)}]$$
$$= \frac{2}{5m^2}$$

Example: Find $(\frac{12y+24}{36}) \div (\frac{y^2+3y+2}{2})$.

$$(\frac{12y+24}{36}) \div (\frac{y^2+3y+2}{2}) = [\frac{12(y+2)}{12 \times 3}] \div [\frac{(y+2)(y+1)}{2}]$$
$$= (\frac{y+2}{3})[\frac{2}{(y+2)(y+1)}]$$
$$= \frac{2}{3(y+1)}$$

Applications

Some problems can be solved using equations with rational expressions. First, write the equation. To solve it, multiply each term by the LCD of all of the fractions. This will cancel out all of the denominators and give an equivalent algebraic equation that can be solved.

Example: The denominator of a fraction is two less than three times the numerator. If 3 is added to both the numerator and the denominator, the new fraction equals $\frac{1}{2}$.

original fraction: $\frac{x}{3x-2}$ revised fraction: $\frac{x+3}{3x+1}$

$\frac{x+3}{3x+1} = \frac{1}{2}$ $2x+6 = 3x+1$ cross multiply

$x = 5$

So the original fraction is $\frac{5}{13}$.

Solving for a Variable in Terms of Another Variable

To solve an algebraic formula for some variable R, use the following steps:

1. Eliminate any parentheses using the distributive property.

2. Multiply every term by the LCD of any fractions to write an equivalent equation without any fractions.

3. Move all of the terms containing the variable R to one side of the equation. Move all of the terms without the variable to the opposite side of the equation.

4. If there are two or more terms containing the variable R, factor only R out of each of those terms as a common factor.

5. Divide both sides of the equation by the number or expression being multiplied times the variable R.

6. Reduce the fractions if possible.

7. Remember that there are restrictions on values allowed for variables because the denominator cannot equal zero.

Examples:

Solve $A = p + prt$ for t.

$$A - p = prt$$
$$\frac{A - p}{pr} = \frac{prt}{pr}$$
$$\frac{A - p}{pr} = t$$

Solve $A = p + prt$ for p.

$$A = p(1 + rt)$$
$$\frac{A}{1 + rt} = \frac{p(1 + rt)}{1 + rt}$$
$$\frac{A}{1 + rt} = p$$

Solve $A = \frac{1}{2}h(b_1 + b_2)$ for b_2.

$$A = \frac{1}{2}hb_1 + \frac{1}{2}hb_2 \qquad \leftarrow \text{step a}$$

$$2A = hb_1 + hb_2 \qquad \leftarrow \text{step b}$$

$$2A - hb_1 = hb_2 \qquad \leftarrow \text{step c}$$

$$\frac{2A - hb_1}{h} = \frac{hb_2}{h} \qquad \leftarrow \text{step d}$$

$$\frac{2A - hb_1}{h} = b_2 \qquad \leftarrow \text{will not reduce}$$

The Laws of Radicals	Examples
1. $(\sqrt[n]{a})^n = a$	$(\sqrt[3]{6})^3 = 6$
2. $\sqrt[n]{ab} = \sqrt[n]{a}\sqrt[n]{b}$	$\sqrt[3]{10} = \sqrt[3]{2 \times 5} = \sqrt[3]{2} \times \sqrt[3]{5}$

Continued on next page

3. $\sqrt[n]{\dfrac{a}{b}} = \dfrac{\sqrt[n]{a}}{\sqrt[n]{b}}$	$\sqrt{\dfrac{3}{7}} = \dfrac{\sqrt{3}}{\sqrt{7}}$
4. $\sqrt[n]{a^m} = (\sqrt[n]{a})^m$	$(2\sqrt[3]{4})(3\sqrt[3]{16}) = (2 \times 3)(\sqrt[3]{4} \times \sqrt[3]{16})$ $= 6\sqrt[3]{4 \times 16} = 6\sqrt[3]{4^3} = 6 \times 4 = 24$
5. $\sqrt[m]{\sqrt[n]{a}} = \sqrt[mn]{a}$	$\sqrt[3]{\sqrt{5}} = \sqrt[3 \times 2]{5} = \sqrt[6]{5}$

Adding and Subtracting Radicals

Addition or subtraction of two or more radicals is achieved by reducing each radical to the simplest form and then combining terms with similar radicals.

Example: Simplify $\sqrt{32} - \sqrt{50} + \sqrt{18}$.
$$\sqrt{32} - \sqrt{50} + \sqrt{18} = \sqrt{16 \cdot 2} - \sqrt{25 \cdot 2} + \sqrt{9 \cdot 2}$$
$$4\sqrt{2} - 5\sqrt{2} + 3\sqrt{2}$$
$$= 2\sqrt{2}$$

Example: Simplify $\sqrt[3]{432} + \sqrt[4]{625} - \sqrt{128}$.
$$\sqrt[3]{432} + \sqrt[4]{625} - \sqrt{128} = \sqrt[3]{2^4 \times 3^3} + \sqrt[4]{5^4} - \sqrt{2^7}$$
$$= 6\sqrt[3]{2} + 5 - 8\sqrt{2}$$

Multiplying and Dividing Radicals

Multiplication and division of radicals are performed using the laws of radicals.

Example: Simplify $(2\sqrt[3]{4})(3\sqrt[3]{16})$.
$$(2\sqrt[3]{4})(3\sqrt[3]{16}) = (2 \times 3)(\sqrt[3]{4} \times \sqrt[3]{16})$$
$$= 6\sqrt[3]{4 \times 16}$$
$$= 6\sqrt[3]{4^3}$$
$$= 6 \times 4 = 24$$

Example: Find $\dfrac{\sqrt[3]{4}}{\sqrt{2}}$.
$$\frac{\sqrt[3]{4}}{\sqrt{2}} = \frac{\sqrt[3]{2^2}}{\sqrt{2}}$$
$$= \frac{2^{\frac{2}{3}}}{2^{\frac{1}{2}}} \qquad \text{See section 6.1 for rules of rational exponents.}$$
$$= 2^{\frac{2}{3} - \frac{1}{2}}$$
$$= 2^{\frac{1}{6}}$$

Example: Simplify $\dfrac{\sqrt[4]{225}}{\sqrt[3]{3}}$.

$$\dfrac{\sqrt[4]{225}}{\sqrt[3]{81}} = \dfrac{\sqrt[4]{5^2 \times 3^2}}{\sqrt[3]{3}}$$

$$= \dfrac{\sqrt[4]{5^2} \times \sqrt[4]{3^2}}{\sqrt[3]{3}}$$

$$= \dfrac{\sqrt[4]{25} \times 3^{\frac{2}{4}}}{3^{\frac{1}{3}}}$$

$$= \sqrt[4]{25} \times 3^{\frac{2}{4} - \frac{1}{3}}$$

$$= \sqrt[4]{25} \times 3^{\frac{1}{6}}$$

$$= \sqrt[4]{25} \times \sqrt[6]{3}$$

Simplifying Radical Expressions

To simplify a radical expression, follow these steps:

1. Factor the number or coefficient completely.

2. For square roots, group like factors in pairs. For cube roots, arrange like factors in groups of three. For nth roots, group like factors in groups of n.

3. For each of these groups, put one of that number outside the radical. Any factors that cannot be combined in groups should be multiplied together and left inside the radical.

4. The index number of a radical is the little number on the front of the radical. For a cube root, the index is 3. If no index appears, then the index is 2 for square roots.

5. For variables inside the radical, divide the index number of the radical into each exponent. The quotient (the answer to the division) is the new exponent to be written on the variable outside the radical. The remainder from the division is the new exponent on the variable remaining inside the radical sign. If the remainder is zero, then the variable no longer appears in the radical sign.

Note: *Remember that the square root of a negative number can be designated by replacing the negative sign inside that square root with an* i *in front of the radical (to signify an imaginary number). Then simplify the remaining positive radical by the normal method. Include the* i *outside the radical as part of the answer.*

If the index number is an odd number, you can still simplify the radical to get a negative solution.

Example:
$$\sqrt{50a^4b^7} = \sqrt{5 \times 5 \times 2 \times a^4 \times b^7} = 5a^2b^3\sqrt{2b}$$

Example:

$$7x\sqrt[3]{16x^5} = 7x\sqrt[3]{2 \times 2 \times 2 \times 2 \times x^5} = 7x \times 2x\sqrt[3]{2x^2} = 14x^2\sqrt[3]{2x^2}$$

An expression with a radical sign can be rewritten using a rational exponent. The radicand becomes the base, which will have the rational exponent. The index number on the front of the radical sign becomes the denominator of the rational exponent. The numerator of the rational exponent is the exponent, which was originally inside the radical sign on the original base. *Note*: If no index number appears on the front of the radical, then it is a 2. If no exponent appears inside the radical, then use a 1 as the numerator of the rational exponent.

If an expression contains rational expressions with different denominators, rewrite the exponents with a common denominator and then change the problem into a radical.

$$a^{\frac{2}{3}}\, b^{\frac{1}{2}}\, c^{\frac{3}{5}} = a^{\frac{20}{30}}\, b^{\frac{15}{30}}\, c^{\frac{18}{30}} = \sqrt[30]{a^{20}\, b^{15}\, c^{18}}$$

Solving Radical Equations

Follow these steps to solve a radical equation:

1. Get a term with a radical alone on one side of the equation.

2. Raise both sides of the equation to a power equal to the index on the radical (that is, square both sides of an equation containing a square root, cube both sides of an equation containing a cube root, etc.). *Do not square (or cube, etc.) each term separately. Square (or cube, etc.) the entire side of the equation.*

3. If there are any radicals remaining, repeat steps 1 and 2 until all radicals are gone.

4. Solve the remaining equation.

5. Check your answers in the original radical equation. Not every answer may check out. If no answer checks out in the original equation, then the answer to the equation is $\varnothing$, the empty set or null set.

Solve and check:

$$\sqrt{2x-8} - 7 = 9 \qquad \text{Get radical alone.}$$
$$\sqrt{2x-8} = 16$$
$$\left(\sqrt{2x-8}\right)^2 = 16^2 \qquad \text{Square both sides.}$$
$$2x - 8 = 256 \qquad \text{Solve for } x.$$
$$2x = 264$$
$$x = 132$$

Note: Since the answers to radical equations must be checked in the original equation anyway, this means that possible answers on a multiple choice test could be immediately substituted into the problem to find the correct answer without having to solve the actual problem.

Check:

$$\sqrt{2(132) - 8} - 7 = 9$$
$$\sqrt{264 - 8} - 7 = 9$$
$$\sqrt{256} - 7 = 9$$
$$16 - 7 = 9 \qquad \text{This answer checks.}$$

Solve and check:

$$\sqrt{5x - 1} - 1 = x \qquad \text{Add 1.}$$
$$(\sqrt{5x - 1})^2 = (x + 1)^2 \qquad \text{Square both sides.}$$
$$5x - 1 = x^2 + 2x + 1 \qquad \text{Solve this equation.}$$
$$0 = x^2 - 3x + 2$$
$$0 = (x - 2)(x - 1)$$
$$x = 2 \qquad x = 1$$

Check both answers:

$$\sqrt{5(2) - 1} - 1 = 2 \qquad \sqrt{5(1) - 1} - 1 = 2$$
$$3 - 1 = 2 \qquad\qquad 2 - 1 = 1$$

Both answers check.

Comparing Radicals

Radicals of the same order can be compared by considering the numbers under the radical sign. Radicals of different orders can be compared after reducing them to radicals of the same order. When an expression has a rational exponent, it can be rewritten using a radical sign. The denominator of the rational exponent becomes the index number on the front of the radical sign. The base of the original expression goes inside the radical sign. The numerator of the rational exponent is an exponent, which can be placed either inside the radical sign on the original base or outside the radical as an exponent on the radical expression. The radical can then be simplified as far as possible.

$$4^{\frac{3}{2}} = \sqrt[2]{4^3} \text{ or } (\sqrt{4})^3 = \sqrt{64} = 8$$
$$16^{\frac{3}{4}} = \sqrt[4]{16^3} \text{ or } (\sqrt[4]{16})^3 = 2^3 = 8$$
$$25^{\frac{-1}{2}} = \frac{1}{25^{\frac{1}{2}}} = \frac{1}{\sqrt{25}} = \frac{1}{5}$$

Example: Compare $\sqrt{5}$ and $\sqrt[3]{11}$.

$$\sqrt{5} = 5^{\frac{1}{2}} \text{ and } \sqrt[3]{11} = 11^{\frac{1}{3}}$$

Here the powers are $\frac{1}{2}$ and $\frac{1}{3}$. The LCD will be 6.

$$\sqrt{5} = 5^{\frac{1}{2}} = 5^{\frac{3}{6}} = (5^3)^{\frac{1}{6}} = (125)^{\frac{1}{6}}, \text{ and}$$
$$\sqrt[3]{11} = 11^{\frac{1}{3}} = 11^{\frac{2}{6}} = (11^2)^{\frac{1}{6}} = 121^{\frac{1}{6}}$$

Now both of the given radicals are of the same power. Therefore, we can compare the bases.

Since $125 > 121$, obviously $\sqrt{5} > \sqrt[3]{11}$.

Example: Arrange the following radicals in ascending order of magnitude:
$\sqrt[3]{2}, \sqrt[4]{3}, \sqrt[6]{5}$

$$\sqrt[3]{2} = 2^{\frac{1}{3}} = 2^{\frac{20}{60}} = (2^{20})^{\frac{1}{60}} = 1,048,576$$

$$\sqrt[4]{3} = 3^{\frac{1}{4}} = 3^{\frac{15}{60}} = (3^{15})^{\frac{1}{60}} = 14,348,907$$

$$\sqrt[6]{5} = 5^{\frac{1}{6}} = 5^{\frac{10}{60}} = (5^{10})^{\frac{1}{60}} = 9,765,625$$

It is clear that $1,048,576 < 9,765,625 < 14,348,907$;
$$\therefore \sqrt[3]{2} < \sqrt[6]{5} < \sqrt[4]{3}.$$

Absolute Value

To solve an absolute value equation, follow these steps:

1. Get the absolute value expression alone on one side of the equation.

2. Split the absolute value equation into two separate equations without absolute value bars. In one equation, the expression inside the absolute value bars is equal to the expression on the other side of the original equation. In the other equation, the expression inside the absolute value bars is equal to the negative of the expression on the other side of the original equation.

3. Now solve each of these equations.

4. Check each answer by substituting it into the original equation (with the absolute value symbol). There will be answers that do not check in the original equation. These answers are discarded because they are extraneous solutions. If all of the answers are discarded as incorrect, then the answer to the equation is $\varnothing$, which is the empty or null set. (Answers of 0, 1, or 2 could be correct.)

To solve an absolute value inequality, follow these steps:

1. Get the absolute value expression alone on one side of the inequality. *Remember*: Dividing or multiplying by a negative number will reverse the direction of the inequality sign.

2. Remember what the inequality sign is at this point.

3. Split the absolute value inequality into two separate inequalities. For the first inequality, rewrite the inequality without the absolute value bars and solve it.

For the next inequality, write the expression inside the absolute value bars, followed by the opposite inequality sign and then by the negative of the expression on the other side of the inequality. Now solve it.

4. If the inequality sign in step 2 is $<$ or $\leq$, the solution is expressed by connecting the solutions of the two inequalities in step 3 by the word *and*. The solution set consists of the points between the two numbers on the number line. If the inequality sign in step 2 is $>$ or $\geq$, the solution is expressed by connecting the solutions of the two inequalities in step 3 by the word *or*. The solution set consists of the points outside the two numbers on the number line.

If an expression inside an absolute value bar is compared to a negative number, the answer can also be either all real numbers or the empty set ($\varnothing$). For instance, $|x + 3| < ^-6$ would have the empty set as the answer, since an absolute value is always positive and will never be less than $^-6$. However, $|x + 3| > ^-6$ would have all real numbers as the answer, since an absolute value is always positive or at least zero, and will never be less than -6. In similar fashion, $|x + 3| = ^-6$ would never check because an absolute value will never give a negative value.

Example: Solve and check: $|2x - 5| + 1 = 12.$

$\qquad |2x - 5| = 11 \qquad$ Get absolute value alone.

Rewrite as two equations and solve separately:

right-hand side positive		right-hand side negative
$2x - 5 = 11$		$2x - 5 = ^-11$
$2x = 16$	and	$2x = ^-6$
$x = 8$		$x = ^-3$

Check: $\|2x - 5\| + 1 = 12$	$\|2x - 5\| + 1 = 12$
$\|2(8) - 5\| + 1 = 12$	$\|2(^-3) - 5\| + 1 = 12$
$\|11\| + 1 = 12$	$\|11\| + 1 = 12$
$12 = 12$	$12 = 12$

Both 8 and $^-3$ check.

Example: Solve and check: $2|x - 7| - 13 \geq 11.$

$\qquad 2|x - 7| \geq 24 \qquad$ Get absolute value alone.

$\qquad |x - 7| \geq 12$

Rewrite as two inequalities and solve separately:

right-hand side positive		right-hand side negative
$x - 7 \geq 12$	or	$x - 7 \leq ^-12$
$x \geq 19$	or	$x \leq ^-5$

Rational functions

A rational function can be written as the ratio of two polynomial expressions. A rational function is given in the form $f(x) = \frac{p(x)}{q(x)}$. In the equation, $p(x)$ and $q(x)$ both represent polynomial functions ($q(x)$ does not equal zero).

Examples of rational functions are $r(x) = \frac{x^2 + 2x + 4}{x - 3}$ and $r(x) = \frac{x}{x - 3}$, which both are ratios of two polynomials.

The branches of rational functions approach asymptotes. Setting the denominator equal to zero and solving will give the value(s) of the vertical asymptotes since the function will be undefined at this point. If the value of $f(x)$ approaches b as $|x|$ increases, the equation $y = b$ is a horizontal asymptote. To find the horizontal asymptote, it is necessary to make a table of values for x that are to the right and left of the vertical asymptotes. The pattern for the horizontal asymptotes will become apparent as $|x|$ increases.

If there is more than one vertical asymptote, remember to choose numbers to the right and left of each one in order to find the horizontal asymptotes and have sufficient points to graph the function.

Setting the numerator to zero and solving for x will give the zero, or root of the function which is graphed as the x intercept.

Example: Graph $f(x) = \frac{3x + 1}{x - 2}$.

$x - 2 = 0$ 1. Set the denominator equal to 0 to find the vertical

$x = 2$ asymptote.

x	f(x)
3	10
10	3.875
100	3.07
1000	3.007
1	-4
-10	2.417
-100	2.93
-1000	2.99

2. Make a table choosing numbers to the right and left of the vertical asymptote

3. Set the numerator equal to zero to find the x intercept
$$3x + 1 = 0$$
$$3x = -1$$
$$x = -\frac{1}{3}$$

4. The pattern shows that as $|x|$ increases, $f(x)$ approaches the value 3 therefore asymptote exists at $y = 3$

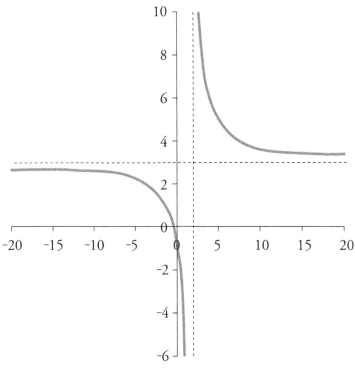

Note that $x = 2$ is excluded from the domain of the function and $y = 3$ is excluded from the range.

In some cases, the restriction on a rational function owing to the denominator being zero will not be a vertical asymptote but simply a hole in the graph. This happens when the value of x that reduces the denominator to zero is also a zero of the numerator.

Example: Plot the function $\frac{x-2}{x^2-4}$.

Factoring the denominator, we see that the denominator goes to zero at $x = -2$ and $x = 2$.

$$\frac{x-2}{x^2-4} = \frac{x-2}{(x+2)(x-2)}$$

There is a vertical asymptote at $x = h - 2$. Since the function can be simplified to the form $\frac{1}{(x+2)}$ by canceling $(x-2)$ from the numerator and denominator, there is no asymptote at $x = 2$. The point $x = 2$, however, must be excluded from the function. Hence, there is a hole in the graph at $x = 2$.

Studying the function, we see that for large values of x the function goes to zero. Thus there is a horizontal asymptote at $y = 0$.

x	y	
-6	$-\frac{1}{4}$	
-4	$-\frac{1}{2}$	
-3	-1	
-2.5	-2	
-1.5	2	
-1	1	
0	$\frac{1}{2}$	
1	$\frac{1}{3}$	
2	$\frac{1}{4}$	(location of hole)
3	$\frac{1}{5}$	

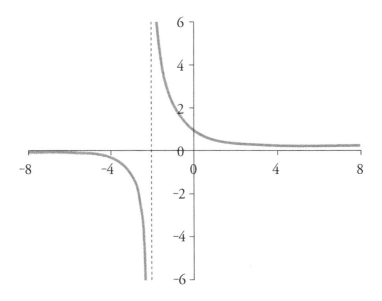

Absolute Value Functions

The absolute value function for a first-degree equation is $y = m|x - h| + k$. Its graph is V-shaped. The point (h, k) is the location of the maximum/minimum point on the graph. The slopes of the two sides of the V are "$\pm m$." The graph opens up if m is positive and down if m is negative.

Following are examples of graphs of absolute value functions.

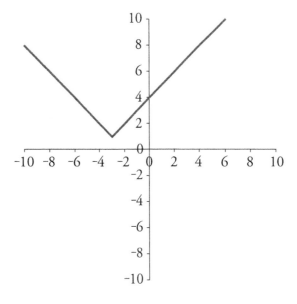

$y = |x + 3| + 1$

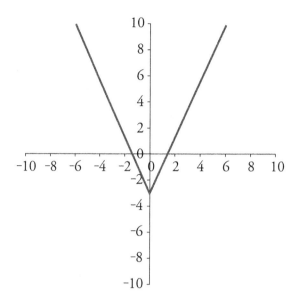

$y = 2|x| - 3$

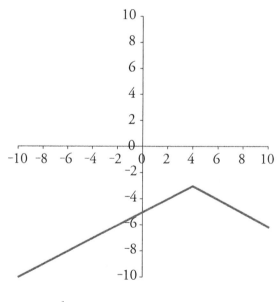

$y = -\frac{1}{2}|x - 4| - 3$

Note that on the first graph, the graph opens up since m is $+1$. Its minimum point is (-3, 1). The slopes of the two upward rays are ± 1. The second graph also opens up since m is positive. Its minimum point is (0, -3). The slopes of the two upward rays are ± 2. The third graph opens downward because m is $-\frac{1}{2}$. The maximum point on the graph is (4, -3). The slopes of the two downward rays are $\pm \frac{1}{2}$.

Radical Functions

Radical functions are those that depend on a root of the independent variable x, typically the square root. Some examples are $f(x) = 3\sqrt{x} + 5$, $f(x) = \sqrt{7 - x}$ and $f(x) = 2\sqrt{x + 3} - 5$.

Plotting a radical function follows a process similar to that of plotting virtually any other function. A set of representative points is needed, and prior knowledge of the domain of the function is helpful (for instance, if only real numbers are considered, the expression under the square root sign must always be positive). Typically, a calculator is needed to find the values of the function for specific variable values.

Plotting a radical function follows a process similar to that of plotting virtually any other function. A set of representative points is needed, and prior knowledge of the domain of the function is helpful (for instance, if only real numbers are considered, the expression under the square root sign must always be positive).

Example: Tabulate and plot the function $y = 3\sqrt{x} + 5$.

x	y
0	5
1	8
4	11
9	14
16	17
25	20

Note that x must always be positive.
Hence the domain of the function is $x \geq 0$.

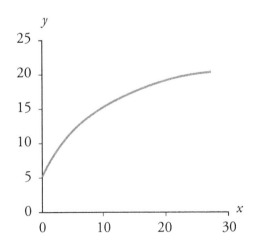

Piecewise Functions

Functions defined by two or more formulas are PIECEWISE FUNCTIONS. The formula used to evaluate piecewise functions varies depending on the value of *x*. The graphs of piecewise functions consist of two or more pieces, or intervals, and are often discontinuous.

> **PIECEWISE FUNCTIONS:** functions defined by two or more formulas

Example 1

$f(x) = x + 1 \quad$ if $x > 2$
$\qquad\; x - 2 \quad$ if $x \leq 2$

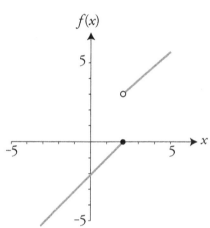

Example 2

$f(x) = x \quad$ if $x \geq 1$
$\qquad\; x^2 \quad$ if $x < 1$

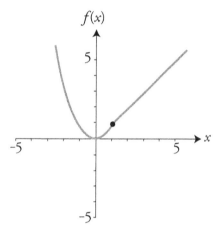

When graphing or interpreting the graph of piecewise functions, it is important to note the points at the beginning and end of each interval because the graph must clearly indicate what happens at the end of each interval. Note that in the graph of Example 1, point (2, 3) is not part of the graph and is represented by an empty circle. On the other hand, point (2, 0) is part of the graph and is represented as a solid circle. Note also that the graph of Example 2 is continuous despite representing a piecewise function.

SKILL 7.3 **Analyze rational, radical, absolute value, and piecewise defined functions in terms of domain, range, and asymptotes**

The restrictions on the domain and range of a function are most easily understood when the function is viewed in graphical form.

The domain of a polynomial function includes all real values of *x*. The range depends on the form of the particular polynomial. For example, the polynomial $f(x) = -x^2 + 5$ has the range $f(x) \leq 5$ whereas $f(x) = -x^3 + 5$ has a range that includes all real numbers.

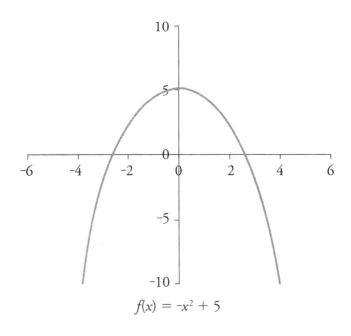

$$f(x) = -x^2 + 5$$

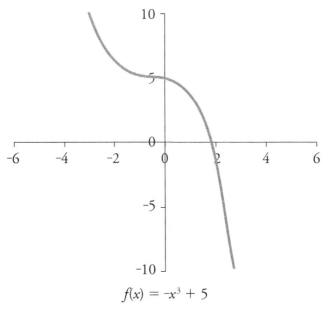

$$f(x) = -x^3 + 5$$

In general, the range of an even polynomial is restricted, and the range of an odd polynomial includes all real numbers.

The domain of a rational function, $\frac{p(x)}{q(x)}$, includes all real values of x except those for which the denominator $q(x)$ is zero. The point $x = \pm 2$, for instance, is excluded from the domain of the function $y = \frac{x}{x^2 - 4}$.

Looking at a graph of a rational function, the points excluded from the domain are the x values for which vertical asymptotes or holes exist. The range of a rational function is determined by its horizontal asymptotes. In cases where the graph of the rational function does not cross the horizontal asymptote, the y value for the horizontal asymptote must be excluded from the range.

When considering $y = \frac{x}{x^2 - 4}$, the domain is all real numbers x, where $x \neq \pm 2$ and the range is all real numbers.

The domain of a radical function is restricted to the x values that will result in a positive number under the square root sign. Thus, radical functions have an upper or lower limit placed on the domain. The restriction on the domain places a corresponding restriction on the range in the form of an upper or lower limit.

Example: Find the domain and range of the function $y = 2\sqrt{x - 3} - 5$.
In order to limit the values within the radical sign to positive numbers, the domain of the function must be limited to $x \geq 3$.

The corresponding range is given by $y \geq -5$.

The graph plotted below displays the domain and range of this function.

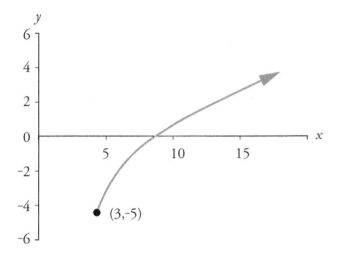

The domain of an absolute value function includes all real numbers. The vertex of the V-shaped function provides the upper or lower limit to the range of the function. For an upright V-shaped function, the vertex is the lower limit of the range. For an upside-down V, the vertex is the upper limit of the range. See the beginning of this competency for examples.

The domain of a piecewise function is simply the union of all points that make up the domain of each piece. Likewise, the range of a piecewise function is the union of all values that make up the range of each piece.

A function may have one or more asymptotes. An **ASYMPTOTE** is a line for which the distance between it and a function or curve is arbitrarily small, especially as the function tends toward infinity in some direction. Asymptotes can be either vertical, horizontal or slant.

The domain of an absolute value function includes all real numbers. The vertex of the V-shaped function provides the upper or lower limit to the range of the function.

ASYMPTOTE: a line for which the distance between it and a function or curve is arbitrarily small, especially as the function tends toward infinity in some direction

Consider, for instance, the plot of the hyperbola defined as follows.

$$g(x) = \pm\sqrt{x^2 + 1}$$

Note, for instance, that as x tends toward infinity, $g(x)$ gets arbitrarily close to x. The graph of $g(x)$ is shown below.

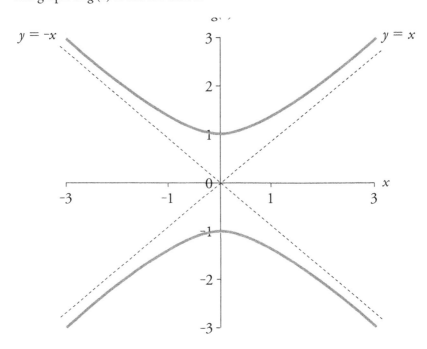

The (slant) asymptotes and their associated functions for this relation are displayed in the graph above as dashed lines.

Vertical and horizontal asymptotes for rational functions are discussed earlier in this competency. A rational function has slant asymptotes if the polynomial in the numerator is of a higher degree than the polynomial in the denominator.

> *A rational function has slant asymptotes if the polynomial in the numerator is of a higher degree than the polynomial in the denominator.*

Example: Find the equation of the slant asymptote for the function $\dfrac{x^2 + 3x + 4}{x - 2}$.

Using long division, we can rewrite the function as

$$\frac{x^2 + 3x + 4}{x - 2} = x + 5 + \frac{14}{x - 2}$$

For large values of x, it is clear that the term $\dfrac{14}{(x - 2)}$ will become very small and the function will tend to follow the line $y = x + 5$.

Thus, the function has two asymptotes, a vertical one at $x = 2$ and a slant asymptote along $y = x + 5$.

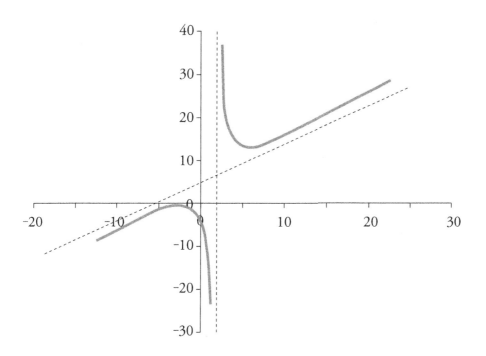

Example: Elly Mae can feed the animals in 15 minutes. Jethro can feed them in 10 minutes. How long will it take them to feed the animals if they work together?

If Elly Mae can feed the animals in 15 minutes, then she could feed $\frac{1}{15}$ of them in 1 minute, $\frac{2}{15}$ of them in 2 minutes, and $\frac{x}{15}$ of them in x minutes. In the same fashion, Jethro could feed $\frac{x}{10}$ of them in x minutes. Together they complete 1 job. The equation is:

$\frac{x}{15} + \frac{x}{10} = 1$

Multiply each term by the LCD (least common denominator) of 30:

$2x + 3x = 30$

$x = 6$ minutes

Example: A salesman drove 480 miles from Pittsburgh to Hartford. The next day he returned the same distance to Pittsburgh in half an hour less time than his original trip took, because he increased his average speed by 4 mph. Find his original speed.

Since distance = rate $\times$ time, then time = $\frac{\text{distance}}{\text{rate}}$.

The form of the equation is original time $- \frac{1}{2}$ hour = shorter return time.

$\frac{480}{x} - \frac{1}{2} = \frac{480}{x + 4}$

Multiplying by the LCD of $2x(x + 4)$, the equation becomes:

$480[2(x + 4)] - 1[x(x + 4)] = 480(2x)$

$960x + 3840 - x^2 - 4x = 960x$

$x^2 + 4x - 3840 = 0$

$(x + 64)(x - 60) = 0$ Either $(x - 60 = 0)$ or $(x + 64 = 0)$ or both $= 0$

$x = 60$ 60 mph is the original speed.

This is the solution since the time cannot be negative. Check your answer

$x + 4 = 64$

$\frac{480}{60} - \frac{1}{2} = \frac{480}{64}$

$8 - \frac{1}{2} = 7\frac{1}{2}$

$7\frac{1}{2} = 7\frac{1}{2}.$

Example: For a cone of height h and radius r, the slant height is given by the formula $s = \sqrt{r^2 + h^2}$. The lateral surface area is represented by πrs and the area of the base by πr^2.

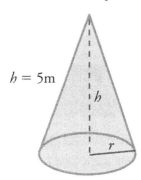

$h = 5\text{m}$

If the lateral surface area of a cone is twice that of its base and the height of the cone is 5m, find the radius.

The problem given may be modeled using the following radical equation:

$$\pi r \sqrt{25 + r^2} = 2\pi r^2.$$

Canceling the common factor πr from both sides and squaring both sides we get

$25 + r^2 = 4r^2$

$\rightarrow 3r^2 = 25$

$\rightarrow r = \sqrt{\frac{25}{3}} = 2.9$

Thus, the radius of the cone is 2.9m.

See also Skill 7.1

DOMAIN III
MEASUREMENT AND GEOMETRY

COMPETENCY 8

UNDERSTAND MEASUREMENT PRINCIPLES AND PROCEDURES

> **SKILL** Analyze the use of various units and unit conversions within the
> **8.1** customary and metric systems

In ancient times, baskets, jars and bowls were used to measure capacity. An inch originated as the length of three barley grains placed end to end. The word "carat," used for measuring precious gems, was derived from carob seeds. Even now, nonstandard units are sometimes used when standard instruments might not be available. For example, students might measure the length of a room by their arm spans. Seeds or stones might be used for measuring weight.

"When you can measure what you are speaking about and express it in numbers, you know something about it; but when you cannot measure it, when you cannot express it in numbers, your knowledge is of a meager and unsatisfactory kind."

—Lord Kelvin

Systems of Units

The Customary (Imperial) System

CUSTOMARY OR IMPERIAL UNITS are the familiar everyday units used in the United States.

CUSTOMARY OR IMPERIAL UNITS: the familiar everyday units used in the United States

Customary System units

Inch, foot, yard and mile are commonly used units of length.

1 yard	=	3 feet	=	36 inches
1 mile	=	1,760 yards		

Rod, furlong, and acre (a unit of area) are less familiar units defined in terms of yards:

1 rod	=	5 ½ yards	=	198 inches
1 furlong	=	220 yards		
1 acre	=	4,840 sq. yards	=	160 sq. rods

The basic unit of weight is pound (lb).

1 pound	=	16 ounces (oz)	=	256 drams
1 ounce	=	16 drams		
Short ton (U.S.)	=	2,000 lb		
Long ton (British)	=	2,240 lb		

The basic unit of liquid measure or liquid capacity is the gallon.

1 gallon	=	4 quarts	=	8 pints	=	16 cups	=	128 ounces

The basic unit of dry measure or dry capacity is the bushel.

1 bushel	=	4 pecks	=	32 dry quarts	=	64 dry pints	=	2,150.42 cubic inches
1 barrel	=	105 dry quarts						

The metric (SI) system

The metric or SI system is commonly used in many countries around the world for making everyday measurements. It is also the standard system used for scientific measurements. The metric system is convenient to use because units at different scales are related by multiples of ten.

The basic metric unit for *length* is the meter (m). The basic metric unit for *weight* or *mass* is the gram (g). The basic metric unit for *volume* is the liter (L).

The following table shows the most commonly used units.

COMMON METRIC UNITS		
1 cm	=	10 mm
1 m	=	1000 mm
1 m	=	100 cm
1 km	=	1000 m
1 L	=	1000 mL
1 kL	=	1000 L
1 g	=	1000 mg
1 kg	=	1000 g

Appropriate units and equivalents

Different units within the same system of measurement are selected based on the scale at which the measurement is being made. For example, the height of a person is measured in feet whereas the distance between two cities is measured in miles. To estimate measurements of familiar objects, it is necessary to first determine the units to be used.

Examples of appropriate units:

LENGTH	
The coastline of Florida	miles or kilometers
The width of a ribbon	inches or millimeters
The thickness of a book	inches or centimeters
The length of a football field	yards or meters
The depth of water in a pool	feet or meters

WEIGHT OR MASS	
A bag of sugar	pounds or grams
A school bus	tons or kilograms
A dime	ounces or grams

CAPACITY	
Bucket of paint for bedroom	gallons or liters
Glass of milk	cups or liters
Bottle of soda	quarts or liters
Medicine for child	ounces or milliliters

To estimate measurements, it is helpful to have a familiar reference with a known measurement. For instance, you can use the knowledge that a dollar bill is about 6 inches long or that a nickel weighs about 5 grams to make estimates of length and weight without actually measuring with a ruler or a balance.

APPROXIMATE MEASUREMENTS OF COMMON ITEMS		
ITEM APPROXIMATELY EQUAL TO	METRIC	IMPERIAL
carton of milk	1 liter	1 quart
yardstick	1 meter	1 yard
distance between highway markers	1 kilometer	1 mile
man's foot	30 centimeters	1 foot
math textbook	1 kilogram	2 pounds
average-sized man	75 kilograms	170 pounds
large paper clip	1 gram	1 ounce
thickness of a dime	2 millimeters	0.1 inch
1 football field	6400 sq. yd.	
boiling point of water	100°C	212°F
freezing point of water	0°C	32°F
1 cup of liquid	240 ml	8 fl. oz.
1 teaspoon	5 ml	

Estimate the measurement of the following items:

The length of an adult cow = _____ meters
The thickness of a compact disc = _____ millimeters
Your height = _____ meters
length of your nose = _____ centimeters
weight of your math textbook = _____ kilograms
weight of an automobile = _____ kilograms
weight of an aspirin = _____ grams

Answers may vary: 2m cow, 2mm disc, 2 m height, 3 cm nose, 1kg book, 1000kg car, 1g aspirin

Conversions: unit analysis

There are many methods for converting measurements to other units within a system or between systems. One method is multiplication of the given measurement by a conversion factor. This conversion factor is the following ratio, which is always equal to unity.

$$\frac{\text{new units}}{\text{old units}} \quad \text{OR} \quad \frac{\text{what you want}}{\text{what you have}}$$

The fundamental feature of *unit analysis* or *dimensional analysis* is that conversion factors may be multiplied together and units cancelled in the same way as numerators and denominators of numerical fractions. The following examples help clarify this point.

Example: Convert 3 miles to yards.

Multiply the initial measurement by the conversion factor, cancel the mile units and solve:

$$\frac{3 \text{ miles}}{1} \times \frac{1760 \text{ yards}}{1 \text{ mile}} = 5280 \text{ yards}$$

Example: It takes Cynthia 45 minutes to get ready each morning. How many hours does she spend getting ready each week?

Multiply the initial measurement by the conversion factors from minutes to hours and from days to weeks, cancel the minute and day units and solve:

$$\frac{45 \text{ min.}}{\text{day}} \times \frac{1 \text{ hour}}{60 \text{ min.}} \times \frac{7 \text{ days}}{\text{week}} = \frac{5.25 \text{ hours}}{\text{week}}$$

Conversion factors for different types of units are listed below.

Conversion factors

MEASUREMENTS OF LENGTH (ENGLISH SYSTEM)		
12 inches (in)	=	1 foot (ft)
3 feet (ft)	=	1 yard (yd)
1760 yards (yd)	=	1 mile (mi)

MEASUREMENTS OF LENGTH (METRIC SYSTEM)		
Kilometer (km)	=	1000 meters (m)
Hectometer (hm)	=	100 meters (m)
Decameter (dam)	=	10 meters (m)

Continued on next page

Meter (m)	=	1 meter (m)
Decimeter (dm)	=	1/10 meter (m)
Centimeter (cm)	=	1/100 meter (m)
Millimeter (mm)	=	1/1000 meter (m)

CONVERSION OF WEIGHT FROM METRIC TO ENGLISH		
28.35 grams (g)	=	1 ounce (oz)
16 ounces (oz)	=	1 pound (lb)
2000 pounds (lb)	=	1 ton (t) (short ton)
1 metric ton (t)	=	1.1 ton (t)

MEASUREMENTS OF WEIGHT (METRIC SYSTEM)		
kilogram (kg)	=	1000 grams (g)
gram (g)	=	1 gram (g)
milligram (mg)	=	1/1000 gram (g)

CONVERSION OF VOLUME FROM ENGLISH TO METRIC		
1 teaspoon (tsp)	≈	5 milliliters
1 fluid ounce	≈	15 milliliters
1 cup	≈	0.24 liters
1 pint	≈	0.47 liters

CONVERSION OF WEIGHT FROM ENGLISH TO METRIC		
1 ounce	≈	28.35 grams
1 pound	≈	0.454 kilogram
1.1 ton	=	1 metric ton

MEASUREMENT OF VOLUME (ENGLISH SYSTEM)		
8 fluid ounces (oz)	=	1 cup (c)
2 cups (c)	=	1 pint (pt)
2 pints (pt)	=	1 quart (qt)
4 quarts (qt)	=	1 gallon (gal)

MEASUREMENT OF VOLUME (METRIC SYSTEM)		
Kiloliter (kl)	=	1000 liters (l)
Liter (l)	=	1 liter (l)
Milliliter (ml)	=	1/1000 liter (ml)

CONVERSION OF VOLUME FROM ENGLISH TO METRIC		
1 teaspoon (tsp)	≈	5 milliliters
1 fluid ounce	≈	29.57 milliliters
1 cup	≈	0.24 liters
1 pint	≈	0.47 liters
1 quart	≈	0.95 liters
1 gallon	≈	3.8 liters

Note: (') represents feet and (") represents inches.

Example: Convert 8750 meters to kilometers.

$$\frac{8750 \text{ meters}}{1} \times \frac{1 \text{ kilometer}}{1000 \text{ meters}} = \underline{\hspace{2cm}} \text{ km}$$
$$= 8.75 \text{ kilometers}$$

Example: 4 mi. = \underline{\hspace{1.5cm}} yd.

$$1760 \text{ yd.} = 1 \text{ mi.}$$
$$4 \text{ mi.} \times 1760 \frac{\text{yd.}}{\text{mi.}} = 7040 \text{ yd.}$$

Square units can be derived with knowledge of basic units of length by squaring the equivalent measurements.

1 square foot (sq. ft. or ft^2) = 144 sq. in.

1 sq. yd. = 9 sq. ft.

1 sq. yd. = 1296 sq. in.

Example: 14 sq. yd. = _____ sq. ft.

1 sq. yd. = 9 sq. ft.

14 sq. yd. $\times \dfrac{9 \text{ sq. ft.}}{\text{sq. yd.}}$ = 126 sq. ft.

Example: A car skidded 170 yards on an icy road before coming to a stop. How long is the skid distance in kilometers?

Since 1 yard ≈ 0.9 meters, multiply 170 yards by 0.9 meters/1 yard.

170 yd. $\times \dfrac{0.9 \text{ m}}{1 \text{ yd.}}$ = 153 m

Since 1000 meters = 1 kilometer, multiply 153 meters by 1 kilometer/1000 meters.

153 m $\times \dfrac{1 \text{ km}}{1000 \text{ m}}$ = 0.153 km

Example: The distance around a race course is exactly 1 mile, 17 feet, and $9\frac{1}{4}$ inches. Approximate this distance to the nearest tenth of a foot.

Convert the distance to feet.

1 mile = 1 = 1760 yards = 1760 $\times$ 3 feet = 5280 feet.

$9\frac{1}{4}$ in. = $\dfrac{37}{4}$ in. $\times \dfrac{1 \text{ ft.}}{12 \text{ in.}}$ = $\dfrac{37}{48}$ ft. = 0.77083 ft.

So 1 mile, 17 ft. and $9\frac{1}{4}$ in. = 5280 ft. + 17 ft. + 0.77083 ft.

= 5297.$\underline{7}$7083 ft.

Now, we need to round to the nearest tenth digit. The underlined 7 is in the tenths place. The digit in the hundredths place, also a 7, is greater than 5. Therefore, the 7 in the tenths place needs to be rounded up to 8 to get a final answer of 5297.8 feet.

Example: If the temperature is 90° F, what is it expressed in Celsius units?

To convert between Celsius (C) and Fahrenheit (F), use the following formula.

$\dfrac{C}{5} = \dfrac{F - 32}{9}$

If F = 90, then C = $5\dfrac{(90 - 32)}{9}$ = $\dfrac{5 \times 58}{9}$ = 32.2.

Example: A map shows a scale of 1 inch = 2 miles. Convert this scale to a numerical ratio so that any unit system (such as metric) can be used to measure distances.

The scale is a ratio—1 inch:2 miles. If either value is converted so that the two values have the same units, then this scale can be converted to a purely numerical ratio. To avoid fractions, convert miles to inches.

$$2 \text{ mi} = 2 \text{ mi} \times \frac{5{,}280 \text{ ft}}{1 \text{ mi}} \times \frac{12 \text{ in.}}{1 \text{ ft.}} = 126{,}720 \text{ in}$$

The ratio is then 1:126,720.

SKILL 8.2 **Apply the concepts of similarity, scale factors, and proportional reasoning to solve measurement problems**

See the Similarity section in Skill 9.4.

SKILL 8.3 **Analyze precision, error, and rounding in measurements and computed quantities**

Most numbers in mathematics are "exact" or "counted." Measurements are "approximate" and usually involve interpolation—for instance, figuring out which mark on the ruler is the closest. Any measurement obtained with a measuring device is approximate. Variations in measurement are defined in terms of precision and accuracy.

PRECISION measures the degree of variation in a particular measurement without reference to a true or real value. If a measurement is precise, it can be made repeatedly with little variation in the result. The precision of a measuring device is the smallest fractional or decimal division on the instrument. The smaller the unit or fraction of a unit on the measuring device, the more precisely it can measure.

The **GREATEST POSSIBLE ERROR** of measurement is always equal to one-half the smallest fraction of a unit on the measuring device. For example, if the smallest unit was mm, then the greatest possible error would be $\pm \frac{1}{2}$ mm.

ACCURACY is a measure of how close the result of measurement comes to the "true" value. In the game of darts, the true value is the bull's eye. If three darts are tossed and each lands on the bull's eye, the dart thrower is both precise (all land near the same spot) and accurate (the darts all land on the "true" value).

PRECISION: measures the degree of variation in a particular measurement without reference to a true or real value

GREATEST POSSIBLE ERROR: a measure is always equal to one-half the smallest fraction of a unit on the measuring device

ACCURACY: a measure of how close the result of measurement comes to the "true" value

TOLERANCE: the greatest allowable measure of error

LOWER LIMIT: the smallest acceptable limit of measurement given a particular tolerance

UPPER LIMIT: the greatest acceptable limit of measurement given a particular tolerance

TOLERANCE INTERVAL: the difference between the upper and lower limits

The greatest allowable measure of error is called the **TOLERANCE**. The least acceptable limit is called the **LOWER LIMIT**, and the greatest acceptable limit is called the **UPPER LIMIT**. The difference between the upper and lower limits is called the **TOLERANCE INTERVAL**. For example, a specification for an automobile part might be 14.625 ± 0.005 mm. This means that the smallest acceptable length of the part is 14.620 mm and the largest acceptable length is 14.630 mm. The tolerance interval is 0.010 mm. One can see how it would be important for automobile parts to be within a set of limits in terms of physical dimensions. If the part is too long or too short, it will not fit properly and vibrations may occur, thereby weakening the part and eventually causing damage to other parts.

Error in measurement may also be expressed by a **percentage of error.** For example, a measurement of 12 feet may be said to be off by 2%. This means that the actual measurement could be between

12 − (2% of 12) and 12 + (2% of 12)

12 − (.02)12 and 12 + (.02)12

11.76 feet and 12.24 feet

To determine the percent error between a measurement of a value and the actual value, use the following formula.

$$\text{Percent Error} = \frac{|\text{Measured} - \text{Actual}|}{\text{Actual}} \times 100$$

Rounding

Error in measurement may also be indicated by the terms "rounded" or "to the nearest." When rounding to a given place value, it is necessary to look at the number in the next smaller place. If this number is 5 or greater, the number in the place to which we are rounding is increased by 1 and all numbers to the right are changed to zero. If the number is smaller than 5, the number in the place to which we are rounding stays the same and all numbers to the right are changed to zero. For example, the length of a side of a square to the nearest inch may be 10 inches. This means that the actual length of the side could be between 9.5 inches and 10.4 inches (since all of these values round to 10).

SKILL 8.4 Apply the concepts of perimeter, circumference, area, surface area, and volume to solve real-world problems

Area Problems

Some problems involve computing the area that remains when sections are cut out of a given figure composed of triangles, squares, rectangles, parallelograms, trapezoids, or circles. The strategy for solving problems of this nature should be to identify the given shapes and choose the correct formulas. Subtract the smaller cut-out shape from the larger shape.

Example: Find the area of one side of the metal in the circular flat washer shown below:

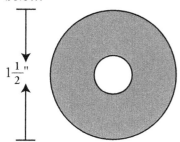

$1\frac{1}{2}$"

1. The shapes are both circles.

2. Use the formula $A = \pi r^2$ for both.
   (Inside diameter is $\frac{3}{8}$")

Area of larger circle
$$A = \pi r^2$$
$$A = \pi(.75^2)$$
$$A = 1.76625 \text{ in}^2$$

Area of smaller circle
$$A = \pi r^2$$
$$A = \pi(.1875^2)$$
$$A = .1103906 \text{ in}^2$$

Area of metal washer = larger area − smaller area
$$= 1.76625 \text{ in}^2 - .1103906 \text{ in}^2$$
$$= 1.65585944 \text{ in}^2$$

Example: You have decided to fertilize your lawn. The shapes and dimensions of your lot, house, pool, and garden are given in the diagram below. The shaded area will not be fertilized. If each bag of fertilizer costs $7.95 and covers 4,500 square feet, find the total number of bags needed and the total cost of the fertilizer.

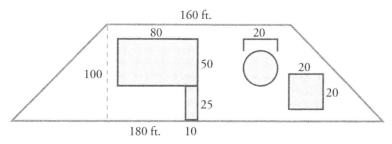

Area of Lot	Area of House	Area of Driveway	Area of Garden	Area of Pool
$A = \frac{1}{2} h(b_1 + b_2)$	$A = LW$	$A = LW$	$A = s^2$	$A = \pi r^2$
$A = \frac{1}{2}(100)(180 + 160)$	$A = (80)(50)$	$A = (10)(25)$	$A = (20)^2$	$A = \pi(10)^2$
$A = 17{,}000 \text{ sq ft}$	$A = 4{,}000 \text{ sq ft}$	$A = 250 \text{ sq ft}$	$A = 400 \text{ sq ft}$	$A = 314.159 \text{ sq ft}$

Total area to fertilize = Lot area − (House + Driveway + Pool + Garden)

$$= 17{,}000 - (4{,}000 + 250 + 314.159 + 400)$$
$$= 12{,}035.841 \text{ sq ft}$$

Number of bags needed = Total area to fertilize/4,500 sq ft bag
$$= 12{,}035.841/4{,}500$$
$$= 2.67 \text{ bags}$$

Since we cannot purchase 2.67 bags we must purchase 3 full bags.

Total cost = Number of bags $\times$ \$7.95
$$= 3 \times \$7.95$$
$$= \$23.85$$

Examining the change in area or volume of a given figure requires first finding the existing area given the original dimensions and then finding the new area given the increased dimensions.

Example: Given the rectangle below, determine the change in area if the length is increased by 5 and the width is increased by 7.

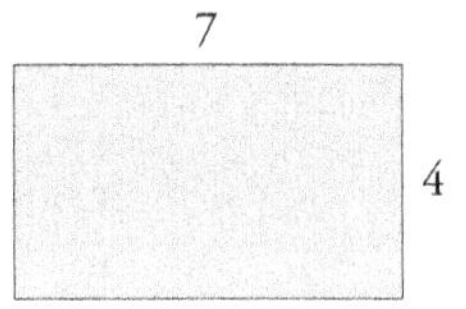

7

4

Draw and label a sketch of the new rectangle.

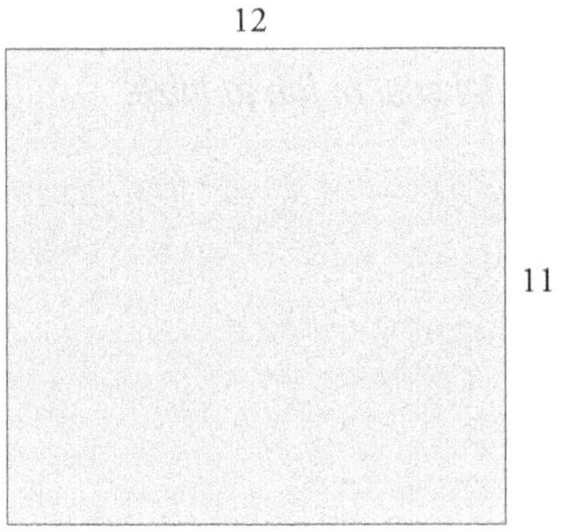

12

11

Find the areas.

Area of original = LW Area of enlarged shape = LW
$$= (7)(4) \qquad\qquad\qquad\qquad\qquad = (12)(11)$$
$$= 28 \text{ units}^2 \qquad\qquad\qquad\qquad = 132 \text{ units}^2$$

The change in area is $132 - 28 = 104 \text{ units}^2$.

To find the area of a compound shape, cut the compound shape into smaller, more familiar shapes, and then compute the total area by adding the areas of the smaller parts.

Example: Find the area of the given shape.

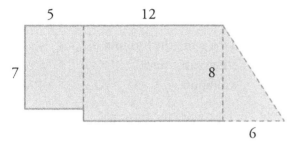

1. Using a dotted line, we have cut the shape into smaller parts that are familiar

2. Use the appropriate formula for each shape and find the sum of all areas

$$\text{Area 1} = LW \qquad\qquad \text{Area 2} = LW \qquad\qquad \text{Area 3} = \tfrac{1}{2}bh$$
$$= (5)(7) \qquad\qquad\quad = (12)(8) \qquad\qquad\quad = \tfrac{1}{2}(6)(8)$$
$$= 35 \text{ units}^2 \qquad\qquad = 96 \text{ units}^2 \qquad\qquad = 24 \text{ units}^2$$

$$\text{Total area} = \text{Area 1} + \text{Area 2} + \text{Area 3}$$
$$= 35 + 96 + 24$$
$$= 155 \text{ units}^2$$

Volume and Surface Area Problems

Use the following formulas to find volume and surface area.

FIGURE	VOLUME	TOTAL SURFACE AREA
Right Cylinder	$\pi r^2 h$	$2\pi rh + 2\pi r^2$
Right Cone	$\dfrac{\pi r^2 h}{3}$	$\pi r \sqrt{r^2 + h^2} + \pi r^2$
Sphere	$\dfrac{4}{3}\pi r^3$	$4\pi r^2$
Rectangular Solid	LWH	$2LW + 2WH + 2LH$

Note: $\sqrt{r^2 + h^2}$ is equal to the slant height of the cone.

Example: Given the figure below, find the volume and the surface area.

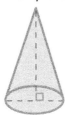

$r = 5$ in

$h = 6.2$ in

Volume $= \frac{\pi r^2 h}{3}$ First write the formula.

$\quad\quad\quad = \frac{1}{3} \pi (5^2)(6.2)$ Then substitute.

$\quad\quad\quad = 162.23333$ cubic inches   Compute.

Surface area $= \pi r \sqrt{r^2 + h^2} + \pi r^2$ First write the formula.

$\quad\quad\quad = \pi 5 \sqrt{5^2 + 6.2^2} + \pi 5^2$ Then substitute.

$\quad\quad\quad = 203.549$ square inches   Compute.

Note: *volume is always given in cubic units, and area is always given in square units.*

Area and Perimeter Problems

FIGURE	AREA FORMULA	PERIMETER FORMULA
Rectangle	LW	$2(L + W)$
Triangle	$\frac{1}{2} bh$	$a + b + c$
Parallelogram	bh	sum of lengths of sides
Trapezoid	$\frac{1}{2} bh(a + b)$	sum of lengths of sides

Example: Find the area and perimeter of a rectangle if its length is 12 inches and its diagonal is 15 inches.

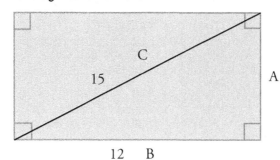

1. Draw and label sketch.
2. Since the height is still needed, use the Pythagorean formula to find the length of the missing leg of the triangle.

$A^2 + B^2 = C^2$

$A^2 + 12^2 = 15^2$

$A^2 = 15^2 - 12^2$

$A^2 = 81$

$A = 9$

Now use this information to find the area and perimeter.

$A = LW$	$P = 2(L + W)$	1. Write formula.
$A = (12)(9)$	$P = 2(12 + 9)$	2. Substitute.
$A = 108$ in^2	$P = 42$ inches	3. Solve.

Circles

Given a circular figure, the formulas are as follows:

$$A = \pi r^2 \quad C = \pi d \text{ or } 2\pi r$$

Example:

If the area of a circle is 50 cm^2, find the circumference.

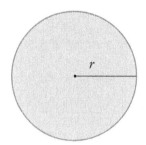

$A = 50$ cm^2

1. Draw a sketch.

2. Determine what is still needed.

Use the area formula to find the radius.

$A = \pi r^2$	1. Write the formula.
$50 = \pi r^2$	2. Substitute.
$\frac{50}{\pi} = r^2$	3. Divide by π.
$15.924 = r^2$	4. Substitute.
$\sqrt{15.924} = \sqrt{r^2}$	5. Take the square root of both sides.
$3.99 \approx r$	6. Compute.

Use the approximate answer (due to rounding) to find the circumference.

$A = 2\pi r$	1. Write the formula.
$C = 2\pi(3.99)$	2. Substitute.
$C \approx 25.057$	3. Compute.

When using formulas to solve a geometry problem, it is helpful to use the same strategies used for general problem solving. First, draw and label a sketch if needed. Second, write down the formula and then substitute in the known values. This will assist in identifying what is still needed (the unknown). Finally, solve the resulting equation.

Being consistent in the strategic approach to problem solving is paramount to teaching the concept as well as solving problems.

Example: Use the appropriate problem-solving strategies to find the solution.

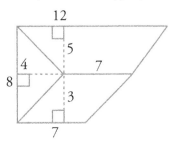

1. Find the area of the given figure.
2. Cut the figure into familiar shapes.
3. Identify what types of figures are given and write the appropriate formulas.

AREA OF FIGURE 1 (TRIANGLE)	AREA OF FIGURE 2 (PARALLELOGRAM)	AREA OF FIGURE 3 (TRAPEZOID)
$A = \frac{1}{2}bh$	$A = bh$	$A = \frac{1}{2}h(a + b)$
$A = \frac{1}{2}(8)(4)$	$A = (7)(3)$	$A = \frac{1}{2}(5)(12 + 7)$
$A = 16$ sq ft	$A = 21$ sq ft	$A = 47.5$ sq ft

Now find the total area by adding the area of all figures:

Total area $= 16 + 21 + 47.5$
$= 84.5$ sq ft

Example: Given the figure below, find the area by dividing the polygon into smaller shapes.

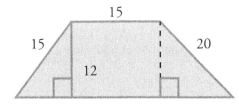

1. Divide the figure into two triangles and a rectangle.
2. Find the missing lengths.
3. Find the area of each part.
4. Find the sum of all of the areas.

Find the base of both right triangles using the Pythagorean formula:

$$a^2 + b^2 = c^2 \qquad\qquad a^2 + b^2 = c^2$$
$$a^2 + 12^2 = 15^2 \qquad\qquad a^2 + 12^2 = 20^2$$
$$a^2 = 225 - 144 \qquad\qquad a^2 = 400 - 144$$
$$a^2 = 81 \qquad\qquad a^2 = 256$$
$$a = 9 \qquad\qquad a = 16$$

AREA OF TRIANGLE 1	AREA OF TRIANGLE 2	AREA OF RECTANGLE
$A = \frac{1}{2}bh$	$A = \frac{1}{2}bh$	$A = LW$
$A = \frac{1}{2}(9)(12)$	$A = \frac{1}{2}(16)(12)$	$A = (15)(12)$
$A = 54$ sq units	$A = 96$ sq units	$A = 180$ sq units

Find the sum of all three figures:

54 + 96 + 180 = 330 square units

Surface Area and Volume of Geometric Solids

To compute the surface area and volume of right prisms, cones, cylinders, spheres, and solids that are combinations of these figures, use the following formulas:

FIGURE	LATERAL AREA	TOTAL AREA	VOLUME
Right Prism	Ph	$2B + Ph$	Bh
Regular Pyramid	$\frac{1}{2}Pl$	$\frac{1}{2}Pl + B$	$\frac{1}{3}Bh$

P = Perimeter; h = height; B = Area of Base; l = slant height

Example: Find the total area of the given figure.

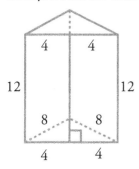

1. Since this is a triangular prism, first find the area of the bases.
2. Find the area of each rectangular lateral face.
3. Add the areas together.

$A = \frac{1}{2}bh$ $A = LW$ 1. Write the formula.

$8^2 = 4^2 + h^2$ 2. Find the height of the base triangle.

$h = \sqrt{48} \approx 6.928$

Then A = .5(8)(6.928) $A = (8)(12)$ 3. Substitute the known values.

A = 27.713 sq units   A = 96 sq units   4. Compute.

Total Area = 2(27.713) + 3(96)

= 343.426 sq units

FIGURE	VOLUME	TOTAL SURFACE AREA	LATERAL AREA
Right Cylinder	$\pi r^2 h$	$2\pi rh + 2\pi r^2$	$2\pi rh$
Right Cone	$\frac{\pi r^2 h}{3}$	$\pi r\sqrt{r^2 + h^2} + \pi r^2$	$\pi r\sqrt{r^2 + h^2}$

Note: $\sqrt{r^2 + h^2}$ is equal to the slant height of the cone.

Example: A water company is trying to decide whether to use traditional cylindrical paper cups or to offer conical paper cups; they both cost the same. The traditional cups are 8 cm wide and 14 cm high. The conical cups are 12 cm wide and 19 cm high. The company will use the cup that holds more water.

Draw and label a sketch of each cup.

$V = \pi r^2 h$ $V = \frac{\pi r^2 h}{3}$ 1. Write a formula.

$V = \pi(4)^2(14)$ $V = \frac{1}{3}\pi(6)^2(19)$ 2. Substitute.

$V = 703.36 \text{ cm}^3$ $V = 715.92 \text{ cm}^3$ 3. Solve.

The choice should be the conical cup, since its volume is greater.

FIGURE	VOLUME	TOTAL SURFACE AREA
Sphere	$\frac{4}{3}\pi r^3$	$4\pi r^2$

Example: How much material is needed to make a basketball that has a diameter of 15 inches? How much air is needed to fill the basketball?

Draw and label a sketch:

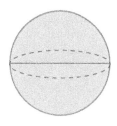

$D = 15$ inches

Total surface area   Volume

$\text{TSA} = 4\pi r^2$ $V = \frac{4}{3}\pi r^3$ 1. Write a formula.

$= 4\pi(7.5)^2$ $= \frac{4}{3}\pi(7.5)^3$ 2. Substitute.

$= 706.5 \text{ in}^2$ $= 1766.25 \text{ in}^3$ 3. Solve.

This represents the total amount of material needed to make the ball.   This represents the total amount of air needed to fill the ball.

COMPETENCY 9
UNDERSTAND EUCLIDEAN GEOMETRY IN TWO AND THREE DIMENSIONS

SKILL Demonstrate knowledge of axiomatic systems and of the axioms of
9.1 non-Euclidean geometries

Plane or Euclidean geometry is a classic example of an axiomatic system. An axiomatic system is composed of terms (or concepts) and axioms, also called postulates, which embody assumptions about the relationships among the terms. From these, theorems are logically derived. A simple example of an axiom is "1 equals 1." This is a statement that we cannot prove, but we accept it as true.

An axiomatic system must be consistent in that there are no contradictions, i.e. there is no statement that you can prove both true and false. Such a statement has no mathematical value because it has no basis in truth. An axiomatic system is said to be complete if a statement and its negation are derivable within that system; therefore, an axiomatic system cannot be both complete and consistent. An example is the relative consistency of absolute geometry with respect to the real number system.

Within an axiomatic system, an axiom is considered independent if it is not derived from other axioms. The system itself is independent when each of its axioms is independent.

The axiomatic system of plane geometry consists of the following:

- **Undefined terms:** For example, points, lines, and planes are intuitively understood but do not have specific, universally accepted definitions

- **Defined terms:** Ray, angle, and triangle are defined using undefined terms.

- **Axioms/Postulates:** These are assumed statements that we accept without proof, similar to undefined terms. For example, the Parallel Postulate states: Given a line and a point not on that line, precisely one line can be drawn that contains the point *and* is parallel to the original line.

- **Theorems:** These are proven statements. With a few axioms given as true, we can prove a multitude of theorems such as the familiar Pythagorean Theorem.

Euclid wrote a set of thirteen books around 330 BCE called the *Elements*. He outlined ten axioms and then deduced 465 theorems. Euclidean geometry is based on the undefined concepts of the point, the line, and the plane.

The fifth of Euclid's axioms (referred to as the Parallel Postulate) was not as readily accepted as the other nine axioms. Many mathematicians throughout the years have attempted to prove that this axiom is not necessary because it could be proved by the other nine. Among the many who attempted to prove this was Carl Friedrich Gauss; his work led to the development of hyperbolic geometry. Elliptical, spherical, or Riemannian geometry was hypothesized by G.F. Bernhard Riemann, who based his work on the theory of surfaces and used models as physical interpretations of the undefined terms that satisfy the axioms.

The variants of the Parallel Postulate that lead to non-Euclidean geometries are based on the number of possible unique lines that can be parallel to a line l, where the potential parallel lines must pass through a specific point not on l.

The variants of the Parallel Postulate that lead to non-Euclidean geometries are based on the number of possible unique lines that can be parallel to a line l, where the potential parallel lines must pass through a specific point not on l.

The chart below lists the fifth axiom (the Parallel Postulate) as it is given in each of the three geometries:

EUCLIDEAN GEOMETRY	SPHERICAL OR RIEMANNIAN GEOMETRY	HYPERBOLIC OR SADDLE GEOMETRY
Through a point not on a line, there is no more than one line parallel to that line.	If l is any line and P is any point not on l, then there are no lines through P that are parallel to l.	If l is any line and P is any point not on l, then there exist at least two lines through P that are parallel to l.

EUCLIDEAN GEOMETRY: the study of flat, two-dimensional space

EUCLIDEAN GEOMETRY is the study of flat, two-dimensional space. Non-Euclidean geometries involve curved surfaces, such as that of a sphere. These geometries have a direct connection to our experiences; for instance, the surface of the Earth is (roughly) spherical. Note the results of the Parallel Postulate for spherical geometry. (A line on a sphere is a so-called great circle, which is a circle of the same radius as the sphere.)

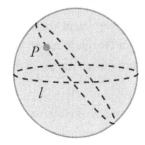

The line through point P is not parallel to line l. Furthermore, it is clear through observation of the figure that, since there is only one great circle through any given point, there are non-collinear parallel lines in spherical geometry. Thus, as is demonstrated by this example, varying the details of the Parallel Postulate leads to various types of non-Euclidean geometries.

Non-Euclidean geometries have application beyond just abstract mathematical theory. For instance, hyperbolic geometry is a central concept in Einstein's theory of relativity.

SKILL 9.2 Use the properties of polygons and circles to solve problems

A **POLYGON** is a simple closed figure composed of line segments. Here we will consider only **CONVEX POLYGONS**, i.e., polygons for which the measure of each internal angle is less than 180°. Of the two polygons shown below, the one on the left is a convex polygon.

POLYGON: a simple closed figure composed of line segments

CONVEX POLYGON: a polygon in which the measure of each internal angle is less than 180 degrees

A **REGULAR POLYGON** is one for which all sides are the same length and all interior angles are the same measure.

The sum of the measures of the interior angles of a polygon can be determined using the following formula, where n represents the number of angles in the polygon.

Sum of $\angle s = 180(n - 2)$

REGULAR POLYGON: a polygon for which all sides are the same length and all interior angles are the same measure

The measure of each angle of a regular polygon can be found by dividing the sum of the measures by the number of angles.

Measure of $\angle = \frac{180(n - 2)}{n}$

Example: Find the measure of each angle of a regular octagon. Since an octagon has eight sides, each angle equals:

$$\frac{180(8 - 2)}{8} = \frac{180(6)}{8} = 135°$$

The sum of the measures of the *exterior angles* of a polygon, taken one angle at each vertex, equals 360°.

The measure of each exterior angle of a regular polygon can be determined using the following formula, where n represents the number of angles in the polygon.

Measure of exterior $\angle$ of regular polygon

$$\angle = 180 - \frac{180(n - 2)}{n} = \frac{360}{n}$$

Example: Find the measure of the interior and exterior angles of a regular pentagon.

Since a pentagon has five sides, each exterior angle measures:

$$\frac{360}{5} = 72°$$

Since each exterior angle is supplementary to its interior angle, the interior angle measures $180 - 72$ or $108°$.

The **AREA OF A REGULAR POLYGON** is represented by the formula $A = \frac{1}{2}\,aP$ where P is the perimeter of the polygon and a is the "apothem" which is defined as the distance from the center of the polygon to an edge. An apothem is perpendicular to a side.

Properties of Quadrilaterals

> **QUADRILATERAL:** a polygon with four sides

A **QUADRILATERAL** is a polygon with four sides. The sum of the measures of the angles of a convex quadrilateral is 360°.

A **TRAPEZOID** is a quadrilateral with exactly one pair of parallel sides.

> **TRAPEZOID:** a quadrilateral with exactly one pair of parallel sides

The two parallel sides of a trapezoid are called the bases, and the two nonparallel sides are called the legs. If the two legs are the same length, then the trapezoid is called an **ISOSCELES TRAPEZOID**.

> **ISOSCELES TRAPEZOID:** a trapezoid with two legs of equal length

The segment connecting the two midpoints of the legs is called the median. The median has the following two properties:

1. The median is parallel to the two bases.

2. The length of the median is equal to one-half the sum of the length of the two bases.

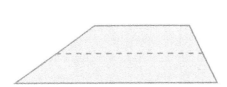

In an isosceles trapezoid, the nonparallel sides are congruent.

An isosceles trapezoid has the following properties:

1. The diagonals of an isosceles trapezoid are congruent.

2. The base angles of an isosceles trapezoid are congruent.

Example: An isosceles trapezoid has a diagonal of 10 and a base angle measuring 30°. Find the measure of the other three angles.

Based on the properties of trapezoids, the measure of the other base angle is 30° and the measure of the other diagonal is 10. The other two angles have a measure of:

$$360 = 30(2) + 2x$$
$$x = 150°$$

The other two angles measure 150° each.

A **PARALLELOGRAM** is a quadrilateral with two pairs of parallel sides. A parallelogram has the following properties:

1. The diagonals bisect each other.

2. Each diagonal divides the parallelogram into two congruent triangles.

3. Both pairs of opposite sides are congruent.

4. Both pairs of opposite angles are congruent.

5. Two adjacent angles are supplementary.

Example: Find the measures of the other three angles of a parallelogram if one angle measures 38°.

Since opposite angles are equal, there are two angles measuring 38°. Since adjacent angles are supplementary, $180 - 38 = 142$. Hence the other two angles measure 142° each.

Example: The measures of two adjacent angles of a parallelogram are 3x + 40 and x + 70. Find the measure of each angle.

$$2(3x + 40) + 2(x + 70) = 360$$
$$6x + 80 + 2x + 140 = 360$$
$$8x + 220 = 360$$
$$8x = 140$$
$$x = 17.5$$
$$3x + 40 = 92.5$$
$$x + 70 = 87.5$$

Thus the angles measure 92.5°, 92.5°, 87.5°, and 87.5°.

A **RECTANGLE** is a parallelogram with a right angle. Since a rectangle is a special type of parallelogram, it exhibits all the properties of a parallelogram. All the

> **PARALLELOGRAM:** a quadrilateral with two pairs of parallel sides

> **RECTANGLE:** a parallelogram with a right angle

angles of a rectangle are right angles because of congruent opposite angles. Additionally, the diagonals of a rectangle are congruent.

RHOMBUS: a parallelogram with all sides equal in length

A **RHOMBUS** is a parallelogram with all sides equal in length. A rhombus has all the properties of a parallelogram. Additionally, its diagonals are perpendicular to each other, and they bisect its angles.

SQUARE: a rectangle with all sides equal in length

A **SQUARE** is a rectangle with all sides equal in length. A square has all the properties of a rectangle and of a rhombus.

TRUE OR FALSE?	
All squares are rhombuses	True
All parallelograms are rectangles	False—*Some* parallelograms are rectangles
All rectangles are parallelograms	True
Some rhombuses are squares	True
Some rectangles are trapezoids	False—Trapezoids have only one pair of parallel sides
All quadrilaterals are parallelograms	False—*Some* quadrilaterals are parallelograms
Some squares are rectangles	False—*All* squares are rectangles
Some parallelograms are rhombuses	True

Example: In rhombus ABCD, side AB = 3x − 7 and side CD = x + 15. Find the length of each side.

Since all the sides are the same length,

$$3x − 7 = x + 15$$
$$2x = 22$$
$$x = 11$$

Since $3(11) − 7 = 26$ and $11 + 15 = 26$, each side measures 26 units.

Properties of Circles

The distance around a circle is called the CIRCUMFERENCE. The ratio of the circumference to the diameter is represented by the Greek letter pi, where $\pi \approx 3.14$. The circumference of a circle is given by the formula $C = 2\pi r$ or $C = \pi d$, where r is the radius of the circle and d is the diameter. The area of a circle is given by the formula $A = \pi r^2$.

> **CIRCUMFERENCE:** the distance around a circle

We can extend the area formula of a regular polygon to obtain the area of a circle by considering the fact that a circle is essentially a regular polygon with an infinite number of sides. The radius of a circle is equivalent to the apothem of a regular polygon. Thus, applying the area formula for a regular polygon to a circle, we get

$$\tfrac{1}{2} \times perimeter \times apothem = \tfrac{1}{2} \times 2\pi r \times r = \pi r^2$$

If two circles have radii that are in a ratio of $a{:}b$, then the following ratios also apply to the circles:

1. The diameters are in the ratio $a{:}b$

2. The circumferences are in the ratio $a{:}b$

3. The areas are in the ratio $a^2{:}b^2$, or the ratio of the areas is the square of the ratio of the radii.

If you draw two radii in a circle, the angle they form with the center as the vertex is a CENTRAL ANGLE. The piece of the circle "inside" the angle is an arc. Just like a central angle, an arc can have any degree measure from 0 to 360. The measure of an arc is equal to the measure of the central angle that forms the arc. Since a diameter forms a semicircle and the measure of a straight angle like a diameter is 180°, the measure of a semicircle is also 180°.

> **CENTRAL ANGLE:** the angle formed by two radii that intersect in the center of a circle

Given two points on a circle, the two points form two different arcs. Except in the case of semicircles, one of the two arcs will always be greater than 180°, and the other will be less than 180°. The arc less than 180° is a MINOR ARC and the arc greater than 180° is a MAJOR ARC.

> **MINOR ARC:** an arc with a measure less than 180°

> **MAJOR ARC:** an arc with a measure greater than 180°.

Examples:

1.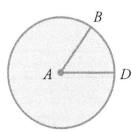

   $m \angle BAD = 45°$

   What is the measure of the major arc *BD*?

   minor arc $BD = m \angle BAD = 45°$

   $360 - 45 =$ major arc *BD*

   Thus, major arc $BD = 315°$.

   A major and minor arc always add up to 360°.

2.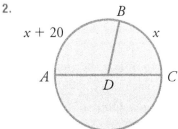

   $\overline{AC}$ is a diameter of circle *D*.

   What is the measure of $\angle BDC$?

   $m \angle ADB + m \angle BDC = 180°$
   $x + 20 + x = 180$
   $2x + 20 = 180$
   $2x = 160$
   $x = 80$

   A diameter forms a semicircle that has a measure of 180°.

   minor arc $BC = 80°$
   $m \angle BDC = 80°$

   A central angle has the same measure as the arc it forms.

Although an arc has a measure associated with the degree measure of a central angle, it also has a length that is a fraction of the circumference of the circle. For each central angle and its associated arc, there is a sector of the circle that resembles a pie piece. The area of such a sector is a fraction of the area of the circle. The fractions used for the area of a sector and length of its associated arc are both equal to the ratio of the central angle to 360°.

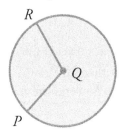

$$\frac{\angle PQR}{360°} = \frac{\text{length of arc } RP}{\text{circumference of circle}} = \frac{\text{area of sector } PQR}{\text{area of circle}}$$

Examples:

1.

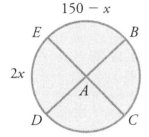

150 − x

2x

$2x + 150 - x = 180$

$x + 150 = 180$

$x = 30$

Arc $ED = 2(30) = 60°$

Circle A has a radius of 4 cm. What is the length of arc ED?

Arc BE and arc ED make a semicircle.

The ratio 60° to 360° is equal to the ratio of arc length ED to the circumference of circle A.

$$\frac{60}{360} = \frac{\text{arc length } ED}{2\pi 4}$$

$$\frac{1}{6} = \frac{\text{arc length}}{8\pi}$$

arc length $= \frac{8\pi}{6} = \frac{4\pi}{3}$

Cross multiply and solve for the arc length.

2.

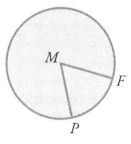

The radius of circle M is 3 cm. The length of arc PF is 2π cm. What is the area of sector MPF?

Circumference of circle

$M = 2\pi(3) = 6\pi$

Area of circle $M = \pi \times 3^2 = 9\pi$

$$\frac{\text{area of } MPF}{9\pi} = \frac{2\pi}{6\pi}$$

Find the circumference and area of the circle.

The ratio of the sector area to the circle area is the same as the arc length to the circumference.

$$\frac{\text{area of } MPF}{9\pi} = \frac{1}{3}$$

area of $MPF = \frac{9\pi}{3}$

area of $MPF = 3\pi$

Solve for the area of the sector.

TANGENT LINE: a line that intersects or touches a circle in exactly one point

A **TANGENT LINE** to a circle intersects or touches the circle in exactly one point. If a radius is drawn to that point, the radius will be perpendicular to the tangent.

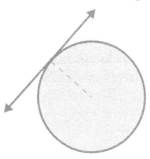

SECANT LINE: a line that intersects a circle in two points

A **SECANT LINE** intersects a circle in two points and includes a **CHORD**, which is a line segment with endpoints on the circle. If a radius or diameter is perpendicular to a chord, the radius will cut the chord into two equal parts, and vice versa.

CHORD: a line segment with endpoints on a circle

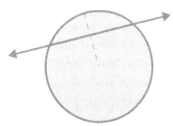

If two chords in the same circle have the same length, the two chords will have arcs that are the same length, and the two chords will be equidistant from the center of the circle. Distance from the center to a chord is measured by finding the length of a segment from the center perpendicular to the chord.

Examples:

1.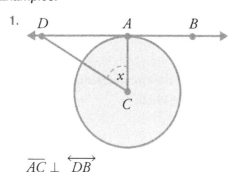

   $\overleftrightarrow{DB}$ is tangent to circle C at A.
   $m\angle ADC = 40°$. Find x.

   $\overline{AC} \perp \overleftrightarrow{DB}$

   A radius is $\perp$ to a tangent at the point of tangency.

   $m\angle DAC = 90°$

   Two segments that are $\perp$ form a 90° angle.

   $40 + 90 + x = 180$

   The sum of the angles of a triangle is 180°.

   $x = 50°$

   Solve for x.

2.

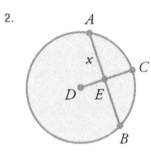

$\overline{CD}$ is a radius and $\overline{CD} \perp$ chord $\overline{AB}$.

$\overline{AB} = 10$. Find x.

$x = \frac{1}{2}(10)$

$x = 5$

If a radius is $\perp$ to a chord, the radius bisects the chord.

An **INSCRIBED ANGLE** is an angle with a vertex is on the circumference of a circle. Such an angle could be formed by two chords, two secants, or a secant and a tangent. An inscribed angle has one arc of the circle in its interior. The measure of the inscribed angle is one-half the measure of its intercepted arc. If two inscribed angles intercept the same arc, the two angles are congruent (i.e. their measures are equal). If an inscribed angle intercepts an entire semicircle, the angle is a right angle.

> **INSCRIBED ANGLE:** an angle with a vertex is on the circumference of a circle

When two chords intersect inside a circle, two sets of vertical angles are formed in the interior of the circle. Each set of vertical angles intercepts two arcs that are across from each other. The measure of an angle formed by two chords in a circle is equal to one-half the sum of the arc intercepted by the angle and the arc intercepted by its vertical angle.

If an angle has its vertex outside of the circle and each side of the angle intersects the circle, then the angle contains two different arcs. The measure of the angle is equal to one-half the difference of the two arcs.

Examples:

1.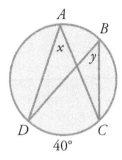

Find *x* and *y*.

$$m \angle DAC = \tfrac{1}{2}(40) = 20°$$

$\angle DAC$ and $\angle DBC$ are both inscribed angles, so each one has a measure equal to one-half the measure of arc *DC*.

$$m \angle DBC = \tfrac{1}{2}(40) = 20°$$

$$x = 20° \text{ and } y = 20°$$

2.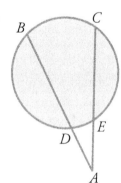

Find the measure of arc *BC* if the measure of arc *DE* is 30° and angle *BAC* = 20°.

$$m \angle BAC = \tfrac{1}{2}(mBC - mDE)$$

$$\rightarrow 2 \times m \angle BAC = mBC - mDE$$

$$\rightarrow mBC = 2 \times m \angle BAC + mDE = 2 \times 20° + 30° = 70°$$

If *two chords intersect inside a circle*, each chord is divided into two smaller segments. The product of the lengths of the two segments formed from one chord equals the product of the lengths of the two segments formed from the other chord.

If *two tangent segments intersect outside of a circle*, the two segments have the same length.

If *two secant segments intersect outside a circle*, a portion of each segment will lie inside the circle and a portion (called the exterior segment) will lie outside the circle. The product of the length of one secant segment and the length of its exterior segment equals the product of the length of the other secant segment and the length of its exterior segment.

If *a tangent segment and a secant segment intersect outside a circle*, the square of the length of the tangent segment equals the product of the length of the secant segment and its exterior segment.

Examples:

1.

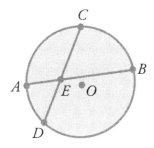

$\overline{AB}$ and $\overline{CD}$ are chords.

$CE = 10$, $ED = x$, $AE = 5$, $EB = 4$

$(AE)(EB) = (CE)(ED)$

Since the chords intersect in the circle, the products of the segment pieces are equal.

$5(4) = 10x$
$20 = 10x$
$x = 2$

Solve for x.

2.

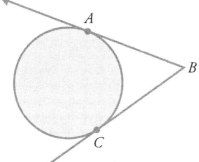

$\overleftrightarrow{AB}$ and $\overleftrightarrow{CD}$ are tangents.

$\overline{AB} = x^2 + x - 2$

$\overline{CB} = 5 - 3x + x^2$

Find the length of $\overline{AB}$ and $\overline{BC}$

$\overline{AB} = x^2 + x - 2$
$\overline{BC} = x^2 - 3x + 5$

Given.

$\overline{AB} = \overline{BC}$

Intersecting tangents are equal.

$x^2 + x - 2 = x^2 - 3x + 5$

Set the expressions equal to each other and solve.

$4x = 7$
$x = 1.75$
$(1.75)^2 + 1.75 - 2 = \overline{AB}$
$\overline{AB} = \overline{BC} = 2.81$

Substitute and solve.

Apply the Pythagorean theorem and its converse

Pythagorean Theorem

RIGHT TRIANGLE: a triangle with one right angle

A **RIGHT TRIANGLE** is a triangle with one right angle. The side opposite the right angle is called the hypotenuse. The other two sides are the legs.

The Pythagorean Theorem states that, for any right triangle, the square of the length of the hypotenuse is equal to the sum of the squares of the lengths of the legs.

The **Pythagorean Theorem** states that, for any right triangle, the square of the length of the **hypotenuse** is equal to the sum of the squares of the lengths of the **legs**. Symbolically, this is stated as:

$$c^2 = a^2 + b^2$$

Example: Given the right triangle below, find the missing side.

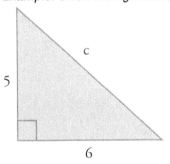

$c^2 = a^2 + b^2$	1. Write formula.
$c^2 = 5^2 + 6^2$	2. Substitute known values.
$c^2 = 61$	3. Take square root.
$c^2 = \sqrt{61}$ or 7.81	4. Solve.

The Converse of the Pythagorean Theorem states that if the square of one side of a triangle is equal to the sum of the squares of the other two sides, then the triangle is a right triangle.

The **Converse of the Pythagorean Theorem** states that if the square of one side of a triangle is equal to the sum of the squares of the other two sides, then the triangle is a right triangle.

Example: Given $\triangle XYZ$, with sides measuring 12, 16, and 20 cm, is this a right triangle?

$$c^2 = a^2 + b^2$$
$$20^2 \underset{?}{=} 12^2 + 16^2$$
$$400 \underset{?}{=} 144 + 256$$
$$400 = 400$$

Yes, the triangle is a right triangle.

This theorem can be expanded to determine if triangles are obtuse or acute.

If the square of the longest side of a triangle is greater than the sum of the squares of the other two sides, then the triangle is an obtuse triangle. If the square of the longest side of a triangle is less than the sum of the squares of the other two sides, then the triangle is an acute triangle.

Example: Given △LMN with sides measuring 7, 12, and 14 inches, is the triangle right, acute, or obtuse?

$14^2 \underset{?}{\underline{}} 7^2 + 12^2$

$196 \underset{?}{\underline{}} 49 + 144$

$196 > 193$

Therefore, the triangle is obtuse.

When an altitude is drawn to the hypotenuse of a right triangle, then the two triangles formed are similar to the original triangle and to each other.

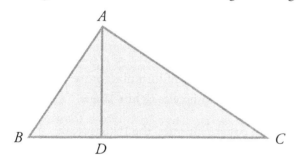

Given right triangle *ABC* with right angle at *A*, altitude *AD* drawn to hypotenuse *BC* at *D*, △*ABC* ~ △*DBA* ~ △*DAC*.

If *a*, *b*, and *c* are positive numbers such that $\frac{a}{b} = \frac{b}{c}$, then *b* is called the GEOMETRIC MEAN of *a* and *c*.

The geometric mean is significant when the altitude is drawn to the hypotenuse of a right triangle.

The length of the altitude is the geometric mean between each segment of the hypotenuse. Also, each leg is the geometric mean between the hypotenuse and the segment of the hypotenuse that is adjacent to the leg.

> *When an altitude is drawn to the hypotenuse of a right triangle, then the two triangles formed are similar to the original triangle and to each other.*

> **GEOMETRIC MEAN:** if *a*, *b*, and *c* are positive numbers such that $\frac{a}{b} = \frac{b}{c}$, then *b* is called the geometric mean of *a* and *c*

Example:

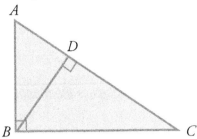

$\triangle ABC$ is a right triangle and $\angle ABC$ is a right angle. $AB = 6$ and $AC = 12$. Find AD, CD, BD, and BC.

$\frac{12}{6} = \frac{6}{AD}$

$12(AD) = 36$

$AD = 3$

$CD = 12 - 3 = 9$

$\frac{3}{BD} = \frac{BD}{9}$

$(BD)^2 = 27$

$BD = \sqrt{27} = \sqrt{9 \times 3} = 3\sqrt{3}$

$\frac{12}{BC} = \frac{BC}{9}$

$(BC)^2 = 108$

$BC = 6\sqrt{3}$

Special Right Triangles

The Pythagorean Theorem can be used to prove a set of formulas for two special cases of triangles. The first is associated with the isosceles right triangle.

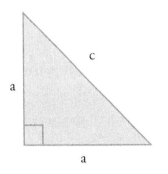

With two congruent sides, the Pythagorean Theorem is set up as

$a^2 + a^2 = c^2$

$2a^2 = c_2$

$a\sqrt{2} = c$

Therefore, the hypotenuse of an isosceles right triangle is always a factor of $\sqrt{2}$ greater than the leg. Since the base angles of an isosceles triangle are congruent, in an isosceles right triangle each base angle is 45°. Another way this special case is named, then, is as a 45–45–90 triangle.

The second special case stems from an equilateral triangle with an altitude (which also bisects the side) to the base.

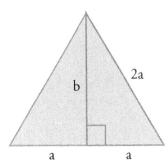

Start again with the Pythagorean Theorem:

$a^2 + b^2 = (2a)^2$

$b^2 = 4a^2 - a^2$

$b^2 = 3a^2$

$b = a\sqrt{3}$

This case, one half of the equilateral triangle, is often referred to as a 30–60–90 triangle. The hypotenuse will be double the smallest side and the side across from the 60° angle will be a factor of $\sqrt{3}$ times the shortest side.

Use these special right triangle relationships to find the lengths of missing sides.

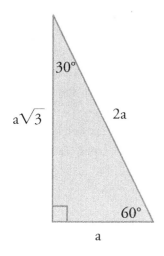

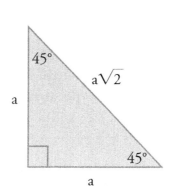

Examples:

1. 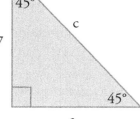   if $8 = a\sqrt{2}$ then $a = \dfrac{8}{\sqrt{2}}$ or 5.657

2.   if $7 = a$ then $c = a\sqrt{2} = 7\sqrt{2}$ or 9.899

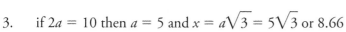

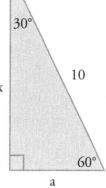

3.   if $2a = 10$ then $a = 5$ and $x = a\sqrt{3} = 5\sqrt{3}$ or 8.66

SKILL Analyze formal and informal geometric proofs, including the use of
9.4 similarity and congruence

EUCLIDEAN GEOMETRY:
the study of the properties
of two-dimensional (planar)
and three-dimensional
(solid) figures

EUCLIDEAN GEOMETRY is the study of the properties of two-dimensional (planar) and three-dimensional (solid) figures. It is based on the undefined concepts of point, line, and plane and a set of self-evident statements or **AXIOMS**. Starting from these building blocks, deductive reasoning is used to prove a set of propositions or theorems about the properties of different geometric figures. The axioms and theorems and the process of formal proof provide a consistent logical framework that can be used to derive further results. The following review of geometric concepts provides a basic overview of proof relating to geometry, as well as the characteristics of various types of polygons, circles, compound shapes, and three-dimensional figures.

AXIOM: a self-evident
mathematical statement

Formal Proofs

DEDUCTIVE REASONING:
the process of arriving at a
conclusion based on other
statements that are known
to be true, such as theo-
rems, axioms, or postulates

DEDUCTIVE REASONING is the process of arriving at a conclusion based on other statements that are known to be true, such as theorems, axioms, or postulates. Valid mathematical arguments are deductive in nature.

A **DIRECT PROOF** demonstrates the truth of a proposition by beginning with the given information and showing that it leads to the proposition through logical steps. An **INDIRECT PROOF** of a proposition can be carried out by demonstrating that the opposite of the proposition is untenable.

DIRECT PROOF: dem-
onstrates the truth of a
proposition by beginning
with the given information
and showing that it leads
to the proposition through
logical steps

A proof of a geometrical proposition is typically presented in a format that has two columns side-by-side. In a two-column proof, the left column consists of the given information or statements that can be proved by deductive reasoning. The right column consists of the reasons used to justify each statement on the left. The right side should identify given information or state the theorems, postulates, definitions, or algebraic properties used to show that the corresponding steps are valid.

INDIRECT PROOF: demonstrates that the opposite of
the proposition is untenable

The following algebraic postulates are frequently used as justifications for statements in two-column geometric proofs:

ALGEBRAIC POSTULATES	
Addition Property	If $a = b$ and $c = d$, then $a + c = b + d$
Subtraction Property	If $a = b$ and $c = d$, then $a - c = b - d$
Multiplication Property	If $a = b$, then $ac = bc$
Division Property	If $a = b$ and $c \neq 0$, then $a/c = b/c$
Reflexive Property	$a = a$
Symmetric Property	If $a = b$, then $b = a$
Transitive Property	If $a = b$ and $b = c$, then $a = c$
Distributive Property	$a(b + c) = ab + ac$
Substitution Property	If $a = b$, then b may be substituted for a in any other expression (a may also be substituted for b)

> *In a two-column proof, the left column consists of the given information or statements that can be proved by deductive reasoning. The right column consists of the reasons used to justify each statement on the left.*

Definitions of Geometric Figures

A POINT is a dimensionless location and has no length, width, or height.

A LINE connects a series of points and continues "straight" infinitely in two directions. Lines extend in one dimension. A line is defined by any two points that fall on the line; therefore, a line may have multiple names.

A LINE SEGMENT is a portion of a line. A line segment is the shortest distance between two endpoints and is named using those endpoints. Line segments therefore have exactly two names (e.g., $\overline{AB}$ or $\overline{BA}$). Because line segments have two endpoints, they have a defined length or distance.

A RAY is a portion of a line that has only one endpoint and continues infinitely in one direction. Rays are named using the endpoint as the first point and any other point on the ray as the second.

Note that the symbol for a line includes two arrows (indicating infinite extent in both directions), the symbol for a ray includes only one arrow (indicating that it has one endpoint), and the symbol for a line segment has no arrows (indicating two endpoints).

> **POINT:** a dimensionless location that has no length, width, or height

> **LINE:** connects a series of points and continues "straight" infinitely in two directions

> **RAY:** a portion of a line that has only one endpoint and continues infinitely in one direction

Example: Using the diagram below, calculate the length of $\overline{AB}$ given that $\overline{AC}$ is 6 *cm and $\overline{BC}$ is twice as long as $\overline{AB}$*

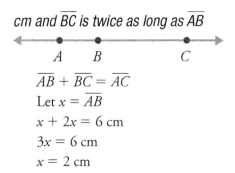

$\overline{AB} + \overline{BC} = \overline{AC}$

Let $x = \overline{AB}$

$x + 2x = 6$ cm

$3x = 6$ cm

$x = 2$ cm

PLANE: a flat surface defined by three points; planes extend indefinitely in two dimensions

A **PLANE** is a flat surface defined by three points. Planes extend indefinitely in two dimensions. A common example of a plane is the *x-y* plane used in the Cartesian coordinate system.

In geometry, the point, line, and plane are key concepts and can be discussed in relation to each other.

Collinear points are all on the same line.

Noncollinear points are not on the same line.

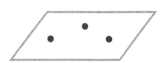

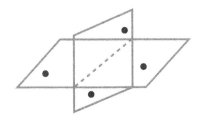

Coplanar points are on the same plane.

Noncoplanar points are not on the same plane.

CONGRUENT: figures that have the same size and shape

Congruence

CONGRUENT figures have the same size and shape; i.e., if one of the figures is super-imposed on the other, the boundaries coincide exactly. Congruent line segments have the same length; congruent angles have equal measures. The symbol $\cong$ is used to indicate that two figures, line segments, or angles are congruent.

The **reflexive**, **symmetric** and **transitive** properties described for algebraic equality relationships may also be applied to congruence. For instance, if $\angle A \cong \angle B$ and $\angle A \cong \angle D$, then $\angle B \cong \angle D$ (transitive property).

The polygons (pentagons) *ABCDE* and *VWXYZ* shown below are congruent since they are exactly the same size and shape.

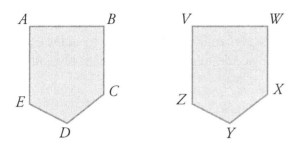

$$ABCDE \cong VWXYZ$$

Corresponding parts are congruent angles and congruent sides. For the polygons shown above:

corresponding angles

$\angle A \leftrightarrow \angle V$

$\angle B \leftrightarrow \angle W$

$\angle C \leftrightarrow \angle X$

$\angle D \leftrightarrow \angle Y$

$\angle E \leftrightarrow \angle Z$

corresponding sides

$AB \leftrightarrow VW$

$BC \leftrightarrow WX$

$CD \leftrightarrow XY$

$DE \leftrightarrow YZ$

$AE \leftrightarrow VZ$

Two triangles are congruent if each of the three angles and three sides of one triangle match up in a one-to-one fashion with congruent angles and sides of the second triangle. To see how the sides and angles match up, it is sometimes necessary to imagine rotating or reflecting one of the triangles so the two figures are oriented in the same position.

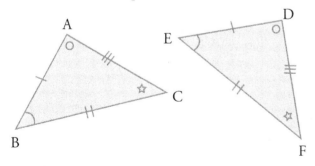

In the example above, the two triangles *ABC* and *DEF* are congruent if these 6 conditions are met:

1. $\angle A \cong \angle D$
2. $\angle B \cong \angle E$
3. $\angle C \cong \angle F$

4. $\overline{AB} \cong \overline{DE}$
5. $\overline{BC} \cong \overline{EF}$
6. $\overline{AC} \cong \overline{DF}$

The congruent angles and segments "correspond" to each other.

It is not always necessary to demonstrate all of the above six conditions to prove that two triangles are congruent. There are several "shortcut" methods described below.

The **SAS POSTULATE** (side-angle-side) states that if two sides and the included angle of one triangle are congruent to two sides and the included angle of another triangle, then the two triangles are congruent.

> **SAS POSTULATE:** also called side-angle-side; states that if two sides and the included angle of one triangle are congruent to two sides and the included angle of another triangle, then the two triangles are congruent

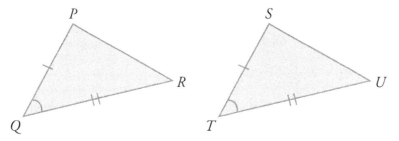

To see why this is true, imagine moving the triangle PQR (shown above) in such a way that the point P coincides with the point S, and line segment PQ coincides with line segment ST. Point Q will then coincide with T, since $PQ \cong ST$. Also, segment QR will coincide with TU, because $\angle Q \cong \angle T$. Point R will coincide with U, because $QR \cong TU$. Since P and S coincide and R and U coincide, line PR will coincide with SU because two lines cannot enclose a space. Thus the two triangles match perfectly point for point and are congruent.

Example: Are the following triangles congruent?

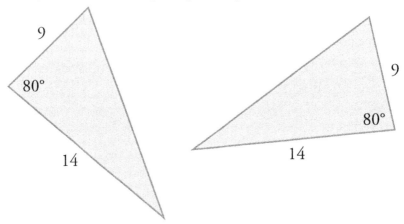

Each of the two triangles has a side that is 14 units and another that is 9 units. The angle included in the sides is 80° in both triangles. Therefore, the triangles are congruent by SAS.

The **SSS POSTULATE** (side-side-side) states that if three sides of one triangle are congruent to three sides of another triangle, then the two triangles are congruent.

> **SSS POSTULATE:** also called side-side-side; states that if three sides of one triangle are congruent to three sides of another triangle, then the two triangles are congruent

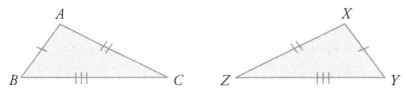

Since $\overline{AB} \cong \overline{XY}$, $\overline{BC} \cong \overline{YZ}$ and $\overline{AC} \cong \overline{XZ}$, then $\triangle ABC \cong \triangle XYZ$.

Example: Given isosceles triangle ABC with D being the midpoint of base $\overline{AC}$, prove that the two triangles ABD and ADC are congruent.

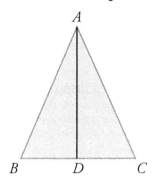

Proof:

1. Isosceles triangle ABC,
   D midpoint of base $\overline{AC}$ Given

2. $\overline{AB} \cong \overline{AC}$ An isosceles triangle has two congruent sides

3. $\overline{BD} \cong \overline{DC}$ Midpoint divides a line into two equal parts

4. $\overline{AD} \cong \overline{AD}$ Reflexive property

5. $\triangle ABD \cong \triangle BCD$ SSS

The **ASA POSTULATE** (angle-side-angle) states that if two angles and the included side of one triangle are congruent to two angles and the included side of another triangle, the triangles are congruent.

> **ASA POSTULATE:** also called angle-side-angle; states that if two angles and the included side of one triangle are congruent to two angles and the included side of another triangle, the triangles are congruent

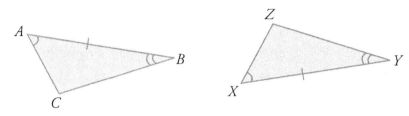

$\angle A \cong \angle X, \angle B \cong \angle Y, \overline{AB} \cong \overline{XY}$ then $\triangle ABC \cong \triangle XYZ$ by ASA

Example: Given two right triangles with one leg (AB and KL) of each measuring 6 cm and the adjacent angle 37°, prove the triangles are congruent.

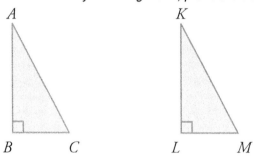

Proof:

1. Right $\triangle ABC$ and $\triangle KLM$ Given
    $AB = KL = 6$ cm
    $m\angle A = m\angle K = 37°$

2. $\overline{AB} \cong \overline{KL}; \angle A \cong \angle K$ Figures with the same measure are congruent

3. $\angle B \cong \angle L$ All right angles arecongruent

4. $\triangle ABC \cong \triangle KLM$ ASA

Example: What method could be used to prove that triangles ABC and AED are congruent?

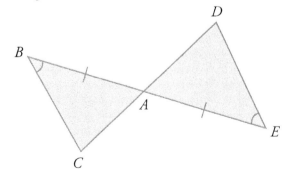

The sides *AB* and *AE* are given as congruent, as are ∠*BAC* and ∠*DEA*. ∠*BAC* and ∠*DEA* are vertical angles and are therefore congruent. Thus triangles Δ*ABC* and Δ*AED* are congruent by the ASA postulate.

The **HL THEOREM** (hypotenuse-leg) is a congruence shortcut that can only be used with right triangles. According to this theorem, if the hypotenuse and leg of one right triangle are congruent to the hypotenuse and leg of the other right triangle, then the two triangles are congruent.

> **HL THEOREM:** states that if the hypotenuse and leg of one right triangle are congruent to the hypotenuse and leg of another right triangle, then the two triangles are congruent

If ∠*B* and ∠*Y* are right angles and $\overline{AC} \cong \overline{XZ}$ (hypotenuse of each triangle), $\overline{AB} \cong \overline{YZ}$ (corresponding leg of each triangle), then Δ*ABC* ≅ Δ*XYZ* by HL.

Proof:

1. ∠*B* ≅ ∠*Y*
   AB ≅ *YZ*
   AC ≅ *XZ*   Given

2. $BC = \sqrt{AC^2 - AB^2} =$ Pythagorean theorem

3. $XY = \sqrt{XZ^2 - YZ^2}$ Pythagorean theorem

4. $XY = \sqrt{AC^2 - AB^2} = BC$ Substitution ($\overline{XZ} \cong \overline{AC}, \overline{YZ} \cong \overline{AB}$)

5. Δ*ABC* ≅ Δ*XYZ*   SAS ($\overline{AB} \cong \overline{YZ}$, ∠*B* ≅ ∠*Y*, $\overline{BC} \cong \overline{XY}$)

Similarity

Two figures that have the same shape are **SIMILAR**. To be the same shape, corresponding angles must be equal. Therefore, polygons are similar if and only if there is a one-to-one correspondence between their vertices such that the corresponding angles are congruent. For similar figures, the lengths of corresponding sides are proportional. The symbol ~ is used to indicate that two figures are similar.

> *For similar figures, the lengths of corresponding sides are proportional.*

> **SIMILAR:** figures that have the same shape but not necessarily the same size are similar

The polygons *ABCDE* and *VWXYZ* shown below are similar.

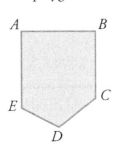 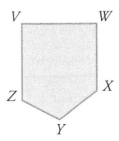

$ABCDE \sim VWXYZ$

Corresponding angles: $\angle A \cong \angle V, \angle B \cong \angle W, \angle C \cong \angle X, \angle D \cong \angle Y, \angle E \cong \angle Z$

Corresponding sides: $\frac{AB}{VW} = \frac{BC}{WX} = \frac{CD}{XY} = \frac{DE}{YZ} = \frac{AE}{VZ}$

Example: Given two similar quadrilaterals, find the lengths of sides x, y, and z.

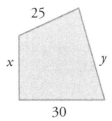 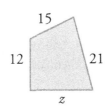

Since corresponding sides are proportional, $\frac{15}{25} = \frac{3}{5}$, so the scale factor is $\frac{3}{5}$.

$$\frac{12}{x} = \frac{3}{5} \qquad \frac{21}{y} = \frac{3}{5} \qquad \frac{z}{30} = \frac{3}{5}$$
$$3x = 60 \qquad 3y = 105 \qquad 5z = 90$$
$$x = 20 \qquad y = 35 \qquad z = 18$$

AA SIMILARITY POSTULATE: states that if two angles of one triangle are congruent to two angles of another triangle, then the triangles are similar

Just as for congruence, there are shortcut methods that can be used to prove triangle similarity.

According to the **AA SIMILARITY POSTULATE**, if two angles of one triangle are congruent to two angles of another triangle, then the triangles are similar. It is obvious that if two of the corresponding angles are congruent, the third set of corresponding angles must be congruent as well. Hence, showing AA is sufficient to prove that two triangles are similar.

SAS SIMILARITY THEOREM: states that if an angle of one triangle is congruent to an angle of another triangle, and the sides adjacent to those angles are in proportion, then the triangles are similar

The **SAS SIMILARITY THEOREM** states that if an angle of one triangle is congruent to an angle of another triangle, and the sides adjacent to those angles are in proportion, then the triangles are similar.

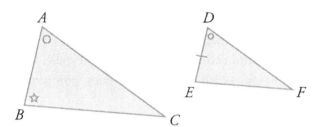

If $\angle A \cong \angle D$ and $\frac{AB}{DE} = \frac{AC}{DF}$, then $\triangle ABC \sim \triangle DEF$.

Example: A graphic artist is designing a logo containing two triangles. The artist wants the triangles to be similar. Determine whether the artist has created similar triangles.

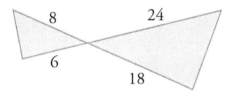

The sides are proportional ($\frac{8}{24} = \frac{6}{18} = \frac{1}{3}$) and vertical angles are congruent. The two triangles are therefore similar by the SAS similarity theorem.

According to the **SSS SIMILARITY THEOREM**, if the sides of two triangles are in proportion, then the triangles are similar.

> **SSS SIMILARITY THEOREM:** states that if the sides of two triangles are in proportion, then the triangles are similar

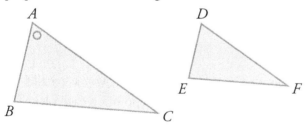

If $\frac{AB}{DE} = \frac{AC}{DF} = \frac{BC}{EF}$, $\triangle ABC \sim \triangle DEF$

Example: Tommy draws and cuts out 2 triangles for a school project. One of them has sides of 3, 6, and 9 inches. The other triangle has sides of 2, 4, and 6 inches. Is there a relationship between the two triangles?

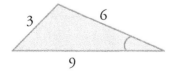 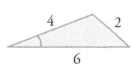

Determine the proportions of the corresponding sides.

$$\frac{2}{3} \qquad \frac{4}{6} = \frac{2}{3} \qquad \frac{6}{9} = \frac{2}{3}$$

The smaller triangle is $\frac{2}{3}$ the size of the large triangle, therefore they are similar triangles by the SSS similarity theorem.

Parallel and Perpendicular Lines and Planes

PARALLEL LINES in two dimensions can be sufficiently defined as lines that do not intersect. In three dimensions, however, this definition is insufficient. Parallel lines in three dimensions are defined as lines for which every pair of nearest points on the lines has a fixed distance.

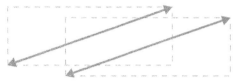

Lines in three dimensions that do not intersect and are not parallel are called **SKEW LINES**. Parallel lines are coplanar; skew lines are not.

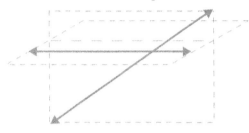

Two planes intersect on a single line. If two planes do not intersect, then they are parallel. Parallel and nonparallel planes are shown in the diagrams below.

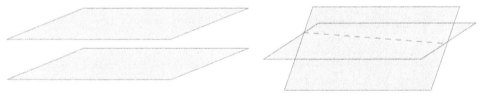

Parallelism between two planes may also be defined in the same way as parallel lines: the distance between any pair of nearest points (one point on each plane) is constant.

Perpendicularity of lines and planes in three dimensions is largely similar to that of two dimensions. Two lines are **PERPENDICULAR LINES** in two or three dimensions if they intersect at a point and form 90° angles between them. Consequently, perpendicular lines are always coplanar.

Notice that, for any line and coincident point on that line, there are an infinite number of perpendicular lines to the line through that point. In two dimensions, there is only one.

PARALLEL LINES: in two dimensions, lines that do not intersect; in three dimensions, lines for which every pair of nearest points on the lines has a fixed distance

SKEW LINES: lines in three dimensions that do not intersect and are not parallel

PERPENDICULAR LINES: when two lines are perpendicular in two or three dimensions they intersect at a point and form 90° angles between them

Two planes are perpendicular if they intersect and the angles formed between them are 90°. For any given plane and line on that plane, there is only one perpendicular plane.

Properties of Parallel Lines

The **PARALLEL POSTULATE** in Euclidean planar geometry states that if a line l is crossed by two other lines m and n (where the crossings are not at the same point on l), then m and n intersect on the side of l on which the sum of the interior angles α and β is less than 180°. This scenario is illustrated below.

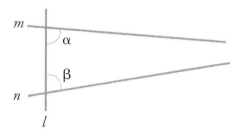

Based on this definition, a number of implications and equivalent formulations can be derived. First, note that the lines m and n intersect on the right-hand side of l above only if $\alpha + \beta < 180°$. This implies that if α and β are both 90° and, therefore, $\alpha + \beta = 180°$, then the lines do not intersect on either side. This is illustrated below.

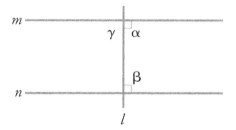

The supplementary angles formed by the intersection of l and m (and the intersection of l and n) must sum to 180°:

$$\alpha + \gamma = 180° \qquad \beta + \delta = 180°$$

Since these sums are both equal to 180°, the lines m and n do not intersect on either side of l. That is to say, these lines are parallel.

Let the nonintersecting lines *m* and *n* used in the above discussion remain parallel, but adjust *l* such that the interior angles are no longer right angles.

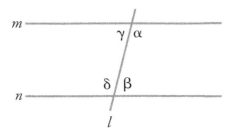

The Parallel Postulate still applies, and it is therefore still the case that $\alpha + \beta = 180°$ and $\gamma + \delta = 180°$. Combined with the fact that $\alpha + \gamma = 180°$ and $\beta + \delta = 180°$, the **ALTERNATE INTERIOR ANGLE THEOREM** can be justified. This theorem states that if two parallel lines are cut by a transversal, the alternate interior angles are congruent.

> **ALTERNATE INTERIOR ANGLE THEOREM:** states that if two parallel lines are cut by a transversal, the alternate interior angles are congruent

By manipulating the four relations based on the above diagram, the relationships between alternate interior angles (γ and β form one set of alternate interior angles, and α and δ form the other) can be established.

$$\alpha = 180° - \beta$$
$$\alpha + \gamma = 180° = 180° - \beta + \gamma$$
$$-\beta + \gamma = 0$$
$$\gamma = \beta$$

By the same reasoning,

$$\gamma = 180° - \delta$$
$$\beta + \delta = 180° = \beta + 180° - \delta$$
$$\beta = \delta$$

> *If two parallel lines are cut by a transversal line, then the corresponding angles are equal.*

One of the consequences of the Parallel Postulate, in addition the Alternate Interior Angle Theorem, is that *corresponding angles* are equal. If two parallel lines are cut by a transversal line, then the corresponding angles are equal. The diagram below illustrates one set of corresponding angles (α and β) for the parallel lines *m* and *n* cut by *l*.

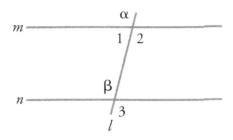

That α and β are equal can be proven as follows.

Proof:

$m\angle\beta = m\angle2$ Alternate Interior Angle Theorem

$m\angle1 + = m\angle2 = 180°$ Supplementary angles

$m\angle2 = 180° - m\angle1$

$m\angle1 + m\angle\alpha = 180°$ Supplementary angles

$m\angle\alpha = 180° - m\angle1$

$m\angle2 = 180° - m\angle1 = m\angle\alpha$

$m\angle2 = m\angle\alpha$

$m\angle\beta = m\angle2 = m\angle\alpha$

$m\angle\beta = m\angle\alpha$

Thus, it has been proven that corresponding angles are equal.

Note that the above proof also demonstrates that vertical angles are equal ($\angle2 = \angle\alpha$). Thus, opposite angles formed by the intersection of two lines (called **vertical angles**) are equal. Furthermore, *alternate exterior angles* (angles α and 1 in the diagram above) are also equal.

Proof:

$m\angle\beta = m\angle3$ Vertical angles

$m\angle\alpha = m\angle2$ Vertical angles

$m\angle\beta = m\angle2$ Alternate Interior Angle Theorem

$m\angle\alpha = m\angle2 = m\angle\beta = m\angle3$

$m\angle\alpha = m\angle3$

Properties of Triangles

The three angles within a triangle are known as the **INTERIOR ANGLES**. The sum of the measures of the interior angles of a triangle is 180°. This property can be justified as follows. Consider a triangle with angles α, β and γ. Draw two parallel lines such that one parallel line coincides with any side of the triangle, and the other parallel line intersects the vertex opposite that side.

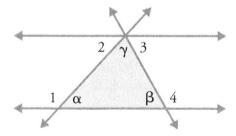

Proof:

$m\angle\alpha = m\angle 2$	Alternate interior angles
$m\angle\beta = m\angle 3$	Alternate interior angles
$m\angle 2 + m\angle 3 + m\angle\gamma = 180°$	Supplementary angles
$m\angle\alpha + m\angle\beta + m\angle\gamma = 180°$	Substitution

Thus, the sum of all the interior angles of a triangle is always 180°.

Example: Can a triangle have two right angles?
No. A right angle measures 90°; therefore, the sum of two right angles would be 180°, and there could not be a third angle.

Example: Can a triangle have two obtuse angles?
No. Since an obtuse angle measures more than 90°, the sum of two obtuse angles would be greater than 180°.

Example: Can a right triangle be obtuse?
No. Once again, the sum of the angles would be more than 180°.

LINEAR PAIR: when two adjacent angles have a common side and their remaining sides form a straight angle

Two adjacent angles form a **LINEAR PAIR** when they have a common side and their remaining sides form a straight angle. Angles in a linear pair are supplementary. An **EXTERIOR ANGLE** of a triangle forms a linear pair with an angle of the triangle.

EXTERIOR ANGLE: an angle that forms a linear pair with an angle of a triangle

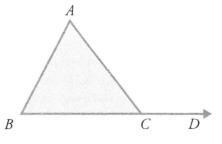

$\angle ACD$ is an exterior angle of triangle ABC, forming a linear pair with $\angle ACB$.

EXTERIOR ANGLE THEOREM: this theorem states that the measure of an exterior angle of a triangle is equal to the sum of the measures of the two nonadjacent interior angles

According to the **EXTERIOR ANGLE THEOREM**, the measure of an exterior angle of a triangle is equal to the sum of the measures of the two nonadjacent interior angles. We can easily demonstrate this by taking the above triangle ABC as an example. In this triangle, $m\angle ABC + m\angle BAC + m\angle ACB = 180°$ (the sum of interior angles of a triangle). Also, $m\angle ACD + m\angle ACB = 180°$ (exterior angle and adjacent interior angle are supplementary). Therefore, $m\angle ACD = m\angle ABC + m\angle BAC$.

Example: In triangle ABC, the measure of ∠A is twice the measure of ∠B. ∠C is 30° more than their sum. Find the measure of the exterior angle formed at ∠C.

Let x = the measure of $\angle B$

$2x$ = the measure of $\angle A$

$x + 2x + 30$ = the measure of $\angle C$

$$x + 2x + x + 2x + 30 = 180$$
$$6x + 30 = 180$$
$$6x = 150$$
$$x = 25$$
$$2x = 50$$

It is not necessary to find the measure of the third angle, since the exterior angle equals the sum of the opposite interior angles. Thus, the exterior angle at $\angle C$ measures 75°.

Concurrence theorems

If three or more segments intersect in a single point, the point is called a **POINT OF CONCURRENCY**. The concurrence theorems given below make statements about the concurrence of the following sets of special segments associated with triangles:

1. **ANGLE BISECTORS:** An angle bisector is a line segment that bisects one of the angles of a triangle. *The three angle bisectors of a triangle intersect in a single point equidistant from all three sides of the triangle.* (Recall that the distance from a point to a side is measured along the perpendicular from the point to the side.) This point is known as the *incenter* and is the center of the *incircle* inscribed within the triangle tangent to each of the three sides.

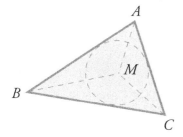

2. **MEDIANS:** A median of a triangle is a segment that connects a vertex to the midpoint of the side opposite from that vertex. *The three medians of a triangle are concurrent and intersect each other in a ratio of 2:1 at the centroid of the triangle.*

POINT OF CONCURRENCY: where three or more segments intersect in a single point

ANGLE BISECTOR: a line segment that bisects one of the angles of a triangle

The three angle bisectors of a triangle intersect in a single point equidistant from all three sides of the triangle.

MEDIAN: a segment of a triangle that connects a vertex to the midpoint of the side opposite from that vertex

The three medians of a triangle are concurrent and intersect each other in a ratio of 2:1 at the centroid of the triangle.

The medians of the triangle *ABC* shown below intersect in the centroid *G* such that $\frac{AG}{GF} = \frac{BG}{GE} = \frac{CG}{GD} = \frac{2}{1}$.

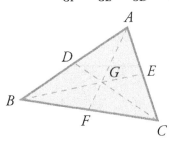

<table>
</table>

ALTITUDE: a segment of a triangle that extends from one vertex and is perpendicular to the side opposite that vertex

3. **ALTITUDES:** An altitude of a triangle is a segment that extends from one vertex and is perpendicular to the side opposite that vertex. In some cases, the side opposite the vertex will need to be extended in order for the altitude to form a perpendicular to the opposite side. The length of the altitude is used when referring to the height of the triangle. *The altitudes of a triangle are concurrent and meet at the orthocenter of the triangle.*

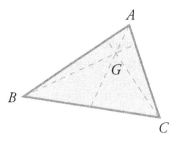

PERPENDICULAR BISECTOR: a segment that bisects one of the sides of a triangle and is perpendicular to it

4. **PERPENDICULAR BISECTORS:** A perpendicular bisector of a triangle bisects one of the sides and is perpendicular to it. *The three perpendicular bisectors of a triangle meet in a point equidistant from the vertices of the triangle.* This point is known as the CIRCUMCENTER and is the center of the CIRCUMCIRCLE that circumscribes the triangles.

The three perpendicular bisectors of a triangle meet in a point equidistant from the vertices of the triangle.

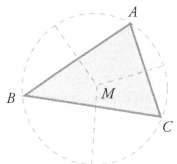

The points of concurrency can lie inside the triangle, outside the triangle, or on one of the sides of the triangle. The following table summarizes this information.

POSSIBLE LOCATION(S) OF THE POINTS OF CONCURRENCY			
	INSIDE THE TRIANGLE	OUTSIDE THE TRIANGLE	ON THE TRIANGLE
Angle Bisectors	X		
Medians	X		
Altitudes	X	X	X
Perpendicular Bisectors	X	X	X

Example: BE and CD are altitudes of equilateral triangle ABC and intersect at the point G. What is the ratio of the area of triangle BDG to the area of triangle ABC?

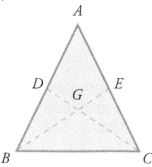

The area of triangle $ABC = \frac{1}{2}AB \times CD$. The area of triangle $BDG = \frac{1}{2}BD \times DG$. Since ABC is an equilateral triangle, the altitudes of the triangles are also medians. Therefore, $BD = \frac{1}{2}AB$ and $GD = \frac{1}{3}CD$. Thus, the area of triangle $BDG = \frac{1}{2}(\frac{1}{2}AB) \times (\frac{1}{3}CD) = \frac{1}{12}AB \times CD$. Hence the area of triangle BDG is one-sixth the area of triangle ABC.

The **TRIANGLE INEQUALITY THEOREM** states that the sum of the lengths of any two sides of a triangle is greater than the length of the remaining side. In the triangle below:

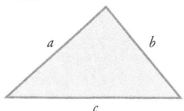

$a + b > c$
$a + c > b$
$b + c > a$

> **TRIANGLE INEQUALITY THEOREM:** states that the sum of the lengths of any two sides of a triangle is greater than the length of the remaining side

If a triangle has an unknown side, the Triangle Inequality Theorem can be applied to determine a reasonable range of possible values for the unknown side.

Example: Determine the range of possible values for the unknown side, p.

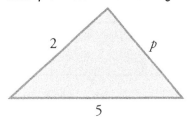

$2 + p > 5$
$2 + 5 > p$
$p + 5 > 2$

The expressions could be arranged to show: $p > 5 - 2$ or $p > 3$
$$7 > p$$
$$p > \text{-}3.$$

> The side of the triangle that is opposite the largest angle is the longest side. The side opposite the smallest angle is the shortest side.

Thus, p is a value between 3 and 7.

An angle-side relationship exists between angles of a triangle and the sides opposite them. The side of the triangle that is opposite the largest angle is the longest side. The side opposite the smallest angle is the shortest side. This rule can be used to determine a reasonable range of measurement for an unknown angle.

SKILL 9.5 — Use nets and cross sections to analyze three-dimensional figures

> If a three-dimensional object is intersected by a plane, the result is a cross section of the object.

If a three-dimensional object is intersected by a plane, the result is a cross section of the object. In the picture below, the striped portion is a cross section of a cube.

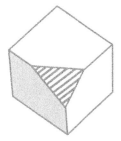

A conic section (e.g., a circle, ellipse, parabola, or hyperbola), for instance, is formed by the intersection of a cone with a plane.

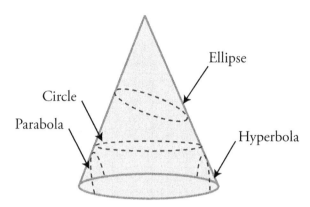

Circles and ellipses are both closed figures. The plane creating the circle cross-section in intersection with the cone is parallel to the base of the cone. Parabolas and hyperbolas are open figures. The plane creating the parabola cross-section in intersection with the cone is parallel to the slant side of the cone.

A **NET** is a two-dimensional figure that can be cut out and folded up to make a three-dimensional solid. Below are models of some regular solids with their corresponding face polygons and nets. Nets clearly show the shape and number of faces of a solid.

> **NET:** a two-dimensional figure that can be cut out and folded up to make a three-dimensional solid

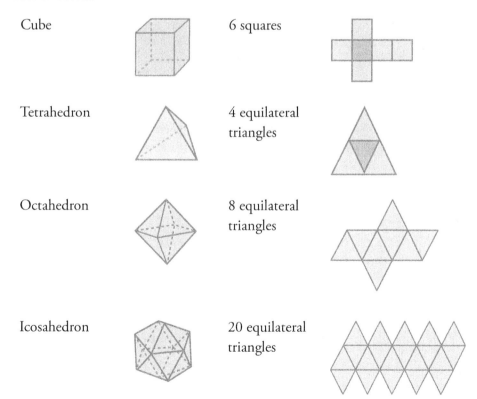

Dodecahedron 12 regular
pentagons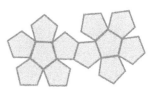

There can be more than one possible net for a particular three-dimensional figure. For instance, here are two more nets for a tetrahedron.

For a polyhedron, the numbers of vertices (V), faces (F), and edges (E) are related by Euler's Formula: $V + F = E + 2$.

Example: How many edges are in a pentagonal pyramid?
A pentagonal pyramid has six vertices and six faces. Using Euler's Formula, compute the number of edges.

$$V + F = E + 2$$
$$6 + 6 = E + 2$$
$$E = 10$$

The figure has 10 edges.

Example: Draw the net of a triangular prism and identify the polygons that make up the faces. How many vertices and edges do triangular prisms have?

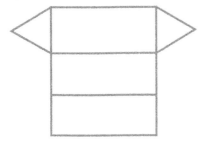

Two triangles and three rectangles are the faces of the figure. There are nine edges (three between the rectangle faces and three on each side where the triangle faces meet the rectangle faces). There are six vertices at the vertices of the two triangle faces.

COMPETENCY 10

UNDERSTAND COORDINATE AND TRANSFORMATIONAL GEOMETRY

SKILL 10.1 Analyze two- and three-dimensional figures using coordinate systems

Any two-dimensional geometric figure can be represented in the Cartesian, or rectangular, coordinate system. The Cartesian, or rectangular, coordinate system is formed by two perpendicular axes (coordinate axes): the x-axis and the y-axis. If the dimensions of a two-dimensional, or planar, figure are known, this coordinate system can be used to create a visual representation of the figure.

Example: Represent an isosceles triangle with two sides of length 4.
Draw the two sides along the x- and y-axes and connect the points (vertices).

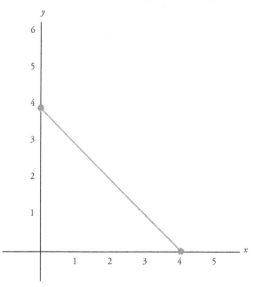

The vertices of the isosceles triangle are found at $(0, 0)$, $(4, 0)$ and $(0, 4)$ with equal sides on the x- and y-axes.

If a polygon is shown in the coordinate plane and the coordinates of the vertices must be determined, then the characteristics of the polygon can be used to this end. Consider the following example.

Example: The rectangle shown in the graph below has sides of length 2 parallel to the y-axis and sides of length 4 parallel to the x-axis. Determine the coordinates of the vertices.

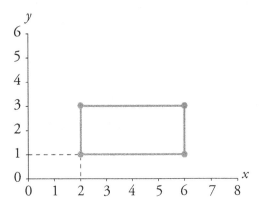

From the graph, it is clear that one of the vertices is located at (2, 1). Using the properties of rectangles (or by inspecting the graph in this case), the other vertices (going in a counter-clockwise direction from the first vertex) are (6, 1), (6, 3), and (2, 3).

Examples that are more difficult may involve polygons with sides that are not parallel to either of the axes. In such cases, knowledge (either given or by inspection) of the location of at least one vertex is necessary, as is the type of polygon (regular or irregular). Calculation of the slopes of the line segments between vertices may be necessary in some cases to determine the location of unknown vertices. This approach is also helpful in cases where, as with the first example, the polygon must be drawn on the coordinate plane. When possible, it is helpful to draw one or more vertices (or entire sides) of a polygon on the axes. This usually simplifies calculation or representation of the remainder of the polygon.

A three-dimensional geometric figure can be plotted using a basic set of three-dimensional axes, as shown below.

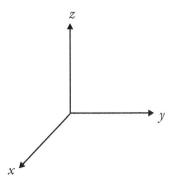

Points can be plotted by traversing the required distance parallel to each axis. Thus, the point (3, 3, 3) is plotted as shown below.

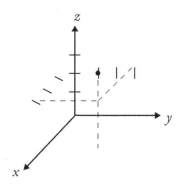

A cube with sides of length 2 can then be represented as shown below.

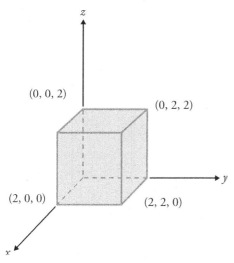

SKILL 10.2 Apply concepts of distance, midpoint, and slope to classify figures and solve problems in the coordinate plane

COORDINATE GEOMETRY involves the application of algebraic methods to geometry. The locations of points in space are expressed in terms of coordinates on a Cartesian plane. The relationships between the coordinates of different points are expressed as equations.

> **COORDINATE GEOMETRY:** the application of algebraic methods to geometry

Proofs using coordinate geometry techniques employ the following commonly used formulae and relationships:

1. **Midpoint formula:** The midpoint (x, y) of the line joining points (x_1, y_1) and (x_2, y_2) is given by $(x, y) = \left(\dfrac{x_1 + x_2}{2}, \dfrac{y_1 + y_2}{2} \right)$

2. **Distance formula:** The distance between points (x_1, y_1) and (x_2, y_2) is given by $D = \sqrt{(x_2 - x_1)^2 + (y_2 - y_1)^2}$

3. **Slope formula:** The slope m of a line passing through the points (x_1, y_1) and (x_2, y_2) is given by $m = \frac{y_2 - y_1}{x_2 - x_1}$

4. **Equation of a line:** The equation of a line is given by $y = mx + b$, where m is the slope of the line and b is the y-intercept, i.e., the y-coordinate at which the line intersects the y-axis.

5. **Parallel and perpendicular lines:** Parallel lines have the same slope. The slope of a line perpendicular to a line with slope m is $\frac{-1}{m}$.

Example: Prove that quadrilateral ABCD with vertices A(-3, 0), B(-1, 0), C(0, 3), and D(2, 3) is in fact a parallelogram using coordinate geometry:

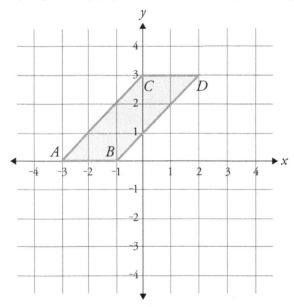

By definition, a parallelogram has diagonals that bisect each other. Using the midpoint formula, $(x, y) = \left(\frac{x_1 + x_2}{2} + \frac{y_1 + y_2}{2}\right)$, find the midpoints of $\overline{AD}$ and $\overline{BC}$.

The midpoint of $\overline{BC} = \left(\frac{-1 + 0}{2}, \frac{0 + 3}{2}\right) = \left(\frac{-1}{2}, \frac{3}{2}\right)$

The midpoint of $\overline{AD} = \left(\frac{-3 + 2}{2}, \frac{0 + 3}{2}\right) = \left(\frac{-1}{2}, \frac{3}{2}\right)$

Since the midpoints of the diagonals are the same, the diagonals bisect each other. Hence the polygon is a parallelogram.

In the above example, the proof involved a specific geometric figure with given coordinates. Coordinate geometry can also be used to prove more general results.

Example: Prove that the diagonals of a rhombus are perpendicular to each other.

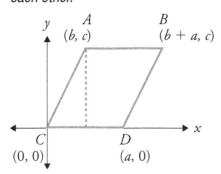

Draw a rhombus *ABCD* with side of length a such that the vertex *C* is at the origin and the side *CD* lies along the x-axis. The coordinates of the corners of the rhombus can then be written as shown above.

The slope m_1 of the diagonal *AD* is given by $m_1 = \dfrac{c}{b-a}$.

The slope m_2 of the diagonal *BC* is given by $m_2 = \dfrac{c}{b+a}$.

The product of the slopes is $m_1 \times m_2 = \dfrac{c}{b-a} \times \dfrac{c}{b+a} = \dfrac{c^2}{b^2-a^2}$.

The length of side $AC = \sqrt{b^2 + c^2} = a$ (since each side of the rhombus is equal to a). Therefore,

$b^2 + c^2 = a^2$

$\rightarrow b^2 - a^2 = -c^2$

$\rightarrow \dfrac{c^2}{b^2 - a^2} = -1$

The product of the slopes of the diagonals $m_1 \times m_2 = -1$.
Hence the two diagonals are perpendicular to each other.

Example: Prove that the line joining the midpoints of two sides of a triangle is parallel to and half the length of the third side.

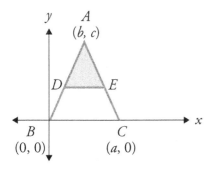

Draw triangle *ABC* on the coordinate plane in such a way that the vertex *B* coincides with the origin and the side *BC* lies along the x-axis. Let point *C* have coordinates $(a, 0)$ and point *A* have coordinates (b, c). Point *D* is the midpoint of side *AB* and point *E* is the midpoint of side *AC*.

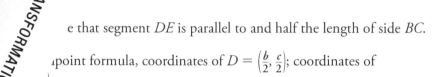

e that segment DE is parallel to and half the length of side BC.

point formula, coordinates of $D = \left(\frac{b}{2}, \frac{c}{2}\right)$; coordinates of

$\frac{}{2}$.

of the line segment DE is then given by $\dfrac{\frac{c}{2} - \frac{c}{2}}{\frac{b+a}{2} - \frac{b}{2}} = 0$, which is equal

slope of the x-axis. Thus DE is parallel to BC.

length of the line segment $DE = \sqrt{\left(\frac{b+a}{2} - \frac{b}{2}\right)^2 + \left(\frac{c}{2} - \frac{c}{2}\right)^2} = \sqrt{\left(\frac{a}{2}\right)^2} = \frac{a}{2}$

the length of DE is half that of side BC.

SKILL 10.3 Analyze conic sections

Conic Sections

> **CONIC SECTION:** the intersection of an infinite cone with a plane

CONIC SECTIONS are the various cross sections of a cone. Even a line and a point may in some sense be considered conic sections, although these are usually not included explicitly as such (they are sometimes called **degenerate conics**, because they include the vertex of the cone). Geometrically, a conic section is the intersection of an infinite cone with a plane.

The general equation for a conic section is:

$$Ax^2 + Bxy + Cy^2 + Dx + Ey + F = 0$$

The value of $B^2 - 4AC$ determines the type of conic. If $B^2 - 4AC$ is less than zero the curve is an ellipse or a circle. If equal to zero, the curve is a parabola. If greater than zero, the curve is a hyperbola.

Ellipses

> **ELLIPSE:** a conic section represented by the equation $\frac{(x-h)^2}{a^2} + \frac{(y-k)^2}{b^2} = 1$

An **ELLIPSE** is a conic section that is formed as shown below.

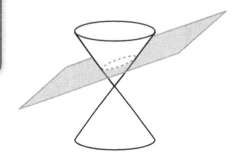

Example graph:

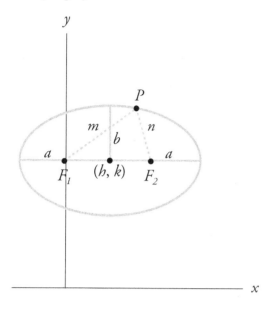

The **FOCI** of an ellipse are located along the major axis on opposite sides of the center such that the sum of the distances from each foci to any given point on the ellipse is always constant, as shown above.

In the above diagram, $m + n$ is a constant, regardless of the position of point P on the ellipse.

> **FOCI:** the foci of an ellipse are located along the major axis such that the sum of the distances from each foci to any given point on the ellipse is always constant

ELLIPSE		
FORM OF EQUATION	$\dfrac{(x - h)^2}{a^2} + \dfrac{(y - k)^2}{b^2} = 1$	$\dfrac{(x - h)^2}{b^2} + \dfrac{(y - k)^2}{a^2} = 1$
(for ellipses where $a^2 > b^2$)	where $c^2 = a^2 - b^2$	where $c^2 = a^2 - b^2$
IDENTIFICATION	horizontal major axis	vertical major axis
SKETCH		
	Continued on next page	

CENTER	(h,k)	(h,k)
FOCI	$(h \pm c, k)$	$(h, k \pm c)$
MAJOR AXIS LENGTH	$2a$	$2a$
MINOR AXIS LENGTH	$2b$	$2b$

Example:

Find all identifying features of the ellipse $2x^2 + y^2 - 4x + 8y - 6 = 0$.

First, begin by writing the equation in standard form for an ellipse.

$2x^2 + y^2 - 4x + 8y - 6 = 0$ 1. Complete the square for each variable.

$2(x^2 - 2x + 1) + (y^2 + 8y + 16) = 6 + 2(1) + 16$

$2(x - 1)^2 + (y + 4)^2 = 24$ 2. Divide both sides by 24.

$\dfrac{(x - 1)^2}{12} + \dfrac{(y + 4)^2}{24} = 1$ 3. Now the equation is in standard form.

Identify known variables: $h = 1, k = -4, a = \sqrt{24}$ or $2\sqrt{6}$,

$b = \sqrt{12}$ or $2\sqrt{3}$

$c^2 = a^2 - b^2 = 24 - 12 = 12, c = 2\sqrt{3}$

Identification: vertical major axis

Center: $(1, -4)$

Foci: $(1, -4 \pm 2\sqrt{3})$

Major axis: $4\sqrt{6}$

Minor axis: $4\sqrt{3}$

Circles

CIRCLE: an ellipse for which the major and minor axes are of equal lengths (that is, a = b). The equation of a circle is
$(x - h)^2 + (y - k)^2 = r^2$

Note that a **CIRCLE**, which is another type of conic section, is simply an ellipse for which the major and minor axes are of equal lengths (that is, $a = b$). The foci then coincide with the center of the ellipse, forming a circle. The equation can then be written in terms of radius r:

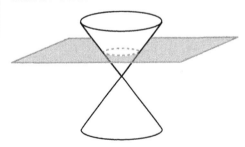

Equation: $(x - h)^2 + (y - k)^2 = r^2$

Example: Write the equation for a circle with center (2, -7) and radius 5

Substitute values into the circle formula:

$$(x - 2)^2 + (y + 7)^2 = 5^2$$
$$(x - 2)^2 + (y + 7)^2 = 25$$

Parabolas

A parabola is a conic section that involves the cross section shown below. A **PARABOLA** is defined by a set of points that are equidistant from a fixed line (the directrix) and a noncollinear fixed point (the focus). The cross section and important parameters are shown below:

> **PARABOLA:** a conic section that is defined by a set of points that are equidistant from a fixed line (the directrix) and a noncollinear fixed point (the focus); the equation of a parabola is $y = a(x - h)^2 + k$

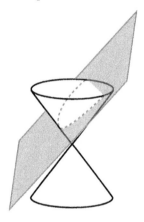

Example graph:

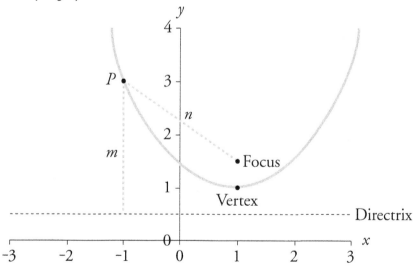

Note that $m = n$ for any point P on the parabola.

PARABOLA		
FORM OF EQUATION	$y = a(x - h)^2 + k$	$x = a(y - k)^2 + h$
IDENTIFICATION	x^2 term, y not squared	y^2 term, x not squared
SKETCH		
AXIS OF SYMMETRY A line through the vertex and focus upon which the parabola is symmetric.	$(x = h)$	$(y = k)$
VERTEX The point where the parabola intersects the axis of symmetry.	(h, k)	(h, k)
FOCUS	$\left(h, k + \dfrac{1}{4a}\right)$	$\left(h + \dfrac{1}{4a}, k\right)$
DIRECTRIX	$y = k - \dfrac{1}{4a}$	$x = h - \dfrac{1}{4a}$
DIRECTION OF OPENING	up if $a > 0$, down if $a < 0$	right if $a > 0$, left if $a < 0$
LENGTH OF LATUS RECTUM A chord through the focus, perpendicular to the axis of symmetry, with endpoints on the parabola.	$\left\|\dfrac{1}{a}\right\|$	$\left\|\dfrac{1}{a}\right\|$

Example:

Find all identifying features of $y = -3x^2 + 6x - 1$.

First, the equation must be put into the general form $y = a(x - h)^2 + k$.

$y = -3x^2 + 6x - 1$ 1. Begin by completing the square.

$= -3(x^2 - 2x + 1) - 1 + 3$

$= -3(x - 1)^2 + 2$ 2. Using the general form of the equation begin to identify known variables.

$a = -3, h = 1, k = 2$

axis of symmetry: $x = 1$

vertex: $(1,2)$

focus: $\left(1, 1\frac{11}{12}\right)$

directrix: $y = 2\frac{1}{12}$

direction of opening: down since $a < 0$

length of latus rectum: $\frac{1}{3}$

Hyperbolas

A **HYPERBOLA** is a conic section as shown below. The hyperbola has two foci and two separate curves, and is similar in some ways to an ellipse. The defining characteristic of a hyperbola is that, for any point P on the hyperbola, the difference between the distances from P to each focus is a constant.

HYPERBOLA: a conic section represented by the equation
$$\frac{(x - h)^2}{a^2} - \frac{(y - k)^2}{b^2} = 1$$

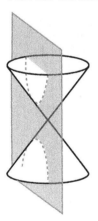

Example graph:

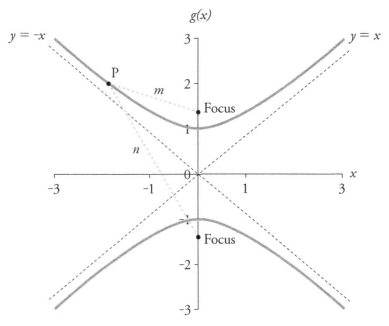

Note that $m - n$ is a constant for any point P on the hyperbola.

HYPERBOLA		
FORM OF EQUATION	$\dfrac{(x - h)^2}{a^2} - \dfrac{(y - k)^2}{b^2} = 1$ where $c^2 = a^2 + b^2$	$\dfrac{(y - k)^2}{a^2} - \dfrac{(x - h)^2}{b^2} = 1$ where $c^2 = a^2 + b^2$
IDENTIFICATION	horizontal transverse axis (y^2 is negative)	vertical transverse axis (x^2 is negative)
SKETCH		
SLOPE OF ASYMPTOTES	$\pm \dfrac{b}{a}$	$\pm \dfrac{a}{b}$
TRANSVERSE AXIS (endpoints are vertices of the hyperbola and go through the center)	$2a$ on x axis	$2a$ on y axis
Continued on next page		

CONJUGATE AXIS (perpendicular to transverse axis at center)	$2b$ on y axis	$2b$ on x axis
CENTER	(h,k)	(h,k)
FOCI	$(h \pm c,k)$	$(h,k \pm c)$
VERTICES	$(h \pm a,k)$	$(h,k \pm a)$

Example:

Find all the identifying features of a hyperbola given its equation.

$$\frac{(x+3)^2}{4} - \frac{(y-4)^2}{16} = 1$$

Identify all known variables: $h = -3$, $k = 4$, $a = 2$, $b = 4$ $c = 2\sqrt{5}$

Slope of asymptotes: $\pm \frac{4}{2}$ or ± 2

Transverse axis: 4 units long

Conjugate axis: 8 units long

Center: $(-3,4)$

Foci: $(-3 \pm 2\sqrt{5},4)$

Vertices: $(-1,4)$ and $(-5,4)$

Example: Find the equation of an ellipse with foci located at (0, 2) and (0, 0) and a minor axis of 2.

First, note that this ellipse is oriented along the y-axis. The expression for the ellipse is then the following, with $b = 1$ as it is half the minor axis.

$$\frac{(x-h)^2}{b^2} + \frac{(y-k)^2}{a^2} = 1$$

The center of the ellipse is located halfway between the foci; by inspection, the center (h, k) is then $(0, 1)$. (Generally, the midpoint formula can be used to find the center when the foci are known.) The length of the major axis can be found using the formula

$$c = \sqrt{|a^2 - b^2|}$$

where c can be deduced from the fact that the foci are 2 units apart.

$$c = 1 = \sqrt{|a^2 - b^2|}$$
$$c^2 = 1 = |a^2 - b^2|$$
$$a^2 - (1)^2 = 1$$
$$a^2 = 2$$
$$a = \sqrt{2}$$

Finally, construct the equation for the ellipse in terms of x and y.

$$x^2 + \frac{(y-1)^2}{2} = 1$$

The plot of this ellipse is shown below.

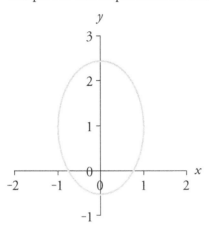

Spheres

A **SPHERE**, whose cross section is a circle, can also be expressed algebraically. The expression for a sphere is simply an extension of the two-dimensional representation of a circle.

$$r^2 = (x-h)^2 + (y-k)^2 + (z-j)^2$$

Here, the center of the sphere is located at (h, k, j), and the radius is r. The above expression can also be viewed as the set of points (x, y, z) equidistant (by length r) from a point (h, k, j). Note that the distance formula uses the same format, where the square root is taken for both sides.

$$r = \sqrt{(x-h)^2 + (y-k)^2 + (z-j)^2}$$

> **SPHERE:** a three-dimenstional circle represented by the equation:
> $r^2 = (x-h)^2 + (y-k)^2 + (z-j)^2$

SKILL 10.4 **Determine the effects of geometric transformations on the graph of a function or relation**

The basic types of transformation are horizontal and vertical shift, horizontal and vertical scaling, and reflection.

Different types of function transformations affect the graph and characteristics of a function in predictable ways. The basic types of transformation are horizontal and vertical shift, horizontal and vertical scaling, and reflection. As an example of the types of transformations, we will consider transformations of the function $f(x) = x^2$.

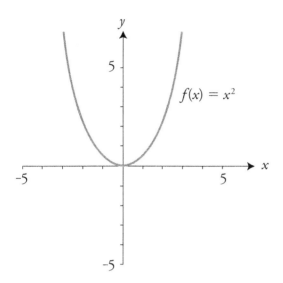

Shifts

Horizontal shifts take the form $g(x) = f(x \pm c)$. For example, we obtain the graph of the function $h(x) = (x + 2)^2$ by shifting the graph of $f(x) = x^2$ two units to the left. The graph of the function $g(x) = (x - 2)^2$ is the graph of $f(x) = x^2$ shifted two units to the right.

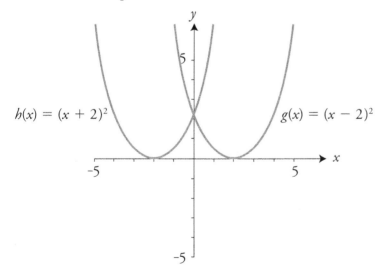

Vertical shifts take the form $g(x) = f(x) \pm c$. For example, we obtain the graph of the function $g(x) = (x^2) - 2$ by shifting the graph of $f(x) = x^2$ two units down. The graph of the function $h(x) = (x^2) + 2$ is the graph of $f(x) = x^2$ shifted two units up.

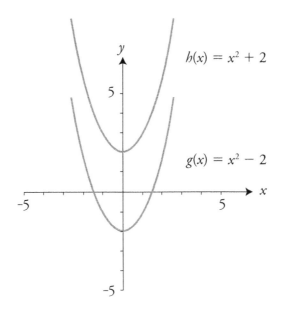

Scaling

Horizontal scaling takes the form $g(x) = f(cx)$. For example, we obtain the graph of the function $g(x) = (2x^2)$ by compressing the graph of $f(x) = x^2$ in the x-direction by a factor of two. If $c > 1$ the graph is compressed in the x-direction, while if $0 < c < 1$ the graph is stretched in the x-direction.

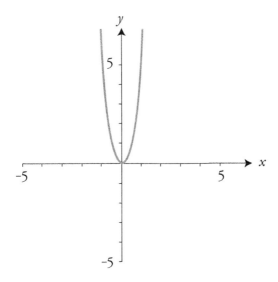

Reflection

A function can be reflected with respect to either axis. A reflection over the x axis is obtained by taking the opposite of the funciton, in other words, changing $f(x)$ into $-f(x)$. The opposite of the function $f(x) = x^2$ is $g(x) = -x^2$.

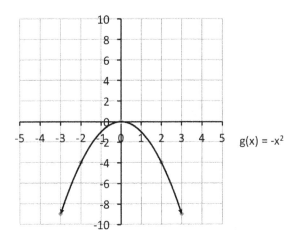

$g(x) = -x^2$

To reflect a function over the y axis, change $f(x)$ into $f(-x)$. Consider the horizontally shifted graph shown earlier, $h(x) = (x + 2)^2$. If x is changed to $-x$, the function becomes $k(x) = (-x + 2)^2$ and will appear as the mirror image of $h(x)$ with respect to the y axis.

SKILL 10.5 **Analyze transformations and symmetries of figures in the coordinate plane**

Transformational Geometry

TRANSFORMATIONAL GEOMETRY is the study of the manipulation of objects through movement, rotation, and scaling. The transformation of an object is called its image. If the original object is labeled with letters, such as *ABCD*, the image can be labeled with the same letters followed by a prime symbol: *A'B'C'D'*. Transformations can be characterized in different ways.

Types of transformations

An **ISOMETRY** is a linear transformation that maintains the dimensions of a geometric figure.

SYMMETRY is exact similarity between two parts or halves, as if one were a mirror image of the other.

A **TRANSLATION** is a transformation that "slides" an object a fixed distance in a given direction. The original object and its translation have the same shape and size, and they face in the same direction.

TRANSFORMATIONAL GEOMETRY: the study of the manipulation of objects through movement, rotation, and scaling

ISOMETRY: a linear transformation that maintains the dimensions of a geometric figure

TRANSLATION: a transformation that "slides" an object a fixed distance in a given direction

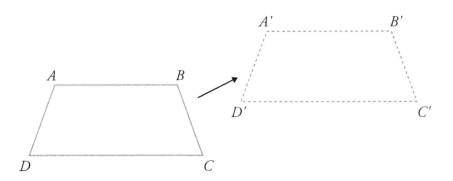

ROTATION: a transformation that turns a figure about a fixed point, which is called the center of rotation

A **ROTATION** is a transformation that turns a figure about a fixed point, which is called the center of rotation. An object and its rotation are the same shape and size, but the figures may be oriented in different directions. Rotations can occur in either a clockwise or a counterclockwise direction.

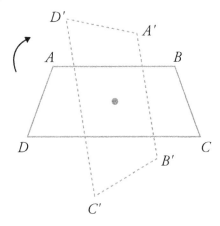

REFLECTION: when an object and another figure have the same shape and size, but they face in opposite directions

An object and its **REFLECTION** have the same shape and size, but the figures face in opposite directions. The line (where a hypothetical mirror may be placed) is called the **line of reflection**. The distance from a point to the line of reflection is the same as the distance from the point's image to the line of reflection.

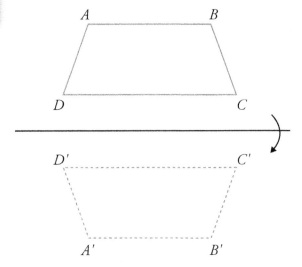

A **GLIDE REFLECTION** involves a combined translation along and a reflection across a single specified line. The characteristic that defines a glide reflection as opposed to a simple combination of an arbitrary translation and arbitrary reflection is that the direction of translation is parallel with the line of reflection. An example of a glide reflection is shown below.

GLIDE REFLECTION: a combined translation along and reflection across a single specified line in which the direction of translation is parallel with the line of reflection

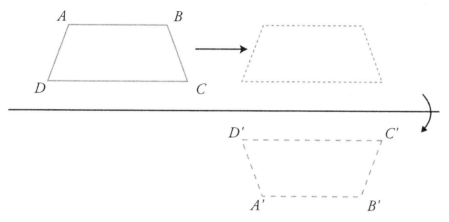

The examples of a translation, a rotation, and a reflection given above are for polygons, but the same principles apply to the simpler geometric elements of points and lines. In fact, a transformation performed on a polygon can be viewed as the same transformation performed on the set of points (vertices) and lines (sides) that compose the polygon. Thus, to perform complicated transformations on a figure, it is helpful to perform the transformations on all the points (or vertices) of the figure, then reconnect the points with lines as appropriate.

Dilation

DILATIONS involve an expansion of a figure and a translation of that figure while maintaining the figure's angles and relative proportions (the translation may be for a distance zero). These two transformations are obtained by first defining a **center of dilation**, C, which is some point that acts like an origin for the dilation. The distance from C to each point in a figure is then altered by a **scale factor**, s. If the magnitude of s is greater than zero, the size of the figure is increased; if the magnitude of s is less than zero, the size is decreased.

DILATION: a simultaneous expansion and translation of a figure while maintaining the figure's angles and relative proportions

The expansion of a geometric figure is a result of the scale factor, s. For instance, if $s = 2$, the expanded figure will be twice the size of the original figure. The translation of a geometric figure is a result of the location of the center of dilation, C. If C is located at the center of the figure, for instance, the figure is dilated without any translation of its center.

Example: Dilate the figure shown by a scale factor of 2 using the origin of the coordinate system as the center of dilation.

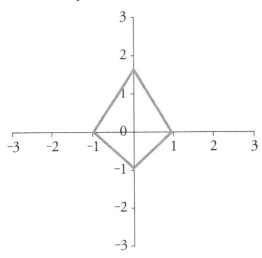

To perform this dilation, the distance between the origin and each point on the figure must be increased by a factor of 2. It is sufficient, however, to simply increase the distance of the vertices of the figure by a factor of 2 and then connect them to form the dilated figure.

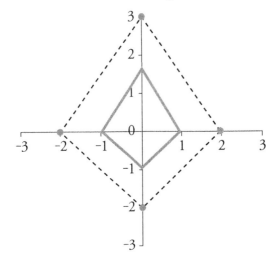

The resulting figure, represented by a dashed line, is the dilation of the original figure.

The points on a figure are dilated by increasing or decreasing their respective distances from a center of dilation, C. As a result, each point P on a figure is essentially translated along the line through P and C. To show that a dilation of this type preserves angles, consider some angle formed by two line segments, with a center of dilation at some arbitrary location. The dilation is for some scale factor s.

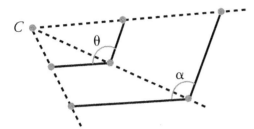

To show that the angles θ and α are equal, it is sufficient to show that the two pairs of overlapping triangles are similar. If they are similar, all the corresponding angles in the figure must be congruent.

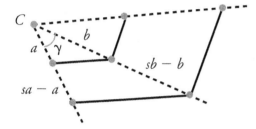

The smaller triangle in this case has sides of lengths a and b and an angle γ between them. The larger triangle has sides of lengths sa (or $sa - a + a = sa$) and sb and an angle γ between them. Thus, by SAS similarity, these two triangles are similar.

Once this reasoning is applied to the other pair of overlapping triangles, it can be shown that angles θ and α are equal. Furthermore, due to the fact that these triangles have been shown to be similar, it is also true that line segments must scale by the same factor, s (this is necessary to maintain the similarity of the triangles above).

As a result of this reasoning, it can be shown that figures that are dilated using an arbitrary scale factor, s, and center of dilation, C, must maintain all angles through the dilation, and all line segments (or sides) of the figure must also scale by s. As a result, figures that are dilated are similar to the original figures.

Figures that are dilated are similar to the original figures.

Since dilations are transformations that maintain similarity of the figures being dilated, they can also be viewed as changes of scale about C. For instance, a dilation of a portion of a map would simply result in a change of the scale of the map.

Multiple transformations (or compositions of transformations) can be performed on a geometrical figure. The order of these transformations may or may not be important. For instance, multiple translations can be performed in any order, as can multiple rotations (around a single fixed point) or reflections (across a single fixed line). The order of the transformations becomes important when several types of transformations are performed or when the point of rotation or the line of reflection change among transformations. For example, consider a translation of a given distance upward and a clockwise rotation by 90° around a fixed point. Changing the order of these transformations changes the result.

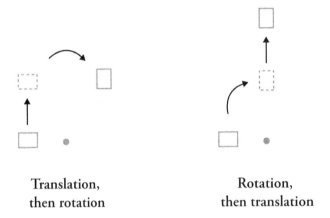

**Translation,
then rotation**

**Rotation,
then translation**

As shown, the final position of the box is different, depending on the order of the transformations. Thus, it is crucial that the proper order of transformations (whether determined by the details of the problem or some other consideration) be followed.

Example: Find the final location of a point at (1, 1) that undergoes the following transformations: rotate 90° counter-clockwise about the origin; translate distance 2 in the negative y direction; reflect about the y-axis.

First, draw a graph of the *x*- and *y*-axes and plot the point at (1, 1).

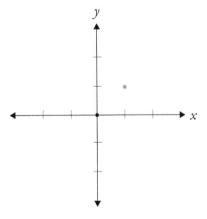

Next, perform the rotation. The center of rotation is the origin and is in the counter-clockwise direction. In this case, the even value of 90° makes the rotation simple to do by inspection. Next, perform a translation of distance 2 in the negative *y* direction (down). The results of these transformations are shown below.

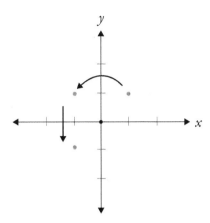

Finally, perform the reflection about the *y*-axis. The final result, shown below, is a point at $(1, -1)$.

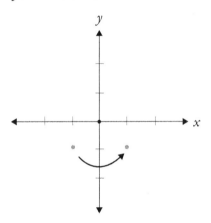

Using this approach, polygons can be transformed on a point-by-point basis.

For some problems, there is no need to work with coordinate axes. For instance, the problem may simply require transformations without respect to any absolute positioning.

Example: Rotate the following regular pentagon by 36° about its center and then reflect it across the horizontal line.

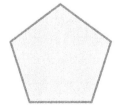

First, perform the rotation. In this case, the direction is not important because the pentagon is symmetric. As it turns out in this case, a rotation of 36° yields the same result as flipping the pentagon vertically (assuming the vertices of the pentagon are indistinguishable).

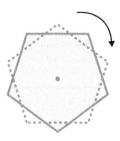

Finally, perform the reflection. Note that the result here is the same as a downward translation (assuming the vertices of the pentagon are indistinguishable).

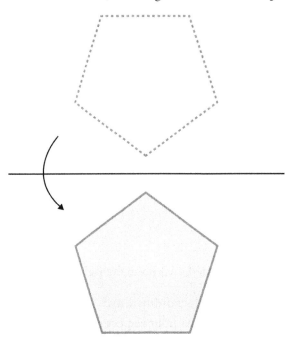

A figure has symmetry when there is an isometry that maps the figure onto itself. A figure has rotational symmetry if there is a rotation of 180 degrees or less that maps the figure onto itself. Point symmetry is where a plane figure can be mapped onto itself by a half-turn or a rotation of 180 degrees around some point.

A figure has **symmetry** when there is an isometry that maps the figure onto itself. A figure has **rotational symmetry** if there is a rotation of 180 degrees or less that maps the figure onto itself. **Point symmetry** is where a plane figure can be mapped onto itself by a half-turn or a rotation of 180 degrees around some point. Thus, point symmetry is a specific type of rotational symmetry. An example of a figure with point symmetry is shown below.

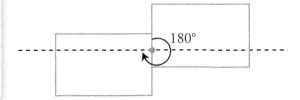

REFLECTIONAL SYMMETRY, or line symmetry, is an isometry that maps the figure onto itself by reflection across a line. An alternative view is that if the figure is folded along a line of symmetry, the two halves will match perfectly. Examples of figures with line symmetry are shown below, with all the potential lines of symmetry marked as broken lines.

REFLECTIONAL SYMMETRY: an isometry that maps the figure onto itself by reflection across a line

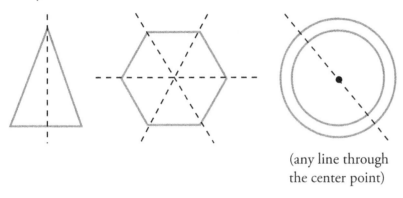

(any line through
the center point)

TRANSLATIONAL SYMMETRY is where an image can be translated in a specific direction to produce the same image. Necessarily, this requires that the image be infinite in extent and repeating in nature. A **TESSELLATION** is an image with translational symmetry. A tessellation or tiling consists of a repeating pattern of figures, which completely cover an area. Below are two examples of art tessellations.

TRANSLATIONAL SYMMETRY: symmetry which allows an image to be translated in a specific direction to produce the same image

TESSELLATION: an image with translational symmetry

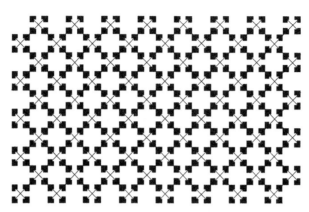

A regular tessellation is made by taking a pattern of polygons that are interlocked and can be extended infinitely. A portion of a tessellation made with hexagons is shown below. This image is made by taking congruent, regular polygons and using them to cover a plane in such a way that there are no holes or overlaps. A semi-regular tessellation is made with polygons arranged exactly the same way at every vertex point. Tessellations occur in frequently in nature. A bee's honeycomb is an example of a tessellation found in nature.

The different types of transformations of geometric figures in the plane, such as translations, rotations, reflections, and dilations, can be represented in the coordinate plane or space (especially when the transformations are complicated or when multiple sequential transformations are to be performed) using vectors and matrices.

Points in a geometric figure, such as vertices, can be treated as a vector with two elements—(x_1, y_1), for instance—that specify the location of the point in some coordinate system. Consider the example below.

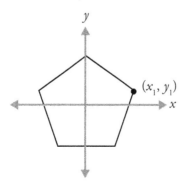

Given that each point on the figure is represented by an ordered pair, a 2 × 2 matrix can be used to perform the transformation. For any given transformation, a particular 2 × 2 matrix $\overline{T}$ can be determined that transforms all the points in the correct manner.

Consider a reflection about the *x*-axis. This transformation results in the following:

$$(x, y) \rightarrow (x, {}^-y)$$

The result of this transformation is shown below for the pentagon given in the diagram above.

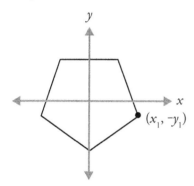

A matrix $\overline{T}$ can be constructed that performs this transformation.

$$\overline{T} \begin{pmatrix} 1 & 0 \\ 0 & -1 \end{pmatrix}$$

Thus:

$$\overline{T} \begin{pmatrix} x \\ y \end{pmatrix} = \begin{pmatrix} 1 & 0 \\ 0 & -1 \end{pmatrix}\begin{pmatrix} x \\ y \end{pmatrix} = \begin{pmatrix} x \\ {}^-y \end{pmatrix}$$

A similar transformation matrix can be constructed for reflections about the *y*-axis or about an arbitrary line (although this latter case is significantly more difficult).

For a translation, it is sufficient to simply construct a vector that is added to each point (x, y) in the figure. This vector is composed of a length for the translation in the *x* direction and a length for the translation in the *y* direction. For instance, to translate a figure a distance *a* in the positive *x* direction and a distance *b* in the negative *y* direction, use a vector $(a, {}^-b)$. The result is shown below for the pentagon.

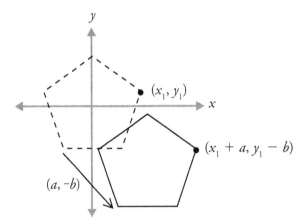

Algebraically, the transformation for the transformed figure in terms of the points (x, y) on the original figure is the following for a general translation (c, d):

$$\begin{pmatrix} x \\ y \end{pmatrix} + \begin{pmatrix} c \\ d \end{pmatrix}$$

Rotations are slightly more complicated transformations. Consider a rotation around the origin of a point specified as (x_1, y_1).

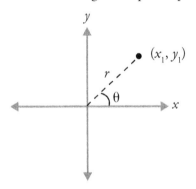

Using polar coordinates, the point can likewise be represented as a distance r from the origin and an angle θ from the x-axis.

$$r = \sqrt{x_1^2 + y_1^2}$$
$$\theta = \arctan \frac{y_1}{x_1}$$

A rotation around the origin simply involves, in this case, changing θ but holding r constant. Consider a rotation α in the counterclockwise direction.

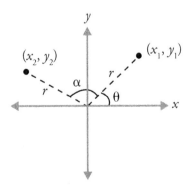

The coordinates of the new point (x_2, y_2) are then the following:

$$x_2 = r \cos (\alpha + \theta)$$
$$y_2 = r \sin (\alpha + \theta)$$

Use the sum formulas for trigonometric functions to expand and then simplify these expressions.

$$x_2 = r (\cos \alpha \cos \theta - \sin \alpha \sin \theta) = (r \cos \theta) \cos \alpha - (r \sin \theta) \sin \alpha$$
$$y_2 = r (\sin \alpha \cos \theta + \cos \alpha \sin \theta) = (r \cos \theta) \sin \alpha + (r \sin \theta) \cos \alpha$$

But $r \cos \theta$ is simply x_1, and $r \sin \theta$ is simply y_1.

$$x_2 = x_1 \cos \alpha - y_1 \sin \alpha$$
$$y_2 = x_1 \sin \alpha + y_1 \cos \alpha$$

Clearly, these two equations can be written in matrix form. Thus, a rotation of point (x_1, y_1) about the origin by angle α can be expressed as follows.

$$\begin{pmatrix} x^2 \\ y^2 \end{pmatrix} = \begin{pmatrix} \cos \alpha & -\sin \alpha \\ \sin \alpha & \cos \alpha \end{pmatrix} \begin{pmatrix} x_1 \\ y_1 \end{pmatrix}$$

This result can be tested using simple cases. For instance, consider a point $(1, 0)$ rotated by π radians.

$$\begin{pmatrix} x^2 \\ y^2 \end{pmatrix} = \begin{pmatrix} \cos \pi & -\sin \pi \\ \sin \pi & \cos \pi \end{pmatrix} \begin{pmatrix} 1 \\ 0 \end{pmatrix} = \begin{pmatrix} -1 & 0 \\ 0 & -1 \end{pmatrix} \begin{pmatrix} 1 \\ 0 \end{pmatrix} = \begin{pmatrix} -1 \\ 0 \end{pmatrix}$$

This result makes intuitive sense. To rotate a figure, simply rotate a set of representative points (such as the vertices); then reconnect them after the rotation. In cases in which a point of rotation is chosen that is not the origin, a change of coordinates to make the origin and the point of rotation coincide may simplify the problem and eliminate the need to handle complicated transformation matrices. Dilations involve a change in the distance r from some point (such as the origin), rather than a change in the angle θ. As with rotations, it is sometimes convenient to perform a change of coordinates so that the center of dilation and the origin of the coordinate system coincide. In such a case, a dilation simply involves multiplying both coordinates of each point in the figure by the dilation factor. Consider the pentagon used above with a dilation factor of 2. For each point (x, y) on the pentagon, the corresponding point (x', y') on the dilated pentagon is simply the following:

$$\begin{pmatrix} x' \\ y' \end{pmatrix} = d \begin{pmatrix} x \\ y \end{pmatrix}$$

where, in this case, the dilation factor d is 2. The result of the dilation is shown below for the pentagon.

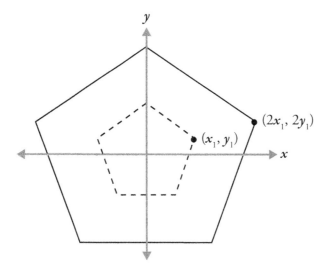

Compound transformations can be made by simply concatenating several transformation operators (whether a multiplicative matrix, a multiplicative constant, or an additive vector).

Example: Find the formula for a transformation involving first a rotation of α counterclockwise around the origin, then a dilation by a factor of 4, then a translation in the positive y direction by 2, and then a clockwise rotation by α.

To solve this problem, consider a point (x, y) on the plane. To rotate counterclockwise by α, use the rotation matrix.

$$\begin{pmatrix} x' \\ y' \end{pmatrix} = \begin{pmatrix} \cos\alpha & -\sin\alpha \\ \sin\alpha & \cos\alpha \end{pmatrix} \begin{pmatrix} x \\ y \end{pmatrix}$$

The dilation simply involves multiplication by a factor of 4.

$$\begin{pmatrix} x'' \\ y'' \end{pmatrix} = 4 \begin{pmatrix} x' \\ y' \end{pmatrix}$$

The translation can be represented as follows.

$$\begin{pmatrix} x''' \\ y''' \end{pmatrix} = \begin{pmatrix} x''' \\ y''' \end{pmatrix} + \begin{pmatrix} 0 \\ 2 \end{pmatrix}$$

The final result requires use of the rotation matrix for $-\alpha$.

$$\begin{pmatrix} \bar{x} \\ \bar{y} \end{pmatrix} = \begin{pmatrix} \cos\alpha & \sin\alpha \\ -\sin\alpha & \cos\alpha \end{pmatrix} \begin{pmatrix} x''' \\ y''' \end{pmatrix}$$

Rewriting the equation in full yields

$$\begin{pmatrix} \bar{x} \\ \bar{y} \end{pmatrix} = \begin{pmatrix} \cos\alpha & \sin\alpha \\ -\sin\alpha & \cos\alpha \end{pmatrix} \left\{ 4 \begin{pmatrix} \cos\alpha & -\sin\alpha \\ \sin\alpha & \cos\alpha \end{pmatrix} \begin{pmatrix} x \\ y \end{pmatrix} + \begin{pmatrix} 0 \\ 2 \end{pmatrix} \right\}$$

Using this formula, any point or set of points can be transformed in the manner specified by the question.

The basic properties of vectors are reviewed in *Skill 16.3.*

DOMAIN IV
TRIGONOMETRY AND CALCULUS

PERSONALIZED STUDY PLAN

PAGE	COMPETENCY AND SKILL	KNOWN MATERIAL/ SKIP IT	BRIEFLY REVIEW eSTICKYNOTES	MAKE eFLASHCARDS	TAKE ADDITIONAL SAMPLE TESTS
201	**11: Understand trigonometric functions**	☐	☐	☐	☐
	11.1: Apply trigonometric functions to solve problems involving distance and angles	☐	☐	☐	☐
	11.2: Apply trigonometric functions to solve problems involving the unit circle	☐	☐	☐	☐
	11.3: Manipulate trigonometric expressions and equations using techniques such as trigonometric identities	☐	☐	☐	☐
	11.4: Analyze the relationship between a trigonometric function and its graph	☐	☐	☐	☐
	11.5: Use trigonometric functions to model periodic relationships	☐	☐	☐	☐
216	**12: Understand differential calculus**	☐	☐	☐	☐
	12.1: Evaluate limits	☐	☐	☐	☐
	12.2: Demonstrate knowledge of continuity	☐	☐	☐	☐
	12.3: Analyze the derivative as the slope of a tangent line and as the limit of the difference quotient	☐	☐	☐	
	12.4: Calculate the derivatives of functions	☐	☐	☐	☐
	12.5: Apply differentiation to analyze the graphs of functions	☐	☐	☐	☐
	12.6: Apply differentiation to solve real-world problems involving rates of change and optimization	☐	☐	☐	☐
237	**13: Understand integral calculus**	☐	☐	☐	☐
	13.1: Analyze the integral as the area under a curve and as the limit of the Riemann sum	☐	☐	☐	☐
	13.2: Calculate the integrals of functions	☐	☐	☐	☐
	13.3: Apply integration to analyze the graphs of functions	☐	☐	☐	☐
	13.4: Apply integration to solve real-world problems	☐	☐	☐	☐

COMPETENCY 11
UNDERSTAND TRIGONOMETRIC FUNCTIONS

Right Triangle Trigonometry

Trigonometric functions can be related to right triangles: each trigonometric function corresponds to a ratio of certain sides of the triangle with respect to a particular angle. Thus, given the generic right triangle diagram below, the following functions can be specified.

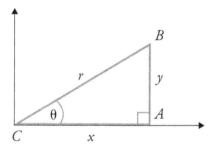

$$\sin\theta = \frac{y}{r} \qquad \csc\theta = \frac{r}{y}$$
$$\cos\theta = \frac{x}{r} \qquad \sec\theta = \frac{r}{x}$$
$$\tan\theta = \frac{y}{x} \qquad \cot\theta = \frac{x}{y}$$

Based on these definitions, the unknown characteristics of a particular right triangle can be calculated based on certain known characteristics. For instance, if the hypotenuse and one of the adjacent angles are both known, the lengths of the other two sides of the triangle can be calculated.

Angle Measures: Degrees and Radians

The argument of a trigonometric function is an angle that is typically expressed in either degrees or radians. A **DEGREE** constitutes an angle corresponding to a sector that is $\frac{1}{360}$th of a circle. Therefore, a circle has 360 degrees. A **RADIAN**, on the other hand, is the angle corresponding to a sector of a circle, where the arc length of the sector is equal to the radius of the circle. In the case of the unit circle (a circle of radius 1), the circumference is 2π. Thus, there are 2π radians in a circle. Conversion between degrees and radians is a simple matter of using the ratio

DEGREE: an angle corresponding to a sector that is $\frac{1}{360}$th of a circle

RADIAN: the angle corresponding to a sector of a circle, where the arc length of the sector is equal to the radius of the circle

between the total degrees in a circle and the total radians in a circle.

$$\text{(degrees)} = \frac{180}{\pi} \times \text{(radians)}$$
$$\text{(radians)} = \frac{\pi}{180} \times \text{(degrees)}$$

Example: Find the side x in the triangle below.

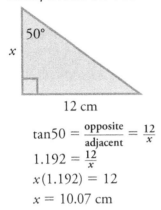

$$\tan 50 = \frac{\text{opposite}}{\text{adjacent}} = \frac{12}{x}$$
$$1.192 = \frac{12}{x}$$
$$x(1.192) = 12$$
$$x = 10.07 \text{ cm}$$

Trigonometric functions can also be applied to nonright triangles by way of the law of sines and the law of cosines. Consider the arbitrary triangle shown below with angles A, B and C and corresponding opposite sides a, b and c.

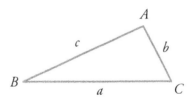

The law of sines is a proportional relationship between the lengths of the sides of the triangle and the opposite angles. The law of sines is given below:

$$\frac{a}{\sin A} = \frac{b}{\sin B} = \frac{c}{\sin C}$$

The law of cosines permits determination of the length of a side of an arbitrary triangle as long as the lengths of the other two sides, along with the angle opposite the unknown side, are known. The law of cosines is given below:

$$c^2 = a^2 + b^2 - 2ab \cos C$$

Example: Find the measure, in degrees, of the acute angles of a right triangle with a hypotenuse measuring 13 in. and legs 5 and 12 inches.

Write trigonometric equations using each acute angle, A and B, where angle A is opposite the leg of length 12 and angle B is opposite the side with length 5.

$$\sin A = \frac{12}{13} \quad \cos B = \frac{12}{13}$$

(Note: these are 2 possible equations; more correct relationships exist)

The variables in these two equations are the angles. To solve a trigonometric equation for an angle, use the inverse trig function. On a calculator, this usually involves pushing the "2nd" button before the trig button.

If $\sin A = \frac{12}{13}$, then $\sin^{-1} \frac{12}{13} = A$

Or "2nd" followed by "sin" followed by $\frac{12}{13}$ should equal approximately 67.4 degrees.

Similarly, $\cos^{-1} \frac{12}{13} = 22.6$ degrees.

Check to see that all 3 angles of the triangle add up to 180 degrees:

$22.6 + 67.4 + 90 = 180$

Example: An inlet is 140 feet wide. The lines of sight from each bank to an approaching ship are 79 degrees and 58 degrees. What are the distances from each bank to the ship?

First, draw an appropriate sketch of the situation with the appropriate labels for the parameters.

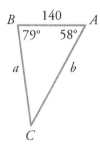

Since the sum of the angles in a triangle is 180°, angle C must be 43°. Use the law of sines to calculate the lengths of sides a and b.

For side b:

$$\frac{b}{\sin 79°} = \frac{140 \text{ feet}}{\sin 43°}$$

$$b = \frac{\sin 79°}{\sin 43°} 140 \text{ feet} \approx 201.5 \text{ feet}$$

And for side a:

$$\frac{a}{\sin 58°} = \frac{140 \text{ feet}}{\sin 43°}$$

$$a = \frac{\sin 58°}{\sin 43°} 140 \text{ feet} \approx 174.1 \text{ feet}$$

Example: Find side b in the triangle below if angle B = 87.5°, a = 12.3, and c = 23.2. (Compute to the nearest tenth.)

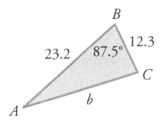

$$b^2 = a^2 + c^2 - (2ac)\cos B$$
$$b^2 = (12.3)^2 + (23.2)^2 - 2(12.3)(23.2)(\cos 87.5)$$
$$b^2 = 664.636$$
$$b = 25.8$$

SKILL 11.2 **Apply trigonometric functions to solve problems involving the unit circle**

Trigonometry and the Unit Circle

Trigonometry can also be understood in terms of a unit circle on the x-y plane. A unit circle has a radius of 1.

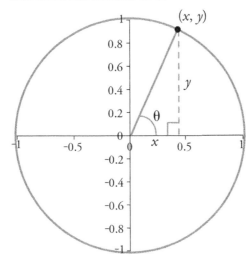

Notice that any given radius forms a right triangle with legs having lengths equal to the position of the point on the circle (x, y). Since the radius is equal to 1, the values of x and y are the following:

$$x = \cos \theta$$
$$y = \sin \theta$$

All the properties of trigonometric relationships for right triangles apply in this case as well.

The unit circle illustrates several properties of trigonometric functions. For example, applying the Pythagorean theorem to the unit circle yields the equation $\cos^2 \theta + \sin^2 \theta = 1$. In addition, the unit circle reveals the periodic nature of trigonometric functions. When we increase the angle θ beyond 2π radians or 360 degrees, the values of x and y coordinates repeat with each revolution. The unit circle also reveals the range of the sine and cosine functions. The values of sine and cosine are always between one and negative one. Finally, the unit circle shows that when the x coordinate of a point on the circle is zero, the tangent function is undefined. Thus, tangent is undefined at the angles $\frac{\pi}{2}, \frac{3\pi}{2}$ and the corresponding angles in all subsequent revolutions.

Example: If sin B = .75, and angle of rotation B is in the second quadrant, find cos B.

Use the Pythagorean theorem as applied to the unit circle: $\cos^2 x + \sin^2 x = 1$

$\cos^2 B + (.75)^2 = 1$

$\cos^2 B = 1 - (.75)^2 = .4375$

$\cos B = \pm \sqrt{.4375} = \pm.66$ (approximately)

But, the ordered pair (cos B, sin B) or (.66, .75) is in the first quadrant. To be in the second quadrant, angle B must rest at (-.66, .75). Therefore the cosine value requested is -.66.

Example: If sin A = $-\frac{1}{2}$ find two possible values for an angle of rotation, A, where 0 < A < 360 degrees.

Given $\sin A = -\frac{1}{2}$, the corresponding unit circle coordinate is $(x, -\frac{1}{2})$. It is not necessary to solve for x, but it is important to realize that x can have two values: one positive and one negative. In other words, angle A could be located in the third quadrant, with a negative value for x, or the fourth quadrant, with a positive value for x. Using the inverse sine function on a calculator yields $\sin^{-1}(-\frac{1}{2}) = -30$. Negative thirty degrees represents an angle of rotation in the fourth quadrant, but does not fit within the boundaries for A as stated in the problem. Realize, then, that rotating clockwise 30 degrees, for -30, is equal to rotating 330 degrees counter clockwise. Additionally, angle A's value in the third quadrant is 30 degrees past 180, or 210. Therefore the two values for angle of rotation A are 210 degrees and 330 degrees.

It is also helpful to know the exact values of specific coordinates on the unit circle. While typing sin 60 on a calculator yields a decimal answer, the ratios of a 30, 60, 90 degree triangle from Geometry point to an exact value of $\sqrt{\frac{3}{2}}$

The following trigonometric values, based on the special case 30–60–90 and 45–45–90 triangles (see section 9.3), should be understood exactly:

$$\sin 30 = \tfrac{1}{2} \qquad \sin 60 = \sqrt{\tfrac{3}{2}}$$

$$\cos 30 = \sqrt{\tfrac{3}{2}} \qquad \cos 60 = \tfrac{1}{2}$$

$$\sin 45 = \cos 45 = \frac{1}{\sqrt{2}} = \sqrt{\tfrac{3}{2}}$$

Furthermore, any angle of rotation with a reference angle measuring 30, 45, or 60 degrees will correspond to these values.

Example: Find the exact value of sin 240.

Since 240 has a reference angle measuring 60 degrees, use the exact value for sin 60 but, because it rests in the third quadrant, the sine value needs to be negative.

Thus $\sin 240 = -\sqrt{\tfrac{3}{2}}$

SKILL 11.3 Manipulate trigonometric expressions and equations using techniques such as trigonometric identities

There are two methods that may be used to prove trigonometric identities. One method is to choose one side of the equation and manipulate it until it equals the other side. The other method is to replace expressions on both sides of the equation with equivalent expressions until both sides are equal.

There are a range of **trigonometric identities**, including reciprocal and Pythagorean identities, as listed below.

RECIPROCAL IDENTITIES		
$\sin x = \dfrac{1}{\csc x}$	$\sin x \csc x = 1$	$\csc x = \dfrac{1}{\sin x}$
$\cos x = \dfrac{1}{\sec x}$	$\cos x \sec x = 1$	$\sec x = \dfrac{1}{\cos x}$
$\tan x = \dfrac{1}{\cot x}$	$\tan x \cot x = 1$	$\cot x = \dfrac{1}{\tan x}$
$\tan x = \dfrac{\sin x}{\cos x}$		$\cot x = \dfrac{\cos x}{\sin x}$

PYTHAGOREAN IDENTITIES		
$\sin^2 x + \cos^2 x = 1$	$1 + \tan^2 x = \sec^2 x$	$1 + \cot^2 x = \csc^2 x$

SUM AND DIFFERENCE AND DOUBLE ANGLE IDENTITIES	
$\sin (A \pm B) = \sin A \cos B \pm \cos A \sin B$	$\cos (A \pm B) = \cos A \cos B \pm \sin A \sin B$
$\sin 2A = 2\sin A \cos A$	$\cos 2A = \cos^2 A - \sin^2 A$

Example: Prove that $\sin^2 x + \cos^2 x = 1$.

Use the definitions of the sine and cosine functions from right triangle trigonometry.

$$\left(\tfrac{y}{r}\right)^2 + \left(\tfrac{x}{r}\right)^2 = 1$$
$$\frac{x^2 + y^2}{r^2} = 1$$

But the numerator of the above fraction, by the Pythagorean theorem, is simply r^2. Then:

$$\frac{r^2}{r^2} = 1$$

The identity has been proven.

Example: Prove that $\cot x + \tan x = \csc x \sec x$.

Use the reciprocal identities to convert the left side of the equation to sines and cosines. Then combine terms using a common denominator.

$$\frac{\cos x}{\sin x} + \frac{\sin x}{\cos x}$$
$$\frac{\cos^2 x}{\sin x \cos x} + \frac{\sin^2 x}{\sin x \cos x} = \frac{\sin^2 x + \cos^2 x}{\sin x \cos x} = \frac{1}{\sin x \cos x}$$

Finally, convert the expression using the reciprocal identities.

$$\frac{1}{\sin x \cos x} = \csc x \sec x$$

The identity is then proven.

The following are some identities for the inverse trigonometric functions:

IDENTITIES FOR THE INVERSE TRIGONOMETRIC FUNCTIONS		
$\csc^{-1}(x)$	$=$	$\sin^{-1}\left(\frac{1}{x}\right)$ for $|x| \geq 1$
$\sec^{-1}(x)$	$=$	$\cos^{-1}\left(\frac{1}{x}\right)$ for $|x| \geq 1$
$\cot^{-1}(x)$	$=$	$\tan^{-1}\left(\frac{1}{x}\right)$ for $x > 0$
	$=$	$\tan^{-1}\left(\frac{1}{x}\right) + \pi$ for $x < 0$
	$=$	$\frac{\pi}{2}$ for $x = 0$

$\sin^{-1} x$	$=$	$\cos^{-1}\left(\sqrt{1-x^2}\right)$	$\cos^{-1} x$	$=$	$\sin^{-1}\left(\sqrt{1-x^2}\right)$
$\tan^{-1} x$	$=$	$\cos^{-1}\left(\frac{1}{\sqrt{1+x^2}}\right)$	$\cos^{-1} x$	$=$	$\tan^{-1}\frac{\sqrt{1-x^2}}{x}$
$\tan^{-1} x$	$=$	$\sin^{-1}\left(\frac{x}{\sqrt{1+x^2}}\right)$	$\sin^{-1} x$	$=$	$\tan^{-1}\left(\frac{x}{\sqrt{1-x^2}}\right)$

Example: Simplify the expression cos(arcsin x) + sin(arccos x)

Note that arcsin and arccos are another way to write the inverse trig functions $\sin^{-1}$ and $\cos^{-1}$

$$\arcsin x = \arccos(\sqrt{1-x^2}) \text{ identity}$$
$$\rightarrow \cos(\arcsin x) = \cos\left[\arccos(\sqrt{1-x^2})\right] = \sqrt{1-x^2}$$
$$\arccos x = \arcsin(\sqrt{1-x^2}) \text{ identity}$$
$$\rightarrow \sin(\arccos x) = \sin\left[\arcsin(\sqrt{1-x^2})\right] = \sqrt{1-x^2}$$

Hence, $\cos(\arcsin x) + \sin(\arccos x) = \sqrt{1-x^2} + \sqrt{1-x^2} = 2\sqrt{1-x^2}$

Example: Using the identities given above, prove the identity
$$\sin^{-1} x + \cos^{-1} x = \frac{\pi}{2}.$$

Since $\sin\left(\frac{\pi}{2}\right) = 1$, the identity may be proven by showing that
$$\sin(\sin^{-1} x + \cos^{-1} x) = 1$$
$$\sin(\sin^{-1} x + \cos^{-1} x) = \sin(\sin^{-1} x)\cos(\cos^{-1} x)$$
$$+ \cos(\sin^{-1} x)\sin(\cos^{-1} x) \quad \text{sine sum formula}$$
$$= x \times x + \sqrt{1-x^2}\,\sqrt{1-x^2} \quad \text{inverse identities}$$
$$= x^2 + 1 - x^2 = 1$$

Other similar identities include the following:
$$\tan^{-1} x + \cot^{-1} x = \frac{\pi}{2}$$
and
$$\sec^{-1} x + \csc^{-1} x = \frac{\pi}{2}.$$

Unlike trigonometric identities, which are true for all values of the defined variable, trigonometric equations and inequalities are true for some, but not all, values of the variable. Most often, trigonometric equations are solved for values between 0 and 360 degrees or between 0 and 2π radians. For inequalities, the solution is often a set of intervals, since trigonometric functions are periodic. Solving trigonometric equations is largely the same as solving algebraic equations. Care must be taken, however, to keep in mind the periodic nature of trigonometric functions. This periodic nature often yields multiple (or an infinite number of) solutions.

Trigonometric identities, including sum and difference formulas, are often indispensable in the problem-solving process. These identities allow many complicated functions to be simplified to forms that are more easily managed algebraically.

Some algebraic operations, such as squaring both sides of an equation, will yield extraneous answers. Avoid incorrect solutions by remembering to check all solutions to be sure they satisfy the original equation.

> *Some algebraic operations, such as squaring both sides of an equation, will yield extraneous answers. Avoid incorrect solutions by remembering to check all solutions to be sure they satisfy the original equation.*

Example: Solve the following equation for x: cos x = 1 − sin x, where $0° \le x \le 360°$.

Start by squaring both sides of the equation.
$$\cos^2 x = (1 - \sin x)^2 = 1 - 2 \sin x + \sin^2 x$$

Substitute using the Pythagorean identity to replace the cosine term.
$$1 - \sin^2 x = 1 - 2 \sin x + \sin^2 x$$

Simplify the results.
$$2 \sin^2 x - 2 \sin x = 0$$
$$\sin x (\sin x - 1) = 0$$

There are two possible solutions to the equation:
$$\sin x = 0 \qquad \text{and} \qquad \sin x = 1$$
$$x = 0°, 180° \qquad\qquad x = 90°$$

Thus, the apparent solutions to the problem are $x = 0°$, 90° and 180°. By checking each solution, however, it is found that $x = 180°$ is not a legitimate solution and must be discarded. The actual solutions to the equation are thus $x = 0°$ and 90°.

Example: Solve the following equation: cos² x = sin² x for 0 ≤ x ≤ 2π.

First, use the Pythagorean identity to convert either the cosine or sine term.

$$\cos^2 x = 1 - \cos^2 x$$

Simplify the results.

$$2\cos^2 x = 1$$
$$\cos^2 x = \frac{1}{2}$$
$$\cos x = \pm \frac{1}{\sqrt{2}}$$

Familiarity with the properties of trigonometric functions should lead to the realization that this solution corresponds to odd integer multiples of $\frac{\pi}{4}$. Alternatively, a calculator can be used to calculate the inverse function. (A detailed review of inverse trigonometric functions is provided earlier.)

$$x = \arccos(\pm \frac{1}{\sqrt{2}})$$

In either case, the solution is the following:

$$x = \frac{\pi}{4}, \frac{3\pi}{4}, \frac{5\pi}{4}, \frac{7\pi}{4}$$

Example: Solve for x: sin x ≥ 0.

Solving a trigonometric inequality involves the same general process that is used in solving any other inequality. In this case, however, the set of solutions includes an infinite number of intervals, rather than a single interval as is the case for some nonperiodic functions. First, replace the inequality symbol with an equal sign. Solve using the inverse function.

$$\sin x = 0$$
$$\arcsin [\sin x] = \arcsin [0]$$
$$x = \arcsin [0]$$

The solutions for x are the following.

$$x = n\pi \quad n = 0, \pm 1, \pm 2, \pm 3, \ldots$$

These solutions are the points at which the sine function crosses the x-axis. Thus, some set of intervals bounded by these solutions is the set of solutions for the inequality. It is apparent that the sine function is greater than zero for x between 0 and π, and negative for x between π and 2π. This pattern then repeats. Thus, sin x is greater than zero between $2n\pi$ and $(2n + 1)\pi$ for $n = 0, \pm 1, \pm 2, \pm 3, \ldots$

$$\sin x \geq 0 \text{ for } 2n\pi \leq x \leq (2n + 1)\pi \text{ where } n = 0, \pm 1, \pm 2, \pm 3, \ldots$$

Note that the endpoints of the intervals are included in the solution set. The validity of this solution can be confirmed by looking at a graph of sin x.

Example: Solve the following equation for x

$$\cos (30 + 45) = \frac{\sqrt{6} - \sqrt{2}}{x}$$

Use the angle sum identity to expand the left side:

$$\cos 30 \cos 45 - \sin 30 \sin 45 = \frac{\sqrt{6} - \sqrt{2}}{x}$$

$$\left(\sqrt{\frac{3}{2}}\right)\left(\frac{1}{\sqrt{2}}\right) - \left(\frac{1}{2}\right)\left(\frac{1}{\sqrt{2}}\right) = \frac{\sqrt{6} - \sqrt{2}}{x}$$

$$\left(\sqrt{\frac{3}{2}}\right)\sqrt{2} - \left(\frac{1}{2}\right)\sqrt{2}$$

$$\frac{\sqrt{3} - 1}{2\sqrt{2}} \qquad \text{multiply the left side by the fraction } \frac{\sqrt{2}}{\sqrt{2}}$$

$$\frac{\sqrt{6} - \sqrt{2}}{4} = \frac{\sqrt{6} - \sqrt{2}}{x}$$

visual inspection shows that $x = 4$

SKILL 11.4 Analyze the relationship between a trigonometric function and its graph

The trigonometric functions sine, cosine, and tangent (and their reciprocals) are **PERIODIC FUNCTIONS**. The values of periodic functions repeat on regular intervals. The period, amplitude, and phase shift are critical properties of periodic functions that can be determined by observation of the graph or by detailed study of the functions themselves.

PERIODIC FUNCTIONS: functions whose values repeat on regular intervals

The **PERIOD** of a function is the smallest domain containing one complete cycle of the function. For example, the period of a sine or cosine function is the distance between the adjacent peaks or troughs of the graph. The **AMPLITUDE** of a function is half the distance between the maximum and minimum values of the function.

The **PHASE SHIFT** of a function is the amount of horizontal displacement of the function from a given reference position.

PERIOD: the smallest domain containing one complete cycle of the function

PHASE SHIFT: the amount of horizontal displacement of the function from a given reference position

Below is a generic sinusoidal graph with the period and amplitude labeled.

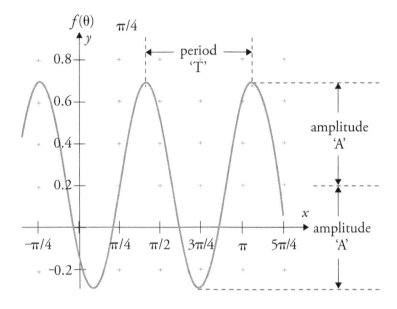

The period and amplitude for the three basic trigonometric functions are provided in the table below.

PERIOD AND AMPLITUDE OF THE BASIC TRIG FUNCTIONS		
Function	**Period (radians)**	**Amplitude**
sin θ	2π	1
cos θ	2π	1
tan θ	π	Undefined

Below are the graphs of the basic trigonometric functions, (a) $y = \sin x$; (b) $y = \cos x$; and (c) $y = \tan x$.

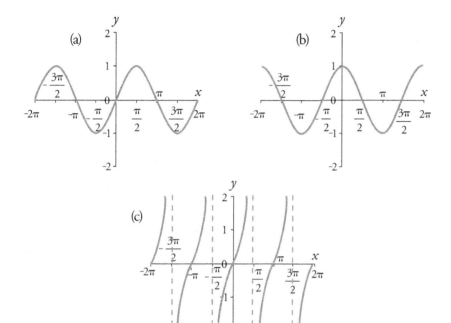

Note that the graph of the tangent function has asymptotes at $x = \frac{2n - 1}{2}\pi$, where $n = 0, \pm1, \pm2, \pm3,\ldots$.

The graphs of the reciprocal trigonometric functions are shown below, with (a) $y = \csc x$; (b) $y = \sec x$; and (c) $y = \cot x$.

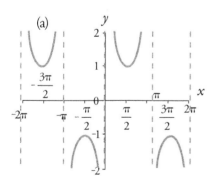

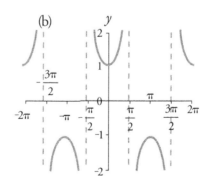

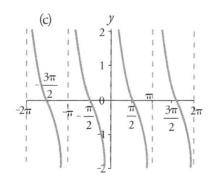

The phase and amplitude for the three reciprocal trigonometric functions are provided in the table below.

PERIOD AND AMPLITUDE OF THE RECIPROCAL TRIG FUNCTIONS		
Function	Period (radians)	Amplitude
$\csc \theta$	2π	Undefined
$\sec \theta$	2π	Undefined
$\cot \theta$	π	Undefined

Inverse Trigonometric Functions

The inverse sine function of x is written as arcsin x or $\sin^{-1} x$ and is the angle for which the sine is x; i.e., $\sin(\arcsin x) = x$. Since the sine function is periodic, many values of arcsin x correspond to a particular x. In order to define arcsin as a function, therefore, its range needs to be restricted.

The function $y = \arcsin x$ has a domain $[-1, 1]$ and range $[-\frac{\pi}{2}, \frac{\pi}{2}]$.

In some books, a restricted inverse function is denoted by a capitalized beginning letter such as in Sin^{-1} or Arctan. The arcsin function is shown below.

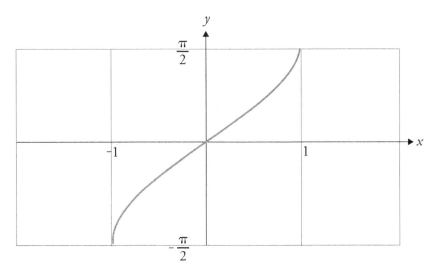

The inverse cosine and tangent functions are defined in the same way: $\cos(\arccos x) = x$; $\tan(\arctan x) = x$.

The function $y = \arccos x$ has a domain $[-1, 1]$ and range $[0, \pi]$. The graph of this function is shown below.

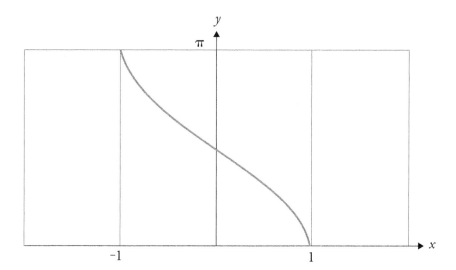

The function $y = \arctan x$ has a domain $[-\infty, +\infty]$ and range $[-\frac{\pi}{2}, \frac{\pi}{2}]$. The plot of the function is shown below.

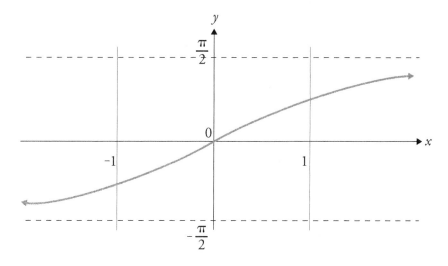

Example: Evaluate the following: (i) sin⁻¹(0) and (ii) arccos(-1)

(i) $\sin(\sin^{-1}(0)) = 0$.

The value of the inverse sine function must lie in the range $[-\frac{\pi}{2}, \frac{\pi}{2}]$. Since 0 is the only argument in the range $[-\frac{\pi}{2}, \frac{\pi}{2}]$ for which the sine function is zero, $\sin^{-1}(0) = 0$.

(ii) $\cos(\arccos(-1)) = -1$

The value of the inverse cosine function must lie in the range $[0, \pi]$. π is the only argument for which the cosine function is equal to -1 in the range $[0, \pi]$. Hence, $\arccos(-1) = \pi$.

Graphing a trigonometric function by hand typically requires a calculator for determining the value of the function for various angles. Nevertheless, simple functions can often be graphed by simply determining the amplitude, period, and phase shift. Once these parameters are known, the graph can be sketched approximately. The amplitude of a simple sine or cosine function is simply the multiplicative constant (or function) associated with the trigonometric function. Thus, $y = 2\cos x$, for instance, has an amplitude of 2. The phase shift is typically just a constant added to the argument of the function. For instance, $y = \sin(x + 1)$ includes a phase shift of 1. A positive phase shift constant indicates that the graph of the function is shifted to the left; a negative phase shift indicates that the graph is shifted to the right.

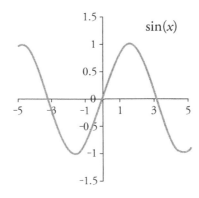

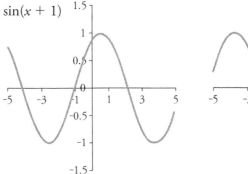

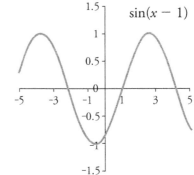

Example: Sketch the graph of the function $f(x) = 4 \sin(2x + \frac{\pi}{2})$.
Notice first that the amplitude of the function is 4. Since there is no constant term added to the sine function, the function is centered on the *x*-axis. Find crucial points on the graph by setting *f* equal to zero and solving for *x* to find the roots.

$$f(x) = 0 = 4 \sin(2x + \tfrac{\pi}{2})$$
$$\sin(2x + \tfrac{\pi}{2}) = 0$$
$$2x + \tfrac{\pi}{2} = n\pi$$

In the above expression, *n* is an integer.

$$2x = (n - \tfrac{1}{2})\pi$$
$$x = (n - \tfrac{1}{2})\tfrac{\pi}{2}$$

So, the roots of the function are at

$$x = \pm\frac{\pi}{4}, \pm\frac{3\pi}{4}, \pm\frac{5\pi}{4}, \dots$$

The maxima and minima of the function are halfway between successive roots. Determine the location of a maximum by testing the function. Try $x = 0$.

$$f(0) = 4\sin(2[0] + \tfrac{\pi}{2}) = 4\sin(\tfrac{\pi}{2}) = 4$$

Thus, f is maximized at $x = 4$. The function can then be sketched.

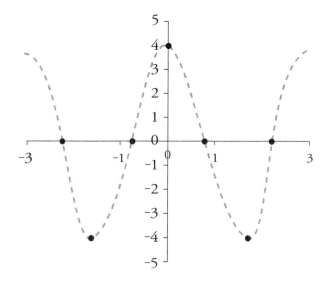

SKILL 11.5 Use trigonometric functions to model periodic relationships

Since trigonometric functions, as seen earlier, can be related to the properties of a circle, they have a cyclical (or periodic) behavior that is suited to modeling periodic phenomena. For instance, the height of a point marked on a wheel, tracked as the wheel rolls, can be modeled using trigonometric functions. The key to modeling such periodic phenomena is identification of the amplitude, period, and phase (if necessary) of the phenomenon. This information allows expression of some parameter of the phenomenon as an equation involving a trigonometric function.

Example: Write an equation for the height of sea waves whose crests pass every 5 seconds and whose peaks are 10 feet above their troughs.

In this case, phase information is not needed since there is no fixed position to form a point of comparison (or origin). Thus, either a sine or cosine function can be used. The amplitude of the waves is half the distance between the peaks and troughs, or 5 feet. The period is simply the inverse of the time between peaks: 0.2 sec^{-1}. The equation for the height h of the waves with respect to time t is

$h = 5\sin(0.2t)$ feet

where t is measured in seconds.

Example: Find an equation to model the length of a 6-foot man's shadow with respect to the angle of the sun in the sky measured relative to the plane of the ground at the man's feet. Assume that the sun is directly overhead at midday.

It is helpful to first draw a diagram of the situation. Since it is assumed that the sun is directly overhead at midday, the situation can be drawn in a single plane.

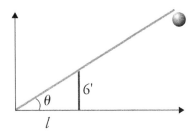

The length l of the shadow can be calculated using the tangent function for the angle θ of the sun in the sky. Use the definition of the tangent to find the function.

$\tan\theta = \dfrac{6'}{l}$

The resulting function can then be written

$l(\theta) = \dfrac{6'}{\tan\theta}$.

To check the result, try some simple cases. For instance, when the sun is overhead, $\theta = 90°$.

$l(90°) = \dfrac{6'}{\tan 90°} = \dfrac{6'}{\infty} = 0'$

Thus, there is no shadow cast when the sun is overhead. Another example is when the sun approaches the horizon. In this case, the shadow should get very long. Try $\theta = 1°$.

$l(1°) = \dfrac{6'}{\tan 1°} = \dfrac{6'}{0.175} = 342.9'$

This answer is at least somewhat intuitive. These checks provide confidence in the equation.

COMPETENCY 12
UNDERSTAND DIFFERENTIAL CALCULUS

Definition of Limit

Informally, the LIMIT of a function is the y value that its graph approaches as the value of x approaches a certain number. The *formal definition of a limit* is as follows.

A function $f(x)$ has a limit L as x approaches the value a, expressed as

$$\lim_{x \to a} f(x) = L$$

if and only if for a given $\varepsilon > 0$ there exists a $\delta > 0$ such that $|f(x) - L| < \varepsilon$ when $0 < |x - a| < \delta$.

This definition essentially means that for a value of x arbitrarily close to a, $f(x)$ must have a value arbitrarily close to L.

> **LIMIT:** the limit of a function is the y value that its graph approaches as the value of x approaches a certain number

Properties of Limits

A function $f(x)$ is CONTINUOUS at $x = a$ if $\lim_{x \to a} f(x)$ exists and is equal to $f(a)$. This essentially means that the graph of the function $f(x)$ does not have a break (or discontinuity) at $x = a$.

> **CONTINUOUS:** a function $f(x)$ is continuous at $x = a$ if $\lim_{x \to a} f(x)$ exists and is equal to $f(a)$. This essentially means that the graph of the function $f(x)$ does not have a break (or discontinuity) at $x = a$

OPERATIONS WITH LIMITS	
Sum Rule for Limits	If $\lim_{x \to a} f(x) = L$, and $\lim_{x \to a} g(x) = M$, then $\lim_{x \to a} (f(x) + g(x)) = L + M$.
	Using the sum rule for limits and the definition of continuity, we can conclude that if functions $f(x)$ and $g(x)$ are continuous at $x = a$—i.e., $L = f(a)$ and $M = g(a)$—then the function $f(x) + g(x)$ is also continuous at $x = a$.
Difference Rule for Limits	If $\lim_{x \to a} f(x) = L$, and $\lim_{x \to a} g(x) = M$, then $\lim_{x \to a} (f(x) - g(x)) = L - M$.
	As before, using the difference rule for limits and the definition of continuity, we can conclude that if functions $f(x)$ and $g(x)$ are continuous at $x = a$ then the function $f(x) - g(x)$ is also continuous at $x = a$.

Continued on next page

Constant Multiple Rule for Limits	If $\lim_{x \to a} f(x) = L$, then, for any constant c, $\lim_{x \to a} (cf(x)) = cL$. Again, we can conclude that if the function $f(x)$ is continuous at $x = a$, then the function $cf(x)$ is also continuous at $x = a$.
Product Rule for Limits	If $\lim_{x \to a} f(x) = L$, and $\lim_{x \to a} g(x) = M$, then, $\lim_{x \to a} (f(x) g(x)) = LM$. Using the definition of continuity, we can conclude that if the functions $f(x)$ and $g(x)$ are continuous at $x = a$, then the function $f(x) g(x)$ is also continuous at $x = a$.
Quotient Rule for Limits	If $\lim_{x \to a} f(x) = L$ and $\lim_{x \to a} g(x) = M$, then $\lim_{x \to a} \dfrac{f(x)}{g(x)} = \dfrac{L}{M}$ for $M \neq 0$. We can conclude that if the functions $f(x)$ and $g(x)$ are continuous at $x = a$, then the function $\dfrac{f(x)}{g(x)}$ is also continuous at $x = a$, provided $g(a)$ is not equal to zero.

Evaluating Limits

In finding a limit, there are two points to remember:

1. Factor the expression completely and cancel all common factors in fractions.

2. Substitute the number that the variable is approaching. In most cases this produces the value of the limit.

If the variable in the limit approaches ∞, factor and simplify first; then examine the result. If the result does not involve a fraction with the variable in the denominator, the limit is usually also equal to ∞. If the variable is in the denominator of the fraction, the denominator is getting larger, which makes the entire fraction smaller. In other words, the limit is zero.

Example: Evaluate the following limits.

1. $\lim_{x \to -3} \left(\dfrac{x^2 + 5x + 6}{x + 3} + 4x \right)$

   First, factor the numerator. Then cancel the common factors.
   $\lim_{x \to -3} \left(\dfrac{(x + 3)(x + 2)}{x + 3} + 4x \right)$
   $\lim_{x \to -3} (x + 2 + 4x) = \lim_{x \to -3} (5x + 2)$
   $5(-3) + 2 = -15 + 2 = -13$

2. $\lim_{x \to \infty} \dfrac{2x^2}{x^5}$

   Cancel the common factors and take the constant outside the limit.
   $2 \lim_{x \to \infty} \dfrac{1}{x^3}$
   Evaluate the limit.
   $2 \dfrac{1}{\infty^3} = 0$

L'Hopital's Rule

In some cases, the evaluation of a limit yields an undefined result. In some such cases, the limit can be evaluated using an alternative method. **L'HOPITAL'S RULE** states that a limit can be evaluated by taking the derivative of both the numerator and denominator and then finding the limit of the resulting quotient. This rule is extremely helpful in cases where simple evaluation of a limit leads to an undefined value (positive or negative infinity). Thus, L'Hopital's rule can be expressed as follows.

$$\lim_{x \to a} \frac{f(x)}{g(x)} = \lim_{x \to a} \frac{f'(x)}{g'(x)}$$

> **L'HOPITAL'S RULE:** states that a limit can be evaluated by taking the derivative of both the numerator and denominator and then finding the limit of the resulting quotient

Example: Evaluate the limit of the function $f(x) = \dfrac{3x - 1}{x^2 + 2x + 3}$ as x approaches infinity.

The limit cannot be evaluated using simple substitution.

$$\lim_{x \to \infty} \frac{3x - 1}{x^2 + 2x + 3} = \frac{3\infty - 1}{\infty^2 + 2\infty + 3} = \frac{\infty}{\infty}$$

Apply L'Hopital's rule by taking the derivative of the numerator and denominator individually.

$$\lim_{x \to \infty} \frac{3x - 1}{x^2 + 2x + 3} = \lim_{x \to \infty} = \frac{3}{2x + 2}$$

$$\lim_{x \to \infty} \frac{3}{2x + 2} = \frac{3}{2x + 2} = 0$$

Example: Evaluate the following limit: $\lim_{x \to 1} \dfrac{\ln x}{x - 1}$.

For $x = 1$, the denominator of the function becomes zero, as does the numerator. Therefore, apply L'Hopital's rule to simplify the limit.

$$\lim_{x \to 1} \frac{\ln x}{x - 1} = \lim_{x \to 1} \frac{\frac{1}{x}}{1}$$

$$\lim_{x \to 1} \frac{\ln x}{x - 1} = \lim_{x \to 1} \frac{1}{x} = \frac{1}{1} = 1$$

SKILL 12.2 Demonstrate knowledge of continuity

Continuity

Recall that the continuity of a function is easily understood graphically as the absence of missing points or breaks in the plot of the function. A more rigorous definition can be formulated, however. A function $f(x)$ is continuous at a point c if all of the following apply:

1. The function $f(x)$ is defined at $x = c$

2. The limit $\lim_{x \to c} f(x)$ exists

3. The limit can be found by substitution: $\lim\limits_{x \to c} f(x) = f(c)$

A function can then be called **continuous** on an open interval (a, b) if the above definition applies to the function for every point c in the interval. The function is also continuous at the points $x = a$ and $x = b$ if $\lim\limits_{x \to a^+} f(x) = f(a)$ and $\lim\limits_{x \to b^-} f(x) = f(b)$ both exist. (The $+/-$ notation simply signifies approaching the limiting value from either the right or left, respectively.) If both of these conditions apply, then the function is continuous on the closed interval $[a, b]$.

Example: Determine whether the function ln x is continuous over the closed interval [0, 1].

One approach is to look at a plot of the function.

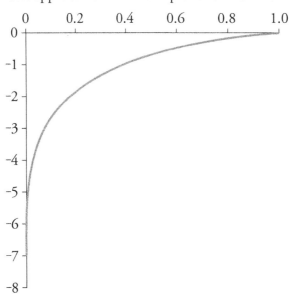

The limit of the function as x approaches zero from the right does not exist. Algebraically, this can be seen by noting that the equation $\ln x = L$ is the same as the equation $e^L = x$. For $x = 0$, the only possible value of L that satisfies this equation is $-\infty$. In other words,

$$\lim\limits_{x \to 0} \ln x = -\infty$$

The limit does not exist, therefore, and the function is not continuous on the closed interval $[0, 1]$. The function is continuous on the open interval $(0, 1)$, however. (It is also continuous on the half-open interval $(0, 1]$.) Note that, for all $x > 0$, x is defined, and for $c > 0$,

$$\lim\limits_{x \to c} \ln x = \ln c$$

Thus, $\ln x$ is continuous over $(0, \infty)$.

Example: Determine if the function shown in the graph is continuous at
x = 2.

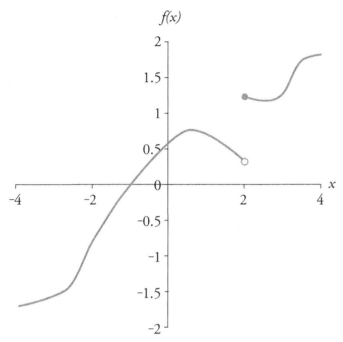

By inspection, it can be seen that the limits of the function as *x* approaches 2 from the right and left are not equal.

$$\lim_{x \to 2^+} f(x) \neq \lim_{x \to 2^-} f(x)$$

As a result, the function does not meet all of the criteria for continuity at $x = 2$ and is therefore discontinuous.

Example: Determine whether the following function is continuous at

$$x = 1: f(x) = \begin{cases} x^2 & x \neq 1 \\ 0 & x = 1 \end{cases}$$

The plot of this piecewise function is shown below.

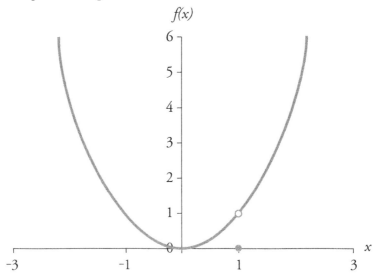

In this case, the function is defined at $x = 1$, and the limits of $f(x)$ as x approaches 1 from both the right and from the left are both equal to 1. Nevertheless, it is not the case that $\lim\limits_{x \to 1} f(x) = f(1)$, since $\lim\limits_{x \to 1} f(x) = 1$ and $f(1) = 0$. Thus, the function is not continuous at $x = 1$.

SKILL 12.3 **Analyze the derivative as the slope of a tangent line and as the limit of the difference quotient**

Derivatives

The **derivative of a function** has two basic interpretations:

1. Instantaneous rate of change

2. Slope of a tangent line at a given point

The following is a list summarizing some of the more common quantities referred to in rate-of-change problems.

- Acceleration
- Area
- Decay
- Distance
- Frequency
- Height
- Population growth
- Position
- Pressure
- Profit
- Sales
- Temperature
- Velocity
- Volume

Derivative and slope

The **SLOPE** of a line is simply the change in the vertical (positive y) direction divided by the change in the horizontal (positive x) direction. Since the slope of a line is constant over the entire domain of the function, any two points can be used to calculate the slope.

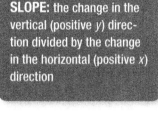

SLOPE: the change in the vertical (positive y) direction divided by the change in the horizontal (positive x) direction

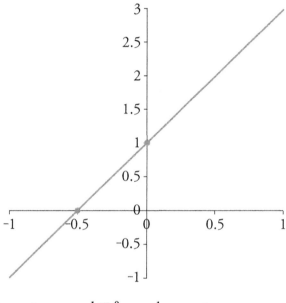

$$\text{slope} = \frac{1-0}{0-(-0.5)} = \frac{1}{0.5} = 2$$

Although the specific approach used for lines cannot be used for curves, it can be used in the general sense if the distance between the points (along the x-axis) becomes zero.

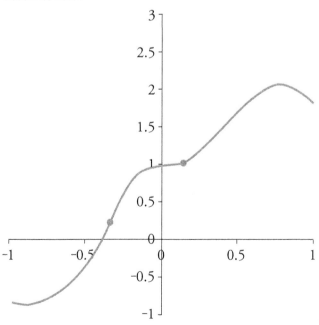

The equation for slope can be written as follows.

$$\text{slope} = \frac{f(x + \Delta x) - f(x)}{\Delta x}$$

This is also known as the **difference quotient.** For a curve defined by the function f, the DIFFERENCE QUOTIENT computes the slope of the secant line through the two points with x-coordinates x and $x + h$. If the two points on the line are chosen sufficiently close together so that the function does not vary significantly from the line between those points, then the difference quotient can serve as a good approximation for the slope (and, therefore, for the derivative as well). The difference quotient is used in the definition of the derivative.

> **DIFFERENCE QUOTIENT:**
> this computes the slope of the secant line through the two points with x-coordinates x and $x + h$

Take the limit as Δx goes to zero. This is the definition of the derivative, which is written as either $f'(x)$ or as $\frac{df(x)}{dx}$.

$$f'(x) = \lim_{\Delta x \to 0} \frac{f(x + \Delta x) - f(x)}{\Delta x}$$

This fundamental definition of the derivative can be used to derive formulas for derivatives of specific types of functions. For instance, consider $f(x) = x^2$. Based on this formula, which defines the slope over an infinitesimal width Δx, the derivative can be seen as the **instantaneous rate of change** of the function.

$$f'(x) = \lim_{\Delta x \to 0} \frac{(x + \Delta x)^2 - x^2}{\Delta x} = \lim_{\Delta x \to 0} \frac{x^2 + 2x\Delta x + \Delta x^2 - x^2}{\Delta x}$$

$$f'(x) = \lim_{\Delta x \to 0} \frac{2x\Delta x + \Delta x^2}{\Delta x} = \lim_{\Delta x \to 0} (2x + \Delta x) = 2x$$

The same approach can be used to show generally, for instance, that $f'(x) = nx^{n-1}$ for $f(x) = x^n$.

The derivative of a function at a point can likewise be interpreted as the **slope of a line tangent to the function** at that same point. Pick a point (for instance, at $x = -3$) on the graph of a function and draw a tangent line at that point. Find the derivative of the function and substitute the value $x = -3$. This result will be the slope of the tangent line.

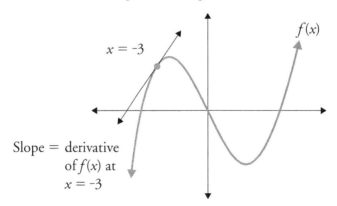

$x = -3$

$f(x)$

Slope = derivative of $f(x)$ at $x = -3$

Properties of the Derivative

The following properties of the derivative allow for differentiation of a wide range of functions (although the process of differentiation may be more or less difficult, depending on the complexity of the function). For illustration, consider two arbitrary functions, $f(x)$ and $g(x)$, and an arbitrary constant, c.

DIFFERENTIATION RULES	
Rule for Multiplicative Constants	$\frac{d}{dx}(cf) = cf'$
Sum and Difference Rules	$\frac{d}{dx}(f + g) = f' + g'$
	$\frac{d}{dx}(f - g) = f' - g'$
Product Rule	$\frac{d}{dx}(fg) = fg' + gf'$
Quotient Rule	$\frac{d}{dx}(\frac{f}{g}) = \frac{gf' - fg'}{g^2}$
Chain Rule	$\frac{df}{dx} = \frac{df}{du}\frac{du}{dx}$

The chain rule, as expressed above, allows for differentiation of composite functions. The variable u can be an independent variable or it can be a function of x. Note that the differential elements du in the numerator of the first factor and in the denominator of the second factor can otherwise cancel, making the right side of the equation identical to the left side.

Derivation of Differentiation Rules

As mentioned previously, the formal definition of the derivative can be used to determine the general form of the derivative for certain families of functions. The formal definition of the derivative is expressed in terms of the limit of a difference quotient, as given below.

$$f'(x) = \lim_{\Delta x \to 0} \frac{f(x + \Delta x) - f(x)}{\Delta x}$$

Using this definition, the derivatives of algebraic functions (including, for instance, polynomial, trigonometric and logarithmic functions) can be derived. In addition, the general differentiation rules above can also be derived by applying in each case the properties of limits to the definition given above.

The use of the formal definition in deriving a general rule of differentiation for a family of functions is best illustrated by way of an example. Consider polynomial functions, as mentioned previously. Note that the sum and difference rules for differentiation, along with the multiplicative constant rule, allow polynomials to be differentiated on a term-by-term basis. Thus, it suffices to simply derive the rule for differentiating the generic term x^n, where n is a constant and x is the variable of the function. Use the formal definition of the derivative given above and substitute this algebraic term for $f(x) =$ (that is, use $f(x) = x^n$).

$$f'(x) = \lim_{\Delta x \to 0} \frac{(x + \Delta x)^n - (x)^n}{\Delta x}$$

Simplify the expression and apply the binomial expansion to the result.

$$f'(x) = \lim_{\Delta x \to 0} \frac{1}{\Delta x}[(x + \Delta x)^n - x^n]$$

$$f'(x) = \lim_{\Delta x \to 0} [\binom{n}{0}x^n + \binom{n}{1}x^{n-1}\Delta x + \binom{n}{2}x^{n-2}(\Delta x)^2 + ... + \binom{n}{n}(\Delta x)^n - x^n]$$

In the above expression, the combinatorial form $\binom{n}{k}$ represents the number of combinations of n objects taken k at a time, or $\frac{n!}{k!(n-k)!}$.

$$f'(x) = \lim_{\Delta x \to 0} \frac{1}{\Delta x}[x^n + nx^{n-1}\Delta x + \binom{n}{2}x^{n-2}(\Delta x)^2 + ... + (\Delta x)^n - x^n]$$

$$f'(x) = \lim_{\Delta x \to 0} \frac{1}{\Delta x}[nx^{n-1}\Delta x + \binom{n}{2}x^{n-2}(\Delta x)^2 + ... + (\Delta x)^n]$$

$$f'(x) = \lim_{\Delta x \to 0} [nx^{n-1} + \binom{n}{2}x^{n-2}\Delta x + ... + (\Delta x)^{n-1}]$$

Note that, with the exception of the first term, all the terms in the brackets have a factor Δx. Thus, when the limit is applied, these terms all become zero, leaving the result of the differentiation.

$$f'(x) = nx^{n-1}$$

This is the well-known rule for differentiating polynomial terms with exponent n.

Example: Find the first derivative of the function $y = 5x^4$.

$$\frac{dy}{dx} = (5)(4)x^{4-1}$$

$$\frac{dy}{dx} = 20x^3$$

Example: Find y' where $y = \frac{1}{4x^3}$.

First, rewrite the function using a negative exponent, then apply the differentiation rule.

$$y' = \frac{1}{4}x^{-3}$$

$$y' = \frac{1}{4}(-3)x^{-3-1}$$

$$y' = -\frac{3}{4}x^{-4} = -\frac{3}{4x^4}$$

Example: Find the first derivative of $y = 3\sqrt{x^5}$.

Rewrite using $\sqrt[z]{x^n} = x^{n/z}$, then take the derivative.

$$y = 3x^{\frac{5}{2}}$$
$$\frac{dy}{dx} = (3)(\tfrac{5}{2})x^{\frac{5}{2}-1}$$
$$\frac{dy}{dx} = (\tfrac{15}{2})x^{\frac{3}{2}}$$
$$\frac{dy}{dx} = 7.5\sqrt{x^3} = 7.5x\sqrt{x}$$

The derivatives of other families of functions can be found in a similar manner. Below is a summary of the rules of differentiation for various transcendental (including trigonometric, logarithmic and exponential) functions.

SUMMARY OF DIFFERENTIATION RULES FOR TRANSCENDENTAL FUNCTIONS	
$\frac{d}{dx}\sin x = \cos x$	$\frac{d}{dx}\csc x = -\csc x \cot x$
$\frac{d}{dx}\cos x = -\sin x$	$\frac{d}{dx}\sec x = \sec x \tan x$
$\frac{d}{dx}\tan x = \sec^2 x$	$\frac{d}{dx}\cot x = -\csc^2 x$
$\frac{d}{dx}\arcsin x = \dfrac{1}{\sqrt{1-x^2}}$	$\frac{d}{dx}\operatorname{arc\,csc} x = -\dfrac{1}{\lvert x\rvert\sqrt{x^2-1}}$
$\frac{d}{dx}\operatorname{arccos} x = -\dfrac{1}{\sqrt{1-x^2}}$	$\frac{d}{dx}\operatorname{arc\,sec} x = \dfrac{1}{\lvert x\rvert\sqrt{x^2-1}}$
$\frac{d}{dx}\arctan x = \dfrac{1}{1+x^2}$	$\frac{d}{dx}\operatorname{arc\,cot} x = -\dfrac{1}{1+x^2}$
$\frac{d}{dx}\ln x = \tfrac{1}{x}$	$\frac{d}{dx}e^x = e^x$

Example: Find the derivative of the function $y = 4e^{x^2}\sin x$.

Apply the appropriate rules (product and chain rules) to the function.

$$\frac{dy}{dx} = 4(\sin x \tfrac{d}{dx}e^{x^2} + e^{x^2}\tfrac{d}{dx}\sin x)$$
$$\frac{dy}{dx} = 4(\sin x[2xe^{x^2}] + e^{x^2}\cos x)$$
$$\frac{dy}{dx} = 8xe^{x^2}\sin x + 4e^{x^2}\cos x$$

Example: Find the derivative of the function $y = \dfrac{5}{e^{\sin x}}$.

Rewrite the function with a negative exponent and use the chain rule.

$$y = 5e^{-\sin x}$$
$$\frac{dy}{dx} = 5\tfrac{d}{dx}e^{-\sin x}$$
$$\frac{dy}{dx} = 5e^{-\sin x}[-\cos x]$$
$$\frac{dy}{dx} = -5e^{-\sin x}\cos x = -\dfrac{5\cos x}{e^{\sin x}}$$

Finding Slope of a Tangent Line at a Point

Using these properties of derivatives, the slopes (and therefore equations) of tangent lines can be found for a wide range of functions. The procedure simply involves finding the slope of the function at the given point using the derivative, then determining the equation of the line using point-slope form.

Example: Find the slope of the tangent line for the given function at the given point: $y = \frac{1}{x-2}$ at (3, 1).

Find the derivative of the function.

$$y' = \frac{d}{dx}(x-2)^{-1}$$
$$y' = (-1)(x-2)^{-2}(1) = -\frac{1}{(x-2)^2}$$

Evaluate the derivative at $x = 3$:

$$y' = -\frac{1}{(3-2)^2} = -1$$

Thus, the slope of the function at the point is -1.

Example: Find the points at which the tangent to the curve $f(x) = 2x^2 + 3x$ is parallel to the line $y = 11x - 5$.

For the tangent line to be parallel to the given line, the only condition is that the slopes are equal. Thus, find the derivative of f, set the result equal to 11, and solve for x.

$$f'(x) = 4x + 3 = 11$$
$$4x = 8$$
$$x = 2$$

To find the y value of the point, simply substitute 2 into f.

$$f(2) = 2(2)^2 + 3(2) = 8 + 6 = 14$$

Thus, the tangent to f is parallel to $y = 11x - 5$ at the point (2, 14) only.

Example: Find the equation of the tangent line to $f(x) = 2e^{x^2}$ at $x = -1$.

To find the tangent line, a point and a slope are needed. The x value of the point is given; the y value can be found by substituting $x = -1$ into f.

$$f(-1) = 2e^{(-1)^2} = 2e$$

Thus, the point is $(-1, 2e)$. The slope is found by substituting -1 into the derivative of f.

$$f'(x) = 2e^{x^2}(2x) = 4xe^{x^2}$$
$$f'(-1) = 4(-1)e^{(-1)^2} = -4e$$

Use the point-slope form of the line to determine the correct equation.

$$y - 2e = -4e(x - [-1])$$
$$y = 2e - 4ex - 4e = -4ex - 2e$$

Thus, the equation of the line tangent to f at $x = -1$ is $y = -4ex - 2e$.

SKILL 12.5 Apply differentiation to analyze the graphs of functions

Differential calculus can be a helpful tool in analyzing functions and the graphs of functions. Derivatives deal with the slope (or rate of change) of a function, and this information can be used to calculate the locations and values of extrema (maxima and minima) and inflection points, as well as to determine information concerning concavity.

Extrema

The concept of **EXTREMA** (maxima and minima) can be differentiated into local (or relative) and global (or absolute) extrema. For instance, consider the following function:

EXTREMA: the minimum and maximum values of a function

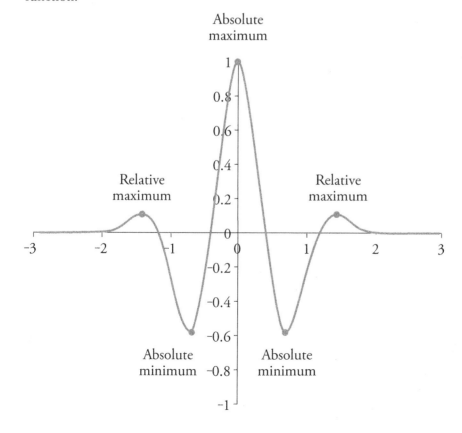

It is apparent that there are a number of peaks and valleys, each of which could, in some sense, be called a maximum or minimum. To allow for greater clarity, local and global extrema can be specified. For instance, the peak at $x = 0$ is the maximum for the entire function. Additionally, the valleys at about $x = \pm 0.7$ both correspond to an (equivalent) minimum for the entire function. These are absolute extrema. On the other hand, the peaks at about $x = \pm 1.4$ are each a maximum for the function within a specific area; thus, they are relative maxima. **RELATIVE EXTREMA** are extreme values of a function over some limited interval. The points at which the derivative of a function is equal to zero are called **CRITICAL POINTS** (the x values are called **CRITICAL NUMBERS**).

By inspection of any graph, it is apparent that all extrema (where the function is continuous on either side of the maximum or minimum point) are located at points where the slope of the function is zero. That is to say, the derivative of the function at an extremum is zero. It is not necessarily the case, however, that all points where the derivative of the function is zero correspond to extrema. Consider the function $y = x^3$, whose graph is shown below.

RELATIVE EXTREMA: extreme values of a function over some limited interval

CRITICAL POINTS: the points at which the derivative of a function is equal to zero

CRITICAL NUMBERS: the critical numbers of a function are the x-values at which the derivative of the function is equal to zero.

The derivative of a function at an extremum is zero. However, not every point at which the derivative is zero is an extremum.

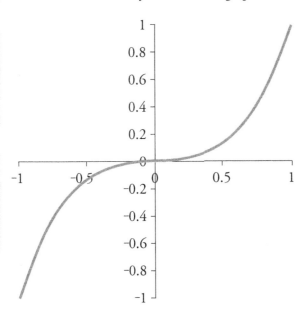

The derivative of y is $3x^2$, and the function is equal to zero only at $x = 0$. Nevertheless, the function y does not have an extremum at $x = 0$. The only cases for which critical points correspond to extrema are when the derivative of the function actually crosses the x-axis. These cases correspond to the function having a positive slope on one side of the critical point and a negative slope on the other. This is a requirement for an extremum. (Notice that, for the plot of $y = x^3$, the function has a positive slope on both sides of the critical point.)

A positive slope on the left side of a critical point and a negative slope on the right side indicate that the critical point is a maximum. If the slope is negative on the left and positive on the right, then the critical point corresponds to a minimum. If the slopes on either side are both positive or both negative, then there is no extremum at the critical point.

Extremum and the second derivative

Whether a critical point is an extremum can be determined using the second derivative f''. A critical point corresponds to a point at which the function f has zero slope. Thus, f' is zero at these points. As noted above, f has a maximum at the critical point only if f' crosses the x-axis. If f' is zero at a point but does not cross the x-axis, then that point is either a maximum or minimum of the function f', i.e., a critical number of f' ($f'' = 0$). As a result, if the critical number of f is also a critical number of f' (i.e., $f'' = 0$), the critical point does not correspond to an extremum of f. The procedure for finding extrema for $f(x)$ is thus as follows.

1. Calculate $f'(x)$.

2. Solve $f'(x) = 0$; the solutions of this equation are the critical numbers.

3. Calculate $f''(x)$.

4. Evaluate $f''(x)$ for each critical number c. If:

    A. $f''(c) = 0$, the critical point is not an extremum of f.

    B. $f''(c) > 0$, the critical point is a minimum of f.

    C. $f''(c) < 0$ the critical point is a maximum of f.

Example: Find the maxima and minima of f(x) = 2x⁴ − 4x² on the closed interval [−2, 1].

First, differentiate the function and set the result equal to zero.

$$\frac{df}{dx} = 8x^3 - 8x = 0$$

Next, solve by factoring to find the critical numbers.

$$8x(x^2 - 1) = 0$$
$$x(x - 1)(x + 1) = 0$$

The solutions for this equation, which are also the critical numbers, are $x = -1$, 0, and 1. For each critical number, it is necessary to determine whether the point corresponds to a maximum, a minimum, or neither.

$$\frac{d^2f}{dx^2} = 24x^2 - 8$$

Test each critical point by substituting into the result above.

$$f''(-1) = 24(-1)^2 - 8 = 24 - 8 = 16 \rightarrow \text{minimum}$$
$$f''(0) = 24(0)^2 - 8 = -8 \rightarrow \text{maximum}$$
$$f''(1) = 24(1)^2 - 8 = 24 - 8 = 16 \rightarrow \text{minimum}$$

The critical numbers correspond to the minima (-1, -2) and (1, -2), and to the maximum (0, 0). The endpoint of the closed interval at $x = -2$ should also be tested to determine if it constitutes an extremum, as such may not be detectable using derivatives (the minimum at the endpoint $x = 1$ was detected, however). This endpoint corresponds to (-2, 16), which is the absolute maximum. Absolute minima exist at (-1, -2) and (1, -2), and a relative maximum exists at (0, 0).

Concavity

A critical number coincides with an inflection point if the curve is concave up on one side of the value and concave down on the other.

The second derivative of a function can also be viewed in terms of concavity. The first derivative reveals whether a curve is increasing or decreasing (rising or falling) from the left to the right. In much the same way, the second derivative relates whether the curve is **concave up** (slope increasing) or **concave down** (slope decreasing). Curves that are concave up can be viewed as "collecting water"; curves that are concave down can be viewed as "dumping water."

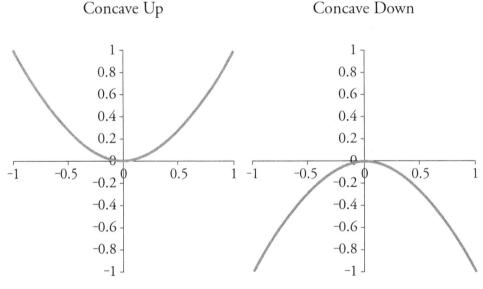

POINT OF INFLECTION:
a point at which a curve changes from being concave up to being concave down (or vice versa)

A **POINT OF INFLECTION** is a point at which a curve changes from being concave up to being concave down (or vice versa). To find these points, find the critical numbers of the first derivative of the function (that is, solve the equation for which the second derivative of the function is set equal to zero). A critical number coincides with an inflection point if the curve is concave up on one side of the value and concave down on the other. The critical number is the x coordinate of the inflection point. To get the y coordinate, plug the critical number into the original function.

Example: Find the inflection points of f(x) = 2x − tan x over the interval
$-\frac{\pi}{2} < x < \frac{\pi}{2}$.

First, calculate the second derivative of *f*.

$$f''(x) = \frac{d^2 f(x)}{dx^2} = \frac{d}{dx}\left[\frac{d}{dx}(2x - \tan x)\right]$$

$$f''(x) = \frac{d}{dx}\left[2 - \sec^2 x\right] = -2\sec x \frac{d}{dx}\sec x$$

$$f''(x) = -2\sec x\,(\sec x \tan x) = -2\sec^2 x \tan x$$

Set the second derivative equal to zero and solve.

$$f''(x) = -2\sec^2 x \tan x = 0$$

The function is zero for either sec $x = 0$ or tan $x = 0$. Only tan $x = 0$, however, has real solutions. This means that the inflection points are at $x = n\pi$, where $n = 0, 1, 2, \ldots$. Within the given interval, however, the only solution is $x = 0$. Substituting this value into the original equation yields the following:

$$f(0) = 2(0) - \tan 0 = 0 - 0 = 0$$

Thus, the inflection point for this function on the interval $-\frac{\pi}{2} < x < \frac{\pi}{2}$ is (0, 0). The plot of the function is shown below, along with the associated inflection point. As hinted earlier, the inflection point can be seen graphically as the point at which the slope changes from an increasing value to a decreasing value (or vice versa).

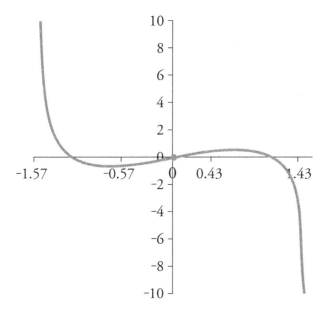

Example: Identify approximately the locations of the extrema (excluding the endpoints) and inflection points for the following graph.

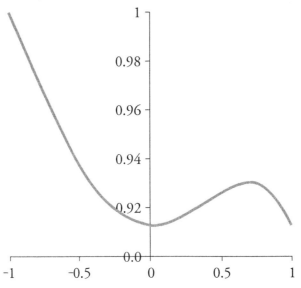

There are two obvious extrema in the graph: a minimum at about (0, .915) and a maximum at about (0.7, 0.93). These extrema are evidently relative extrema, since the function (at least apparently) has both larger and smaller values elsewhere. There is also an obvious concavity shift between the maximum and minimum. The inflection point is at about (0.35, 0.92). The extrema and inflection points are shown marked below.

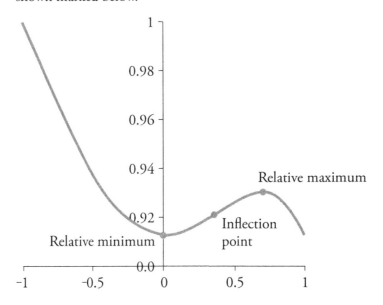

Optimization Problems

Extreme value problems, also known as **max-min problems** or **optimization problems**, entail using the first derivative to find values that either maximize or minimize some quantity, such as area, profit, or volume. The derivative is a critical tool in solving these types of problems. Follow these steps to solve an extreme value (optimization) problem.

1. Write an equation for the quantity to be maximized or minimized.

2. Use the other information in the problem to write secondary equations.

3. Use the secondary equations for substitutions, and rewrite the original equation in terms of only one variable.

4. Find the derivative of the primary equation (Step 1) and the critical numbers of this derivative.

5. Substitute these critical numbers into the primary equation. The value that produces either the largest or smallest result can be used to find the solution.

Example: A manufacturer wishes to construct an open box from a square piece of metal by cutting squares from each corner and folding up the sides. The metal is 12 feet on each side. What are the dimensions of the squares to be cut out such that the volume of the box is maximized?

First, draw a figure that represents the situation. Assume that the squares to be cut from the metal have sides of length x. Noting that the metal has sides of length 12 feet, this leaves $12 - 2x$ feet remaining on each side after the squares are cut out.

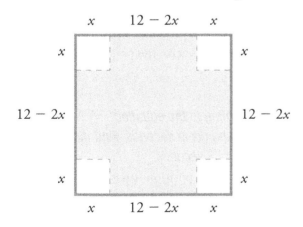

The volume $V(x)$ of the box formed when the sides are folded up is the following:
$$V(x) = x(12 - 2x)^2$$

Simplify and take the first derivative of the result.
$$V(x) = x(144 - 48x + 4x^2) = 4x^3 - 48x^2 - 144x$$
$$V'(x) = 12x^2 - 96x + 144$$

Set the first derivative to zero and solve by factoring.
$$V'(x) = 12x^2 - 96x + 144 = 0$$
$$(x - 6)(x - 2) = 0$$

The solutions are then $x = 2$ feet and $x = 6$ feet. Note that if $x = 6$ feet, the sides of the box become zero in width. This, therefore, is not a legitimate solution. Choose $x = 2$ feet as the solution that leads to the largest volume of the box.

Problems Involving Rectilinear Motion

If a particle (such as a car, bullet, or other object) is moving along a line, then the position of the particle can be expressed as a function of time.

The first derivative of the position function yields the velocity function.

The rate of change of position with respect to time is the velocity of the object; thus, the first derivative of the position function yields the velocity function for the particle. Substituting a value for time into this expression provides the instantaneous velocity of the particle at that time. The absolute value of the derivative is the speed (magnitude of the velocity) of the particle. A positive value for the velocity indicates that the particle is moving forward (that is, in the positive x direction); a negative value indicates the particle is moving backward (that is, in the negative x direction).

The second derivative of the position function (which is also the first derivative of the velocity function) yields the acceleration function.

The acceleration of the particle is the rate of change of the velocity. The second derivative of the position function (which is also the first derivative of the velocity function) yields the acceleration function. If a value for time produces a positive acceleration, the particle's velocity is increasing; if it produces a negative value, the particle's velocity is decreasing. If the acceleration is zero, the particle is moving at a constant speed.

Example: A particle moves along a line according to the equation
$s(t) = 20 + 3t - 5t^2$, where s is in meters and t is in seconds. Find the position, velocity, and acceleration of the particle at t = 2 seconds.
To find the position, simply use $t = 2$ in the given position function. Note that the initial position of the particle is $s(0) = 20$ meters.
$$s(2) = 20 + 3(2) - 5(2)^2$$
$$s(2) = 20 + 6 - 20 = 6m$$

To find the velocity of the particle, calculate the first derivative of $s(t)$ and then evaluate the result for $t = 2$ seconds.

$$s'(t) = v(t) = 3 - 10t$$
$$v(2) = 3 - 10(2) = 3 - 20 = \text{-17m/s}$$

Finally, for the acceleration of the particle, calculate the second derivative of $s(t)$ (also equal to the first derivative of $v(t)$) and evaluate for $t = 2$ seconds.

$$s''(t) = v'(t) = a(t) = \text{-10m/s}^2$$

Since the acceleration function $a(t)$ is a constant, the acceleration is always -10m/s² (the velocity of the particle decreases every second by 10 meters per second).

Related Rate Problems

Some rate problems may involve functions with different parameters that are each dependent on time. In such a case, implicit differentiation may be required. Often, related rate problems give certain rates in the description, thus eliminating the need to have specific functions of time for every parameter. Related rate problems are otherwise solved in the same manner as other similar problems.

Example: A spherical balloon is inflated such that its radius is increasing at a constant rate of 1 inch per second. What is the rate of increase of the volume of the balloon when the radius is 10 inches?

First, write the equation for the volume of a sphere in terms of the radius, r.

$$V(r) = \tfrac{4}{3}\pi r^3$$

Differentiate the function implicitly with respect to time, t, by using the chain rule.

$$\frac{dV(r)}{dt} = \tfrac{4}{3}\pi \frac{d}{dt}(r^3)$$
$$\frac{dV(r)}{dt} = \tfrac{4}{3}\pi(3r^2)\frac{dr}{dt} = 4\pi r^2\frac{dr}{dt}$$

To find the solution to the problem, use the radius value $r = 10$ inches and the rate of increase of the radius $\frac{dr}{dt} = 1\text{in/sec}$. Calculate the resulting rate of increase of the volume, $\frac{dV(r)}{dt}$.

$$\frac{dV(10)}{dt} = 4\pi(10\text{in})^2\,1\text{in/sec} = 400\pi\text{in}^3/\text{sec} \approx 1257\ \text{in}^3/\text{sec}$$

The problem is thus solved.

COMPETENCY 13
UNDERSTAND INTEGRAL CALCULUS

Riemann Sums

> **RIEMANN SUM:** the sum of the areas of a set of rectangles that is used to approximate the area under the curve of a function

The formal definition of an integral is based on the RIEMANN SUM. A Riemann sum is the sum of the areas of a set of rectangles that is used to approximate the area under the curve of a function. Given a function f defined over some closed interval $[a, b]$, the interval can be divided into a set of n arbitrary partitions, each of length Δx_i. Within the limits of each partition, some value $x = c_i$ can be chosen such that Δx_i and $f(c_i)$ define the width and height (respectively) of a rectangle. The sum of the aggregate of all the rectangles defined in this manner over the interval $[a, b]$ is the Riemann sum.

Consider, for example, the function $f(x) = x^2 + 1$ over the interval $[0, 1]$. The plot of the function is shown below.

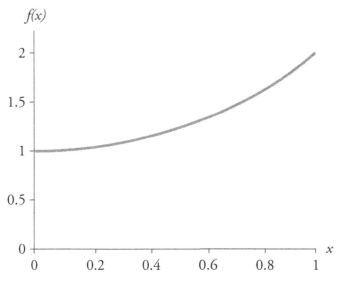

Partition the interval into segments of width 0.2 along the x-axis, and choose the function value $f(c_i)$ at the center of each interval. This function value is the height of the respective rectangle.

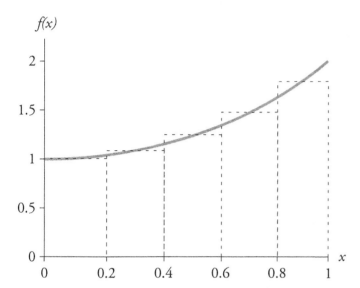

The Riemann sum for this case is expressed below.

$$\sum_{i=1}^{5} 0.2f(0.2i - 0.1) = 1.33$$

This expression is the sum of the areas of all the rectangles shown above. This is an approximation of the area under the curve of the function (and a reasonably accurate one, as well—the actual area is $\frac{4}{3}$).

Generally, the Riemann sum for arbitrary partitioning and selection of the values c_i is the following:

$$\sum_{i=1}^{n} f(c_i)\Delta x_i$$

where c_i is within the closed interval defined by the partition Δx_i.

Definite Integrals

The **DEFINITE INTEGRAL** is defined as the limit of the Riemann sum as the widths of the partitions Δx_i go to zero (and, consequently, n goes to infinity). Thus, the definite integral can be expressed mathematically as follows:

$$\int_{a}^{b} f(x)dx = \lim_{\Delta x_m \to 0} \sum_{i=1}^{n} f(c_i)\Delta x_i$$

where Δx_m is the width of the largest partition. If the partitioning of the interval is such that each partition has the same width, then the definition can be written as follows:

$$\int_{a}^{b} f(x)dx = \lim_{\Delta x \to 0} \sum_{i=1}^{n} f(c_i)\Delta x_i$$

Note that $n = \frac{b-a}{\Delta x}$ in this case.

The definite integral, therefore, is the area under the curve of $f(x)$ over the interval $[a, b]$. By taking the limit of the Riemann sum, the number of rectangles used to find the area under the curve becomes infinite and, therefore, the error in the

DEFINITE INTEGRAL: the limit of the Riemann sum as the widths of the partitions Δx_i go to zero (and, consequently, n goes to infinity)

The definite integral, is the area under the curve of f(x) over the interval [a, b].

result goes to zero (since the width of each rectangle becomes infinitesimal).

Integrals of algebraic functions

Since we have outlined the formal definition of a definite integral, it is helpful to understand the process of deriving the **integrals of algebraic functions** based on this definition. The following example illustrates this process using the Riemann sum. The process can be summarized with the following basic steps:

1. Partition the interval into n segments of equal width

2. Substitute the value of the function into the Riemann sum using the x value at the center of each subinterval

3. Write the sum in closed form

4. Take the limit of the result as n approaches infinity

Example: For f(x) = x², find the values of the Riemann sum over the interval [0, 1] using n subintervals of equal width, each evaluated at the right endpoint of each subinterval. Find the limit of the Riemann sum.

Take the interval $[0, 1]$ and subdivide it into n subintervals, each of length $\frac{1}{n}$.

$$\Delta x = \frac{1}{n}$$

The endpoints of the ith subinterval are

$$\frac{i-1}{n} \quad \frac{i}{n}$$

$$\Delta x = \frac{1}{n}$$

Let $x_i = \frac{i}{n}$ be the right endpoint. Draw a line of length $f(x_i) = \left(\frac{i}{n}\right)^2$ at the right-hand endpoint.

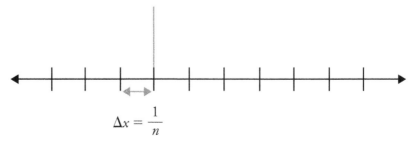

$$\Delta x = \frac{1}{n}$$

Draw a rectangle.

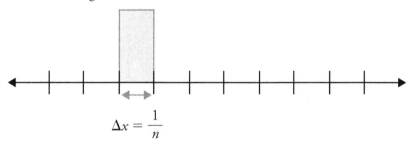

$$\Delta x = \frac{1}{n}$$

The area of this rectangle is $f(x)\Delta x$.

$$f(x)\Delta x = \left(\tfrac{i}{n}\right)^2 \tfrac{1}{n} = \tfrac{i^2}{n^3}$$

Now draw all n rectangles (drawing below not to scale).

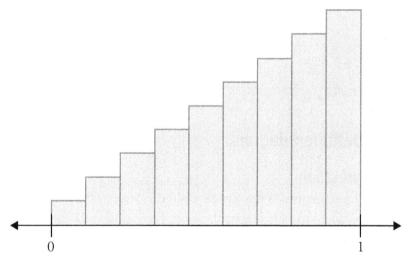

0   1

The sum of the area of these rectangles is the following.

$$\sum_{i=1}^{n} \frac{i^2}{n^3} = \frac{1}{n^3} \sum_{i=1}^{n} i^2$$

The sum can be evaluated by substituting the series formula for the sum of the squares.

$$\frac{1}{n^3}\sum_{i=1}^{n} i^2 = \frac{1}{n^3}\frac{n(n+1)(2n+1)}{6}$$

This is the Riemann sum for n subdivisions of the interval [0, 1]. Finally, to evaluate the integral, take the limit as n approaches infinity.

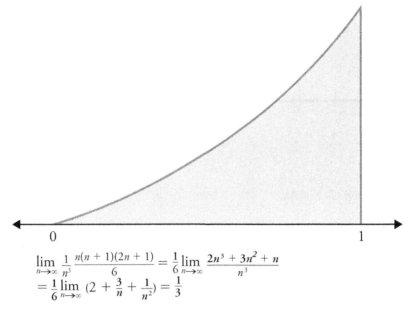

$$\lim_{n\to\infty} \frac{1}{n^3} \frac{n(n+1)(2n+1)}{6} = \frac{1}{6}\lim_{n\to\infty} \frac{2n^3 + 3n^2 + n}{n^3}$$
$$= \frac{1}{6}\lim_{n\to\infty} (2 + \frac{3}{n} + \frac{1}{n^2}) = \frac{1}{3}$$

This is the correct answer. Thus,

$$\int_0^1 x^2\,dx = \frac{1}{3}$$

Understanding Definite Integrals

Geometrical interpretation

Geometrically, the definite integral is the area between the curve of the function $f(x)$ and the x-axis over some specified interval. Since, in general, $f(x)$ is not piecewise linear, the use of rectangles, trapezoids or other polygons (in finite numbers) is not sufficient to accurately calculate this area (unless additional mathematical machinery is brought to bear). For instance, although two triangles can approximate the area under the curve of the function shown in the graph below, they do not do so exactly.

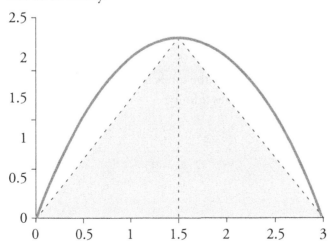

Numerical interpretation

Numerically, the definite integral is an area of a region defined by the product of a height and a width.

$$\int_a^b f(x)\,dx$$

In this case, the height is $f(x)$, and the width is dx. The height is continuously changing, so the width dx is infinitesimally small. Thus, the integral is a calculation of the product of the variable height and the constant width over the interval $[a, b]$.

Analytical interpretation

Analytically, as seen in the previous section, the definite integral is the limit of the Riemann sum as the number of subintervals (n) of a specific width (Δx) approaches infinity. Since it is apparent that larger rectangles generally provide less accuracy in the Riemann sum than do smaller rectangles, taking the limit as n approaches infinity is in fact a matter of increasing the accuracy of the result. In the limit, the Riemann sum is perfectly accurate. This concept is illustrated in the graphs below, where the increasing accuracy of the Riemann sum as n increases is apparent.

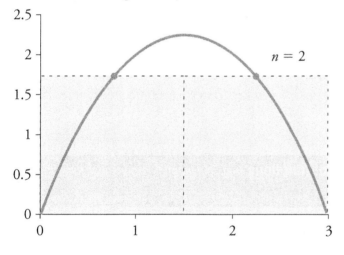

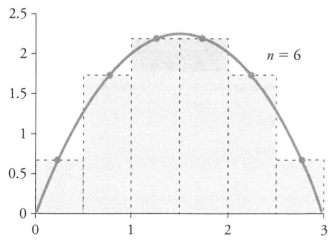

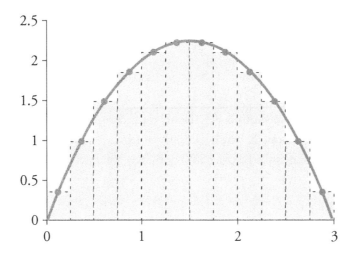

Again, notice how the accuracy of the area estimate using rectangles increases as n increases. This is the rationale behind the use of the limit for the Riemann sum, which yields the definite integral.

Thus, the limit of the Riemann sum increases the accuracy of the approximation to the area of a curve. In the limit, the accuracy is infinite. That is to say, the result is equal to the definite integral, which is the exact area under the curve on the specified interval.

$$\int_a^b f(x)\,dx = \lim_{\Delta x_n \to 0} \sum_{i=1}^n f(c_i)\Delta x_i$$

SKILL 13.2 Calculate the integrals of functions *(e.g., polynomial, exponential, logarithmic)*

Basic Integration Rules

The following summarizes some of the basic rules for integration in terms of some common functions.

BASIC INTEGRATION RULES			
Integration Involving Constants	$\int 0\,dx = C$	$\int k\,dx = kx + C$	$\int kf(x)\,dx = k\int f(x)\,dx$
Integration of Sums or Differences of Functions	$\int [f(x) + g(x)]\,dx = \int f(x)\,dx + \int g(x)\,dx$ $\int [f(x) - g(x)]\,dx = \int f(x)\,dx - \int g(x)\,dx$		
Power Rule	$\int x^n\,dx = \dfrac{x^{n+1}}{n+1} + C$ for $n \neq 1$		

Continued on next page

Trigonometric Functions	$\int \sin x \, dx = -\cos x + C$	$\int \cos x \, dx = \sin x + C$
	$\int \tan x \, dx = \ln|\cos x| + C$	$\int \cot x \, dx = \ln|\sin x| + C$
	$\int \csc x \, dx = \ln|\csc x + \cot x| + C$	$\int \sec x \, dx = \ln|\sec x + \tan x| + C$
	$\int \sec^2 x \, dx = \tan x + C$	$\int \sec x \tan x \, dx = \sec x + C$
	$\int \csc^2 x \, dx = -\cot x + C$	$\int \csc x \cot x \, dx = -\csc x + C$
Logometric Functions	$\int \ln x \, dx = x\ln x - x + C$	$\int \frac{1}{x} dx = \ln|x| + C$
Exponential Functions	$\int e^x \, dx = e^x + C$	

Example: Find $\int[\, x^3 + 5x^2 - 3\,]dx$

Separate the terms:

$\int x^3 \, dx + 5\int x^2 \, dx - \int 3 \, dx$

$\frac{1}{(3+1)}x^4 + 5\frac{1}{(2+1)}x^3 - 3x + C$

$\frac{x^4}{4} + \frac{5x^3}{3} - 3x + C$

A definite integral asks for the integration to be evaluated over a bounded region. The above example can be repeated as a definite integral as follows:

Find $\int\limits_{3}^{6}[\, x^3 + 5x^2 - 3\,]dx$

$\int[\, x^3 + 5x^2 - 3\,]dx = \frac{x^4}{4} + \frac{5x^3}{3} - 3x \Big|_{3}^{6}$

$\frac{6^4}{4} + \frac{5(6)^3}{3} - 3(6) - \left[\frac{3^4}{4} + \frac{5(3)^3}{3} - 3(3)\right] = 666 - 56.25 = 609.75$

The above rules are helpful for finding the antiderivatives of functions, but they are far from complete, since they do not permit in any obvious manner integration of composite functions or functions with arguments other than simply *x*. To this end, several helpful strategies can be applied.

Integrating by u-Substitution

If a function is expressed in terms of another function (that is, if it is a composite function), then a **change of variables** permits integration through conversion of the expression into a form similar to a form given in the rules above.

Consider a composite function $f(g(x))$ in the context of the following integral:

$\int f(g(x)) \, g'(x)dx$

An example of such a composite function might be $f(x) = (x + 1)^2$ or $f(x) = \sin(x^3)$. Assign $g(x)$ a new variable name, u. Then differentiate $g(x)$ in terms of x and rearrange the differentials.

$$u = g(x)$$
$$\frac{dg(x)}{dx} = g'(x) = \frac{du}{dx}$$
$$du = g'(x)dx$$

Use this result in the indefinite integration of the composite function:

$$\int f(g(x))g'(u)dx = \int f(u)du$$

With this simple substitution (sometimes called a u-substitution), the integral can be made to look like one of the general forms. It is sometimes necessary to experiment with different u-substitutions to find one that works (finding a u that allows complete elimination of x from the integral is not always trivial). Follow these steps for integration by substitution:

1. Select an appropriate value for u to perform the substitution.

2. Differentiate u as shown above.

3. Substitute u and du into the integral to eliminate x.

4. Evaluate the integral.

5. Substitute $g(x)$ back into the result to get the antiderivative.

When dealing with definite integrals that require u-substitution, the only difference is that the limits of integration must be modified in accordance with the choice of u. Thus:

$$\int_a^b f(g(x))g'(u)dx = \int_{g(a)}^{g(b)} f(u)du$$

Example: Evaluate the following antiderivative: $\int 2\,x[\sin(x^2) + \cos(x^2)]dx$.
First, split the integral into two parts.

$$\int 2\,x[\sin(x^2) + \cos(x^2)]dx = \int 2\,x\sin(x^2)\,dx + \int 2\,x\cos(x^2)\,dx$$

Next, select an appropriate value for u. In this case, choose $u = x^2$. Then:

$$du = 2x\,dx$$

Rewrite the integral in terms of u.

$$\int \sin(x^2)2x\,dx + \int \cos(x^2)2xdx = \int \sin u\,du + \int \cos u\,du$$

This result is in a form for which the antiderivative can be found easily.

$$\int \sin u\,du + \int \cos u\,du = -\cos u + \sin u + C$$

Substitute the definition of u back into the result to get the antiderivative in terms of x.

$$-\cos u + \sin u + C = -\cos(x^2) + \sin(x^2) + C$$

Example: Evaluate the following antiderivative: $\int e^{\sin x}\cos x dx$.

Try choosing $u = \cos x$.

$du = {}^-\sin x\, dx$

Substitute into the integral.

$\int e^{\sin x}\cos x dx = -\int \frac{ue^{\sin x}}{\sin x}\, du$

Note that there is no apparent way to eliminate x from the integral. Thus, this choice of u should be abandoned. Instead, try $u = \sin x$.

$du = \cos x dx$

Substitute into the integral, as before.

$\int e^{\sin x}\cos x dx = \int e^{u} du$

This choice of u was successful. Evaluate the antiderivative and substitute the definition of u back into the result.

$\int e^{u} du = e^{u} + C = e^{\sin x} + C$

Example: Evaluate the definite integral $\int \frac{1}{x\ln x}\, dx$ *over the interval* $[e, e^{e}]$.

Substitute using $u = \ln x$. Then, $du = \frac{1}{x}dx$.

$\int\frac{1}{x\ln x}dx = \int\frac{1}{xu}x du = \int\frac{1}{u}du$

Evaluate the integral and apply the limits of integration, which, using $u = \ln x$, lead to the interval $[\ln e, \ln e^{e}] = [1, e]$.

$\int\frac{1}{u}du = \ln u\Big|_{1}^{e}$

$\ln u\Big|_{1}^{e} = \ln e - \ln 1 = 1 - 0 = 1$

Integration by Parts

Another useful technique for evaluating complicated integrals is integration by parts. Since this method is itself complicated, it should only be used as a last resort if simpler methods of integration are not successful. Integration by parts requires two substitutions. To remember the formula for integration by parts, it is helpful to remember that it is based on the product rule of differentiation for two functions, u and v.

$\frac{d}{dx}(uv) = u\frac{dv}{dx} + v\frac{du}{dx}$

Naturally, then, integrating this result should return the product uv.

$\int\frac{d}{dx}(uv)dx = \int d(uv) = uv$

$\int[u\frac{dv}{dx} + v\frac{du}{dx}]dx = \int u dv + \int v du$

Rewrite the equation and rearrange to get the formula for integration by parts:

$uv = \int u dv + \int v du$

$\int u dv = uv - \int v du$

Thus, by identifying substitution functions for u and v, a method for integration is available. Proper selection of u and v is crucial to making this technique work. Use the following steps to perform integration by parts.

1. Choose dv as the most complicated part of the integral that can be integrated by itself.

2. Choose u as the part of the integral that remains after the dv substitution is made. Preferably, the derivative of u should be simpler than u.

3. Integrate dv to get v.

4. Differentiate u to get du.

5. Rewrite the integral in the form $\int u\,dv = uv - \int v\,du$.

6. Integrate $\int v\,du$.

7. If you cannot integrate $v\,du$, go back to the first step and try a different set of substitutions.

Example: Find the antiderivative of the following function: $\int xe^{3x}dx$.
First, choose $dv = e^{3x}dx$ and $u = x$. Calculate du and v.

$$dv = e^{3x}dx \qquad u = x$$
$$\int dv = \int e^{3x}dx \qquad du = dx$$
$$v = \frac{e^{3x}}{3}$$

Substitute these results into the formula for integration by parts:
$$\int u\,dv = \int xe^{3x}dx = uv - \int v\,du = \frac{xe^{3x}}{3} - \int \frac{e^{3x}}{3}dx$$

The substitutions fit in this case, and the integration can now be performed easily.
$$\int xe^{3x}dx = \frac{xe^{3x}}{3} - \int \frac{e^{3x}}{3}dx = \frac{xe^{3x}}{3} - \frac{e^{3x}}{9} + C$$
$$\int xe^{3x}dx = \frac{e^{3x}}{3}\left(x - \frac{1}{3}\right) + C$$

This is the correct solution to the problem.

Example: Evaluate the following indefinite integral: $\int x \cos x\, dx$
Try choosing $u = x$ and $dv = \cos x\, dx$.
$$du = dx \qquad\qquad \int dv = \int \cos x\, dx$$
$$v = \sin x$$

Substitute into the formula for integration by parts:
$$\int u\,dv = \int x\cos x\,dx = uv - \int v\,du = x\sin x - \int \sin x\,dx$$

The choices of u and dv work, so the integral can be evaluated to find the result.

$$\int x\cos x\,dx = x\sin x + \cos x + C$$

Apply integration to analyze the graphs of functions

Applications of Integrals

Area under a curve

Taking the integral of a function and evaluating it over some interval on x provides the *total area under the curve* (or, more formally, the *area bounded by the curve and the x-axis*). Thus, the areas of geometric figures can be determined when the figure can be cast as a function or set of functions in the coordinate plane. Remember, though, that regions above the x-axis have "positive" area and regions below the x-axis have "negative" area. It is necessary to account for these positive and negative values when finding the area under curves. The boundaries between positive and negative regions are delineated by the roots of the function. Follow these steps to find the total area under the curve:

1. Determine the interval or intervals on which the area under the curve is to be found. If portions of the function are negative, a given interval may need to be divided appropriately if all areas are to be considered positive.

2. Integrate the function.

3. Evaluate the integral once for each interval.

4. If any of the intervals evaluates to a negative number, reverse the sign (equivalently, take the absolute value of each integral).

5. Add the value of all the integrals to get the area under the curve.

Example: Find the area under the following function on the given interval:
$f(x) = \sin x; [0, 2\pi].$
First, find the roots of the function on the interval.

$$f(x) = \sin x = 0$$
$$x = 0, \pi$$

The function $\sin x$ is positive over $[0, \pi]$ (since $\sin\frac{\pi}{2} = 1$) and negative over $[\pi, 2\pi]$ (since $\sin\frac{3\pi}{2} = -1$). Use these intervals for the integration to find the area A under the curve.

$$A = \int_0^{2\pi} |\sin x| dx = \left|\int_0^{\pi}\sin x \, dx\right| + \left|\int_{\pi}^{2\pi}\sin x \, dx\right|$$
$$A = \left|-\cos x\big|_0^{\pi}\right| + \left|-\cos x\big|_{\pi}^{2\pi}\right| = |-\cos \pi + \cos 0| + |-\cos 2\pi + \cos \pi|$$
$$A = |1 + 1| + |-1 - 1| = 2 + 2 = 4$$

Thus, the total area under the curve of $f(x) = \sin x$ on the interval $[0, 2\pi]$ is 4 square units.

Area between two curves

Finding the *area between two curves* is similar to finding the area under one curve. The general process involves integrating the absolute value of the difference between the two functions over the interval of interest. In some instances, it is necessary to find the intervals over which the difference is positive and over which the difference is negative. For the former, the integral can simply be taken with no modifications; for the latter, however, the result of the integral must be negated. To find the points at which the difference between the functions changes from positive to negative (or vice versa), simply set the functions equal to each other and solve. Take the absolute value of each portion of the integral (that is, each integral over a portion of the interval) and add all the parts. This yields the total area between the curves.

Example: Find the area of the regions bounded by the two functions on the indicated interval: $f(x) = x + 2$ and $g(x) = x^2$ on [−2, 3].

The integral of interest is the following:

$$\int_{-2}^{3} |f(x) - g(x)| dx$$

To eliminate the need to use the absolute value notation inside the integral, find the values for which $f(x) = g(x)$.

$$f(x) = x + 2 = g(x) = x^2$$
$$x^2 - x - 2 = 0 = (x - 2)(x + 1)$$

The functions are then equal at $x = -1$ and $x = 2$. Perform the integration over the intervals defined by these values.

$$\int_{-2}^{3} |f(x) - g(x)| dx = \left| \int_{-2}^{-1} f(x) - g(x) \, dx \right| + \left| \int_{-1}^{2} f(x) - g(x) \, dx \right| + \left| \int_{2}^{3} f(x) - g(x) \, dx \right|$$

The antiderivative of $f(x) - g(x)$ is the following (ignoring the constant of integration).

$$\int [f(x) - g(x)] dx = \int (x + 2 - x^2) dx = \frac{x^2}{2} + 2x - \frac{x^3}{3}$$

Evaluate over the intervals above.

$$\int_{-2}^{3} |f(x) - g(x)| dx = \left| \left[\frac{x^2}{2} + 2x - \frac{x^3}{3} \right]_{-2}^{-1} \right| + \left| \left[\frac{x^2}{2} + 2x - \frac{x^3}{3} \right]_{-1}^{2} \right| + \left| \left[\frac{x^2}{2} + 2x - \frac{x^3}{3} \right]_{2}^{3} \right|$$

$$\left| \left[\frac{x^2}{2} + 2x - \frac{x^3}{3} \right]_{-2}^{-1} \right| = \left| (\tfrac{1}{2} - 2 + \tfrac{1}{3}) - (\tfrac{4}{2} - 4 + \tfrac{8}{3}) \right| = \left| -\tfrac{7}{6} - \tfrac{2}{3} \right| = \tfrac{11}{6}$$

$$\left| \left[\frac{x^2}{2} + 2x - \frac{x^3}{3} \right]_{-1}^{2} \right| = \left| (\tfrac{4}{2} + 4 - \tfrac{8}{3}) - (\tfrac{1}{2} - 2 + \tfrac{1}{3}) \right| = \left| \tfrac{10}{3} + \tfrac{7}{6} \right| = \tfrac{27}{6}$$

$$\left| \left[\frac{x^2}{2} + 2x - \frac{x^3}{3} \right]_{2}^{3} \right| = \left| (\tfrac{9}{2} + 6 - \tfrac{27}{3}) - (\tfrac{4}{2} + 4 - \tfrac{8}{3}) \right| = \left| \tfrac{3}{2} - \tfrac{10}{3} \right| = \tfrac{11}{6}$$

The sum of these individual parts is $\frac{49}{6}$.

Volumes of solids of revolution

An area bounded by a curve (or curves) and revolved about a line is called a SOLID OF REVOLUTION. To find the volume of such a solid, the disc method (called the washer method if the solid has an empty interior of some form) works in most instances. Imagine slicing through the solid perpendicular to the line of revolution. The cross section should resemble either a disc or a washer. The washer method involves finding the sum of the volumes of all "washers" that compose the solid, using the following general formula:

$$V = \pi(r_1^2 - r_2^2)t$$

where V is the volume of the washer, r_1 and r_2 are the interior and exterior radii, and t is the thickness of the washer.

SOLID OF REVOLUTION:
an area bounded by a curve (or curves) and revolved about a line

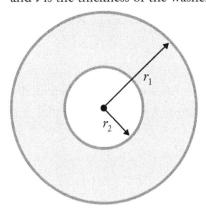

Depending on the situation, the radius is the distance from the line of revolution to the curve; or if there are two curves involved, the radius is the difference between the two functions. The thickness is dx if the line of revolution is parallel to the x-axis and dy if the line of revolution is parallel to the y-axis. The integral is then the following, where dV is the differential volume of a washer.

$$\int dV = \int \pi(r_1^2 - r_2^2)dt$$
$$V = \pi\int(r_1^2 - r_2^2)dt$$

It is assumed here that r_1 is the outer radius and r_2 is the inner radius. For the disc method, where only one radius is needed, $r_2 = 0$.

Example: Find the volume of the solid of revolution made by revolving $f(x) = 9 - x^2$ about the x-axis on the interval [0, 3].

This problem can be solved using the disc method. First, note that the radius is $9 - x^2$ and the thickness of the disc is dx. Write the appropriate integral as follows.

$$V = \pi\int_0^3 (9 - x^2)^2 dx$$

Next, expand the radius term and evaluate the integral.

$$V = \pi\int_0^3 (81 - 18x^2 + x^4)dx$$
$$V = \pi[81x - \frac{18}{3}x^3 + \frac{1}{5}x^5]_0^3$$
$$V = \pi[81(3) - \frac{18}{3}(3)^3 + \frac{1}{5}(3)^5]$$
$$V = \pi[243 - 162 + 48.6] = 129.6\pi \approx 406.9$$

The volume is thus approximately 406.9 cubic units.

Arc Length

Finding the arc length of a curve is another useful application of integration. The ARC LENGTH is the distance traversed by a curve over a given interval. Geometrically, the distance d between two points (x_1, y_1) and (x_2, y_2) is given by the following formula.

> **ARC LENGTH:** the distance traversed by a curve over a given interval

$$d = \sqrt{(x_2 - x_1)^2 + (y_2 - y_1)^2}$$

If the points are only an infinitesimal distance apart (ds, which is the differential arc length), then the above expression can be written as follows in differential form:

$$ds = \sqrt{dx^2 + dy^2}$$

Factor out the dx term:

$$ds = \sqrt{1 + (\frac{dy}{dx})^2} \quad dx$$

But $\frac{dy}{dx}$ is simply the derivative of a function $y(x)$ (which can be expressed as $f(x)$ instead). Thus, the integral of the above expression over the interval $[a, b]$ yields the formula for the arc length.

$$\int ds = = \int_a^b \sqrt{1 + [f'(x)]^2}dx$$

Example: Find the distance traversed by the function f(x) = ln (cos x) on the interval $[-\frac{\pi}{4}, \frac{\pi}{4}]$.

Use the formula for arc length s, applying trigonometric identities as appropriate.

$$s = \int \sqrt{1 + [\frac{d}{dx}\ln(\cos x)]^2} = \int \sqrt{1 + [\frac{\sin x}{\cos x}]^2}dx$$
$$s = \int \sqrt{1 + [\tan x]^2}dx = \int \sqrt{1 + \tan^2 x}\,dx = \int \sqrt{\sec^2 x}\,dx$$
$$s = \int \sec x\,dx$$

Evaluate the integral over the limits of integration.

$$s = \int_{-\pi/4}^{\pi/4} \sec x\,dx = \ln(\sec x + \tan x)|_{-\pi/4}^{\pi/4}$$
$$s = \ln(\sec \frac{\pi}{4} + \tan \frac{\pi}{4}) - \ln(\sec [-\frac{\pi}{4}] + \tan [\frac{\pi}{4}])$$
$$s = \ln(\sqrt{2} + 1) - \ln(\sqrt{2} - 1) \approx 1.763$$

The result is approximately 1.763 units.

Linear motion

Integral calculus, in addition to differential calculus, is a powerful tool for analysis of problems involving linear motion. The derivative of the position (or displacement) function is the velocity function, and the derivative of a velocity function is the acceleration function. As a result, the antiderivative of an acceleration function is a velocity function, and the antiderivative of a velocity function is a position (or displacement) function. Solving word problems of this type involve converting the information given into an appropriate integral expression. To find the constant of integration, use the conditions provided in the problem (such as an initial displacement, velocity, or acceleration).

The antiderivative of an acceleration function is a velocity function, and the antiderivative of a velocity function is a position (or displacement) function.

Example: A particle moves along the x-axis with acceleration $a(t) = 3t - 1 \frac{cm}{sec^2}$. At time $t = 4$ seconds, the particle is moving to the left at 3 cm per second. Find the velocity of the particle at time $t = 2$ seconds.

Evaluate the antiderivative of the acceleration function $a(t)$ to get the velocity function $v(t)$ along with the unknown constant of integration C.

$$v(t) = \int a(t) dt = \int (3t - 1) dt$$
$$v(t) = \frac{3t^2}{2} - t + C$$

Use the condition that at time $t = 4$ seconds, the particle has a velocity of -3 cm/sec.

$$v(4) = \frac{3(4)^2}{2} - 4 + C = -3$$
$$\frac{48}{2} - 4 + C = -3$$
$$C = -3 + 4 - 24 = -23 \frac{cm}{sec}$$

Now evaluate $v(t)$ at time $t = 2$ seconds to get the solution to the problem.

$$v(t) = \frac{3t^2}{2} - t - 23 \frac{cm}{sec}$$
$$v(2) = \frac{3(2)^2}{2} - 2 - 23 \frac{cm}{sec} = 6 - 25 \frac{cm}{sec} = -19 \frac{cm}{sec}$$

Example: Find the displacement function of a particle whose acceleration is described by the equation $a(t) = 3\sin 2t$. Assume that the particle is initially motionless at the origin.

Find the antiderivative of the acceleration function $a(t)$ to get the velocity function $v(t)$.

$$v(t) = \int 3 \sin 2t \, dt = -\frac{3}{2}\cos 2t + C$$

Note that the initial velocity is zero; thus:

$$v(0) = 0 = -\frac{3}{2} \cos 2(0) + C = -\frac{3}{2} + C$$
$$C = \frac{3}{2}$$
$$v(t) = \frac{3}{2} (1 - \cos 2t)$$

Find the antiderivative of the velocity function to get the displacement function $s(t)$.

$$s(t) = -\int \frac{3}{2}(1 - \cos 2t)dt = -\frac{3}{2}(t - \frac{1}{2}\sin 2t) + C'$$

The initial position is at the origin, so C' can be found.

$$s(0) = 0 = -\frac{3}{2}(0 - \frac{1}{2}\sin 2(0)) + C'$$
$$s(0) = 0 = -\frac{3}{2}(0 - 0) + C'$$
$$C' = 0$$
$$s(t) = \frac{3}{2}(t - \frac{1}{2}\sin 2t)$$

This last result is the solution to the problem. A necessary (but not sufficient) check of the answer is to differentiate $s(t)$ twice and compare with $a(t)$.

$$s'(t) = \frac{3}{2}(1 - \cos 2t)$$
$$s''(t) = 3 \sin 2t = a(t)$$

SKILL 13.4 Apply integration to solve real-world problems

In addition to problems involving area and volume calculations and linear motion (*see Skill 13.3*), integration is useful in the realm of physics for calculating other parameters as well. Work is defined as the product of the force acting on an object and the distance that the object moves. If the force is constant, this product is easily computable; if the force is variable, however, the work W must be calculated using the following integral, where $F(x)$ is the force and the object is moved from a to b.

$$W = \int_a^b F(x)dx$$

Example: An object of mass 4 kilograms is initially at rest. How much work is required to accelerate the object (at a constant rate) to 4 meters per second by the time the object reaches 4 meters from its initial position?

The force on a mass is defined as the product of the mass and the acceleration. In this case, the acceleration and the mass are both constant. Use the integral for calculating work as follows.

$$W = \int_0^4 ma\ dx = m\int_0^4 a\ dx$$

Note, however, that the result is the mass multiplied by the velocity function.

$$\int a\,dx = v(x) = ax + C$$

Solve for a and C using the fact that the initial velocity is zero and the velocity at

4 meters is 4 meters per second.

$$v(0) = 0 = a(0) + C = C$$
$$C = 0$$
$$v(4) = 4 = a(4)$$
$$a = 1\,\frac{\text{meter}}{\text{sec}^2}$$
$$v(x) = x$$

Now calculate the result by evaluating the integral and substituting for m and a.

$$W = m \int_0^4 a\, dx = (4\text{kg})(1\,\tfrac{\text{meter}}{\text{sec}^2})[x]_0^4 \text{ meter}$$
$$W = 16\text{kg}\,\frac{\text{m}^2}{\text{sec}^2}$$

This result can also be written as 16 Newtons (or 16 N).

DOMAIN V
STATISTICS, PROBABILITY, AND DISCRETE MATHEMATICS

COMPETENCY 14
UNDERSTAND PRINCIPLES AND TECHNIQUES OF STATISTICS

SKILL **Use appropriate formats for organizing and displaying data**
14.1

Displaying Statistical Data

The data obtained from sampling may be categorical (e.g., yes or no responses) or numerical. In both cases, results are displayed using a variety of graphical techniques. Geographical data is often displayed superimposed on maps.

Histograms

The most common form of graphical display used for numerical data obtained from random sampling is the histogram. A trend line can be superimposed on a histogram to observe the general shape of the distribution. In some cases, the trend line may also be fitted to a probability density function.

If the data set is large, it may be expressed in compact form as a FREQUENCY DISTRIBUTION. The number of occurrences of each data point is the FREQUENCY of that value. The RELATIVE FREQUENCY is defined as the frequency divided by the total number of data points. Since the sum of the frequencies equals the number of data points, the relative frequencies add up to 1. The relative frequency of a data point, therefore, represents the probability of occurrence of that value. Thus, a distribution consisting of relative frequencies is known as a PROBABILITY DISTRIBUTION. The CUMULATIVE FREQUENCY of a data point is the sum of the frequencies from the beginning up to that point.

A histogram is used to display a discrete frequency distribution graphically. It shows the counts of data in different ranges, the center of the data set, the spread of the data, and whether there are any outliers. It also shows whether the data has a single mode or more than one.

FREQUENCY DISTRIBUTION: divides a set of data into classes or intervals

FREQUENCY: the number of occurrences of a given value in a data set

RELATIVE FREQUENCY: the frequency divided by the total number of data points

PROBABILITY DISTRIBUTION: a distribution consisting of relative frequencies

CUMULATIVE FREQUENCY: the sum of the frequencies from the beginning up to a given point

A histogram is used to display a discrete frequency distribution graphically.

Example: The table below shows the summary of some test results, where people scored a total number of points ranging from 0 to 45. The total range of points has been divided into bins 0–5, 6–10, 11–15, and so on. The frequency for the first bin (labeled 5) is the number of people who scored points ranging from 0 to 5; the frequency for the second bin (labeled 10) is the number of people who scored points ranging from 6 to 10; and so on.

Points	Frequency	Cumulative Frequency	Relative Frequency
5	1	1	0.009
10	4	5	0.035
15	12	17	0.105
20	22	39	0.193
25	30	69	0.263
30	25	94	0.219
35	13	107	0.114
40	6	113	0.053
45	1	114	0.009

The histogram of the probability distribution is given below:

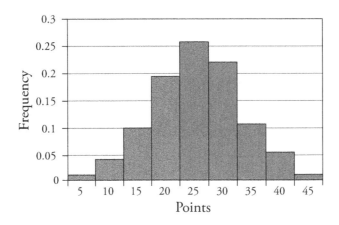

The probability distribution can be used to calculate the probability of a particular test score occurring in a certain range. For instance, the probability of a test score lying between 15 and 30 is given by the sum of the areas (assuming width of 1) of the three middle bins in the histogram above:

$$0.193 + 0.263 + 0.219 = 0.675$$

Bar graphs

Bar graphs are used to compare various quantities using bars of different lengths.

Example: A class had the following grades: 4 As, 9 Bs, 8 Cs, 1 D, 3 Fs.
Graph these on a bar graph.

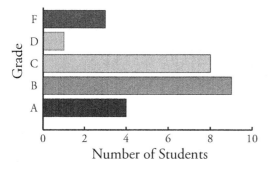

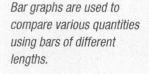

Bar graphs are used to compare various quantities using bars of different lengths.

Line graphs

Line graphs are used to show trends, often over a period of time.

Example: Graph the following information using a line graph.

Line graphs are used to show trends, often over a period of time.

THE NUMBER OF NATIONAL MERIT FINALISTS/SCHOOL YEAR						
School	90-91	91-92	92-93	93-94	94-95	95-96
Central	3	5	1	4	6	8
Wilson	4	2	3	2	3	2

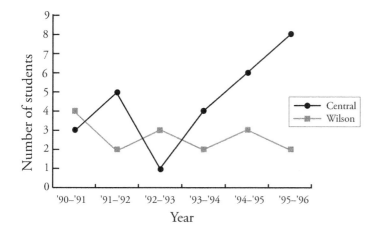

Circle graphs (pie charts)

Circle graphs or **pie charts** show the relationships of various parts of a data set to each other and to the whole. Each part is shown as a percentage of the total and occupies a proportional sector of the circular area. To make a circle graph, total all the information that is to be included on the graph. Determine the central angle to be used for each sector of the graph using the following formula:

$$\frac{\text{information}}{\text{total information}} \times 360° = \text{degrees in central} \angle$$

Lay out the central angles according to these sizes, label each section and include its percentage.

Example: Graph this information on a circle graph:

MONTHLY EXPENSES	
Rent	$400
Food	$150
Utilities	$75
Clothes	$75
Church	$100
Misc.	$200

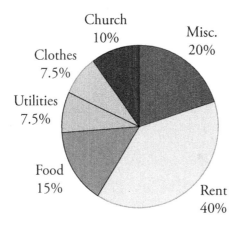

Scatter plots

Scatter plots compare two characteristics of the same group of things or people and usually consist of a large body of data. They show how much one variable is affected by another. The relationship between the two variables is their

CORRELATION. The closer the data points come to making a straight line when plotted, the closer the correlation.

Choosing a Regression Model

It is often helpful to use regression to construct a more general trend or distribution based on sample data. To select an appropriate model for the regression, a representative set of data must be examined. It is often helpful, in this case, to plot the data and review it visually on a graph. In this manner, it is relatively simple to select a general class of functions (linear, quadratic, exponential, etc.) that might be used to model the data. There are two basic aspects of regression: selection of an appropriate curve that best fits the data and quantification of the "goodness of fit" of that curve. For instance, if a line can be constructed that passes through every data point of a distribution, then that line is a perfect fit to the data (and, obviously, linear regression is an appropriate choice for the model). If the distribution of data points seems to bear no particular resemblance to the line, then linear regression is probably not a wise choice, and a quantification of the goodness of fit should reflect this fact.

There are two basic aspects of regression: selection of an appropriate curve that best fits the data and quantification of the "goodness of fit" of that curve.

The following discussion summarizes least squares linear regression analysis. The same principles can be applied to other forms of regression (such as quadratic or exponential).

The Method of Least Squares

Given a set of data, a curve approximation can be fitted to the data by using the **METHOD OF LEAST SQUARES**. The best-fit curve, defined by the function $f(x)$, is assumed to approximate a set of data with coordinates (x_i, y_i) by minimizing the sum of squared differences between the curve and the data. Mathematically, the sum of these squared differences (errors) can be written as follows for a data set with n points.

$$S = \sum_{i=1}^{n} [f(x_i) - y_i]^2$$

Thus, the best-fit curve approximation to a set of data (x_i, y_i) is $f(x)$ such that S is minimized.

Shown below is a set of data and a linear function that approximates it. The vertical distances between the data points and the line are the errors that are squared and summed to find S.

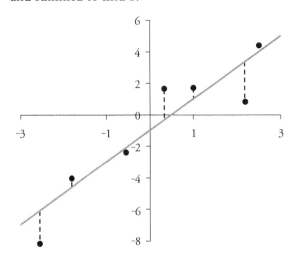

Linear Least Squares Regression

If the curve $f(x)$ that is used to approximate a set of data by minimizing the sum of squared errors (or RESIDUALS), S, is linear, then $f(x)$ is called a least squares regression line. The process of determining $f(x)$ is called LINEAR LEAST SQUARES REGRESSION. In this case, $f(x)$ has the following form:

$$f(x) = ax + b$$

Given a set of data $\{(x_1, y_1), (x_2, y_2), (x_3, y_3), \ldots (x_n, y_n)\}$, the sum S for linear regression is the following.

$$S = \sum_{i=1}^{n} [ax_i + b - y_i]^2$$

To find $f(x)$, it is necessary to find a and b. This can be done by minimizing S. Since S is a function of both a and b, S must be minimized through the use of partial derivatives. (A partial derivative is exactly the same as a full derivative, except that all variables other than the one being differentiated are treated as constants. Partial derivatives often use the symbol ∂ in place of d.) Therefore, find the partial derivative with respect to a and the partial derivative with respect to b.

$$\frac{\partial S}{\partial a} = \frac{\partial}{\partial a} \sum_{i=1}^{n} [ax_i + b - y_i]^2 \quad \frac{\partial S}{\partial b} = \frac{\partial}{\partial b} \sum_{i=1}^{n} [ax_i + b - y_i]^2$$

RESIDUALS: the difference between an observed data value and the value predicted by a regression model

LINEAR LEAST SQUARES REGRESSION: the difference between an observed data value and the value predicted by a regression model

$$\frac{\partial S}{\partial a} = \sum_{i=1}^{n} 2a\,[ax_i + b - y_i] \qquad \frac{\partial S}{\partial b} = \sum_{i=1}^{n} 2[ax_i + b - y_i]$$

Set these equal to zero. This yields a system of equations that can be solved to find a and b. Although the algebra is somewhat involved, it is not conceptually difficult. The results are given below.

$$a = \frac{n\sum_{i=1}^{n} x_i y_i - \sum_{i=1}^{n} x_i \sum_{i=1}^{n} y_i}{n\sum_{i=1}^{n} x_i^2 - [\sum_{i=1}^{n} x_i]^2}$$

Note that the average x value for the data (which is the sum of all x values divided by n) and the average y value for the data (which is the sum of all y values divided by n) can be used to simplify the expression. The average x value is defined as $\bar{x}$, and the average y value is defined as $\bar{y}$.

$$a = \frac{\sum_{i=1}^{n} x_i y_i - n\bar{x}\bar{y}}{\sum_{i=1}^{n} x_i^2 - n\bar{x}^2}$$

Since the expression for b is complicated, it suffices to write the above expression for b in terms of a.

$$b = \frac{1}{n}\left(\sum_{i=1}^{n} y_i - a\sum_{i=1}^{n} x_i\right)$$
$$b = \bar{y} - a\bar{x}$$

Thus, given a set of data, the linear least squares regression line can be found by calculating a and b as shown above.

> *A partial derivative is exactly the same as a full derivative, except that all variables other than the one being differentiated are treated as constants. Partial derivatives often use the symbol ∂ in place of d.*

Correlation coefficient

The **CORRELATION COEFFICIENT**, r, can be used as a measure of the quality of $f(x)$ as a fit to the data set. The value of r ranges from zero (for a poor fit) to one (for a good fit). The correlation coefficient formula is given below.

$$r^2 = \frac{[\sum_{i=1}^{n} x_i y_i - \frac{1}{n}\sum_{i=1}^{n} x_i \sum_{i=1}^{n} y_i]^2}{[\sum_{i=1}^{n} x_i^2 - \frac{1}{n}(\sum_{i=1}^{n} x_i)^2][\sum_{i=1}^{n} y_i^2 - \frac{1}{n}(\sum_{i=1}^{n} y_i)^2]}$$

$$r^2 = \frac{(\sum_{i=1}^{n} x_i y_i - n\bar{x}\bar{y})^2}{(\sum_{i=1}^{n} x_i^2 - n\bar{x}^2)(\sum_{i=1}^{n} y_i^2 - n\bar{y}^2)}$$

> **CORRELATION COEFFICIENT:** a value between 0 and 1 that measures how well a particular model "fits" a particular set of data

Example: A company has collected data comparing the ages of its employees to their respective incomes (in thousands of dollars). Find the line that best fits the data (using a least squares approach). Also calculate the correlation coefficient for the fit. The data is given below in the form of (age, income).

$$\{(35, 42), (27, 23), (54, 43), (58, 64), (39, 51), (31, 40)\}$$

The data are plotted in the graph below.

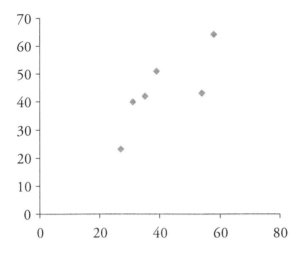

Note that there are six pieces of data. It is helpful to first calculate the following sums:

$$\sum_{i=1}^{6} x_i = 35 + 27 + 54 + 58 + 39 + 31 = 244$$

$$\sum_{i=1}^{6} y_i = 42 + 23 + 43 + 64 + 51 + 40 = 263$$

$$\sum_{i=1}^{6} x_i y_i = 35(42) + 27(23) + 54(43) + 58(64) + 39(51) + 31(40) = 11354$$

$$\sum_{i=1}^{6} x_i^2 = 35^2 + 27^2 + 54^2 + 58^2 + 39^2 + 31^2 = 10716$$

$$\sum_{i=1}^{6} y_i^2 = 42^2 + 23^2 + 43^2 + 64^2 + 51^2 + 40^2 = 12439$$

Based on these values, the average x and y values are given below.

$$\bar{x} = \frac{244}{6} \approx 40.67$$

$$\bar{y} = \frac{263}{6} \approx 43.83$$

To find the equation of the least squares regression line, calculate the values of a and b.

$$a = \frac{\sum_{i=1}^{n} x_i y_i - n\bar{x}\bar{y}}{\sum_{i=1}^{n} x_i^2 - n\bar{x}^2} = \frac{11354 - 6\,(40.67)\,(43.83)}{10716 - 6\,(40.67)^2} \approx 0.832$$

$$b = \bar{y} - a\bar{x} = 43.83 - 0.832\,(40.67) = 9.993$$

Thus, the equation of the least squares regression line is

$$f(x) = 0.832x + 9.993$$

This result can be displayed on the data graph to ensure that there are no egregious errors in the result.

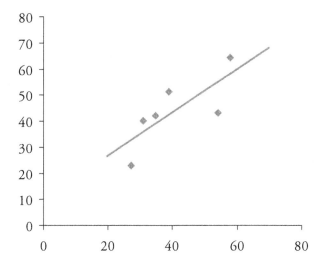

The regression line in the graph above appears to do a good job of approximating the trend of the data. To quantify how well the line fits the data, calculate the correlation coefficient using the formula given above.

$$r^2 = \frac{(11354 - 6\,(40.67)\,(43.83))^2}{(10716 - 6\,(40.67)^2)(12439 - 6\,(43.83)^2)}$$

$$r^2 = \frac{(658.603)^2}{(791.707)(912.587)} = 0.600$$

$$r = 0.775$$

Thus, the fit to the data is reasonably good.

Calculators and Regression

Modern handheld calculators, especially graphing calculators, often have built-in tools for handling multiple types of regression. After entering the data (in the form of lists, for instance), the calculator's regression functions can be employed. It is usually best to test several different regressions (if no particular model is obviously appropriate) and to compare the associated residual or correlation coefficient values for each function. For instance, it may be best to test a data set using both linear and exponential models. By comparing the correlation coefficient, the better-fitting curve can be determined. In this case, the closer the value is to unity, the better the fit. Of course, it is necessary to know the features of a particular calculator, as well as its limitations, to accurately employ regression functions.

The Exponential Distribution

The **exponential distribution** is for continuous random variables and has the following form.

$$f(x) = \lambda e^{-\lambda x}$$

Here, $x \geq 0$. The parameter λ is called the **rate parameter**. For instance, the exponential distribution is often applied to failure rates. If a certain device has a failure rate of λ failures per hour, then the probability that a device has failed at time T hours is

$$P(T) = \lambda \int_0^T e^{-\lambda t}\, dt = -\lambda \frac{1}{\lambda} e^{-\lambda t}\Big|_0^T = -[e^{-\lambda t} - e^0] = 1 - e^{-\lambda t}$$

Example: Testing has revealed that a newly designed widget has a failure rate of 1 per 5,000 hours of use. What is the probability that a particular part will be operational after a year of continual use?

Use the formula given above for the exponential distribution.
$$P(1 \text{ year}) = 1 - e^{-\lambda(1 \text{ year})}$$

Write λ in terms of failures per year.
$$\lambda = \frac{1 \text{ failure}}{5,000 \text{ hours}} \left(\frac{24 \text{ hours}}{1 \text{ day}}\right)\left(\frac{365 \text{ days}}{1 \text{ year}}\right) = 1.752 \frac{\text{failures}}{\text{year}}$$

Then
$$P(1 \text{ year}) = 1 - e^{-1.752(1)} = 1 - 0.173 = 0.827$$

Thus, there is an 82.7% probability that the device will be operational after one year of continual use.

SKILL 14.3 **Analyze the use of measures of central tendency and variability**

Statistics for Discrete Distributions

Mean, Median, and Mode

MEAN: for discrete data, the value obtained by adding all the data values and then dividing by the total number of values

The mean, median, and mode are measures of central tendency (i.e., the average or typical value) in a data set. They can be defined both for discrete and continuous data sets. For discrete data, the **MEAN** is the average of the data items, or the value obtained by adding all the data values and dividing by the total number of data items. For a data set of n items with data values $x_1, x_2, x_3, \ldots x_n$, the mean is given by

$$\bar{x} = \frac{x_1 + x_2 + x_3 + \ldots + x_n}{n}$$

WEIGHTED AVERAGE: the mean of a set of data in which each individual datum has an associated probability or weight

The **WEIGHTED AVERAGE** is the mean of a set of data in which each individual datum has an associated probability or weight. For data values $x_1, x_2, x_3, \ldots x_n$, with associated probabilities (or weights) $p(x_1), p(x_2), p(x_3), \ldots p(x_n)$, the mean value is

$$\bar{x} = x_1 p(x_1) + x_2 p(x_2) + x_3 p(x_3) + \ldots + x_n p(x_n) = \sum_i x_i p(x_i)$$

This is the most general definition of the mean.

The MEDIAN is found by putting the data in order from smallest to largest and selecting the value in the middle (or the average of the two values in the middle if the number of data items is even). The MODE is the most frequently occurring datum. There can be more than one mode in a data set.

> **MEDIAN:** found by putting the data in order from smallest to largest and selecting the value in the middle

> **MODE:** the most frequently occurring datum in a data set

Example: Find the mean, median, and mode of the test scores listed below:

85	77	65
92	90	54
88	85	70
75	80	69
85	88	60
72	74	95

Mean: Sum of all scores ÷ number of scores = 78

Median: Put the numbers in order from smallest to largest. Pick the middle number.

54 60 65 69 70 72 74 75 | 77 80 | 85 85 85 88 88 90 92 95

Two values are in the middle.

Therefore, the median is average of the two numbers in the middle, or 78.5. The mode is the most frequent number, or 85.

Range, variance, and standard deviation

The RANGE is a measure of variability that is calculated by subtracting the smallest value from the largest value in a set of discrete data.

> **RANGE:** found by subtracting the smallest data value from the largest

The VARIANCE and STANDARD DEVIATION are measures of the "spread" of data around the mean. It is noteworthy that descriptive statistics involving such parameters as variance and standard deviation can be applied to a set of data that spans the entire population (population parameters, typically represented using Greek symbols) or to a set of data that only constitutes a portion of the population (sample statistics, typically represented by Latin letters).

> **VARIANCE:** a measure of the "spread" of data about the mean

When making informal inferences about a population based on sample statistics, it is important to ensure that the sample is collected in a manner that adequately represents the population (see the discussion of surveys and sampling below). The confidence in an inference based on sample statistics can increase when, for instance, the size of the sample space approaches that of the population, or when the sampling approach is designed to take into account known aspects of

> **STANDARD DEVIATION:** also a measure of the "spread" of data about the mean; the standard deviation is the square root of the variance

the population. Insofar as the sample represents the population, sample statistics approach (and can be equal to, in some cases) population parameters.

The mean of a set of data, whether for a population (μ) or for a sample ($\bar{x}$), uses the formula discussed above and can be represented as either a set of individual data or as a set of data with associated frequencies. The variance and standard deviation for the population differ slightly from those of a sample. The population variance (σ^2) and the population standard deviation (σ) are as follows.

$$\sigma^2 = \frac{1}{n} \Sigma (x_i - \mu)^2$$
$$\sigma = \sqrt{\sigma^2}$$

For a sample, the data does not include the entire population. As a result, it should be expected that the sample data might not be perfectly representative of the population. To account for this shortcoming in the sample variance (s^2) and standard deviation (s), the sum of the squared differences between the data and the mean is divided by ($n - 1$) instead of just n. This increases the variance and standard deviation slightly, which in turn increases slightly the data spread to account for the possibility that the sample may not accurately represent the population.

$$s^2 = \frac{1}{n - 1} \Sigma (x_i - \bar{x})^2$$
$$s = \sqrt{s^2}$$

Example: Calculate the range, variance, and standard deviation for the following data set: {3, 3, 5, 7, 8, 8, 8, 10, 12, 21}.

The range is simply the largest data value minus the smallest. In this case, the range is $21 - 3 = 18$.

To calculate the variance and standard deviation, first calculate the mean. If it is not stated whether a data set constitutes a population or sample, assume it is a population. (In this case, if the data were labeled as "ages of the 10 people in a room," this would be a population. If the data were labeled "ages of males at a crowded circus event," the data would be a sample.)

$$\mu = \frac{3 + 3 + 5 + 7 + 8 + 8 + 8 + 10 + 12 + 21}{10} = 8.5$$

Use this mean to calculate the variance.

$$\sigma^2 = \frac{1}{10} \Sigma (x_i - 8.5)^2$$
$$\sigma^2 = \frac{1}{10} \{(3 - 8.5)^2 + (3 - 8.5)^2 + (5 - 8.5)^2 + \ldots + (21 - 8.5)^2\}$$
$$\sigma^2 = \frac{246.5}{10} = 24.65$$

The standard deviation is

$$\sigma = \sqrt{\sigma^2} = \sqrt{24.65} \approx 4.96$$

Statistics for Continuous Distributions

The *range* for a continuous data distribution is the same as that for a discrete distribution: the largest value minus the smallest value. Calculation of the mean, variance, and standard deviation are similar, but slightly different. Since a continuous distribution does not permit a simple summation, integrals must be used. The mean μ of a distribution function $f(x)$ is expressed below.

$$\mu = \int_{-\infty}^{\infty} xf(x)\,dx$$

The variance σ^2 over also has an integral form, and has a form similar to that of a discrete distribution.

$$\sigma^2 = \int_{-\infty}^{\infty} (x - \mu)^2\, f(x)\,dx$$

The standard deviation σ is simply

$$\sigma = \sqrt{\sigma^2}$$

Example: Calculate the standard deviation of a data distribution function f(x), where

$$f(x) = \begin{cases} 0 & x < 1 \\ -2x^2 + 2 & -1 \leq x \leq 1 \\ 0 & x > 1 \end{cases}$$

First calculate the mean of the function. Since the function is zero except between 1 and -1, the integral can likewise be evaluated from -1 to 1.

$$\mu = \int_{-1}^{1} (-2x^2 + 2)x\,dx$$

$$\mu = -2\int_{-1}^{1} (x^3 - x)\,dx$$

$$\mu = -2\,[\tfrac{x^4}{4} - \tfrac{x^2}{2}]_{x=-1}^{x=1}$$

$$\mu = -2\,\{[\tfrac{(1)^4}{4} - \tfrac{(1)^2}{2}] - [\tfrac{(-1)^4}{4} + \tfrac{(-1)^2}{2}]\} = 0$$

The mean can also be seen clearly by the fact that the graph of the function $f(x)$ is symmetric about the y-axis, indicating that its center (or mean) is at $x = 0$. Next, calculate the variance of f.

$$\sigma^2 = \int_{-1}^{1} (x - 0)^2\, (-2x^2 + 2)\,dx = -2\int_{-1}^{1} x^2(x^2 - 1)\,dx$$

$$\sigma^2 = -2\int_{-1}^{1} (x^4 - x^2)\,dx$$

$$\sigma^2 = -2[\tfrac{x^5}{5} - \tfrac{x^3}{3}]_{x=-1}^{x=1} = -2\{[\tfrac{(1)^5}{5} - \tfrac{(1)^3}{3}] - [\tfrac{(-1)^5}{5} - \tfrac{(-1)^3}{3}]\}$$

$$\sigma^2 = -2\{\tfrac{1}{5} - \tfrac{1}{3} - (-\tfrac{1}{5}) + (-\tfrac{1}{3})\} = -2(\tfrac{2}{5} - \tfrac{2}{3})$$

$$\sigma^2 = \tfrac{8}{15} \approx 0.533$$

The standard deviation is

$$\sigma = \sqrt{\sigma^2} = \sqrt{\tfrac{8}{15}} \approx 0.730$$

Probability density functions

A large data set of continuous data is often represented using a probability distribution expressed as a **PROBABILITY DENSITY FUNCTION**. The integral of the probability density function over a certain range gives the probability of a data point being in that range of values. The integral of the probability density function over the whole range of values is equal to 1.

> **PROBABILITY DENSITY FUNCTION:** the integral of the probability density function over a certain range gives the probability of a data point being in that range of values

The *mean* value for a distribution of a variable x represented by a probability density function $f(x)$ is given by

$$\int_{-\infty}^{+\infty} x f(x)\,dx$$

(Compare this with its discrete counterpart $\bar{x} = \Sigma\, x_i f_i'$).

The *median* is the upper bound for which the integral of the probability density function is equal to 0.5; i.e., if $\int_{-\infty}^{a} f(x)\,dx = 0.5$, then a is the median of the distribution.

The *mode* is the maximum value or values of the probability density function within the range of the function.

> *If a distribution is skewed to the right, the mean is greater than the median. If a distribution is skewed to the left, the mean is smaller than the median.*

As mentioned before, the mean and median are very close together for symmetric distributions. If a distribution is skewed to the right, the mean is greater than the median. If a distribution is skewed to the left, the mean is smaller than the median.

Example: Find the mean, median, and mode for the distribution given by the probability density function

$$f(x) = \begin{cases} 4x(1 - x^2) & 0 \le x \le 1 \\ 0 \end{cases}$$

otherwise

$$\text{Mean} = \int_{0}^{1} 4x^2(1 - x^2)\,dx = \frac{4x^3}{3}\Big|_0^1 - \frac{4x^5}{5}\Big|_0^1 = \frac{4}{3} - \frac{4}{5} = \frac{20 - 12}{15} = \frac{8}{15} = 0.53$$

If $x = a$ is the median, then

$$\int_{0}^{a} 4x(1 - x^2)\,dx = 0.5$$
$$\rightarrow \frac{4x^2}{2}\Big|_0^a - \frac{4x^4}{4}\Big|_0^a = 0.5$$
$$\rightarrow 2a^2 - a^4 = 0.5$$
$$\rightarrow 2a^4 - 4a^2 + 1 = 0$$

Solving for a yields

$$a^2 = \frac{4 \pm \sqrt{16 - 8}}{4} = 1 \pm \frac{2\sqrt{2}}{4} = 1 - \frac{\sqrt{2}}{2} \text{ (to keep } x \text{ within the range 0 to 1)}$$
$$a = \sqrt{1 - \frac{1}{\sqrt{2}}} = 0.54$$

The mode is obtained by taking the derivative of the probability density function and setting it to zero as shown below. (Notice that the second derivative is negative at $x = 0.58$, and, hence, this is clearly a maximum.)

$$\frac{d}{dx}(4x - 4x^3) = 4 - 12x^2 = 0$$
$$\rightarrow 12x^2 = 4$$
$$\rightarrow x^2 = \frac{1}{3}$$
$$\rightarrow x = \frac{1}{\sqrt{3}} = 0.58$$

SKILL 14.4 Analyze the effects of bias and sampling techniques

Statistical studies typically involve a large number of people or a large pool of data known as the **POPULATION**. In most cases, it is impractical or impossible to collect data from every member, and therefore a representative sample has to be chosen. The process of selecting a sample must be undertaken with extreme care to ensure that it truly represents a population.

> **POPULATION:** in a statistical study, a large number of people or a large pool of data

In addition to deciding what kind of sample will be selected, one must also select the sample statistic to be used. Different sample statistics can be used to estimate a particular population parameter. In order to estimate a population mean, for instance, one can use the sample median or the sample mean. One way to evaluate whether a sample statistic accurately reflects the value of a population parameter is by studying the characteristics of a sampling distribution. For a study that involves a sample of size n, for example, different samples of the same size and same type will produce slightly different values for the same statistic. A **SAMPLE STATISTIC**, therefore, is a random variable that follows a probability distribution. Informal inferences about the shape, symmetry, mean, and variance of this sampling distribution can help in selection of the appropriate sampling statistic or estimator.

> **SAMPLE STATISTIC:** a random variable that follows a probability distribution

For an **UNBIASED ESTIMATOR**, i.e., a sample statistic that accurately reflects a population parameter, the sampling distribution mean is equal to the estimated population parameter and the distribution is centered at the population parameter. The shape of the sample distribution approaches a normal distribution as the sample size increases. Since consistency between samples is desired in the choice of an estimator, a smaller standard deviation indicates a better estimator.

> **UNBIASED ESTIMATOR:** a sample statistic that accurately reflects a population parameter

Surveys and Sampling

In cases where the number of events or individuals is too large to collect data on each one, scientists collect information from only a small percentage. This is

SAMPLING OR SUR-VEYING: when scientists collect information from only a small percentage of a numbers of events or individuals because the data pool is too large

known as **SAMPLING** or **SURVEYING**. If sampling is done correctly, it should give the investigator nearly the same information he would have obtained by testing the entire population. The survey must be carefully designed, considering both the sampling technique and the size of the sample.

There are a variety of sampling techniques, both random and nonrandom. Random sampling is also known as probability sampling, since the methods of probability theory can be used to ascertain the odds that the sample is representative of the whole population. Statistical methods may be used to determine how large a sample is necessary to give an investigator a specified level of certainty (95% is a typical confidence interval). Conversely, if an investigator has a sample of certain size, those same statistical methods can be used to determine how confident one can be that the sample accurately reflects the whole population.

A good estimator for a 95% confidence interval calculates the margin of error as $\pm \frac{1}{\sqrt{n}}$, where n is the sample size. This reciprocal formula supports the notion that a larger sample size results in a smaller margin of error, or a more reliable survey.

Example: 1000 people were surveyed about their preferred source for news. 52% of respondents sited television as their main news source. The margin of error for these results is estimated to be $\pm \frac{1}{\sqrt{1000}} = \pm .032$ *or* $\pm 3.2\,\%.$

The 95% confidence interval, then, is built from 3.2% on either side of the 52% response, providing the interval (48.8%, 55.2%)

A truly random sample must choose events or individuals without regard to time, place, or result. Simple random sampling is ideal for populations that are relatively homogeneous with respect to the data being collected.

In some cases an accurate representation of distinct sub-populations requires stratified random sampling or quota sampling. For instance, if men and women are likely to respond very differently to a particular survey, the total sample population can be separated into these two subgroups and then a random group of respondents selected from each subgroup. This kind of sampling not only provides balanced representation of different subgroups, it also allows comparison of data between subgroups.

Stratified sampling is sometimes proportional; i.e., the number of samples selected from each subgroup reflects the fraction of the whole population represented by the subgroup.

Sometimes compromises must be made to save time, money, or effort. For instance, when conducting a phone survey, calls are typically made only in a certain geographical area and at a certain time of day. This is an example of **cluster random sampling**. There are three stages to cluster or area sampling:

1. The target population is divided into many regional clusters (groups).

2. A few clusters are randomly selected for study.

3. A few subjects are randomly chosen from within a cluster.

4. Systematic random sampling involves the collection of a sample at defined intervals (for instance, every tenth part to come off a manufacturing line). Here, it is assumed that the population is ordered randomly and that there is no hidden pattern that may compromise the randomness of the sampling.

Nonrandom sampling is also known as nonprobability sampling. **Convenience sampling** is the method of choosing items arbitrarily and in an unstructured manner from the frame. **Purposive sampling** targets a particular section of the population. **Snowball sampling** (e.g., having survey participants recommend others) and **expert sampling** are other types of nonrandom sampling. Obviously, nonrandom samples are far less representative of the whole population than random ones. They may, however, be the only methods available or may meet the needs of a particular study.

COMPETENCY 15
UNDERSTAND PRINCIPLES AND TECHNIQUES OF PROBABILITY

SKILL 15.1 **Determine probabilities of simple and compound events and conditional probabilities**

Elements of Probability

The **PROBABILITY** of an outcome, given a **RANDOM EXPERIMENT** (a structured, repeatable experiment for which the outcome cannot be predicted or, alternatively, for which the outcome is dependent on "chance"), is the relative frequency of the outcome. The **RELATIVE FREQUENCY** of an outcome is the number of times an experiment yields that outcome for a very large (ideally, infinite) number of

> **RANDOM EXPERIMENT:** a structured, repeatable experiment for which the outcome cannot be predicted

trials. For instance, if a "fair" coin is tossed a very large number of times, then the relative frequency of a "heads-up" outcome is 0.5, or 50% (that is, one out of every two trials, on average, should be heads up). The probability is this relative frequency.

In probability theory, the **SAMPLE SPACE** is a list of all possible outcomes of an experiment. For example, the sample space of tossing two coins is the set {HH, HT, TT, TH}, where H is heads and T is tails, and the sample space of rolling a six-sided die is the set {1, 2, 3, 4, 5, 6}. When conducting experiments with a large number of possible outcomes, it is important to determine the size of the sample space. The size of the sample space can be determined by using the fundamental counting principles and the rules of combinations and permutations.

A **RANDOM VARIABLE** is a function that corresponds to the outcome of some experiment or event, which is in turn dependent on "chance." For instance, the result of a tossed coin is a random variable: the outcome is either heads or tails, and each outcome has an associated probability. A **DISCRETE VARIABLE** is one that can only take on certain specific values. For instance, the number of students in a class can only be a whole number (e.g., 15 or 16, but not 15.5). A **CONTINUOUS VARIABLE**, such as the weight of an object, can take on a continuous range of values.

The probabilities for the possible values of a random variable constitute the **PROBABILITY DISTRIBUTION** for that random variable. Probability distributions can be discrete, as with the case of the tossing of a coin (there are only two possible distinct outcomes), or they can be continuous, as with the outside temperature at a given time of day. In the latter case, the probability is represented as a continuous function over a range of possible temperatures, and finite probabilities can only be measured in terms of ranges of temperatures rather than specific temperatures. That is to say, for a continuous distribution, it is not meaningful to say "the probability that the outcome is x"; instead, only "the probability that the outcome is between x and $\triangle x$" is meaningful. (Note that if each potential outcome in a continuous distribution has a non-zero probability, then the sum of all the probabilities would be greater than 1, since there are an infinite number of potential outcomes.)

Example: Find the sample space and construct a probability distribution for tossing a six-sided die (with numbers 1 through 6) for which even numbers are twice as likely as odd numbers to come up on a given roll (assume the even numbers are equally likely and the odd numbers are equally likely).

The sample space is simply the set of all possible outcomes that can arise in a given trial. For this die, the sample space is {1, 2, 3, 4, 5, 6}. To construct the associated probability distribution, note first that the sum of the probabilities must equal 1.

SAMPLE SPACE: a list of all possible outcomes of an experiment

RELATIVE FREQUENCY: the number of times an experiment yields a given outcome for a very large number of trials

RANDOM VARIABLE: a function that corresponds to the outcome of some experiment or event

DISCRETE VARIABLE: a variable that can only take on certain specific values

CONTINUOUS VARIABLE: a variable that can take on a continuous range of values

PROBABILITY DISTRIBUTION: the probabilities for the possible values of a random variable

Let the probability of rolling an odd number (1, 3, or 5) be x; the probability of rolling an even number (2, 4, or 6) is then $2x$.

$$1 = p(1) + p(2) + p(3) + p(4) + p(5) + p(6) = 3x + 6x = 9x$$
$$x = \frac{1}{9}$$

The probability distribution can be shown as a histogram below.

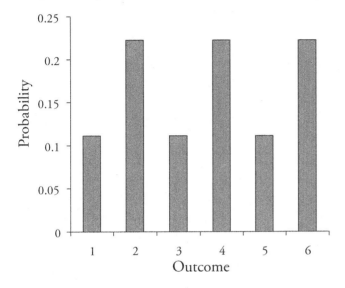

The sum of the probabilities for all the possible outcomes of a discrete distribution (or the integral of the continuous distribution over all possible values) must be equal to unity. The expected value of a probability distribution is the same as the **mean value** of a probability distribution. The **EXPECTED VALUE** is thus a measure of the central tendency or average value for a random variable with a given probability distribution.

A **BERNOULLI TRIAL** is an experiment whose outcome is random and can be either of two possible outcomes, which are called "success" or "failure." Tossing a coin would be an example of a Bernoulli trial. The probability of success is represented by p, with the probability of failure being $q = 1 - p$. Bernoulli trials can be applied to any real-life situation in which there are only two possible outcomes. For example, concerning the birth of a child, the only two possible outcomes for the sex of the child are male and female.

Probability can also be expressed in terms of odds. **ODDS** are defined as the ratio of the number of favorable outcomes to the number of unfavorable outcomes. The sum of the favorable outcomes and the unfavorable outcomes should always equal the total possible outcomes.

> **EXPECTED VALUE:** a measure of the central tendency or average value for a random variable with a given probability distribution

> **BERNOULLI TRIAL:** an experiment whose outcome is random and can be either of two possible outcomes, which are called "success" or "failure"

> **ODDS:** the ratio of the number of favorable outcomes to the number of unfavorable outcomes

For example, given a bag of 12 red marbles and 7 green marbles, compute the odds of randomly selecting a red marble.

Odds of getting red $= \frac{12}{7}$

Odds of not getting red $= \frac{7}{12}$

In the case of flipping a coin, it is equally likely that a head or a tail will be tossed. The odds of tossing a head are 1:1. This is called **even odds**.

A **simple event** is a single event such as a coin toss. A **compound event** is a combination of two or more simple events that may or may not be dependent on each other.

Dependent and Independent Events

DEPENDENT EVENTS occur when the probability of the second event depends on the outcome of the first event. For example, consider the following two events: the home team wins the semifinal round (event A) and the home team wins the final round (event B). The probability of event B is contingent on the probability of event A. If the home team fails to win the semifinal round, it has a zero probability of winning the final round. On the other hand, if the home team wins the semifinal round, then it may have a finite probability of winning the final round. Symbolically, the probability of event B given event A is written $P(B|A)$.

> **DEPENDENT EVENTS:** events that occur when the probability of the second event depends on the outcome of the first event

The **CONDITIONAL PROBABILITY** can be calculated according to the following definition (the symbol $\cap$ means "and," $\cup$ means "or," and $P(x)$ means "the probability of x"):

$$P(B|A) = \frac{P(A \cap B)}{P(A)}$$

> **CONDITIONAL PROBABILITY:** the probability that event B will occur, given that event A has occurred

Consider a pair of dice: one red and one green. First the red die is rolled, followed by the green die. It is apparent that these events do not depend on each other, since the outcome of the roll of the green die is not affected by the outcome of the roll of the red die. Thus the events are **INDEPENDENT EVENTS**. The total probability of two independent events can be found by multiplying the separate probabilities.

$$P(A \cap B) = P(A)P(B)$$
$$P(A \cap B) = \left(\frac{1}{6}\right)\left(\frac{1}{6}\right) = \frac{1}{36}$$

> **INDEPENDENT EVENTS:** when the probability of a second event occurring does not depend on the probability of the first event occurring

> *The total probability of two independent events can be found by multiplying the separate probabilities.*

Replacement

In many instances, events are not independent. Suppose a jar contains 12 red marbles and 8 blue marbles. If a marble is selected at random and then replaced, the probability of picking a certain color is the same in the second trial as it is in the first trial. If the marble is *not* replaced, then the probability of picking a certain color is *not* the same in the second trial, because the total number of marbles is decreased by 1. This is an illustration of conditional probability. If R_n signifies selection of a red marble on the nth trial and B_n signifies selection of a blue marble on the nth trial, then the probability of selecting a red marble in two trials *with replacement* is

$$P(R_1 \cap R_2) = P(R_1)P(R_2) = (\tfrac{12}{20})(\tfrac{12}{20}) = \tfrac{144}{400} = 0.36$$

The probability of selecting a red marble in two trials *without replacement* is

$$P(R_1 \cap R_2) = P(R_1)P(R|R_1) = (\tfrac{12}{20})(\tfrac{11}{19}) = \tfrac{132}{360} \approx 0.367$$

Example: A car has a 75% probability of traveling 20,000 miles without breaking down. It has a 50% probability of traveling 10,000 additional miles without breaking down if it first makes it to 20,000 miles without breaking down. What is the probability that the car reaches 30,000 miles without breaking down?

Let event A be that the car reaches 20,000 miles without breaking down.

$$P(A) = 0.75$$

Event B is that the car travels an additional 10,000 miles without breaking down (assuming it didn't break down for the first 20,000 miles). Since event B is contingent on event A, write the probability as follows:

$$P(B|A) = 0.50$$

Use the conditional probability formula to find the probability that the car travels 30,000 miles ($A \cap B$) without breaking down.

$$P(B|A) = \frac{P(A \cap B)}{P(A)}$$
$$0.50 = \frac{P(A \cap B)}{0.75}$$
$$P(A \cap B) = (0.50)(0.75) = 0.375$$

Thus, the car has a 37.5% probability of traveling 30,000 consecutive miles without breaking down.

SKILL 15.2 Use counting principles to calculate probabilities

The following discussion uses the symbols $\cap$ to mean "and," $\cup$ to mean "or," and $P(x)$ to mean "the probability of x." Also, $N(x)$ means "the number of ways that x can occur."

The Addition Rule

The ADDITION PRINCIPLE OF COUNTING states that if A and B are arbitrary events, then

$$N(A \cup B) = N(A) + N(B) - N(A \cap B).$$

ADDITION PRINCIPLE OF COUNTING: if A and B are arbitrary events, then $N(A \cup B) = N(A) + N(B) - N(A \cap B)$

Furthermore, if A and B are **MUTUALLY EXCLUSIVE EVENTS**, then
$$N(A \cup B) = N(A) + N(B).$$

> **MUTUALLY EXCLUSIVE EVENTS:** events that cannot occur together or have no outcomes in common

Correspondingly, the probabilities associated with arbitrary events are
$$P(A \cup B) = P(A) + P(B) - P(A \cap B).$$

For mutually exclusive events, the probabilities are
$$P(A \cup B) = P(A) + P(B).$$

Example: In how many ways can you select a black card or a jack from an ordinary deck of playing cards?

Let B denote selection of a black card and let J denote selection of a jack. Then, since half the cards (26) are black and four are jacks,
$$N(B) = 26$$
$$N(J) = 4$$

Also, since a card can be both black and a jack (the jack of spades and the jack of clubs),
$$N(B \cap J) = 2.$$

Thus, the solution is
$$N(B \cup J) = N(B) + N(J) - N(B \cap J) = 26 + 4 - 2 = 28.$$

Example: A travel agency offers 40 possible trips: 14 to Asia, 16 to Europe, and 10 to South America. In how many ways can you select a trip to Asia or Europe through this agency?

Let A denote selection of a trip to Asia and let E denote selection of a trip to Europe. Since these are mutually exclusive events, then
$$N(A \cup E) = N(A) + N(E) = 14 + 16 = 30.$$

Therefore, there are 30 ways you can select a trip to Asia or Europe.

The Multiplication Rule

> **MULTIPLICATION PRINCIPLE OF COUNTING FOR DEPENDENT EVENTS:** if A and B are arbitrary events, then the number of ways that A and B can occur in a two-stage experiment is given by $N(A \cap B) = N(A)N(B|A)$ where $N(B|A)$ is the number of ways B can occur given that A has already occurred

The **MULTIPLICATION PRINCIPLE OF COUNTING FOR DEPENDENT EVENTS** states that if A and B are arbitrary events, then the number of ways that A and B can occur in a two-stage experiment is given by
$$N(A \cap B) = N(A)N(B|A),$$

where $N(B|A)$ is the number of ways B can occur given that A has already occurred. This expression is also known as the joint probability of events A and B. If A and B are independent events (events for which the probability of one event is not dependent on the outcome of another event), then
$$N(A \cap B) = N(A)N(B).$$

Also, the probabilities associated with arbitrary events are

$$P(A \cap B) = P(A)P(B \mid A).$$

For independent events, the probabilities are

$$P(A \cap B) = P(A)P(B).$$

Example: In how many ways can two jacks from an ordinary deck of 52 cards be drawn in succession if the first card is not replaced into the deck before the second card is drawn (that is, without replacement)?

This is a two-stage experiment. Let A be selection of a jack in the first draw and let B be selection of a jack in the second draw. It is clear that

$$N(A) = 4.$$

If the first card drawn is a jack, however, then there are only three remaining jacks remaining for the second draw. Thus, drawing two cards without replacement means the events A and B are dependent, and

$$N(B \mid A) = 3.$$

The solution is

$$N(A \cap B) = N(A)N(B \mid A) = (4)(3) = 12.$$

Example: How many six-letter code "words" can be formed if repetition of letters is not allowed?

Since these are code words, a word does not have to be in the dictionary; for example, *abcdef* could be a code word. Since the experiment requires choosing each letter without replacing the letters from previous selections, the experiment has six stages.

Repetition is not allowed; thus, there are 26 choices for the first letter, 25 for the second, 24 for the third, 23 for the fourth, 22 for the fifth, and 21 for the sixth. Therefore, if A is the selection of a six-letter code word without repetition, then

$$N(A) = (26)(25)(24)(23)(22)(21) = 165,765,600$$

There are over 165 million ways to choose a six-letter code word with six unique letters.

Finite Probability

Using the fundamental counting principles described above, finite probability problems can be solved. Generally, finding the probability of a particular event or set of events involves dividing the number of ways the particular event can take place by the total number of possible outcomes for the experiment. Thus, by appropriately counting these possible outcomes using the above rules, probabilities can be determined.

Example: Determine the probability of rolling three even numbers on three successive rolls of a six-sided die.

This is a three-stage experiment. First, determine the total number of possible outcomes for three rolls of a die. For each roll,

$$N(\text{roll}) = 6.$$

There are three possible even rolls for a die: 2, 4, and 6.

$$N(\text{even}) = 3$$

The probability of rolling an even number on any particular roll is

$$P(\text{even}) = \frac{N(\text{even})}{N(\text{roll})} = \frac{3}{6} = \frac{1}{2}.$$

For three successive rolls, use the multiplication rule for mutually exclusive events.

$$P(3 \text{ even rolls}) = P(\text{even})^3 = \left(\frac{1}{2}\right)^3 = \frac{1}{8} = 0.125$$

Thus, the probability of rolling three successive even numbers using a six-sided die is 0.125.

SKILL 15.3 Use a variety of graphical representations to calculate probabilities

Probabilities can be calculated by finding the ratios of areas of geometric regions. In the context of probability distributions, probabilities correspond to areas under the probability density function. For instance, the total area under the probability density curve should be unity (since the probability of some outcome for an experiment must be one). The ratio of the area under the curve for some particular value or range of values for the random variable to the total area (unity) is the probability of that value or range of values.

VENN DIAGRAM: represents events or sets of events as shapes that depict the relationships of these events by overlapping (or not overlapping)

Likewise, probabilities can be represented using a **VENN DIAGRAM**, which represents events or sets of events as shapes that depict the relationships of these events by overlapping (or not overlapping). For example, let the rectangle below represent all the possible outcomes of the random selection of a card from a standard deck. Let oval A be all the outcomes for which a spade is chosen, and let oval B be all the outcomes for which a jack is chosen. Since there is one choice that falls within both of these categories (the jack of spades), the ovals overlap.

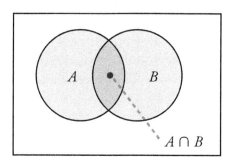

If the shapes correspond to areas that are to scale with their probabilities, then a Venn diagram can be used to calculate probabilities using ratios of these areas. Consider, for instance, the flip of a fair coin. The diagram for this case is shown below. (Although this may not be strictly considered a Venn diagram, depending on the definition of such, it does relay the same idea.)

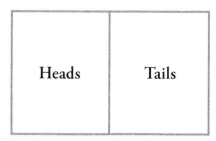

Notice that the total area A is divided evenly between "heads" $\left(\frac{A}{2}\right)$ and "tails" $\left(\frac{A}{2}\right)$. Thus, the probability of heads (or tails) is

$$\frac{A}{2} = \frac{1}{2}.$$

Another Venn diagram is shown below for a six-sided die.

1	4
2	5
3	6

Again, the possibility of a particular outcome or range of outcomes can be found by using ratios of the associated areas. In both the cases above, there are no possible outcomes beyond those shown, so the Venn diagrams do not show any area outside these outcomes.

Geometric probability describes situations that involve shapes and measures. For example, given a 10-inch string, we can determine the probability of cutting the string so that one piece is at least 8 inches long. If the cut occurs in the first or last two inches of the string, one of the pieces will be at least 8 inches long.

String

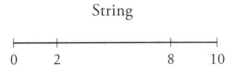

Thus, the probability of such a cut is $\frac{2 + 2}{10} = \frac{4}{10} = \frac{2}{5}$ or 40%.

Other geometric probability problems involve the ratio of areas. For example, to determine the likelihood of randomly hitting a defined area of a dartboard (pictured below) we determine the ratio of the target area to the total area of the board.

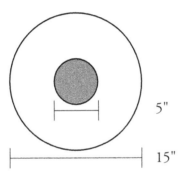

Given that a randomly thrown dart lands somewhere on the board, the probability that it hits the target area is the ratio of the areas of the two circles. Thus, the probability, P, of hitting the target is

$$P = \frac{(2.5)^2\pi}{(7.5)^2\pi} \times 100 = \frac{6.25}{56.25} \times 100 = 11.1\%.$$

SKILL 15.4 **Select simulations that model real-world events**

Probability Simulations
Simulations of random events or variables can be helpful in making informal inferences about theoretical probability distributions. Although simulations can involve use of physical situations that bear some similarity to the situation of interest, oftentimes simulations involve computer modeling.

Pseudorandom numbers
One of the crucial aspects of modeling probability using a computer program is the need for a random number that can be used to "randomize" the aspect of the program that corresponds to the event or variable. Although there is no function on a computer that can provide a truly random number, most programming

languages have some function designed to produce a pseudorandom number. A **PSEUDORANDOM NUMBER** is not truly random, but it is sufficiently unpredictable that it can be used as a random number in many contexts.

Pseudorandom numbers can serve as the basis for simulation of rolling a die, flipping a coin, selecting an object from a collection of different objects, and a range of other situations. If, for instance, the pseudorandom number generator produces a number between 0 and 1, simply divide up that range in accordance with the probabilities of each particular outcome. (For instance, assign 0 to 0.5 as heads and 0.5 to 1 as tails for the flip of a fair coin.) By performing a number of simulated trials and tallying the results, empirical probability distributions can be created.

Ideally, as the number of trials goes to infinity, the empirical probability distribution should approach the theoretical distribution. As a result, by performing a sufficiently large number of trials (this number must be at least somewhat justified for the particular situation), one should be able to make informal inferences based on the data. Such inferences, however, must take into account the limitations of the computer, such as the inability to perform an infinite number of trials in finite time and the numerical inaccuracies that are an inherent part of computer programming.

> **PSEUDORANDOM NUMBER:** a number that is not truly random but that is sufficiently unpredictable that it can be used as a random number in many contexts

SKILL 15.5 Analyze uniform, binomial, and normal probability distributions

A **UNIFORM** distribution has the same probability value for all values of the variable. A discrete uniform distribution has a finite number of outcomes and each outcome is equally likely. For instance, a regular six-sided die has a uniform distribution since each of the six outcomes is equally likely. A continuous uniform distribution or rectangular distribution (so called since the plot of the probability density function $P(x)$ has a rectangular shape) on the interval $[a, b]$ is given by

> **UNIFORM:** a distribution has the same probability value for all values of the variable

$$P(x) = \begin{cases} 0 & \text{for } x < a \\ \dfrac{1}{b-a} & \text{for } a \le x \le b \\ 0 & \text{for } x > b \end{cases}$$

The constant value of the probability density function is determined by the requirement that the integral of the function over the specified interval be 1 as shown below.

$$\int_a^b P(x)\,dx = \int_a^b \frac{1}{b-a}\,dx = \frac{x}{b-a}\Big|_a^b = \frac{b}{b-a} - \frac{a}{b-a} = \frac{b-a}{b-a} = 1$$

The Normal Distribution

> **NORMAL DISTRIBUTION:** the probability distribution associated with most sets of real-world data; also called a bell curve

A **NORMAL DISTRIBUTION** (frequently called a bell curve) is the probability distribution associated with most sets of real-world data. A normal distribution has a **continuous random variable** X with mean μ and variance σ^2. The normal distribution has the following form.

$$f(x) = \frac{1}{\sigma\sqrt{2\pi}}\, e^{-\frac{1}{2}\left(\frac{x-\mu}{\sigma}\right)^2}$$

The total area under the normal curve is 1. Thus,

$$\int_{-\infty}^{\infty} f(x)\,dx = 1$$

Since the area under the curve of this function is 1, the distribution can be used to determine probabilities through integration. If a continuous random variable x follows the normal distribution, then the probability that x has a value between a and b is

$$P(a < X \le b) = \int_{a}^{b} f(x)\,dx = F(b) - F(a)$$

Since this integral is difficult to evaluate analytically, tables of values are often used. Often, however, the tables use the integral

$$\frac{1}{\sqrt{2\pi}}\int_{a}^{b} e^{-\frac{t^2}{2}}\,dt = F(b) - F(a)$$

To use this form, simply convert x values to t values using

$$t = \frac{x_i - \mu}{\sigma}$$

where x_i is a particular value for the random variable X. This formula is often called the **Z-SCORE**.

> **Z-SCORE:** this score gives the number of standard deviations between a data value x and the mean of the x distribution

Example: Albert's Bagel Shop's morning customer load follows a normal distribution, with mean (average) 50 and standard deviation 10. Determine the probability that the number of customers on a particular morning will be less than 42.

First, convert to a form that allows use of normal distribution tables:

$$t = \frac{x - \mu}{\sigma} = \frac{42 - 50}{10} = -0.8$$

Next, use a table to find the probability corresponding to the z-score. The actual integral in this case is

$$P(X < 42) = \frac{1}{\sqrt{2\pi}} \int_{-\infty}^{-0.8} e^{-\frac{t^2}{2}}\,dt$$

The table gives a value for $x = 0.8$ of 0.7881. To find the value for $x < -0.8$, subtract this result from 1.

$$P(X < 42) = 1 - 0.7881 = 0.2119$$

This means that there is about a 21.2% chance that there will be fewer than 42 customers in a given morning.

Example: The scores on Mr. Rogers' statistics exam follow a normal distribution with mean 85 and standard deviation 5. A student is wondering about the probability that she will score between a 90 and a 95 on her exam.

To compute $P(90 < x < 95)$, first compute the z-scores for each raw score.

$$z_{90} = \frac{90 - 85}{5} = 1$$

$$z_{95} = \frac{95 - 85}{5} = 2$$

Use the tables to find $P(1 < z < 2)$. To do this, subtract as follows.

$$P(1 < z < 2) = P(z < 2) - P(z < 1)$$

The table yields

$$P(1 < z < 2) = 0.9772 - 0.8413 = 0.1359$$

It can then be concluded that there is a 13.6% chance that the student will score between a 90 and a 95 on her exam.

The Binomial Distribution

The **binomial distribution** is a probability distribution for discrete random variables and is expressed as follows.

$$f(x) = \binom{n}{x} p^x q^{n-x}$$

where a sequence of n trials of an experiment are performed and where p is the probability of "success" and q is the probability of "failure." The value x is the number of times the experiment yields a successful outcome. Notice that this probability function is the product of p^x (the probability of successful outcomes in x trials) and q^{n-x} (the probability of unsuccessful outcomes in the remainder of the trials). The factor $\binom{n}{x}$ indicates that the x successful trials can be chosen $\binom{n}{x}$ ways (combinations) from the n total trials. (In other words, the successful trials may occur at different points in the sequence.)

Example: A loaded coin has a probability 0.6 of landing heads up. What is the probability of getting three heads in four successive tosses?

Use the binomial distribution. In this case, p is the probability of the coin landing heads up, and $q = 1 - p$ is the probability of the coin landing tails up. Also, the number of "successful" trials (heads up) is 3. Then,

$$f(3) = \binom{4}{3} (0.6)^3 (1 - 0.6)^{4-3}$$

$$f(3) = \frac{4!}{3!(4-3)!} (0.6)^3 (0.4)^1$$

$$f(3) = \frac{24}{6(1)} (0.216)(0.4) = 0.3456$$

Thus, there is a 34.56% chance that the loaded coin will land heads up three out of four times.

COMPETENCY 16
UNDERSTAND PRINCIPLES OF DISCRETE MATHEMATICS

SKILL 16.1 Apply concepts of permutations and combinations to solve problems

Permutations and Combinations

PERMUTATION: the number of possible arrangements of n items, without repetition, where order of selection is important

COMBINATION: the number of possible arrangements of n items, without repetition, where order of selection is not important

A **PERMUTATION** is the number of possible arrangements of n items, without repetition, where order of selection is important.

A **COMBINATION** is the number of possible arrangements of n items, without repetition, where order of selection is not important.

Example: If any two numbers are selected from the set {1, 2, 3, 4}, list the possible permutations and combinations.

Combinations	Permutations
12, 13, 14, 23, 24, 34: six ways	12, 21, 13, 31, 14, 41, 23, 32, 24, 42, 34, 43: twelve ways

Note that the list of permutations includes 12 and 21 as separate possibilities since the order of selection is important. In the case of combinations, however, the order of selection is not important and, therefore, 12 is the same combination as 21. Hence, 21 is not listed separately as a possibility.

The number of permutations and combinations may also be found by using the formulae given below.

The number of possible permutations in selecting r objects from a set of n is given by

$$_nP_r = \frac{n!}{(n-r)!}$$

The notation nPr is read "the number of permutations of n objects taken r at a time."

In our example, two objects are being selected from a set of four.

$$_4P_2 = \frac{4!}{(4-2)!}$$ Substitute known values.
$$_4P_2 = 12$$

The number of possible combinations in selecting r objects from a set of n is given by

$$_nC_r = \frac{n!}{(n - r)!r!}$$ The number of combinations when r objects are selected from n objects.

In our example,

$$_4C_2 = \frac{4!}{(4 - 2)!2!}$$ Substitute known values.
$$_4C_2 = 6$$

Objects arranged in a row

It can be shown that $_nP_n$, the number of ways n objects can be arranged in a row, is equal to $n!$. We can think of the problem as n positions being filled, one at a time. The first position can be filled in n ways using any one of the n objects. Since one of the objects has already been used, the second position can be filled only in $n - 1$ ways. Similarly, the third position can be filled in $n - 2$ ways, and so on. Hence, the total number of possible arrangements of n objects in a row is given by

$$_nP_n = n(n - 1)(n - 2)........1 = n!$$

Example: Five books are placed in a row on a bookshelf. In how many different ways can they be arranged?

The number of possible ways in which 5 books can be arranged in a row is $5! = 1 \times 2 \times 3 \times 4 \times 5 = 120$.

The formula given above for $_nP_r$, *the number of possible permutations of* r *objects selected from* n *objects,* can also be proven in a similar manner. If r positions are filled by selecting from n objects, the first position can be filled in n ways, the second position can be filled in $n - 1$ ways, and so on (as shown before). The rth position can be filled in $n - (r - 1) = n - r + 1$ ways. Hence,

$$_nP_r = n(n - 1)(n - 2).....(n - r + 1) = \frac{n!}{(n - r)!}$$

The formula for the *number of possible combinations of* r *objects selected from* n, $_nC_r$, may be derived by using the above two formulae. For the same set of r objects, the number of permutations is $r!$. All of these permutations, however, correspond to the same combination. Hence,

$$_nC_r = \frac{_nP_r}{r!} = \frac{n!}{(n - r)!r!}$$

Objects arranged in a ring

The number of permutations of n objects in a ring is given by $(n - 1)!$. This can be demonstrated by considering the fact that the number of permutations of n objects in a row is $n!$. When the objects are placed in a ring, moving every object one place to its left will result in the same arrangement. Moving each object two places to its left will also result in the same arrangement. We can continue this kind of movement up to n places to get the same arrangement. Thus the count $n!$ is n times too many when the objects are arranged in a ring. Hence, the number of permutations of n objects in a ring is given by $\frac{n!}{n} = (n - 1)!$.

Example: There are 20 people at a meeting. Five of them are selected to lead a discussion. How many different combinations of five people can be selected from the group? If the five people are seated in a row, how many different seating permutations are possible? If the five people are seated around a circular table, how many possible permutations are there?

The number of possible combinations of 5 people selected from the group of 20 is

$$_{20}C_5 = \frac{20!}{15!5!} = \frac{16 \times 17 \times 18 \times 19 \times 20}{1 \times 2 \times 3 \times 4 \times 5} = \frac{1860480}{120} = 15{,}504$$

The number of possible permutations of the five seated in a row is

$$_{20}P_5 = \frac{20!}{15!} = 16 \times 17 \times 18 \times 19 \times 20 = 1{,}860{,}480$$

The number of possible permutations of the five seated in a circle is

$$\frac{_{20}P_5}{5} = \frac{20!}{5 \times 15!} = \frac{16 \times 17 \times 18 \times 19 \times 20}{5} = 372{,}096$$

Sets containing like objects

If the set of n objects contains some objects that are exactly alike, the number of permutations will again be different than $n!$. For instance, if n_1 of the n objects are exactly alike, then switching those objects among themselves will result in the same arrangement. Since we already know that n_1 objects can be arranged in $n_1!$ ways, n! must be reduced by a factor of $n_1!$ to get the correct number of permutations. Thus, the number of permutations of n objects of which n_1 are exactly alike is given by $\frac{n!}{n_1!}$. Generalizing this, *we can say that the number of different permutations of* n *objects of which* n$_1$ *are alike,* n$_2$ *are alike, …,* n$_j$ *are alike, is*

$$\frac{n!}{n_1! \, n_2! \dots n_j!} \text{ where } n_1 + n_2 \dots + n_j = n$$

Example: A box contains 3 red, 2 blue, and 5 green marbles. If all the marbles are taken out of the box and arranged in a row, how many different permutations are possible?

The number of possible permutations is

$$\frac{10!}{3!2!5!} = \frac{6 \times 7 \times 8 \times 9 \times 10}{6 \times 2} = 2520$$

Sequences and Series

Sequences and series can take on a vast range of different forms and patterns. Sequences and series are essentially two different representations of a set of numbers: a sequence is the set of numbers, and a series is the sum of the terms of the sequence. That is, a sequence such as

$$a_1, a_2, a_3, \ldots$$

has a corresponding series S such that

$$S = a_1 + a_2 + a_3 + \ldots$$

Two of the most common forms of series are the arithmetic and geometric series, both of which are discussed below.

A sequence is a set of numbers; a series is the sum of the terms of a sequence.

Arithmetic series

A finite series of numbers for which the difference between successive terms is constant is called an **ARITHMETIC SERIES**. An arithmetic series with n terms can be expressed as follows, where a and d are constants. (The constant a is the first term, and d is the difference between successive terms.)

$$a + (a + d) + (a + 2d) + (a + 3d) + \ldots (a + [n - 1]d)$$

To derive the general formula, examine the series sum for several small values of n.

ARITHMETIC SERIES: a finite series of numbers for which the difference between successive terms is constant

n	Sum
1	a
2	$2a + d$
3	$3a + 3d$
4	$4a + 6d$
5	$5a + 10d$
6	$6a + 15d$
. . .	. . .
n	$na + d\sum\limits_{i=1}^{n-1} i$

The result in the table for n terms is found by examining the pattern of the previous series. All that is necessary, then, is to determine a closed expression for the summation.

By inspection, it can be seen that the product of n and $(n + 1)$, divided by 2, is the expression for the sum of $1 + 2 + 3 + 4 + 5 + \ldots + n$. Then:

$$\sum_{i=1}^{n} i = \tfrac{1}{2}n(n + 1)$$

An simple derivation of this relationship may be made as follows:

$$S_n = 1 + 2 + 3 + \ldots + n$$

Writing the terms in reverse order:

$$S_n = n + (n - 1) + (n - 2) + \ldots + 1$$

Adding the two expressions for S_n term by term, we get

$$2S_n = (1 + n) + (2 + n - 1) + (3 + n - 2) + \ldots (n + 1)$$
$$= (1 + n) + (1 + n) + (1 + n) + \ldots (n + 1)$$
$$= n(n + 1)$$

Therefore, $S_n = \dfrac{n(n + 1)}{2}$

For the general case (with first term a and common difference d), therefore, the sum for a series with n terms is given by

$$na + d\sum_{i=1}^{n-1} i = na + d\frac{(n - 1)(n)}{2} = \tfrac{1}{2}n(2a + d(n - 1))$$

Often, closed formulas for series such as the arithmetic series must be found by inspection, as a more rigorous derivation is difficult. The result can be proven using mathematical induction, however.

Example: Calculate the sum of the series 1 + 5 + 9 + ... + 57.

This is an arithmetic series, as the difference between successive terms, d, is constant ($d = 4$). Determine the total number of terms by subtracting the first term from the last term, dividing by d, and adding 1.

$$n = \frac{57 - 1}{4} + 1 = \frac{56}{4} + 1 = 14 + 1 = 15$$

That this approach works can be seen by testing simple examples. For instance, if the series is $1 + 5 + 9$, then

$$n = \frac{9 - 1}{4} + 1 = \frac{8}{4} + 1 = 2 + 1 = 3$$

There are indeed three terms in this simple series.

Next, apply the formula, noting that $a = 1$.

$$\tfrac{1}{2}n[2a + d(n - 1)] = \tfrac{1}{2}(15)[2(1) + (4)(15 - 1)]$$
$$= \tfrac{15}{2}[2 + 4(14)] = \tfrac{15}{2}(58) = 435$$

Thus, the answer is 435.

Geometric series

A **GEOMETRIC SERIES** is a series whose successive terms are related by a common factor (rather than the common difference of the arithmetic series). Assuming that a is the first term of the series and r is the common factor, the general n-term geometric series can be written as follows.

$$a + ar + ar^2 + ar^3 + \dots + ar^{n-1}$$

The geometric series can also be written using sum notation.

$$a + ar + ar^2 + \dots + ar^{n-1} = \sum_{i=0}^{n-1} ar^i$$

To derive the closed-form expression for this finite series, let the sum for n terms be defined as S_n. Multiply S_n by r.

$$S_n = a + ar + ar^2 + \dots + ar^{n-1}$$
$$rS_n = ar + ar^2 + ar^3 + \dots + ar^n$$

Note that if a is added to this new series, the result is the sum S_{n+1}, which has $n + 1$ terms.

$$a + rS_n = a + ar + ar^2 + ar^3 + \dots + ar^n = S_{n+1}$$

But S_{n+1} is simply $S_n + ar^n$, so the above expression can be written solely in terms of S_n.

$$a + rS_n = S_{n+1} = S_n + ar^n$$

Rearrange the result to obtain a simple formula for the geometric series.

$$a + rS_n = S_n + ar^n$$
$$a - ar^n = S_n - rS_n$$
$$a(1 - r^n) = S_n(1 - r)$$
$$S_n = a\frac{1 - r^n}{1 - r}$$

Infinite geometric series

The infinite geometric series is the limit of S_n as n approaches infinity.

$$a + ar + ar^2 + \dots = \lim_{n \to \infty} a\frac{1 - r^n}{1 - r}$$

Three cases are of interest: $r \geq 1$, $r \leq -1$, and $-1 < r < 1$. To determine the limit in each case, first apply L'Hopital's rule.

$$\lim_{n \to \infty} a\frac{1 - r^n}{1 - r} = a\lim_{n \to \infty} \frac{\frac{d}{dr}(1 - r^n)}{\frac{d}{dr}(1 - r)} = a\lim_{n \to \infty} \frac{-nr^{n-1}}{-1}$$

$$\lim_{n \to \infty} a\frac{1 - r^n}{1 - r} = a\lim_{n \to \infty} nr^{n-1}$$

Thus, it can be seen that if r is either 1 or -1, the limit goes to infinity due to the factor n. The same reasoning applies if r is greater than 1 or less than -1. For $-1 < r < 1$, rearrange the original form of the limit.

$$\lim_{n \to \infty} a\frac{1 - r^n}{1 - r} = a\frac{1 - r^\infty}{1 - r}$$

GEOMETRIC SERIES: a series whose successive terms are related by a common factor

Since the magnitude of r is less than 1, r^∞ must be zero. This yields a closed form for the infinite geometric series, which converges only if $-1 < r < 1$.

$$a + ar + ar^2 + \ldots = \frac{a}{1 - r}$$

Example: Evaluate the following series: $1 + \frac{1}{2} + \frac{1}{4} + \frac{1}{8} + \ldots$.

Note that this series is an infinite geometric series with $a = 1$ and $r = \frac{1}{2}$ (or 0.5).

Use the formula to evaluate the series.

$$1 + \frac{1}{2} + \frac{1}{4} + \frac{1}{8} + \ldots = \frac{a}{1 - r} = \frac{1}{1 - 0.5} = \frac{1}{0.5} = 2$$

The answer is thus 2.

Modeling Phenomena with Sequences and Series

Arithmetic and geometric sequences and series can be used to model various phenomena and are especially useful for financial mathematics. Compound interest, annuities, and mortgages can all be modeled using sequences and series. Growth and decay problems, such as those that arise in physics and other sciences, can also be modeled using sequences and series.

Compound interest

Compound interest can be modeled by deriving a general formula for the total amount of money available after a principal deposit P has accrued interest at rate of r (a decimal) compounded n times annually for t years. The same sequence-based approach to modeling compound interest is illustrative and can be applied in a similar manner to the various aspects of annuities and mortgages as well. Interest is compounded n times per year, so, after each interval, the total balance accrues interest at a rate $\frac{r}{n}$. For the first instance,

$$A_1 = P + \frac{r}{n}P = P\left(1 + \frac{r}{n}\right)$$

In the second instance,

$$A_2 = A_1 + \frac{r}{n}A_1 = A_1\left(1 + \frac{r}{n}\right)$$

The pattern continues. Note that if the expression is written out fully, then:

$$A_2 = A_1\left(1 + \frac{r}{n}\right) = P\left(1 + \frac{r}{n}\right)^2$$

The pattern that emerges from this approach can be expressed generally for a sequence with n terms:

$$A_n = P\left(1 + \frac{r}{n}\right)^n$$

A_n is the total amount (principal plus accrued interest) after one year. Thus, for t years, the total balance is the following.

$$A = P\left(1 + \frac{r}{n}\right)^{nt}$$

If the interest is compounded continuously, then the formula becomes the limit of the above expression as n approaches infinity.

$$A = \lim_{n \to \infty} [P(1 + \tfrac{r}{n})^{nt}]$$

By rearranging this expression, a simpler form of the limit can be found.

$$A = P \lim_{n \to \infty} [(1 + \tfrac{1}{n/r})^{n/r}]^{rt} = P \lim_{n/r \to \infty} [(1 + \tfrac{1}{n/r})^{n/r}]^{rt}$$

Evaluating the limit reveals the balance after t years with continuously compounded interest.

$$A = Pe^{rt}$$

Example: Calculate the interest accrued after 3 years for $1,000 in a savings account that compounds the interest monthly at an annual rate of 3%.

Use the formula derived above, where $t = 3$, $n = 12$, $P = 1,000$, and $r = 0.03$.

$$A = P(1 + \tfrac{r}{n})^{nt} = \$1000(1 + \tfrac{0.03}{12})^{(12)(3)} = \$1000(1.0025)^{36}$$
$$A = \$1094.05$$

Thus, the total interest accrued is $94.05.

Example: What is the total balance after 5 years in a savings account with an annual continuously compounded interest rate of 1% if the initial deposit is $500?

Use the expression for continuously compounded interest, substituting all the relevant information described in the problem.

$$A = Pe^{rt} = \$500e^{(0.01)(5)} = \$500e^{0.05}$$
$$A = \$525.64$$

Iteration and Recursive Patterns and Relations

A RECURRENCE RELATION is an equation that defines a sequence recursively; in other words, each term of the sequence is defined as a function of the preceding terms. For instance, the formula for the balance of an interest-bearing savings account after t years, which is given above in closed form (that is, explicit form), can be expressed recursively as follows.

$$A_t = A_{t-1} (1 + \tfrac{r}{n})^n \qquad \text{where } A_0 = P$$

Here, r is the annual interest rate and n is the number of times the interest is compounded per year. Mortgage and annuity parameters can also be expressed in recursive form. Calculation of a past or future term by applying a recursive formula multiple times is called ITERATION.

RECURRENCE RELATION: an equation that defines a sequence recursively; in other words, each term of the sequence is defined as a function of the preceding terms

ITERATION: the process of calculating a past or future term by applying a recursive formula multiple times

Sequences of numbers can be defined by iteratively applying a recursive pattern. For instance, the Fibonacci sequence is defined as follows.

$$F_i = F_{i-1} + F_{i-2} \qquad \text{where } F_0 = 0 \text{ and } F_1 = 1$$

Applying this recursive formula gives the sequence $\{0, 1, 1, 2, 3, 5, 8, 13, 21, \ldots\}$.

It is sometimes difficult or impossible to write recursive relations in explicit or closed form. In such cases, especially when computer programming is involved, the recursive form can still be helpful. When the elements of a sequence of numbers or values depend on one or more previous values, then it is possible that a recursive formula could be used to summarize the sequence.

If a value or number from a later point in the sequence (that is, other than the beginning) is known and it is necessary to find previous terms, then the indices of the recursive relation can be adjusted to find previous values instead of later ones. Consider, for instance, the Fibonacci sequence.

$$F_i = F_{i-1} + F_{i-2}$$
$$F_{i+2} = F_{i+1} + F_i$$
$$F_i = F_{i+2} - F_{i+1}$$

Thus, if any two consecutive numbers in the Fibonacci sequence are known, then the previous numbers of the sequence can be found (in addition to the later numbers).

Example: Write a recursive formula for the following sequence: $\{2, 3, 5, 9, 17, 33, 65, \ldots\}$.

By inspection, it can be seen that each number in the sequence is equal to twice the previous number, less 1. If the numbers in the sequence are indexed such that, for the first number, $i = 1$, and so on, then the recursion relation is the following.

$$N_i = 2N_{i-1} - 1$$

Example: If a recursive relation is defined by $N_i = N_{i-1}^2$ and the fourth term is 65,536, what is the first term?

Adjust the indices of the recursion and then solve for N_i.

$$N_{i+1} = N_i^2$$
$$N_i = \sqrt{N_{i+1}}$$

Use this relationship to backtrack to the first term.

$$N_3 = \sqrt{N_4} = \sqrt{65{,}536} = 256$$
$$N_2 = \sqrt{N_3} = \sqrt{256} = 16$$
$$N_1 = \sqrt{N_2} = \sqrt{16} = 16$$

The first term of the sequence is thus 4.

Converting between Recursive and Closed Forms

It helpful in some situations to convert between the recursive form and closed form of a function. Given a closed-form representation of a function, the recursive form can be found by writing out the corresponding series or sequence and then determining a pattern or formula that accurately represents that series or sequence. Consider, for instance, the mortgage principal formula in recursive form:

$$A_i = A_{i-1}(1 + \tfrac{r}{n}) - M \qquad \text{where } A_0 = P$$

Here, A_i is the remaining principal on the mortgage after the ith payment, r is the annual interest rate, which is compounded n times annually, and M is the monthly payment. The initial value P is the original loan amount for the mortgage. To obtain a closed-form expression for this recursive formula, first write out the terms of the corresponding sequence.

$$A_0 = P$$
$$A_1 = P(1 + \tfrac{r}{n}) - M$$
$$A_2 = A_1(1 + \tfrac{r}{n}) - M = P(1 + \tfrac{r}{n})^2 - M(1 + \tfrac{r}{n}) - M$$
$$A_3 = A_2(1 + \tfrac{r}{n}) - M = P(1 + \tfrac{r}{n})^3 - M(1 + \tfrac{r}{n})^2 - M(1 + \tfrac{r}{n}) - M$$

This pattern continues until $i = k$, where k is the total number of payments in the mortgage term. Note that the term A_k can be written as follows, where $z = 1 + \tfrac{r}{n}$:

$$A_k = Pz^k - M\{z^{k-1} + z^{k-2} + \ldots z^2 + z + 1\}$$

But the expression in the curly brackets is simply a geometric series, which can be written in closed form as

$$z^{k-1} + z^{k-2} + \ldots z^2 + z + 1 = \tfrac{1 - z^k}{1 - z}$$

Thus, the closed form expression for the principle remaining after k payments on the mortgage is

$$A_k = Pz^k - M\tfrac{1 - z^k}{1 - z} \qquad \text{where } z = 1 + \tfrac{r}{n}$$

The process for converting from closed form to recursive form is similar (it is essentially the reverse of the process described above). Simply write out the terms, determine the pattern and then write the ith value in terms of the $(i-1)$st or $(i+1)$st value.

SKILL 16.3 **Perform operations on matrices and vectors**

Vectors

A **VECTOR** is any quantity that has **magnitude** (or length) and **direction**. For instance, unlike temperature (which is just a scalar), velocity is a vector because it has magnitude (speed) and direction (the direction of travel). Because vectors do not have specified locations, they can be translated as long as their direction and magnitude remain the same. A vector is often written in the same form as a point; for instance, a vector can be written as (x_1, y_1, z_1). In this case, the direction and magnitude of the vector are defined by a ray that starts at the origin and terminates at the point (x_1, y_1, z_1).

Because vectors do not have specified locations, they can be translated as long as their direction and magnitude remain the same.

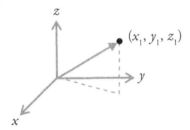

As noted before, however, the vector is not confined to the location shown above. The magnitude of a vector is simply the distance from the origin to the point (x_1, y_1, z_1). If $\vec{A} = (x_1, y_1, z_1)$, then the magnitude is written as $|\vec{A}|$.

$$|\vec{A}| = \sqrt{x_1^2 + y_1^2 + z_1^2}$$

Note that the direction of a vector can be written as a unit vector $\vec{u}$ of length 1, such that

$$\vec{A} = \vec{u}|\vec{A}|$$

Vectors obey the laws of associativity, commutativity, identity, and additive inverses:

$$\vec{A} + (\vec{B} + \vec{C}) = (\vec{A} + \vec{B}) + \vec{C}$$
$$\vec{A} + \vec{B} = \vec{B} + \vec{A}$$
$$\vec{A} + 0 = \vec{A}$$
$$\vec{A} + (-\vec{A}) = 0$$

As such, vectors have some of the same properties as real numbers.

Matrices

Matrices are slightly more complicated than vectors, and operations involving matrices likewise require more subtle analysis. In fact, vectors can simply be viewed as a type of matrix. Like vectors, matrices obey some of the same rules and principles as do real numbers; in other cases, however, such as commutativity, matrices and real numbers differ.

A **MATRIX** is an ordered set of numbers written in rectangular form. An example matrix is shown below.

$$\begin{pmatrix} 0 & 3 & 1 \\ 4 & 2 & 3 \\ 1 & 0 & 2 \end{pmatrix}$$

> **MATRIX:** an ordered set of numbers written in rectangular form

Since this matrix has 3 rows and 3 columns, it is called a 3×3 matrix. The element in the second row of the third column would be denoted as $3_{2,\,3}$. In general, a matrix with r rows and c columns is an $r \times c$ matrix.

> *In general, a matrix with r rows and c columns is an r × c matrix.*

Matrix addition and subtraction obey the rules of associativity, commutativity, identity, and additive inverse.

$$\overline{A} + (\overline{B} + \overline{C}) = (\overline{A} + \overline{B}) + \overline{C}$$
$$\overline{A} + \overline{B} = \overline{B} + \overline{A}$$
$$\overline{A} + 0 = \overline{A}$$
$$\overline{A} + (-\overline{A}) = 0$$

Addition, Subtraction, and Scalar Multiplication of Vectors

Addition and subtraction of two vectors $\overrightarrow{A} = (x_1, y_1, z_1)$ and $\overrightarrow{B} = (x_2, y_2, z_2)$ can be performed by adding or subtracting corresponding components of the vectors.

$$\overrightarrow{A} + \overrightarrow{B} = (x_1 + x_2, y_1 + y_2, z_1 + z_2)$$
$$\overrightarrow{A} - \overrightarrow{B} = (x_1 - x_2, y_1 - y_2, z_1 - z_2)$$

Geometrically, addition involves placing the tail of $\overrightarrow{B}$ on the head of $\overrightarrow{A}$, as shown below. The result is a vector that starts from the tail of $\overrightarrow{A}$ and ends at the head of $\overrightarrow{B}$.

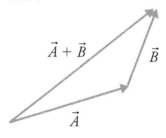

Subtraction of two vectors involves the same process, except that the direction of $\overrightarrow{B}$ must be reversed.

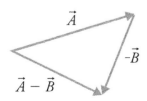

Multiplication of a vector by a scalar simply involves multiplying each component by the scalar.

$$\vec{cA} = (cx_1, cy_1, cz_1)$$

Geometrically, this operation extends the length of the vector by a factor c.

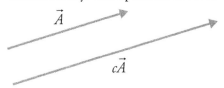

Vector Multiplication

Vector multiplication takes two forms: the dot product (or scalar product) and the **cross product** (or vector product). The **DOT PRODUCT** is calculated by multiplying corresponding components of two vectors. The operator for this product is typically a small dot ($\cdot$).

$$\vec{A} \cdot \vec{B} = x_1x_2 + y_1y_2 + z_1z_2$$

> **DOT PRODUCT:** the product of two vectors is found by multiplying corresponding components of the vectors; the result is a scalar

Notice that the dot product yields a single scalar value. Also note that the magnitude of a vector can be written in terms of the dot product.

$$|\vec{A}| = \sqrt{\vec{A} \cdot \vec{A}}$$

Geometrically, the dot product is a projection of one vector onto another.

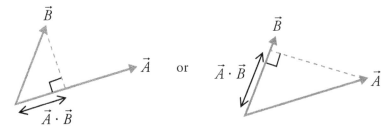

It can be shown that the dot product of two vectors is equivalent to the following:

$$\vec{A} \cdot \vec{B} = |\vec{A}| |\vec{B}| \cos \theta$$

> If two vectors are perpendicular, then their dot product is zero.

It is clear, both from the geometric and the algebraic definitions of the dot product, that if two vectors are perpendicular, then their dot product is zero.

The cross product of two vectors, typically symbolized by a "$\times$" operator, yields a third vector. The cross product is defined as follows.

$$\vec{A} \times \vec{B} = (y_1z_2 - y_2z_1, z_1x_2 - z_2x_1, x_1y_2, x_2y_1)$$

> **CROSS PRODUCT:** a third vector that is perpendicular to both original vectors (that is, to the plane formed by the two original vectors)

Geometrically, the **CROSS PRODUCT** of $\vec{A}$ and $\vec{B}$ is a third vector that is perpendicular to both $\vec{A}$ and $\vec{B}$ (that is, to the plane formed by $\vec{A}$ and $\vec{B}$), with the direction defined by the so-called right-hand screw rule. If a right-hand screw is turned in the direction from $\vec{A}$ to $\vec{B}$, the direction in which the screw advances is the direction of the cross product.

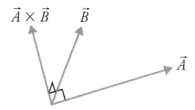

The magnitude of $\vec{A} \times \vec{B}$ is the area of the parallelogram defined by $\vec{A}$ and $\vec{B}$.

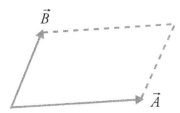

The magnitude of the cross product can also be written as follows. $|\vec{A} \times \vec{B}| = |\vec{A}||\vec{B}|\sin\theta$

From both the algebraic and geometric definitions of the cross product, it is apparent that if two vectors are parallel, their cross product is zero.

If two vectors are parallel, their cross product is zero.

Multiplication of vectors, either by the dot product or cross product, obeys the rule of distibutivity, where $*$ symbolizes either $\cdot$ or $\times$.
$$\vec{A} * (\vec{B} + \vec{C}) = \vec{A} * \vec{B} + \vec{A} * \vec{C}$$

Only the dot product obeys commutativity, however. There is a similar rule for cross products, though.
$$\vec{A} \cdot \vec{B} = \vec{B} \cdot \vec{A}$$
$$\vec{A} \times \vec{B} = -\vec{B} \times \vec{A}$$

Example: Find the cross product $\vec{a} \times \vec{b}$, where $\vec{a}$ = (-1, 4, 2) and $\vec{b}$ = (3, -1, 4).

Use the expression given to calculate the cross product.
$$\vec{a} \times \vec{b} = (4 \cdot 4 - (-1) \cdot 2, 2 \cdot 3 - 4 \cdot (-1), (-1) \cdot (-1) - 3 \cdot 4)$$
$$\vec{a} \times \vec{b} = (16 + 2, 6 + 4, 1 - 12) = (18, 10, -11)$$

Example: Find the follo wing for $\vec{a}$ = (1, 2, 3), $\vec{b}$ = (2, 3, 1) and c = 2c($\vec{a} \cdot \vec{b}$).

First, find the dot product; then multiply. Note that the result must be a scalar.
$$c(\vec{a} \cdot \vec{b}) = 2[1(2) + 2(3) + 3(1)] = 2[11] = 22$$

Addition, Subtraction, and Multiplication of Matrices

Matrices can be added or subtracted only if their dimensions are the same. To add (subtract) compatible matrices, simply add (subtract) the corresponding elements, as with the example below for 2×2 matrices.

$$\begin{pmatrix} a_{11} & a_{12} \\ a_{21} & a_{22} \end{pmatrix} + \begin{pmatrix} b_{11} & b_{12} \\ b_{21} & b_{22} \end{pmatrix} = \begin{pmatrix} a_{11} + b_{11} & a_{12} + b_{12} \\ a_{21} + b_{21} & a_{22} + b_{22} \end{pmatrix}$$

Multiplication of matrices is more complicated, except for the case of multiplication by a scalar. The product of a matrix and a scalar is found by multiplying each element of the matrix by the scalar.

$$c\begin{pmatrix} a_{11} & a_{12} \\ a_{21} & a_{22} \end{pmatrix} = \begin{pmatrix} ca_{11} & ca_{12} \\ ca_{21} & ca_{22} \end{pmatrix}$$

Multiplication of two matrices is only defined if the number of columns in the first matrix is equal to the number of rows in the second matrix.

Multiplication of two matrices is only defined if the number of columns in the first matrix is equal to the number of rows in the second matrix. Matrix multiplication is not necessarily commutative. Given an $n \times m$ matrix ($\overline{A}$) multiplied by an $m \times p$ matrix ($\overline{B}$) (multiplied in that order), the product is an $n \times p$ matrix. Each element C_{ij} in the product matrix is equal to the sum of each element in the ith row of the $n \times m$ matrix multiplied by each corresponding element in the jth column of the $m \times p$ matrix. Thus, each element C_{ij} of the product matrix $\overline{AB}$ is equal to the following, where $\overline{AB} = \overline{C}$:

$$C_{ij} = \sum_{k-1}^{m} A_{ik}B_{kj}$$

Consider the following example.

$$\begin{pmatrix} 1 & 2 & 3 \\ 4 & 5 & 6 \end{pmatrix} \begin{pmatrix} 7 \\ 8 \\ 9 \end{pmatrix}$$

The solution is found as follows.

$$\begin{pmatrix} 1 & 2 & 3 \\ 4 & 5 & 6 \end{pmatrix} \begin{pmatrix} 7 \\ 8 \\ 9 \end{pmatrix} = \begin{pmatrix} (1)(7) + (2)(8) + (3)(9) \\ (4)(7) + (5)(8) + (6)(9) \end{pmatrix} = \begin{pmatrix} 50 \\ 122 \end{pmatrix}$$

Matrix multiplication obeys the rules of associativity and distributivity, but not commutativity.

$$\overline{A}(\overline{BC}) = (\overline{AB})\overline{C}$$
$$\overline{A}(\overline{B} + \overline{C}) = \overline{AB} + \overline{AC}$$
$$(\overline{B} + \overline{C})\overline{A} = \overline{BA} + \overline{CA}$$

Example: Determine the product $\overline{AB}$ of the following matrices.

$$\overline{A} = \begin{pmatrix} -1 & 2 & 8 \\ 4 & -3 & 7 \\ 0 & 1 & 4 \end{pmatrix} \quad \overline{B} = \begin{pmatrix} 0 & 5 & 0 \\ 7 & -2 & -1 \\ -8 & 0 & 3 \end{pmatrix}$$

The product AB is a 3×3 matrix. The first column of AB is the dot product of the first column of B with each row of A.

$$\overline{AB} = \begin{pmatrix} -1 & 2 & 8 \\ 4 & -3 & 7 \\ 0 & 1 & 4 \end{pmatrix} \begin{pmatrix} 0 & 5 & 0 \\ 7 & -2 & -1 \\ -8 & 0 & 3 \end{pmatrix} = \begin{pmatrix} 0 + 14 - 64 & \cdot & \cdot \\ -21 - 56 & \cdot & \cdot \\ 7 - 32 & \cdot & \cdot \end{pmatrix}$$

The other columns of AB are found using the same approach for the other columns of B.

$$\overline{AB} = \begin{pmatrix} -50 & -9 & 22 \\ -77 & 26 & 24 \\ -25 & -2 & 11 \end{pmatrix}$$

SKILL 16.4 Apply set theory to solve problems

Properties of Sets

Set theory is a helpful tool for organizing and describing information in mathematics. Any collection of elements can be considered a set. For instance, a set could be as simple as {banana, apple, pear} or as complicated as $\mathbb{C}$, the set of complex numbers. Two basic set operations are union (symbolized by ∪) and intersection (symbolized by ∩). Two sets that have no members in common are **disjoint**.

The **UNION** (∪) of two sets is the set of all the numbers that are in either the first or the second set or in both sets.

> If set A = {-7, -2, 0, 1, 3, 4, 5, 6} and set B = {-5, -3, 0, 1, 2, 3, 5}, then A ∪ B is {-7, -5, -3, -2, 0, 1, 2, 3, 4, 5, 6}.

> **UNION:** in two sets, the set of all the numbers, which are in either the first or the second set or in both sets

The **INTERSECTION** (∩) of two sets is the set of numbers that are in both sets.

> A(∩) B is {0, 1, 3, 5}.

> **INTERSECTION:** in two sets of numbers, the numbers that are in both sets

We can illustrate the union and intersection of sets A and B with a Venn diagram.

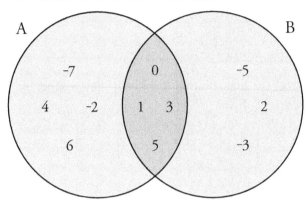

The union of the two sets would be the entire Venn diagram, whereas the intersection would be the area in the middle of the diagram where the two circles overlap.

NULL SET: called the empty set; it does not contain any numbers

The **NULL SET** is also called the empty set; it is the set that does not contain any numbers. The null set can be expressed two different ways: either { } or ∅. {0} is not the null set, since it does have one element, zero.

DISJOINT SETS: sets that have no elements in common

If sets A and B did not contain 0, 1, 3, and 5, they would be disjoint sets. **DISJOINT SETS** are sets that have no elements in common. They would look like this:

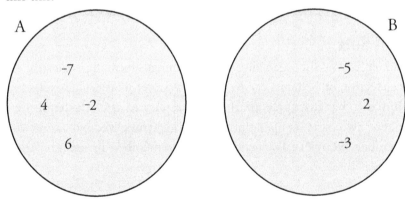

Example: Find the union of {a, b, c} and {d, e, f}.
Solution: {a, b, c} ∪ {d, e, f} = {a, b, c, d, e, f}

Example: Find the intersection of {a, b, c, d} and {b, d, e, f}.
Solution: {a, b, c, d} ∩ {b, d, e, f} = {b, d}

SUBSET: set A is a subset of set B if every element of set A is an element of set B

Set A is a **SUBSET** of set B if every element of set A is an element of set B.

Example: Set A = {Virginia, Rhode Island}; Set B = {the United States}

A ⊆ B

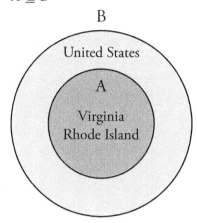

The result of a union of two sets contains all the elements found in each set. Thus, for instance, the union of the set of irrational numbers and the set of rational numbers is the set of real numbers.

The result of an intersection of two sets contains all the elements that are common to both sets. The intersection of the sets of irrational and rational numbers is an empty set (or null set) because there are no numbers that are both rational and irrational (the two sets are disjoint).

Example: Find the union and intersection of the sets of real and complex numbers.

The set of real numbers is expressed as $\mathbb{R}$, and the set of complex numbers is expressed as $\mathbb{C}$. Since the set of real numbers is contained in the set of complex numbers, the following can be written:

$$\mathbb{R} \cup \mathbb{C} = \mathbb{C}$$

For the intersection, only the real numbers are common to both sets. Thus:

$$\mathbb{R} \cap \mathbb{C} = \mathbb{R}$$

Sets may have a limited number of elements or an infinite number.

The ordering of the elements in a set is not relevant, although a certain order may be imposed for convenience when writing all or some portion of the elements of a set. For instance, the set of the first four natural numbers can be equivalently written {1, 2, 3, 4} or {4, 2, 1, 3} (or any other arrangement).

Sets may also be written in a conditional form that specifies a certain collection of elements. For instance, $\{x : x \geq 3\}$ specifies the set of x such that x is greater than or equal to 3. Another example is $\{x : x \in \mathbb{Z}\}$, which is the set of integers (this set could be written more simply as just $\mathbb{Z}$).

SAMPLE TEST

Sample Test:
Mathematical Processes and Number Sense

(Average) (Skill 1.1)

1. Identify the correct sequence of sub-skills required for solving and graphing inequalities involving absolute value in one variable, such as $|x + 1| \leq 6$.

    A. Understanding absolute value, graphing inequalities, solving systems of equations

    B. Graphing inequalities on a Cartesian plane, solving systems of equations, simplifying expressions with absolute value

    C. Plotting points, graphing equations, graphing inequalities

    D. Solving equations with absolute value, solving inequalities, graphing conjunctions and disjunctions

(Rigorous) (Skill 1.1)

2. Mr. Lacey is using problem solving to help students develop their math skills. He gives the class a box of pencils. He says that the pencils have to be divided so that each student has the same number of pencils. What step should come first in problem solving?

    A. Find a strategy to solve the problem

    B. Identify the problem

    C. Count the number of pencils

    D. Make basic calculations

(Average) (Skill 1.2)

3. Estimate the sum of $1498 + 1309$.

    A. 2900

    B. 2850

    C. 2800

    D. 2600

(Average) (Skill 1.2)

4. The mass of a Chips Ahoy cookie is about:

    A. 1 kilogram

    B. 1 gram

    C. 15 grams

    D. 15 milligrams

(Average) (Skill 1.3)

5. What would be the total cost of a suit for $295.99 and a pair of shoes for $69.95 including 6.5% sales tax?

    A. $389.73

    B. $398.37

    C. $237.86

    D. $315.23

(Rigorous)(Skill 1.3)

6. Convert $\overline{.63}$ into a fraction in simplest form.

    A. $\frac{63}{100}$

    B. $\frac{7}{11}$

    C. $6\frac{3}{10}$

    D. $\frac{2}{3}$

(Easy) (Skill 1.3)

7. A student had 60 days to appeal the results of an exam. If the results were received on March 23, what was the last day that the student could appeal?

   A. May 21

   B. May 22

   C. May 23

   D. May 24

(Average) (Skill 1.3)

8. Evaluate: $\frac{1}{3} - \frac{1}{2} + \frac{1}{6}$

   A. $\frac{5}{6}$

   B. $\frac{2}{3}$

   C. 0

   D. 1

(Rigorous) (Skill 1.4)

9. The volume of water flowing through a pipe varies directly with the square of the radius of the pipe. If the water flows at a rate of 80 liters per minute through a pipe with a radius of 4 cm, at what rate would water flow through a pipe with a radius of 3 cm?

   A. 45 liters per minute

   B. 6.67 liters per minute

   C. 60 liters per minute

   D. 4.5 liters per minute

(Rigorous) (Skill 1.4)

10. Joe reads 20 words/min., and Jan reads 80 words/min. How many minutes will it take Joe to read the same number of words that it takes Jan 40 minutes to read?

    A. 10

    B. 20

    C. 80

    D. 160

(Easy) (Skill 1.4)

11. If three cups of concentrate are needed to make 2 gallons of fruit punch, how many cups are needed to make 5 gallons?

    A. 6 cups

    B. 7 cups

    C. 7.5 cups

    D. 10 cups

(Rigorous) (Skill 2.1)

12. Kindergarten students are doing a butterfly art project. They fold paper in half. On one half, they paint a design. Then they fold the paper closed and reopen. The resulting picture is a butterfly with matching sides. What math principle does this demonstrate?

    A. Slide

    B. Rotate

    C. Symmetry

    D. Transformation

(Average) (Skill 2.1)

13. Express in symbols: "*x* is greater than seven and less than or equal to fifteen."

   A. $7 < x \leq 15$

   B. $7 > x \geq 15$

   C. $15 \leq x < 7$

   D. $7 < x = 15$

(Easy) (Skill 2.3)

14. The following statement about inductive reasoning is not accurate:

   A. Inductive reasoning involves making inference from specific facts to general principles.

   B. Inductive reasoning involves making inference from general principles to specific facts.

   C. Inductive reasoning is generally weaker than deductive reasoning.

   D. Mathematical proofs are not inductive.

(Average) (Skill 2.4)

15. The contrapositive of the statement "If I am hungry I eat" is:

   A. If I eat then I am hungry.

   B. If I am not hungry I do not eat.

   C. If I do not eat I am not hungry.

   D. None of the above

(Rigorous) (Skill 2.4)

16. Which of the following is a simple statement that can be assigned a truth value?

   A. It is sunny today.

   B. Please put away the books.

   C. The wind blew and the leaves fell.

   D. They will stay home or they will go to the mall.

(Rigorous) (Skill 2.4)

17. What is the negation of a statement of the form "*p* and *q*"?

   A. not *p* and not *q*

   B. not *p* and *q*

   C. not *p* or not *q*

   D. *p* or not *q*

(Average) (Skill 3.1)

18. Given W = whole numbers

   N = natural numbers

   Z = integers

   R = rational numbers

   I = irrational numbers

   which of the following is not true?

   A. $R \subset I$

   B. $W \subset Z$

   C. $Z \subset R$

   D. $N \subset W$

(Rigorous) (Skill 2.3)

19. Which expression below is equivalent to the expression $14 - 2(3x + 5) - 8x$

   A. $88x$

   B. $28x + 60$

   C. $-5x + 17$

   D. $-14x + 4$

(Easy) (Skill 3.1)

20. How many real numbers lie between −1 and +1?

A. 0

B. 1

C. 17

D. An infinite number

(Easy) (Skill 3.2)

21. The conjugate of $4 + 5i$ is

A. $-4 + 5i$

B. $4 - 5i$

C. $4i + 5$

D. $4i - 5$

(Average) (Skill 3.2)

22. Simplify: $(6 + 3i) - (4 - 2i)$

A. $2 + 5i$

B. $2 + i$

C. $10 + 5i$

D. $2 - 2i$

(Rigorous) (Skill 3.2)

23. Simplify: $\frac{10}{1 + 3i}$

A. $-1.25(1 - 3i)$

B. $1.25(1 - 3i)$

C. $1 + 3i$

D. $1 - 3i$

(Average) (Skill 5.3)

24. Which statement below best represents the algorithm for fraction division?

A. Multiply the means and the extremes, then equate the two.

B. Multiply the numerators and the denominators to create a fraction answer.

C. Rewrite the quotient as the product of the first fraction and the reciprocal of the second fraction.

D. Rewrite the quotient as the product of the first fraction and the opposite of the second fraction.

(Average) (Skill 3.3)

25. Which of the following sets is closed under division?

I) {½, 1, 2, 4}

II) {-1, 1}

III) {-1, 0, 1}

A. I only

B. II only

C. III only

D. I and II

(Easy) (Skill 3.4)

26. Find the LCM of 27, 90, and 84.

A. 90

B. 3,780

C. 204,120

D. 1,260

(Average) (Skill 3.4)

27. Which of the following is always composite if x is odd, y is even, and both x and y are greater than or equal to 2?

    A. $x + y$

    B. $3x + 2y$

    C. $5xy$

    D. $5x + 3y$

(Rigorous) (Skill 5.4)

28. Which ordered pair listed below best follows the pattern represented in the given graph?

    A. $(0, 0)$

    B. $(2, 6)$

    C. $(4, 9)$

    D. $(5, 5)$

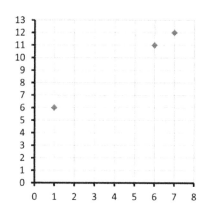

(Average) (Skill 3.4)

29. Find the GCF of $2^2 \times 3^2 \times 5$ and $2^2 \times 3 \times 7$.

    A. $2^5 \times 3^3 \times 5 \times 7$

    B. $2 \times 3 \times 5 \times 7$

    C. $2^2 \times 3$

    D. $2^3 \times 3^2 \times 5 \times 7$

Patterns, Algebra, and Functions

(Easy) (Skill 4.1)

30. Which set illustrates a function?

    A. $\{(0, 1)\ (0, 2)\ (0, 3)\ (0, 4)\}$

    B. $\{(3, 9)\ (-3, 9)\ (4, 16)\ (-4, 16)\}$

    C. $\{(1, 2)\ (2, 3)\ (3, 4)\ (1, 4)\}$

    D. $\{(2, 4)\ (3, 6)\ (4, 8)\ (4, 16)\}$

(Average) (Skill 4.2)

31. Given $f(x) = 3x - 2$ and $g(x) = x^2$, determine $g(f(x))$.

    A. $3x^2 - 2$

    B. $9x^2 + 4$

    C. $9x^2 - 12x + 4$

    D. $3x^3 - 2$

(Average) (Skill 4.2)

32. $f(x) = 3x - 2;\ f^{-1}(x) =$

    A. $3x + 2$

    B. $\frac{x}{6}$

    C. $2x - 3$

    D. $\frac{(x + 2)}{3}$

(Average) (Skill 4.3)

33. State the domain of the function $f(x) = \frac{3x - 6}{x^2 - 25}$.

    A. $x \neq 2$

    B. $x \neq 5, -5$

    C. $x \neq 2, -2$

    D. $x \neq 5$

(Average) (Skill 4.3)

34. Give the domain for the function over the set of real numbers:

$$y = \frac{3x + 2}{2x^2 - 3}$$

A. All real numbers

B. All real numbers, $x \neq 0$

C. All real numbers, $x \neq -2$ or 3

D. All real numbers, $x \neq \frac{\pm\sqrt{6}}{2}$

(Rigorous) (Skill 4.4)

35. Which equation is represented by the graph below?

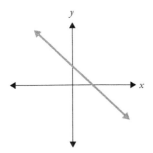

A. $x - y = 3$

B. $x - y = -3$

C. $x + y = 3$

D. $x + y = -3$

(Rigorous) (Skill 4.4)

36. What is the equation of the graph below?

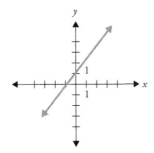

A. $2x + y = 2$

B. $2x - y = -2$

C. $2x - y = 2$

D. $2x + y = -2$

(Average) (Skill 4.4)

37. Three less than four times a number is five times the sum of that number and 6. Which equation could be used to solve this problem?

A. $3 - 4n = 5(n + 6)$

B. $3 - 4n + 5n = 6$

C. $4n - 3 = 5n + 6$

D. $4n - 3 = 5(n + 6)$

(Rigorous) (Skill 5.1)

38. Which graph represents the equation of $y = x^2 + 3x$?

A.

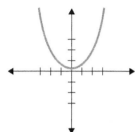

B.

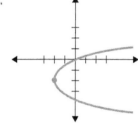

C.

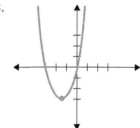

D.

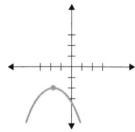

(Average) (Skill 5.1)

39. Which equation is graphed below?

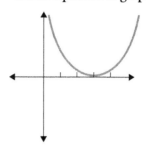

A. $y = 4(x + 3)^2$

B. $y = 4(x - 3)^2$

C. $y = 3(x - 4)^2$

D. $y = 3(x + 4)^2$

(Average) (Skill 5.2)

40. Solve for x: $3x + 5 \geq 8 + 7x$

A. $x \geq -\frac{3}{4}$

B. $x \leq -\frac{3}{4}$

C. $x \geq \frac{3}{4}$

D. $x \leq \frac{3}{4}$

(Average) (Skill 5.6)

41. Identify the expression below that does not represent the phrase "half of M."

A. $\frac{1}{2}M$

B. $\frac{M}{2}$

C. $M \div \frac{1}{2}$

D. $0.5M$

(Easy) (Skill 5.2)

42. The formula for solving a quadratic equation is:

    A. $x = \dfrac{-b \pm \sqrt{b^2 - 4ac}}{2a}$

    B. $x = \dfrac{-b \pm \sqrt{b^2 - 4a}}{2a}$

    C. $x = \dfrac{b \pm \sqrt{b^2 - 4ac}}{2a}$

    D. $x = \dfrac{b \pm \sqrt{b^3 - 4ac}}{2a}$

(Rigorous) (Skill 5.3)

43. Solve for x and y:

    $x = 3y + 7$
    $7x + 5y = 23$

    A. $(-1, 4)$

    B. $(4, -1)$

    C. $\left(\dfrac{-29}{7}, \dfrac{-26}{7}\right)$

    D. $(10, 1)$

(Rigorous) (Skill 5.3)

44. Solve the system of equations for x, y, and z.

    $3x + 2y - z = 0$
    $2x + 5y = 8z$
    $x + 3y + 2z = 7$

    A. $(-1, 2, 1)$

    B. $(1, 2, -1)$

    C. $(-3, 4, -1)$

    D. $(0, 1, 2)$

(Rigorous) (Skill 5.4)

45. Find the zeroes of $f(x) = x^3 + x^2 - 14x - 24$.

    A. $4, 3, 2$

    B. $3, -8$

    C. $7, -2, -1$

    D. $4, -3, -2$

(Easy) (Skill 5.4)

46. How many roots does the polynomial $x^4 + 3x^3 - 7x^2 + x + 4$ have?

    A. 2

    B. 3

    C. 4

    D. 5

(Rigorous) (Skill 5.4)

47. The solutions to the polynomial equation $x^4 - 4x^3 - 9x^2 + 16x + 20 = 0$ are given by

    A. $\{-2, -1, 2, 5\}$

    B. $\{-1, 0, 1, 5\}$

    C. $\{-2, 0, 1, 5\}$

    D. $\{-1, 1, 2, 5\}$

(Average) (Skill 5.5)

48. What is the slope of any line parallel to the line $2x + 4y = 4$?

    A. -2

    B. -1

    C. $-\dfrac{1}{2}$

    D. 2

(Average) (Skill 5.5)

49. The discriminant of a quadratic equation is evaluated and determined to be -3. The equation has:

    A. One real root

    B. One complex root

    C. Two roots, both real

    D. Two roots, both complex

(Average) (Skill 5.6)

50. The path, d, of a projectile shot into the air with an initial velocity of 20 m/s is modeled by the function $d(t) = 20t - 5t^2$. When will the projectile hit the ground?

A. after 20 seconds

B. after 5 seconds

C. after 4 seconds

D. after 1 seconds

(Rigorous) (Skill 5.6)

51. A boat travels 30 miles upstream in three hours. It makes the return trip in one and a half hours. What is the speed of the boat in still water?

A. 10 mph

B. 15 mph

C. 20 mph

D. 30 mph

(Average) (Skill 6.1)

52. Which of the following is equivalent to $\sqrt[b]{x^a}$?

A. $x^{a/b}$

B. $x^{b/a}$

C. $a^{x/b}$

D. $b^{x/a}$

(Rigorous) (Skill 6.1)

53. Evaluate $3^{\frac{1}{2}}(9^{\frac{1}{3}})$.

A. $27^{\frac{5}{6}}$

B. $9^{\frac{7}{12}}$

C. $3^{\frac{5}{6}}$

D. $3^{\frac{6}{7}}$

(Average) (Skill 6.1)

54. $(3.8 \times 10^{17}) \times (.5 \times 10^{-12})$

A. 19×10^5

B. 1.9×10^5

C. 1.9×10^6

D. 1.9×10^7

(Rigorous) (Skill 6.1)

55. Simplify $\dfrac{\frac{3}{4}x^2y^{-3}}{\frac{2}{3}xy}$

A. $\frac{1}{2}xy^{-4}$

B. $\frac{1}{2}x^{-1}y^{-4}$

C. $\frac{9}{8}xy^{-4}$

D. $\frac{9}{8}xy^{-2}$

(Average) (Skill 6.2)

56. Which equation corresponds to the logarithmic statement: $\log_x k = m$?

A. $x^m = k$

B. $k^m = x$

C. $x^k = m$

D. $m^x = k$

(Average) (Skill 6.2)

57. Solve for x: $10^{x-3} + 5 = 105$.

A. 3

B. 10

C. 2

D. 5

(Average) (Skill 6.3)

58. Which of the following is the graph of the function $3^x - 4$?

A.

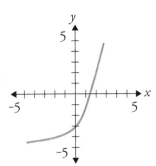

B.

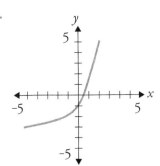

C.

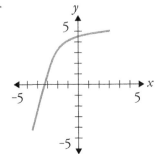

D.

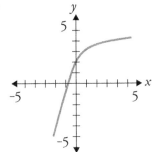

(Rigorous) (Skill 6.4)

59. After 5730 years, a given amount of carbon-14 decays to half the original amount. If A_0 is the original amount, A is the current amount and t is the number of years elapsed, the exponential decay model for carbon-14 is

A. $A = A_0 e^{\frac{-t}{5730}}$

B. $A = A_0 e^{-5730\,t}$

C. $A = A_0 e^{\frac{\ln 0.5}{5730}\,t}$

D. $A = A_0 e^{\frac{t}{5730}}$

(Rigorous) (Skill 7.1)

60. Solve for x: $|\,2x + 3\,| > 4$

A. $-\frac{7}{2} > x > \frac{1}{2}$

B. $-\frac{1}{2} > x > \frac{7}{2}$

C. $x < \frac{7}{2}$ or $x > -\frac{1}{2}$

D. $x < -\frac{7}{2}$ or $x > \frac{1}{2}$

(Rigorous) (Skill 7.1)

61. Graph the solution: $|\,x\,| + 7 < 13$

A.

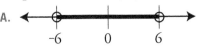

B.

C.

D.

(Average) (Skill 7.1)

62. Solve for x: $18 = 4 + |\,2x\,|$

A. $\{-11, 7\}$

B. $\{-7, 0, 7\}$

C. $\{-7, 7\}$

D. $\{-11, 11\}$

(Average) (Skill 7.2)

63. Graphs of functions $f(x) = \sqrt{x+1}$ and $g(x) = \sqrt{4-x}$ are shown below. What is the domain of the function $f(x) + g(x)$?

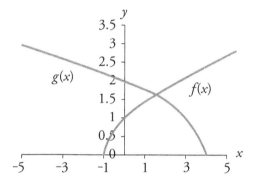

A. $-\infty \le x \le 4$

B. $-1 \le x \le 4$

C. $-1 \le x \le \infty$

D. $-\infty \le x \le \infty$

(Average) (Skill 7.3)

64. Find the domain of the function $\sqrt{6 - x^2}$.

A. $x \ge \sqrt{6}$

B. $-\sqrt{6} \le x \le \sqrt{6}$

C. $0 \le x \le \sqrt{6}$

D. $x \ge 0$

(Average) (Skill 7.3)

65. The rational function $\dfrac{2x+1}{2x^2 - x - 1}$ has

A. A vertical asymptote at $x = 1$

B. A horizontal asymptote at $y = 0$

C. A hole at $x = -\frac{1}{2}$

D. All of the above

(Rigorous) (Skill 7.4)

66. Ralph and Rhonda can paint a barn together in 4 hours. If Ralph needs 6 more hours than Rhonda to paint the barn by himself, how many hours does Rhonda need to paint the barn by herself?

A. 5

B. 6

C. 7

D. 8

Measurement and Geometry

(Easy) (Skill 8.1)

67. 3 km is equivalent to:

A. 300 cm

B. 300 m

C. 3000 cm

D. 3000 m

(Average) (Skill 8.1)

68. The speed of light in space is about 3×10^8 meters per second. Express this in kilometers per hour.

A. 1.08×10^9 km/hr

B. 3.0×10^{11} km/hr

C. 1.08×10^{12} km/hr

D. 1.08×10^{15} km/hr

(Rigorous) (Skill 8.2)

69. If the area of the base of a cone is tripled, the volume will be

A. the same as the original

B. 9 times the original

C. 3 times the original

D. 3π times the original

(Average) (Skill 8.2)

70. Given similar polygons with corresponding sides 6 and 8, what is the area of the smaller polygon if the area of the larger is 64?

    A. 48

    B. 36

    C. 144

    D. 78

(Average) (Skill 8.2)

71. In similar polygons, if the perimeters are in a ratio of $x : y$, the sides are in a ratio of:

    A. $x : y$

    B. $x^2 : y^2$

    C. $2x : y$

    D. $\frac{1}{2}x : y$

(Easy) (Skill 8.3)

72. Which word best describes a set of measured values that are all very similar but that all deviate significantly from the expected result?

    A. Perfect

    B. Precise

    C. Accurate

    D. Appropriate

(Average) (Skill 8.3)

73. A man's waist measures 90 cm. What is the greatest possible error for the measurement?

    A. ± 1 m

    B. ± 8 cm

    C. ± 1 cm

    D. ± 5 mm

(Average) (Skill 8.4)

74. Find the surface area of a box that is 3 feet wide, 5 feet tall, and 4 feet deep.

    A. 47 sq. ft.

    B. 60 sq. ft.

    C. 94 sq. ft.

    D. 188 sq. ft.

(Rigorous) (Skill 8.4)

75. Given a 30 meter by 60 meter garden with a circular fountain with a 5 meter radius, calculate the area of the portion of the garden not occupied by the fountain.

    A. 1,721 m^2

    B. 1,879 m^2

    C. 2,585 m^2

    D. 1,015 m^2

(Rigorous) (Skill 8.4)

76. The length of a picture frame is 2 inches greater than its width. If the area of the frame is 143 square inches, what is its width?

    A. 11 inches

    B. 13 inches

    C. 12 inches

    D. 10 inches

(Easy) (Skill 9.1)

77. Which of the following statements about an axiom is not true?

    A. An axiom is a self-evident statement.

    B. Axioms can be used to deduce theorems.

    C. An axiom can be proven.

    D. An axiom includes undefined terms.

(Average) (Skill 9.2)

78. Which of the following statements about a trapezoid is incorrect?

    A. It has one pair of parallel sides

    B. The parallel sides are called bases

    C. If the two bases are the same length, the trapezoid is called isosceles

    D. The median is parallel to the bases

(Rigorous) (Skill 9.2)

79. What is the degree measure of an interior angle of a regular 10-sided polygon?

    A. 18°

    B. 36°

    C. 144°

    D. 54°

(Rigorous) (Skill 9.2)

80. What is the measure of minor arc AD, given that the measure of arc PS is 40° and $m < K = 10°$?

    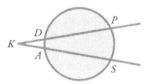

    A. 50°

    B. 20°

    C. 30°

    D. 25°

(Rigorous) (Skill 9.3)

81. Ginny and Nick head back to their respective colleges after being home for the weekend. They leave their house at the same time and drive for 4 hours. Ginny drives due south at the average rate of 60 miles per hour and Nick drives due east at the average rate of 60 miles per hour. What is the straight-line distance between them, in miles, at the end of the 4 hours?

    A. $120\sqrt{2}$

    B. 240

    C. $240\sqrt{2}$

    D. 288

(Average) (Skill 9.3)

82. If $AB = 12$, determine BC.

    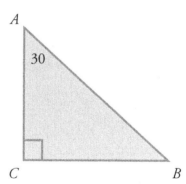

    A. 6

    B. 4

    C. $6\sqrt{3}$

    D. $3\sqrt{6}$

(Average) (Skill 9.3)

83. If a ship sails due south 6 miles, then due west 8 miles, how far is it from the starting point?

  A. 100 miles

  B. 10 miles

  C. 14 miles

  D. 48 miles

(Easy) (Skill 9.4)

84. Which term most accurately describes two coplanar lines without any common points?

  A. Perpendicular

  B. Parallel

  C. Intersecting

  D. Skew

(Average) (Skill 9.4)

85. Which theorem can be used to prove $\triangle BAK \cong \triangle MKA$?

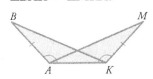

  A. *SSS*

  B. *ASA*

  C. *SAS*

  D. *AAS*

(Average) (Skill 9.4)

86. Prove $\triangle HYM \cong \triangle KZL$, given $\overline{XZ} \cong \overline{XY}$, $\angle KLM \cong \angle HML$ and $\overline{YL} \cong \overline{MZ}$

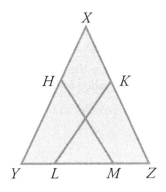

1. $\overline{XZ} \cong \overline{XY}$ 1. Given

2. $\angle HYL \cong \angle KZM$ 2. ?

3. $\angle KLM \cong \angle HML$ 3. Given

4. $\overline{YL} \cong \overline{MZ}$ 4. Given

5. $\overline{LM} \cong \overline{LM}$ 5. ?

6. $\overline{YM} \cong \overline{LZ}$ 6. Add

7. $\triangle HYM \cong \triangle KZL$ 7. ASA

Which could be used to justify steps 2 and 5?

  A. CPCTC, Identity

  B. Isosceles Triangle Theorem, Identity

  C. SAS, Reflexive

  D. Isosceles Triangle Theorem, Reflexive

(Rigorous) (Skill 9.4)

87. Which of the following statements is true about the number of degrees in each angle?

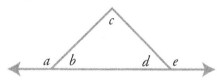

A. $a + b + c = 180°$

B. $a = e$

C. $b + c = e$

D. $c + d = e$

(Average) (Skill 10.2)

88. Compute the distance from $(-2, 7)$ to the line $x = 5$.

A. -9

B. -7

C. 5

D. 7

(Rigorous) (Skill 10.2)

89. Given $K(-4, y)$ and $M(2, -3)$ with midpoint $L(x, 1)$, determine the values of x and y.

A. $x = -1, y = 5$

B. $x = 3, y = 2$

C. $x = 5, y = -1$

D. $x = -1, y = -1$

(Rigorous) (Skill 10.2)

90. Line p has a negative slope and passes through the point $(0, 0)$. If line q is perpendicular to line p, which of the following must be true?

A. Line q has a negative y-intercept.

B. Line q passes through the point $(0, 0)$.

C. Line q has a positive slope.

D. Line q has a positive y-intercept.

(Rigorous) (Skill 10.3)

91. Which equation represents a circle with a diameter whose endpoints are $(0, 7)$ and $(0, 3)$?

A. $x^2 + y^2 + 21 = 0$

B. $x^2 + y^2 - 10y + 21 = 0$

C. $x^2 + y^2 - 10y + 9 = 0$

D. $x^2 - y^2 - 10y + 9 = 0$

(Average) (Skill 10.3)

92. The vertex for the parabola represented by $y = -x^2 + 4x - 1$ is given by the point

A. $(2, 5)$

B. $(2, -5)$

C. $(2, 3)$

D. $(2, -3)$

(Rigorous) (Skill 10.3)

93. Find the length of the major axis of $x^2 + 9y^2 = 36$.

A. 4

B. 6

C. 12

D. 8

(Rigorous) (Skill 10.4)

94. What transformations have been applied to the function $f(x)$ shown below to obtain function $g(x)$?

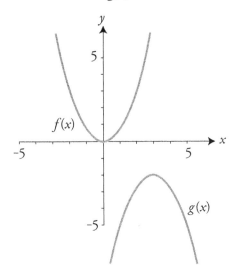

A. Reflection over *x*-axis, translation 3 units to the right, translation 2 units down

B. Translation 3 units to the right, translation 2 units down, reflection over *x*-axis

C. Translation 2 units down, translation 3 units to the right, reflection over *x*-axis

D. Reflection over *y* axis, translation 3 units to the right, translation 2 units down

(Easy) (Skill 10.5)

95. A glide reflection involves

A. A translation and dilation

B. A reflection and dilation

C. A translation and a reflection

D. A reflection and a rotation

(Average) (Skill 10.5)

96. A point at $(1, 2)$ on a Cartesian coordinate plane is translated two units to the left, reflected in the *y*-axis and then reflected in the *x*-axis. What is its final position?

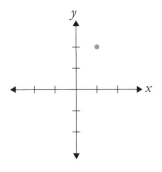

A. $(3, 2)$

B. $(-1, 2)$

C. $(-2, 1)$

D. $(1, -2)$

Trigonometry and Calculus

(Average) (Skill 11.1)

97. Determine the measures of angles *A* and *B*.

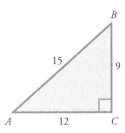

A. $A = 30°, B = 60°$

B. $A = 60°, B = 30°$

C. $A = 53°, B = 37°$

D. $A = 37°, B = 53°$

(Average) (Skill 11.1)

98. For an acute angle x, $\sin x = 0.6$. What is $\cot x$?

    A. $\frac{5}{3}$

    B. 0.75

    C. 1.33

    D. 11

(Easy) (Skill 11.3)

99. Which of the following is a Pythagorean identity?

    A. $\sin^2 \theta - \cos^2 \theta = 1$

    B. $\sin^2 \theta + \cos^2 \theta = 1$

    C. $\cos^2 \theta - \sin^2 \theta = 1$

    D. $\cos^2 \theta - \tan^2 \theta = 1$

(Average) (Skill 11.3)

100. Which expression is not identical to $\sin x$?

    A. $\sqrt{1 - \cos^2 x}$

    B. $\tan x \cos x$

    C. $\frac{1}{\csc x}$

    D. $\frac{1}{\sec x}$

(Average) (Skill 11.3)

101. Which expression is equivalent to $1 - \sin^2 x$?

    A. $1 - \cos^2 x$

    B. $1 + \cos^2 x$

    C. $\frac{1}{\sec x}$

    D. $\frac{1}{\sec^2 x}$

(Rigorous) (Skill 11.3)

102. The trigonometric expression $\frac{\tan \theta + \cot \theta}{\tan \theta}$ is identical to

    A. $\sin^2 \theta$

    B. $\cos^2 \theta$

    C. $\sec^2 \theta$

    D. $\csc^2 \theta$

(Rigorous) (Skill 11.3)

103. Solve $2\cos x + 1 = 0$.

    A. $\frac{2\pi}{3} + 2n\pi, \frac{4\pi}{3} + 2n\pi$ where n is an integer

    B. $\frac{2\pi}{3} + 2n\pi$ where n is an integer

    C. $\frac{2\pi}{3} + n\pi$ where n is an integer

    D. $\frac{\pi}{3} + 2n\pi$ where n is an integer

(Rigorous) (Skill 11.5)

104. A boy tosses a ball at a velocity of 20m/s to his friend 20 m away. At what angle θ from the horizontal was the ball tossed given that the range of a projectile R $= \frac{1}{10} v^2 \sin 2\theta$ m where v is the initial velocity of the ball?

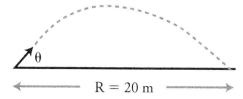

    A. 20°

    B. 15°

    C. 30°

    D. 25°

(Easy) (Skill 12.1)

105. L'Hopital's rule provides a method to evaluate which of the following?

A. Limit of a function

B. Derivative of a function

C. Sum of an arithmetic series

D. Sum of a geometric series

(Average) (Skill 12.1)

106. Find the following limit: $\lim\limits_{x \to 2} \frac{x^2 - 4}{x - 2}$

A. 0

B. Infinity

C. 2

D. 4

(Rigorous) (Skill 12.1)

107. Find the following limit: $\lim\limits_{x \to 0} \frac{\sin 2x}{5x}$

A. Infinity

B. 0

C. 0.4

D. 1

(Rigorous) (Skill 12.1)

108. Evaluate $\lim\limits_{x \to 0} \frac{e^{3x} - 1}{2x}$.

A. $-\frac{1}{2}$

B. 0

C. -1

D. $\frac{3}{2}$

(Rigorous) (Skill 12.3)

109. The equation of the tangent line to the curve $x^4 + x^2 + 1$ at $x = 1$ is

A. $y = 6x + 3$

B. $y = -6x + 3$

C. $y = 6x - 3$

D. $y = -6x - 3$

(Rigorous) (Skill 12.3)

110. Find the slope of the line tangent to $y = 3x(\cos x)$ at $(\frac{\pi}{2}, \frac{\pi}{2})$.

A. $-\frac{3\pi}{2}$

B. $\frac{3\pi}{2}$

C. $\frac{\pi}{2}$

D. $-\frac{\pi}{2}$

(Rigorous) (Skill 12.3)

111. Find the equation of the line tangent to $y = 3x^2 - 5x$ at $(1, -2)$.

A. $y = x - 3$

B. $y = 1$

C. $y = x + 2$

D. $y = x$

(Rigorous) (Skill 12.4)

112. Find the first derivative of the function: $f(x) = x^3 - 6x^2 + 5x + 4$

A. $3x^3 - 12x^2 + 5x$

B. $3x^2 - 12x^2 - 5$

C. $3x^2 - 12x^2 + 9$

D. $3x^2 - 12x^2 + 5$

(Rigorous) (Skill 12.5)

113. Find the absolute maximum obtained by the function $y = 2x^2 + 3x$ on the interval $x = 0$ to $x = 3$.

  A. $-\dfrac{3}{4}$

  B. $-\dfrac{4}{3}$

  C. 0

  D. 27

(Average) (Skill 12.5)

114. How does the function $y = x^3 + x^2 + 4$ behave from $x = 1$ to $x = 3$?

  A. Increasing, then decreasing

  B. Increasing

  C. Decreasing

  D. Neither increasing nor decreasing

(Rigorous) (Skill 12.6)

115. An open cylindrical container has a surface area of 5 square feet. What should be the radius r and height h of the container so that the volume is maximized?

  A. $r = 0.73, h = 0.73$

  B. $r = 1, h = 1$

  C. $r = 1, h = 0.5$

  D. $r = 0.67, h = 0.73$

(Rigorous) (Skill 13.2)

116. Find the antiderivative for $4x^3 - 2x + 6 = y$

  A. $x^4 - x^2 + 6x + C$

  B. $x^4 - \dfrac{2}{3}x^3 + 6x + C$

  C. $12x^2 - 2 + C$

  D. $\dfrac{4}{3}x^4 - x^2 + 6x + C$

(Rigorous) (Skill 13.2)

117. Find the antiderivative for the function $y = e^{3x}$.

  A. $3x(e^{3x}) + C$

  B. $3(e^{3x}) + C$

  C. $\dfrac{1}{3}(e^x) + C$

  D. $\dfrac{1}{3}(e^{3x}) + C$

(Rigorous) (Skill 13.2)

118. Evaluate: $\int_0^2 (x^2 + x - 1)dx$

  A. $\dfrac{11}{3}$

  B. $\dfrac{8}{3}$

  C. $-\dfrac{8}{3}$

  D. $-\dfrac{11}{3}$

(Average) (Skill 13.2)

119. Evaluate: $\int_1^2 (3x^2 + \dfrac{1}{x^2})dx$

  A. 12.25

  B. 7.5

  C. 8.25

  D. 5.5

(Average) (Skill 13.3)

120. Find the area under the function $y = x^2 + 4$ from $x = 3$ to $x = 6$.

  A. 75

  B. 21

  C. 96

  D. 57

(Average) (Skill 13.4)

121. If the velocity of a body is given by $v = 16 - t^2$, find the distance traveled from $t = 0$ until the body comes to a complete stop.

    A. 16

    B. 43

    C. 48

    D. 64

(Rigorous) (Skill 13.4)

122. A ball is thrown up with an initial velocity of 15m/s. The acceleration due to gravity (about 10 m/s²) slows it down until it stops and falls back to the ground. At any time t after the ball is thrown, the velocity v and the distance traveled upwards s are given by

    A. $v = 15 + 10t; s = 15t + 5t^2$

    B. $v = 15 - 10t; s = 15t - 5t^2$

    C. $v = 15 - 10t; s = 15t - 10t^2$

    D. $v = 10t; s = 10t^2$

Statistics, Probability, and Discrete Mathematics

(Easy) (Skill 14.1)

123. What conclusion can be drawn from the graph below?

MLK Elementary School
Student Enrollment

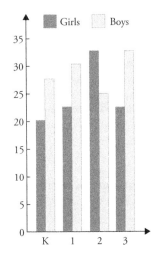

A. The number of students in first grade exceeds the number in second grade

B. There are more boys than girls in the entire school

C. There are more girls than boys in the first grade

D. Third grade has the largest number of students

(Easy) (Skill 14.1)

124. The pie chart below shows sales at an automobile dealership for the first four months of a year. What percentage of the vehicles were sold in April?

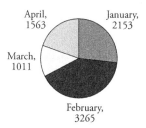

April, 1563
January, 2153
March, 1011
February, 3265

A. More than 50%

B. Less than 25%

C. Between 25% and 50%

D. None

(Easy) (Skill 14.1)

125. Which statement is true about George's budget?

A. George spends the greatest portion of his income on food

B. George spends twice as much on utilities as he does on his mortgage

C. George spends twice as much on utilities as he does on food

D. George spends the same amount on food and utilities as he does on mortgage

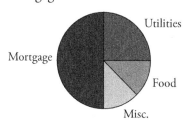

Utilities
Mortgage
Food
Misc.

(Average) (Skill 14.1)

126. Which type of graph uses symbols to represent quantities?

A. Bar graph

B. Line graph

C. Pictograph

D. Circle graph

(Average) (Skill 14.2)

127. Linear least squares regression is performed on a data set and the correlation coefficient is found to be 0.98. This implies that the quality of fit is:

A. Poor

B. Fair

C. Good

D. Excellent

(Easy) (Skill 14.2)

128. The following stem and leaf plot shows rainfall data in inches over several consecutive days. What is the median value?

0	7
1	3 9
2	1 5 7 8
3	0 3 4 6 6 9
4	3 5 5 7 8
5	0 0 3 5
10	3

A. 3.6 in

B. 3.9 in

C. 4.3 in

D. 3.4 in

(Easy) (Skill 14.3)

129. Compute the median for the following data set:

{12, 19, 13, 16, 17, 14}

A. 14.5

B. 15.17

C. 15

D. 16

(Rigorous) (Skill 14.3)

130. Half the students in a class scored 80% on an exam, and most of the rest scored 85%, except for one student who scored 10%. Which would be the best measure of central tendency for the test scores?

A. Mean

B. Median

C. Mode

D. Either the median or the mode because they are equal

(Rigorous) (Skill 14.3)

131. The probability density function for an exponential distribution is given by $f(x) = 2e^{-2x}$; $x \geq 0$. What is the median value for the variable x?

A. 0.35

B. 0.5

C. 2.0

D. 0.45

(Rigorous) (Skill 14.3)

132. Compute the standard deviation for the following set of temperatures:
(37, 38, 35, 37, 38, 40, 36, 39)

A. 37.5

B. 1.5

C. 0.5

D. 2.5

(Easy) (Skill 14.4)

133. Systematic random sampling involves

    A. choosing items arbitrarily and in an unstructured manner

    B. targeting a particular section of the population

    C. the collection of a sample at defined intervals

    D. proportional sampling from subgroups

(Easy) (Skill 15.1)

134. A jar contains 3 red marbles, 5 white marbles, 1 green marble, and 15 blue marbles. If one marble is picked at random from the jar, what is the probability that it will be red?

    A. $\frac{1}{3}$

    B. $\frac{1}{8}$

    C. $\frac{3}{8}$

    D. $\frac{1}{24}$

(Easy) (Skill 15.1)

135. If a horse will probably win three races out of ten, what are the odds that he will win?

    A. 3:10

    B. 7:10

    C. 3:7

    D. 7:3

(Average) (Skill 15.2)

136. A sack of candy has 3 peppermints, 2 butterscotch drops, and 3 cinnamon drops. One candy is drawn and replaced, then another candy is drawn; what is the probability that both will be butterscotch?

    A. $\frac{1}{2}$

    B. $\frac{1}{28}$

    C. $\frac{1}{4}$

    D. $\frac{1}{16}$

(Rigorous) (Skill 15.2)

137. A die is rolled several times. What is the probability that a 3 will not appear before the third roll of the die?

    A. $\frac{1}{3}$

    B. $\frac{25}{216}$

    C. $\frac{25}{36}$

    D. $\frac{1}{216}$

(Rigorous) (Skill 15.2)

138. If there are three people in a room, what is the probability that at least two of them will share a birthday? (Assume a year has 365 days.)

    A. 0.67

    B. 0.05

    C. 0.008

    D. 0.33

(Rigorous) (Skill 15.3)

139. A circular disc of radius 1 ft is placed on a 6 ft by 6 ft square table. The center of the disc may be placed on any point on the table top. What is the probability that the entire disk will be on top of the table without any portion hanging over the edge?

A. $\frac{4}{9}$

B. $\frac{25}{36}$

C. $\frac{1}{2}$

D. $\frac{16}{25}$

(Average) (Skill 16.1)

140. A school has 15 male teachers and 35 female teachers. In how many ways can they form a committee with 2 male teachers and 4 female teachers on it?

A. 525

B. 5,497,800

C. 88

D. 263,894,400

(Average) (Skill 16.2)

141. Which of the following is a recursive definition of the sequence {1, 2, 2, 4, 8, 32, ...}?

A. $N_i = 2N_{i-1}$

B. $N_i = 2N_{i-2}$

C. $N_i = N^2_{i-1}$

D. $N_i = N_{i-1}N_{i-2}$

(Average) (Skill 16.2)

142. What is the sum of the first 20 terms of the geometric sequence (2, 4, 8, 16, 32, ...)?

A. 2,097,150

B. 1,048,575

C. 524,288

D. 1,048,576

(Rigorous) (Skill 16.2)

143. Find the sum of the first one hundred terms in the progression.

(–6, –2, 2, ...)

A. 19,200

B. 19,400

C. –604

D. 604

(Average) (Skill 16.2)

144. {1, 4, 7, 10, . . .}

What is the 40th term in this sequence?

A. 43

B. 121

C. 118

D. 120

(Easy) (Skill 16.3)

145. The scalar multiplication of the number 3 with the matrix $\begin{pmatrix} 2 & 1 \\ 3 & 5 \end{pmatrix}$ yields:

A. 33

B. $\begin{pmatrix} 6 & 1 \\ 9 & 5 \end{pmatrix}$

C. $\begin{pmatrix} 2 & 3 \\ 3 & 15 \end{pmatrix}$

D. $\begin{pmatrix} 6 & 3 \\ 9 & 15 \end{pmatrix}$

(Easy) (Skill 16.3)

146. Find the sum of the following matrices.

$$\begin{pmatrix} 6 & 3 \\ 9 & 15 \end{pmatrix} + \begin{pmatrix} 4 & 7 \\ 1 & 0 \end{pmatrix}$$

A. $\begin{pmatrix} 10 & 10 \\ 10 & 15 \end{pmatrix}$

B. $\begin{pmatrix} 13 & 7 \\ 9 & 16 \end{pmatrix}$

C. 45

D. $\begin{pmatrix} 20 \\ 25 \end{pmatrix}$

(Average) (Skill 16.3)

147. The product of two matrices can be found only if:

A. The number of rows in the first matrix is equal to the number of rows in the second matrix

B. The number of columns in the first matrix is equal to the number of columns in the second matrix

C. The number of columns in the first matrix is equal to the number of rows in the second matrix

D. The number of rows in the first matrix is equal to the number of columns in the second matrix

(Rigorous) (Skill 16.3)

148. Evaluate the following matrix product

$$\begin{pmatrix} 2 & 1 & 3 \\ 2 & 2 & 4 \end{pmatrix} \begin{pmatrix} 6 & 5 \\ 2 & 1 \\ 2 & 7 \end{pmatrix}$$

A. $\begin{pmatrix} 20 & 32 & 24 \\ 24 & 40 & 48 \end{pmatrix}$

B. $\begin{pmatrix} 20 & 32 \\ 40 & 24 \\ 24 & 48 \end{pmatrix}$

C. 116

D. $\begin{pmatrix} 20 & 32 \\ 24 & 40 \end{pmatrix}$

(Average) (Skill 16.3)

149. Given a vector with horizontal component 5 and vertical component 6, determine the length of the vector.

A. 61

B. $\sqrt{61}$

C. 30

D. $\sqrt{30}$

(Average) (Skill 16.4)

150. Determine the number of subsets of set K. $K = \{4, 5, 6, 7\}$

A. 15

B. 16

C. 17

D. 18

Answer Key

ANSWER KEY								
1. D	18. A	35. C	52. A	69. C	86. D	103. A	120. A	137. B
2. B	19. D	36. B	53. B	70. B	87. C	104. B	121. B	138. C
3. C	20. D	37. D	54. B	71. A	88. D	105. A	122. B	139. A
4. C	21. B	38. C	55. C	72. B	89. A	106. D	123. B	140. B
5. A	22. A	39. B	56. A	73. D	90. C	107. C	124. B	141. D
6. B	23. D	40. B	57. D	74. C	91. B	108. D	125. C	142. A
7. B	24. C	41. C	58. A	75. A	92. C	109. C	126. C	143. A
8. C	25. B	42. A	59. C	76. A	93. C	110. A	127. D	144. C
9. A	26. B	43. B	60. D	77. C	94. A	111. A	128. A	145. D
10. D	27. C	44. A	61. A	78. C	95. C	112. D	129. C	146. A
11. C	28. C	45. D	62. C	79. C	96. D	113. D	130. B	147. C
12. C	29. C	46. C	63. B	80. B	97. D	114. B	131. A	148. D
13. A	30. B	47. A	64. B	81. C	98. C	115. A	132. B	149. B
14. A	31. C	48. C	65. D	82. A	99. B	116. A	133. C	150. B
15. C	32. D	49. D	66. B	83. B	100. D	117. D	134. B	
16. A	33. B	50. C	67. D	84. B	101. D	118. B	135. C	
17. C	34. D	51. B	68. A	85. C	102. D	119. B	136. D	

29   18   11   24

24

(19%
Math Process

$\frac{24}{29}$

24%
Patterns

$\frac{30}{37}$

19%
Geo.

$\frac{19}{30}$

19%
Trig

$\frac{12}{26}$

19%
stats

$\frac{22}{28}$

$= 70\%$

RIGOR TABLE	
Rigor level	**Questions**
Easy 25%	7, 11, 14, 20, 21, 26, 30, 42, 46, 67, 72, 77, 84, 95, 99, 105, 123, 124, 125, 128, 129, 133, 134, 135, 145, 146
Average 50%	1, 3, 4, 5, 8, 13, 15, 18, 22, 24, 25, 27, 29, 31, 32, 33, 34, 37, 39, 40, 41, 48, 49, 50, 52, 54, 56, 57, 58, 62, 63, 64, 65, 68, 70, 71, 73, 74, 78, 82, 83, 85, 86, 88, 92, 96, 97, 98, 100, 101, 106, 114, 119, 120, 121, 126, 127, 136, 140, 141, 142, 144, 147, 149, 150
Rigorous 50%	2, 6, 9, 10, 12, 16, 17, 19, 23, 28, 35, 36, 38, 43, 44, 45, 47, 51, 53, 55, 59, 60, 61, 66, 69, 75, 76, 79, 80, 81, 87, 89, 90, 91, 93, 94, 102, 103, 104, 107, 108, 109, 110, 111, 112, 113, 115, 116, 117, 118, 122, 130, 131, 132, 137, 138, 139, 143, 148

Sample Test with Rationales: Mathematical Processes and Number Sense

(Average) (Skill 1.1)

1. Identify the correct sequence of sub-skills required for solving and graphing inequalities involving absolute value in one variable, such as $|x + 1| \leq 6$.

    A. Understanding absolute value, graphing inequalities, solving systems of equations

    B. Graphing inequalities on a Cartesian plane, solving systems of equations, simplifying expressions with absolute value

    C. Plotting points, graphing equations, graphing inequalities

    D. Solving equations with absolute value, solving inequalities, graphing conjunctions and disjunctions

Answer: D.

The steps listed in answer D would look like this for the given example:

If $|x + 1| \leq 6$, then $-6 \leq x + 1 \leq 6$, which means $-7 \leq x \leq 5$. Then the inequality would be graphed on a number line and would show that the solution set is all real numbers between -7 and 5, including -7 and 5.

(Rigorous) (Skill 1.1)

2. Mr. Lacey is using problem solving to help students develop their math skills. He gives the class a box of pencils. He says that the pencils have to be divided so that each student has the same number of pencils. What step should come first in problem solving?

    A. Find a strategy to solve the problem

    B. Identify the problem

    C. Count the number of pencils

    D. Make basic calculations

Answer: B.

The first step in problem solving is always to identify the problem.

(Average) (Skill 1.2)

3. Estimate the sum of $1498 + 1309$.

    A. 2900

    B. 2850

    C. 2800

    D. 2600

Answer: C.

As this is an estimate, you add 1500 and 1300 to get 2800.

(Average) (Skill 1.2)

4. The mass of a Chips Ahoy cookie is about:

    A. 1 kilogram

    B. 1 gram

    C. 15 grams

    D. 15 milligrams

Answer: C.

Since an ordinary cookie would not weigh as much as 1 kilogram or as little as 1 gram or 15 milligrams, the only reasonable answer is 15 grams.

(Average) (Skill 1.3)

5. **What would be the total cost of a suit for $295.99 and a pair of shoes for $69.95 including 6.5% sales tax?**

   A. $389.73

   B. $398.37

   C. $237.86

   D. $315.23

Answer: A.

Before the tax, the total comes to $365.94. Then .065($365.94) = $23.79. With the tax added on, the total bill is $365.94 + $23.79 = $389.73. (A quicker way is 1.065($365.94) = $389.73.)

(Rigorous)(Skill 1.3)

6. **Convert $.\overline{63}$ into a fraction in simplest form.**

   A. $\frac{63}{100}$

   B. $\frac{7}{11}$

   C. $6\frac{3}{10}$

   D. $\frac{2}{3}$

Answer: B.

Let N = .636363.... Then, multiplying both sides of the equation by 100 or 10^2 (because there are two repeated numbers) yields 100N = 63.636363... Next, subtract the two equations to get 99N = 63 or N = $\frac{63}{99}$ = $\frac{7}{11}$.

(Easy) (Skill 1.3)

7. **A student had 60 days to appeal the results of an exam. If the results were received on March 23, what was the last day that the student could appeal?**

   A. May 21

   B. May 22

   C. May 23

   D. May 24

Answer: B.

Recall: 30 days in April and 31 in March. 8 days in March + 30 days in April + 22 days in May brings him to a total of 60 days on May 22.

(Average) (Skill 1.3)

8. **Evaluate: $\frac{1}{3} - \frac{1}{2} + \frac{1}{6}$**

   A. $\frac{5}{6}$

   B. $\frac{2}{3}$

   C. 0

   D. 1

Answer: C.

$$\frac{1}{3} - \frac{1}{2} + \frac{1}{6} = \frac{2}{6} - \frac{3}{6} + \frac{1}{6} = \frac{2-3+1}{6} = 0$$

(Rigorous) (Skill 1.4)

9. **The volume of water flowing through a pipe varies directly with the square of the radius of the pipe. If the water flows at a rate of 80 liters per minute through a pipe with a radius of 4 cm, at what rate would water flow through a pipe with a radius of 3 cm?**

   A. 45 liters per minute

   B. 6.67 liters per minute

   C. 60 liters per minute

   D. 4.5 liters per minute

Answer: A.

Set up the direct variation: $\frac{V}{r^2} = \frac{V}{r^2}$. Substitution yields $\frac{80}{16} = \frac{V}{9}$. Solve for V to get 45 liters per minute.

(Rigorous) (Skill 1.4)

10. Joe reads 20 words/min., and Jan reads 80 words/min. How many minutes will it take Joe to read the same number of words that it takes Jan 40 minutes to read?

   A. 10

   B. 20

   C. 80

   D. 160

Answer: D.

If Jan reads 80 words/minute, she will read 3200 words in 40 minutes.

$$\frac{3200}{20} = 160$$

At 20 words per minute, it will take Joe 160 minutes to read 3200 words.

(Easy) (Skill 1.4)

11. If three cups of concentrate are needed to make 2 gallons of fruit punch, how many cups are needed to make 5 gallons?

   A. 6 cups

   B. 7 cups

   C. 7.5 cups

   D. 10 cups

Answer: C.

Set up the proportion $\frac{3}{2} = \frac{x}{5}$, cross multiply to obtain $15 = 2x$, then divide both sides by 2.

(Rigorous) (Skill 2.1)

12. Kindergarten students are doing a butterfly art project. They fold paper in half. On one half, they paint a design. Then they fold the paper closed and reopen. The resulting picture is a butterfly with matching sides. What math principle does this demonstrate?

   A. Slide

   B. Rotate

   C. Symmetry

   D. Transformation

Answer: C.

By folding the painted paper in half, the design is mirrored on the other side, creating symmetry and reflection. The butterfly design is symmetrical about the center.

(Average) (Skill 2.1)

13. Express in symbols: "x is greater than seven and less than or equal to fifteen."

   A. $7 < x \le 15$

   B. $7 > x \ge 15$

   C. $15 \le x < 7$

   D. $7 < x = 15$

Answer: A.

(Easy) (Skill 2.3)

14. The following statement about inductive reasoning is not accurate:

    A. Inductive reasoning involves making inference from specific facts to general principles.

    B. Inductive reasoning involves making inference from general principles to specific facts.

    C. Inductive reasoning is generally weaker than deductive reasoning.

    D. Mathematical proofs are not inductive.

    Answer: A.

    By definition, inductive reasoning is generalization from specific facts. It is weaker than deductive reasoning since one could, in theory, always find a specific counterexample to the generalization. For instance, from an observation of many black ravens one can conclude that all ravens are black. If someone sees a white raven, however, the conclusion will become invalid. Mathematical proofs are deductive in nature.

(Average) (Skill 2.4)

15. The contrapositive of the statement "If I am hungry I eat" is:

    A. If I eat then I am hungry.

    B. If I am not hungry I do not eat.

    C. If I do not eat I am not hungry.

    D. None of the above

    Answer: C.

    The contrapositive of the statement "if p then q" is given by "if not q then not p."

(Rigorous) (Skill 2.4)

16. Which of the following is a simple statement that can be assigned a truth value?

    A. It is sunny today.

    B. Please put away the books.

    C. The wind blew and the leaves fell.

    D. They will stay home or they will go to the mall.

    Answer: A.

    The statement in B cannot be assigned a truth value. C and D are compound statements formed by joining simple statements using the connectives "and" and "or."

(Rigorous) (Skill 2.4)

17. What is the negation of a statement of the form "p and q"?

    A. not p and not q

    B. not p and q

    C. not p or not q

    D. p or not q

    Answer: C.

    The negation of p and q is (not p) or (not q).

(Average) (Skill 3.1)

18. Given W = whole numbers

    N = natural numbers

    Z = integers

    R = rational numbers

    I = irrational numbers

    which of the following is not true?

    A. $R \subset I$

    B. $W \subset Z$

    C. $Z \subset R$

    D. $N \subset W$

    Answer: A.

    The rational numbers are not a subset of the irrational numbers. All of the other statements are true.

(Rigorous) (Skill 2.3)

19. Which expression below is equivalent to the expression $14 - 2(3x + 5) - 8x$

    A. $88x$

    B. $28x + 60$

    C. $-5x + 17$

    D. $-14x + 4$

    Answer: D

    Order of operations requires that multiplication is performed before addition or subtraction. The multiplication in this case requires application of the distributive property.

    $14 - 2(3x + 5) - 8x$

    $14 - 6x - 10 - 8x$

    $-6x - 8x + 14 - 10$

    by the commutative property

    $-14x + 4$

(Easy) (Skill 3.1)

20. How many real numbers lie between -1 and $+1$?

    A. 0

    B. 1

    C. 17

    D. An infinite number

    Answer: D.

    There are an infinite number of real numbers between any two real numbers.

(Easy) (Skill 3.2)

21. The conjugate of $4 + 5i$ is

    A. $-4 + 5i$

    B. $4 - 5i$

    C. $4i + 5$

    D. $4i - 5$

    Answer: B.

    By definition, the conjugate of a complex number is obtained by changing the sign of its imaginary part.

(Average) (Skill 3.2)

22. Simplify: $(6 + 3i) - (4 - 2i)$

    A. $2 + 5i$

    B. $2 + i$

    C. $10 + 5i$

    D. $2 - 2i$

    Answer: A.

    Use the rules of addition and subtraction for complex numbers. $(6 + 3i) - (4 - 2i)$ $= 6 + 3i - 4 + 2i = 2 + 5i$

(Rigorous) (Skill 3.2)

23. Simplify: $\frac{10}{1+3i}$

 A. $-1.25(1-3i)$

 B. $1.25(1-3i)$

 C. $1+3i$

 D. $1-3i$

Answer: D.

Multiplying numerator and denominator by the conjugate yields

$$\frac{10}{1+3i} \times \frac{1-3i}{1-3i} = \frac{10(1-3i)}{1-9i^2} = \frac{10(1-3i)}{1-9(-1)} = \frac{10(1-3i)}{10} = 1-3i.$$

(Average) (Skill 5.3)

24. **Which statement below best represents the algorithm for fraction division?**

 A. Multiply the means and the extremes, then equate the two.

 B. Multiply the numerators and the denominators to create a fraction answer.

 C. Rewrite the quotient as the product of the first fraction and the reciprocal of the second fraction.

 D. Rewrite the quotient as the product of the first fraction and the opposite of the second fraction.

Answer: C

When dividing fractions, the problem is best rewritten as multiplication by the reciprocal of the fraction following the division symbol. For instance:

$$\frac{2}{3} \div \frac{5}{12} = \frac{2}{3} \times \frac{12}{5} = \frac{8}{5}$$

(Average) (Skill 3.3)

25. Which of the following sets is closed under division?

 I) {½, 1, 2, 4}

 II) {-1, 1}

 III) {-1, 0, 1}

 A. I only

 B. II only

 C. III only

 D. I and II

Answer: B.

I is not closed because $\frac{4}{0.5} = 8$ and 8 is not in the set. III is not closed because $\frac{1}{0}$ is undefined. II is closed because $\frac{-1}{1} = -1, \frac{1}{-1} = -1, \frac{1}{1} = 1, \frac{-1}{-1} = 1$ are all in the set.

(Easy) (Skill 3.4)

26. **Find the LCM of 27, 90, and 84.**

 A. 90

 B. 3,780

 C. 204,120

 D. 1,260

Answer: B.

To find the LCM of the above numbers, factor each into its prime factors and multiply each common factor the maximum number of times it occurs. Thus, $27 = 3 \times 3 \times 3$; $90 = 2 \times 3 \times 3 \times 5$; $84 = 2 \times 2 \times 3 \times 7$; LCM $= 2 \times 2 \times 3 \times 3 \times 3 \times 5 \times 7 = 3,780$.

(Average) (Skill 3.4)

27. Which of the following is always composite if x is odd, y is even, and both x and y are greater than or equal to 2?

A. $x + y$

B. $3x + 2y$

C. $5xy$

D. $5x + 3y$

Answer: C.

A composite number is a number that is not prime. The prime number sequence begins 2, 3, 5, 7, 11, 13, 17, ... To determine which of the expressions is always composite, experiment with different values of x and y, such as $x = 3$ and $y = 2$, or $x = 5$ and $y = 2$. It turns out that $5xy$ will always be an even number and, therefore, composite if $y = 2$.

(Rigorous) (Skill 5.4)

28. Which ordered pair listed below best follows the pattern represented in the given graph?

A. $(0, 0)$

B. $(2, 6)$

C. $(4, 9)$

D. $(5, 5)$

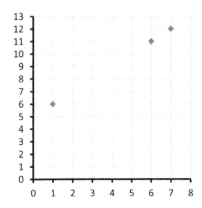

Answer: C

The point $(4, 9)$ is in line with the given data points. Therefore they all represent a shared linear pattern or equation.

(Average) (Skill 3.4)

29. Find the GCF of $2^2 \times 3^2 \times 5$ and $2^2 \times 3 \times 7$.

A. $2^5 \times 3^3 \times 5 \times 7$

B. $2 \times 3 \times 5 \times 7$

C. $2^2 \times 3$

D. $2^3 \times 3^2 \times 5 \times 7$

Answer: C.

Choose the number of each prime factor that is in common.

Patterns, Algebra, and Functions

(Easy) (Skill 4.1)

30. Which set illustrates a function?

A. $\{(0, 1)\ (0, 2)\ (0, 3)\ (0, 4)\}$

B. $\{(3, 9)\ (-3, 9)\ (4, 16)\ (-4, 16)\}$

C. $\{(1, 2)\ (2, 3)\ (3, 4)\ (1, 4)\}$

D. $\{(2, 4)\ (3, 6)\ (4, 8)\ (4, 16)\}$

Answer: B.

Each number in the domain can only be matched with one number in the range. A is not a function because 0 is mapped to 4 different numbers in the range. In C, 1 is mapped to two different numbers. In D, 4 is also mapped to two different numbers.

(Average) (Skill 4.2)

31. Given $f(x) = 3x - 2$ and $g(x) = x^2$, determine $g(f(x))$.

    A. $3x^2 - 2$

    B. $9x^2 + 4$

    C. $9x^2 - 12x + 4$

    D. $3x^3 - 2$

Answer: C.

The composite function $g(f(x))$ is $(3x - 2)^2 = 9x^2 - 12x + 4$.

(Average) (Skill 4.2)

32. $f(x) = 3x - 2; f^{-1}(x) =$

    A. $3x + 2$

    B. $\frac{x}{6}$

    C. $2x - 3$

    D. $\frac{(x + 2)}{3}$

Answer: D.

To find the inverse, $f^{-1}(x)$, of the given function, reverse the variables in the given equation, $y = 3x - 2$, to get $x = 3y - 2$. Then solve for y as follows:

$x + 2 = 3y$, and $y = \frac{x + 2}{3}$

(Average) (Skill 4.3)

33. State the domain of the function $f(x) = \frac{3x - 6}{x^2 - 25}$.

    A. $x \neq 2$

    B. $x \neq 5, -5$

    C. $x \neq 2, -2$

    D. $x \neq 5$

Answer: B.

The values 5 and -5 must be omitted from the domain because if x took on either of those values, the denominator of the fraction would have a value of 0. Therefore the fraction would be undefined. Thus, the domain of the function is all real numbers x not equal to 5 and -5.

(Average) (Skill 4.3)

34. Give the domain for the function over the set of real numbers:

    $y = \frac{3x + 2}{2x^2 - 3}$

    A. All real numbers

    B. All real numbers, $x \neq 0$

    C. All real numbers, $x \neq -2$ or 3

    D. All real numbers, $x \neq \frac{\pm\sqrt{6}}{2}$

Answer: D.

Solve the denominator for 0. These values will be excluded from the domain.

$$2x^2 - 3 = 0$$
$$2x^2 = 3$$
$$x^2 = \frac{3}{2}$$
$$x = \sqrt{\frac{3}{2}} = \sqrt{\frac{3}{2}} \times \sqrt{\frac{2}{2}} = \frac{\pm\sqrt{6}}{2}$$

(Rigorous) (Skill 4.4)

35. Which equation is represented by the graph below?

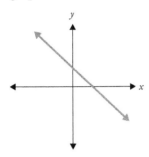

A. $x - y = 3$

B. $x - y = -3$

C. $x + y = 3$

D. $x + y = -3$

Answer: C.

By looking at the graph, we can determine the slope to be -1 and the y-intercept to be 3. Write the slope intercept form of the line as $y = -1x + 3$. Add x to both sides to obtain $x + y = 3$, the equation in standard form.

(Rigorous) (Skill 4.4)

36. What is the equation of the graph below?

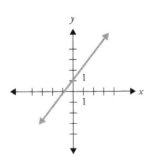

A. $2x + y = 2$

B. $2x - y = -2$

C. $2x - y = 2$

D. $2x + y = -2$

Answer: B.

By observation, we see that the graph has a y-intercept of 2 and a slope of $\frac{2}{1} = 2$. Therefore its equation is $y = mx + b = 2x + 2$. Rearranging the terms gives $2x - y = -2$.

(Average) (Skill 4.4)

37. Three less than four times a number is five times the sum of that number and 6. Which equation could be used to solve this problem?

A. $3 - 4n = 5(n + 6)$

B. $3 - 4n + 5n = 6$

C. $4n - 3 = 5n + 6$

D. $4n - 3 = 5(n + 6)$

Answer: D.

Be sure to enclose the sum of the number and 6 in parentheses.

(Rigorous) (Skill 5.1)

38. Which graph represents the equation of $y = x^2 + 3x$?

A.

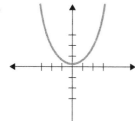

B.

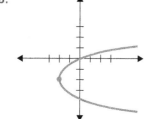

C.

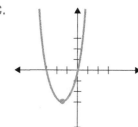

D.

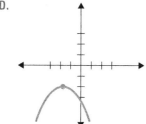

Answer: C.

Answer B is not the graph of a function. Answer D is the graph of a parabola where the coefficient of x^2 is negative. Answer A appears to be the graph of $y = x^2$. To find the x-intercepts of $y = x^2 + 3x$, set $y = 0$ and solve for x: $0 = x^2 + 3x = x(x + 3)$ to get $x = 0$ or $x = -3$. Therefore, the graph of the function intersects the x-axis at $x = 0$ and $x = -3$. The correct answer is C.

(Average) (Skill 5.1)

39. Which equation is graphed below?

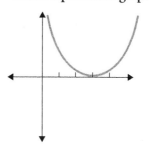

A. $y = 4\,(x + 3)^2$

B. $y = 4\,(x - 3)^2$

C. $y = 3\,(x - 4)^2$

D. $y = 3\,(x + 4)^2$

Answer: B.

Since the vertex of the parabola is three units to the left, we choose the solution where 3 is subtracted from x, and then the quantity is squared.

(Average) (Skill 5.2)

40. Solve for x: $3x + 5 \geq 8 + 7x$

A. $x \geq -\dfrac{3}{4}$

B. $x \leq -\dfrac{3}{4}$

C. $x \geq \dfrac{3}{4}$

D. $x \leq \dfrac{3}{4}$

Answer: B.

Using additive equality, $-3 \geq 4x$. Divide both sides by 4 to obtain $-\dfrac{3}{4} \geq x$. Carefully determine which answer choice is equivalent.

(Average) (Skill 5.6)

41. Identify the expression below that does not represent the phrase "half of M."

    A. $\frac{1}{2}M$

    B. $\frac{M}{2}$

    C. $M \div \frac{1}{2}$

    D. $0.5M$

Answer: C

Choice C actually equates to $2M$, or "twice M," rather than "half of M."

(Easy) (Skill 5.2)

42. The formula for solving a quadratic equation is:

    A. $x = \dfrac{-b \pm \sqrt{b^2 - 4ac}}{2a}$

    B. $x = \dfrac{-b \pm \sqrt{b^2 - 4a}}{2a}$

    C. $x = \dfrac{b \pm \sqrt{b^2 - 4ac}}{2a}$

    D. $x = \dfrac{b \pm \sqrt{b^3 - 4ac}}{2a}$

Answer: A.

Option B is missing the factor c from the term $4ac$ within the square root. Option C does not have the minus sign with the term b in the numerator. Option D has b cubed instead of squared within the square root symbol and lacks the minus sign before the first b. A is thus the correct choice.

(Rigorous) (Skill 5.3)

43. Solve for x and y:

    $x = 3y + 7$
    $7x + 5y = 23$

    A. $(-1, 4)$

    B. $(4, -1)$

    C. $(\frac{-29}{7}, \frac{-26}{7})$

    D. $(10, 1)$

Answer: B.

Substituting x in the second equation results in $7(3y + 7) + 5y = 23$. Solve by distributing and grouping like terms: $26y + 49 = 23$, $26y = -26$, $y = -1$. Substitute y into the first equation to obtain x.

(Rigorous) (Skill 5.3)

44. Solve the system of equations for x, y, and z.

    $3x + 2y - z = 0$
    $2x + 5y = 8z$
    $x + 3y + 2z = 7$

    A. $(-1, 2, 1)$

    B. $(1, 2, -1)$

    C. $(-3, 4, -1)$

    D. $(0, 1, 2)$

Answer: A.

Multiplying equation 1 by 2, and equation 2 by -3, and then adding together the two resulting equations gives $-11y + 22z = 0$. Solving for y gives $y = 2z$. In the meantime, multiplying equation 3 by -2 and adding it to equation 2 gives $-y - 12z = -14$. Then substituting $2z$ for y, yields the result $z = 1$. Subsequently, one can easily find that $y = 2$, and $x = -1$.

(Rigorous) (Skill 5.4)

45. Find the zeroes of $f(x) = x^3 + x^2 - 14x - 24$.

    A. 4, 3, 2

    B. 3, -8

    C. 7, -2, -1

    D. 4, -3, -2

Answer: D.

Possible rational roots of the equation $0 = x^3 + x^2 - 14x - 24$ are all the positive and negative factors of 24. By substituting into the equation, we find that -2 is a root, and therefore that $x + 2$ is a factor. By performing the long division $\frac{(x^3 + x^2 - 14x - 24)}{(x + 2)}$, we can find that another factor of the original equation is $x^2 - x - 12$ or $(x - 4)(x + 3)$. Therefore the zeros of the original function are -2, -3, and 4.

(Easy) (Skill 5.4)

46. How many roots does the polynomial $x^4 + 3x^3 - 7x^2 + x + 4$ have?

    A. 2

    B. 3

    C. 4

    D. 5

Answer: C.

According to the Fundamental Theorem of Algebra, a polynomial expression of degree n must have n roots. Since this is a 4th degree polynomial, it has 4 roots.

(Rigorous) (Skill 5.4)

47. The solutions to the polynomial equation $x^4 - 4x^3 - 9x^2 + 16x + 20 = 0$ are given by

    A. {-2, -1, 2, 5}

    B. {-1, 0, 1, 5}

    C. {-2, 0, 1, 5}

    D. {-1, 1, 2, 5}

Answer: A.

Since 5 occurs in all the choices, it must be a solution of the equation. Dividing the polynomial by $x - 5$ using synthethic division we get

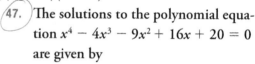

Thus $x^4 - 4x^3 - 9x^2 + 16x + 20 = (x - 5)(x^3 + x^2 - 4x - 4)$

Factoring the rest of the expression by grouping

$x^3 + x^2 - 4x - 4 = x^2(x + 1) - 4(x + 1) = (x + 1)(x^2 - 4) = (x + 1)(x + 2)(x - 2)$

Hence the other 3 solutions are -1, -2 and 2.

(Average) (Skill 5.5)

48. What is the slope of any line parallel to the line $2x + 4y = 4$?

A. -2

B. -1

C. $-\frac{1}{2}$

D. 2

Answer: C.

The formula for slope is $y = mx + b$, where m is the slope. Lines that are parallel have the same slope.

$2x + 4y = 4$
$4y = -2x + 4$
$y = \frac{-2x}{4} + 1$
$y = \frac{-1}{2}x + 1$

(Average) (Skill 5.5)

49. The discriminant of a quadratic equation is evaluated and determined to be -3. The equation has:

A. One real root

B. One complex root

C. Two roots, both real

D. Two roots, both complex

Answer: D.

The discriminant is the number under the radical sign. Since it is negative, the two roots of the equation are complex.

(Average) (Skill 5.6)

50. The path, d, of a projectile shot into the air with an initial velocity of 20 m/s is modeled by the function $d(t) = 20t - 5t^2$. When will the projectile hit the ground?

A. after 20 seconds

B. after 5 seconds

C. after 4 seconds

D. after 1 seconds

Answer: C.

When the projectile returns to the ground, $d(t) = 0$. Solve:

$0 = 20t - 5t^2$
$0 = 5t(4 - t)$
$t = \{0, 4\}$

$t = 0$ seconds represents the moment when the projectile begins its journey, so $t = 4$ seconds is when the journey ends, and the projectile returns to the ground.

(Rigorous) (Skill 5.6)

51. A boat travels 30 miles upstream in three hours. It makes the return trip in one and a half hours. What is the speed of the boat in still water?

A. 10 mph

B. 15 mph

C. 20 mph

D. 30 mph

Answer: B.

Let $x =$ the speed of the boat in still water and $c =$ the speed of the current.

	Rate	Time	Distance
Upstream	$x - c$	3	30
Downstream	$x + c$	1.5	30

Solve the system:

$3x - 3c = 30$

$1.5x + 1.5c = 30$

(Average) (Skill 6.1)

52. Which of the following is equivalent to $\sqrt[b]{x^a}$?

    A. $x^{a/b}$

    B. $x^{b/a}$

    C. $a^{x/b}$

    D. $b^{x/a}$

Answer: A.

The bth root, expressed in the form $\sqrt[b]{}$, can also be written as an exponential, $1/b$. Writing the expression in this form, $(x^a)^{1/b}$, and then multiplying exponents yields $x^{a/b}$.

(Rigorous) (Skill 6.1)

53. Evaluate $3^{\frac{1}{2}}(9^{\frac{1}{3}})$.

    A. $27^{\frac{5}{6}}$

    B. $9^{\frac{7}{12}}$

    C. $3^{\frac{5}{6}}$

    D. $3^{\frac{6}{7}}$

Answer: B.

Getting the bases the same yields $3^{\frac{1}{2}} 3^{\frac{2}{3}}$. Adding exponents yields $3^{\frac{7}{6}}$. Additional manipulation of exponents produces $3^{\frac{7}{6}} = 3^{\frac{14}{12}} = (3^2)^{\frac{7}{12}} = 9^{\frac{9}{12}}$.

(Average) (Skill 6.1)

54. $(3.8 \times 10^{17}) \times (.5 \times 10^{-12})$

    A. 19×10^5

    B. 1.9×10^5

    C. 1.9×10^6

    D. 1.9×10^7

Answer: B.

Multiply the decimals and add the exponents.

(Rigorous) (Skill 6.1)

55. Simplify $\dfrac{\frac{3}{4} x^2 y^{-3}}{\frac{2}{3} xy}$

    A. $\frac{1}{2} xy^{-4}$

    B. $\frac{1}{2} x^{-1} y^{-4}$

    C. $\frac{9}{8} xy^{-4}$

    D. $\frac{9}{8} xy^{-2}$

Answer: C.

Simplify the complex fraction by inverting the denominator and multiplying: $\frac{3}{4} \left(\frac{3}{2}\right) = \frac{9}{8}$, then subtract exponents to obtain the correct answer.

(Average) (Skill 6.2)

56. Which equation corresponds to the logarithmic statement: $\log_x k = m$?

    A. $x^m = k$

    B. $k^m = x$

    C. $x^k = m$

    D. $m^x = k$

    Answer: A.

    By definition of log form and exponential form, $\log_x k = m$ corresponds to $x^m = k$.

(Average) (Skill 6.2)

57. Solve for x: $10^{x-3} + 5 = 105$.

    A. 3

    B. 10

    C. 2

    D. 5

    Answer: D.

    Simplify: $10^{x-3} = 100$. Taking the logarithm to base 10 of both sides yields $(x - 3)\log_{10} 10 = \log_{10} 100$. Thus, $x - 3 = 2$ and $x = 5$.

(Average) (Skill 6.3)

58. Which of the following is the graph of the function $3^x - 4$?

    A.

    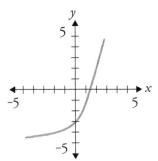

    B.

    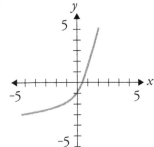

    C.

    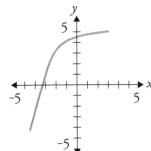

    D.

    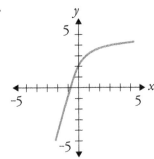

    Answer: A

    Note the x and y intercepts. When $x = 0$, $y = -3$ and $y = 0$ when $x = 1.25$.

(Rigorous) (Skill 6.4)

59. After 5730 years, a given amount of carbon-14 decays to half the original amount. If A_0 is the original amount, A is the current amount and t is the number of years elapsed, the exponential decay model for carbon-14 is

A. $A = A_0 e^{\frac{-t}{5730}}$

B. $A = A_0 e^{-5730\,t}$

C. $A = A_0 e^{\frac{\ln 0.5}{5730}\,t}$

D. $A = A_0 e^{\frac{t}{5730}}$

Answer: C.

The general form of the exponential decay model is $A = A_0 e^{rt}$. We can use the fact that the half life of carbon-14 is 5730 years to find the constant r.

When $t = 5730$, $A = \frac{A_0}{2}$. Therefore

$$\frac{A_0}{2} = A_0 e^{5730r}$$
$$\rightarrow \frac{1}{2} = e^{5730r}$$

Taking the natural logarithm of both sides

$$\ln \frac{1}{2} = 5730r$$
$$\rightarrow r = \frac{\ln 0.5}{5730}$$

(Rigorous) (Skill 7.1)

60. Solve for x: $|2x + 3| > 4$

A. $-\frac{7}{2} > x > \frac{1}{2}$

B. $-\frac{1}{2} > x > \frac{7}{2}$

C. $x < \frac{7}{2}$ or $x > -\frac{1}{2}$

D. $x < -\frac{7}{2}$ or $x > \frac{1}{2}$

Answer: D.

The quantity within the absolute value symbols must be either > 4 or < -4. Solve the two inequalities $2x + 3 > 4$ or $2x + 3 < -4$.

(Rigorous) (Skill 7.1)

61. Graph the solution: $|x| + 7 < 13$

A.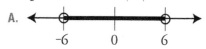

B.

C.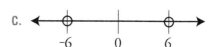

D.

Answer: A.

Solve by adding −7 to each side of the inequality. Since the absolute value of x is less than 6, x must be between −6 and 6. The end points are not included so the circles on the graph are hollow.

(Average) (Skill 7.1)

62. Solve for x: $18 = 4 + |2x|$

A. $\{-11, 7\}$

B. $\{-7, 0, 7\}$

C. $\{-7, 7\}$

D. $\{-11, 11\}$

Answer: C.

Using the definition of absolute value, two equations are possible: $18 = 4 + 2x$ or $18 = 4 - 2x$. Solving for x gives $x = 7$ or $x = -7$.

(Average) (Skill 7.2)

63. Graphs of functions $f(x) = \sqrt{x+1}$ and $g(x) = \sqrt{4-x}$ are shown below. What is the domain of the function $f(x) + g(x)$?

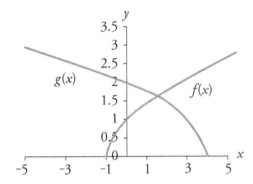

A. $-\infty \leq x \leq 4$

B. $-1 \leq x \leq 4$

C. $-1 \leq x \leq \infty$

D. $-\infty \leq x \leq \infty$

Answer: B.

For the function $f(x)$, the expression under the square root sign $x + 1$ must be zero or greater, i.e. $x \geq -1$. For the function $g(x)$, $4 - x$ must be zero or greater, i.e. $x \leq 4$. For the function $f(x) + g(x)$ both conditions must be satisfied.

(Average) (Skill 7.3)

64. Find the domain of the function $\sqrt{6 - x^2}$.

A. $x \geq \sqrt{6}$

B. $-\sqrt{6} \leq x \leq \sqrt{6}$

C. $0 \leq x \leq \sqrt{6}$

D. $x \geq 0$

Answer: B.

The expression under the square root sign cannot be negative. Hence we must have $6 - x^2 \geq 0; \rightarrow x^2 \leq 6; \rightarrow x \leq \sqrt{6}$ and $x \geq -\sqrt{6}$

(Average) (Skill 7.3)

65. The rational function $\dfrac{2x + 1}{2x^2 - x - 1}$ has

A. A vertical asymptote at $x = 1$

B. A horizontal asymptote at $y = 0$

C. A hole at $x = -\dfrac{1}{2}$

D. All of the above

Answer: D.

Factoring the denominator we get $2x^2 - x - 1 = (2x + 1)(x - 1)$. Since the factor $2x + 1$ can be cancelled with the numerator, there is no asymptote at $x = -\dfrac{1}{2}$ but a hole in the graph. There is a vertical asymptote at $x = 1$ since the denominator goes to zero for that value of x. Also, the function goes to zero for large values of x. Hence there is a horizontal asymptote at the x-axis.

(Rigorous) (Skill 7.4)

66. Ralph and Rhonda can paint a barn together in 4 hours. If Ralph needs 6 more hours than Rhonda to paint the barn by himself, how many hours does Rhonda need to paint the barn by herself?

A. 5

B. 6

C. 7

D. 8

Answer: B.

Let the number of hours Rhonda needs to paint the barn by herself be x. Then Ralph needs $x + 6$ hours to paint the barn by himself.

In 1 hour Rhonda paints $\frac{1}{x}$ of the barn and Ralph paints $\frac{1}{(x + 6)}$ of the barn.

In 4 hours Rhonda paints $\frac{4}{x}$ of the barn and Ralph paints $\frac{4}{(x + 6)}$ of the barn.

Since both of them together paint the whole barn in 4 hours, we can write

$$\frac{4}{x} + \frac{4}{x + 6} = 1$$
$$\rightarrow \frac{4x + 24 + 4x}{x(x + 6)} = 1$$
$$\rightarrow 8x + 24 = x^2 + 6x$$
$$\rightarrow x^2 - 2x - 24 = 0$$
$$\rightarrow (x - 6)(x + 4) = 0$$

The solutions to the above equation are $x = 6$, and $x = -4$. Since in this case we cannot have a negative answer, the number of hours Rhonda needs to paint the barn by herself is 6.

Measurement and Geometry

(Easy) (Skill 8.1)

67. 3 km is equivalent to:

A. 300 cm

B. 300 m

C. 3000 cm

D. 3000 m

Answer: D.

To change kilometers to meters, move the decimal 3 places to the right.

(Average) (Skill 8.1)

68. The speed of light in space is about 3×10^8 meters per second. Express this in kilometers per hour.

A. 1.08×10^9 km/hr

B. 3.0×10^{11} km/hr

C. 1.08×10^{12} km/hr

D. 1.08×10^{15} km/hr

Answer: A.

$$3 \times 10^8 \frac{m}{s} = 3 \times 10^8 \frac{m}{s} \times \frac{1\text{km}}{1000m} \times \frac{3600s}{1\text{ hr}}$$
$$= 108 \times 10^7 \frac{\text{km}}{\text{hr}} = 1.08 \times 10^9 \frac{\text{km}}{\text{hr}}$$

(Rigorous) (Skill 8.2)

69. If the area of the base of a cone is tripled, the volume will be

A. the same as the original

B. 9 times the original

C. 3 times the original

D. 3π times the original

Answer: C.

The formula for the volume of a cone is $V = \frac{1}{3}Bh$ where B is the area of the circular base and h is the height. If the area of the base is tripled, the volume becomes $V = \frac{1}{3}(3B)h = Bh$, or three times the original area.

(Average) (Skill 8.2)

70. Given similar polygons with corresponding sides 6 and 8, what is the area of the smaller polygon if the area of the larger is 64?

    A. 48

    B. 36

    C. 144

    D. 78

    Answer: B.

    In similar polygons, the areas are proportional to the squares of the sides.
    $$\frac{36}{64} = \frac{x}{64}$$

(Average) (Skill 8.2)

71. In similar polygons, if the perimeters are in a ratio of $x : y$, the sides are in a ratio of:

    A. $x : y$

    B. $x^2 : y^2$

    C. $2x : y$

    D. $\frac{1}{2}x : y$

    Answer: A.

    The sides are in the same ratio.

(Easy) (Skill 8.3)

72. Which word best describes a set of measured values that are all very similar but that all deviate significantly from the expected result?

    A. Perfect

    B. Precise

    C. Accurate

    D. Appropriate

    Answer: B.

A set of measurements that are close to the same value are precise. Measurements that are close to the actual (or expected) value are accurate. In this case, the set of measurements described in the question are best summarized as precise.

(Average) (Skill 8.3)

73. A man's waist measures 90 cm. What is the greatest possible error for the measurement?

    A. ± 1 m

    B. ± 8 cm

    C. ± 1 cm

    D. ± 5 mm

    Answer: D.

    The greatest possible error of measurement is always equal to one-half the smallest fraction of a unit on the measuring device.

(Average) (Skill 8.4)

74. Find the surface area of a box that is 3 feet wide, 5 feet tall, and 4 feet deep.

    A. 47 sq. ft.

    B. 60 sq. ft.

    C. 94 sq. ft.

    D. 188 sq. ft.

    Answer: C.

    Assume the base of the rectangular solid (box) is 3 by 4, and the height is 5. Then the surface area of the top and bottom together is $2(12) = 24$. The sum of the areas of the front and back are $2(15) = 30$, and the sum of the areas of the sides are $2(20) = 40$. The total surface area is therefore 94 square feet.

(Rigorous) (Skill 8.4)

75. Given a 30 meter by 60 meter garden with a circular fountain with a 5 meter radius, calculate the area of the portion of the garden not occupied by the fountain.

   A. 1,721 m²

   B. 1,879 m²

   C. 2,585 m²

   D. 1,015 m²

   Answer: A.

   Find the area of the garden and then subtract the area of the fountain: $30(60) - \pi(5)^2$ or approximately 1,721 square meters.

(Rigorous) (Skill 8.4)

76. The length of a picture frame is 2 inches greater than its width. If the area of the frame is 143 square inches, what is its width?

   A. 11 inches

   B. 13 inches

   C. 12 inches

   D. 10 inches

   Answer: A.

   First, set up the equation for the problem. If the width of the picture frame is w, then $w(w + 2) = 143$. Next, solve the equation to obtain w. Using the method of completing squares yields $w^2 + 2w + 1 = 144$; $(w + 1)^2 = 144$; $w + 1 = \pm 12$. Thus $w = 11$ or -13. Since the width cannot be negative, the correct answer is 11.

(Easy) (Skill 9.1)

77. Which of the following statements about an axiom is not true?

   A. An axiom is a self-evident statement.

   B. Axioms can be used to deduce theorems.

   C. An axiom can be proven.

   D. An axiom includes undefined terms.

   Answer: C.

   By definition axioms are self-evident statements that cannot be proven.

(Average) (Skill 9.2)

78. Which of the following statements about a trapezoid is incorrect?

   A. It has one pair of parallel sides

   B. The parallel sides are called bases

   C. If the two bases are the same length, the trapezoid is called isosceles

   D. The median is parallel to the bases

   Answer: C.

   A trapezoid is isosceles if the two legs (not bases) are the same length.

(Rigorous) (Skill 9.2)

79. What is the degree measure of an interior angle of a regular 10-sided polygon?

   A. 18°

   B. 36°

   C. 144°

   D. 54°

Answer: C.

The formula for finding the measure of each interior angle of a regular polygon with n sides is $\frac{(n-2)180}{n}$. For $n = 10$, $\frac{8(180)}{10} = 144$.

(Rigorous) (Skill 9.2)

80. What is the measure of minor arc AD, given that the measure of arc PS is $40°$ and $m < K = 10°$?

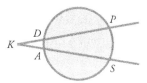

A. $50°$

B. $20°$

C. $30°$

D. $25°$

Answer: B.

The formula relating the measure of angle K and the two arcs it intercepts is $m\angle K = \frac{1}{2}(mPS - mAD)$. Substituting the known values yields $10 = \frac{1}{2}(40 - mAD)$. Solving for mAD gives an answer of 20 degrees.

(Rigorous) (Skill 9.3)

81. Ginny and Nick head back to their respective colleges after being home for the weekend. They leave their house at the same time and drive for 4 hours. Ginny drives due south at the average rate of 60 miles per hour and Nick drives due east at the average rate of 60 miles per hour. What is the straight-line distance between them, in miles, at the end of the 4 hours?

A. $120\sqrt{2}$

B. 240

C. $240\sqrt{2}$

D. 288

Answer: C.

Draw a picture.

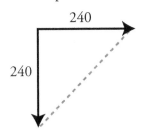

We have a right triangle, so we can use the Pythagorean Theorem to find the distance between the two points.

$240^2 + 240^2 = c^2$
$(2)240^2 = c^2$
$240\sqrt{2} = c^2$

(Average) (Skill 9.3)

82. If $AB = 12$, determine BC.

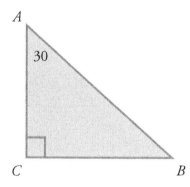

A. 6

B. 4

C. $6\sqrt{3}$

D. $3\sqrt{6}$

Answer: A.

In a 30-60-90 right triangle, the leg opposite the 30° angle is half the length of the hypotenuse.

(Average) (Skill 9.3)

83. If a ship sails due south 6 miles, then due west 8 miles, how far is it from the starting point?

A. 100 miles

B. 10 miles

C. 14 miles

D. 48 miles

Answer: B.

Draw a right triangle with legs of 6 and 8. Find the hypotenuse using the Pythagorean Theorem:
$6^2 + 8^2 = c^2 = 36 + 64 = 100$
Therefore, $c = 10$ miles.

(Easy) (Skill 9.4)

84. Which term most accurately describes two coplanar lines without any common points?

A. Perpendicular

B. Parallel

C. Intersecting

D. Skew

Answer: B.

By definition, parallel lines are coplanar lines without any common points.

(Average) (Skill 9.4)

85. Which theorem can be used to prove $\triangle BAK \cong \triangle MKA$?

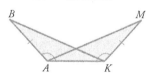

A. SSS

B. ASA

C. SAS

D. AAS

Answer: C.

Since side AK is common to both triangles, the triangles can be proved congruent by using the Side-Angle-Side Postulate.

(Average) (Skill 9.4)

86. Prove $\triangle HYM \cong \triangle KZL$, given $\overline{XZ} \cong \overline{XY}$, $\angle KLM \cong \angle HML$ and $\overline{YL} \cong \overline{MZ}$

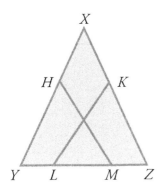

1. $\overline{XZ} \cong \overline{XY}$	1. Given
2. $\angle HYL \cong \angle KZM$	2. ?
3. $\angle KLM \cong \angle HML$	3. Given
4. $\overline{YL} \cong \overline{MZ}$	4. Given
5. $\overline{LM} \cong \overline{LM}$	5. ?
6. $\overline{YM} \cong \overline{LZ}$	6. Add
7. $\triangle HYM \cong \triangle KZL$	7. ASA

Which could be used to justify steps 2 and 5?

A. CPCTC, Identity

B. Isosceles Triangle Theorem, Identity

C. SAS, Reflexive

D. Isosceles Triangle Theorem, Reflexive

Answer: D.

The Isosceles Triangle Theorem states that the base angles are congruent, and the Reflexive property states that every segment is congruent to itself.

(Rigorous) (Skill 9.4)

87. **Which of the following statements is true about the number of degrees in each angle?**

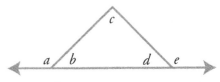

A. $a + b + c = 180°$

B. $a = e$

C. $b + c = e$

D. $c + d = e$

Answer: C.

In any triangle, an exterior angle is equal to the sum of the remote interior angles.

(Average) (Skill 10.2)

88. **Compute the distance from $(-2, 7)$ to the line $x = 5$.**

A. -9

B. -7

C. 5

D. 7

Answer: D.

The line $x = 5$ is a vertical line passing through $(5, 0)$ on the Cartesian plane. By observation, the distance along the horizontal line from the point $(-2, 7)$ to the line $x = 5$ is 7 units.

(Rigorous) (Skill 10.2)

89. Given $K(-4, y)$ and $M(2, -3)$ with midpoint $L(x, 1)$, determine the values of x and y.

    A. $x = -1, y = 5$

    B. $x = 3, y = 2$

    C. $x = 5, y = -1$

    D. $x = -1, y = -1$

    Answer: A.

    The formula for finding the midpoint (a, b) of a segment passing through the points (x_1, y_1) and (x_2, y_2) is $(a, b) = (\frac{x_1 + x_2}{2}, \frac{y_1 + y_2}{2})$. Setting up the corresponding equations from this information yields $x = \frac{-4 + 2}{2}$ and $1 = \frac{y - 3}{2}$. Solving for x and y yields $x = -1$ and $y = 5$.

(Rigorous) (Skill 10.2)

90. Line p has a negative slope and passes through the point $(0, 0)$. If line q is perpendicular to line p, which of the following must be true?

    A. Line q has a negative y-intercept.

    B. Line q passes through the point $(0, 0)$.

    C. Line q has a positive slope.

    D. Line q has a positive y-intercept.

Answer: C.

Draw a picture to help you visualize the problem.

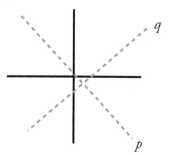

Choices (A) and (D) are not correct because line q could have a positive or a negative y-intercept. Choice (B) is incorrect because line q does not necessarily pass through $(0, 0)$. Since line q is perpendicular to line p, which has a negative slope, it must have a positive slope.

(Rigorous) (Skill 10.3)

91. Which equation represents a circle with a diameter whose endpoints are $(0, 7)$ and $(0, 3)$?

    A. $x^2 + y^2 + 21 = 0$

    B. $x^2 + y^2 - 10y + 21 = 0$

    C. $x^2 + y^2 - 10y + 9 = 0$

    D. $x^2 - y^2 - 10y + 9 = 0$

Answer: B.

With a diameter going from $(0, 7)$ to $(0, 3)$, the diameter of the circle must be 4, the radius must be 2, and the center of the circle must be at $(0, 5)$. Using the standard form for the equation of a circle, we get $(x - 0)^2 + (y - 5)^2 = 2^2$. Expanding yields $x^2 + y^2 - 10y + 21 = 0$.

(Average) (Skill 10.3)

92. The vertex for the parabola represented by $y = -x^2 + 4x - 1$ is given by the point

   A. (2, 5)

   B. (2, -5)

   C. (2, 3)

   D. (2, -3)

Answer: C.

Completing the square on the right hand side of the equation:

$y = -x^2 + 4x - 1 = -(x^2 - 4x + 4) + 3$
$= -(x - 2)^2 + 3$

Thus in the standard form for a parabola we have $y - 3 = (x - 2)^2$ and the vertex is given by (2, 3).

(Rigorous) (Skill 10.3)

93. Find the length of the major axis of $x^2 + 9y^2 = 36$.

   A. 4

   B. 6

   C. 12

   D. 8

Answer: C.

Dividing by 36 yields $\frac{x^2}{36} + \frac{y^2}{4} = 1$, which implies that the ellipse intersects the x-axis at 6 and -6. Therefore, the length of the major axis is 12. (The ellipse intersects the y-axis at 2 and -2.)

(Rigorous) (Skill 10.4)

94. What transformations have been applied to the function $f(x)$ shown below to obtain function $g(x)$?

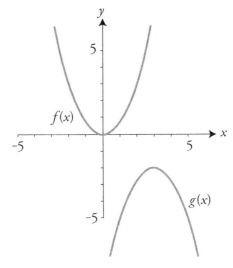

   A. Reflection over x-axis, translation 3 units to the right, translation 2 units down

   B. Translation 3 units to the right, translation 2 units down, reflection over x-axis

   C. Translation 2 units down, translation 3 units to the right, reflection over x-axis

   D. Reflection over y axis, translation 3 units to the right, translation 2 units down

Answer: A.

Notice that choices A, B, and C have the same transformations but in different order. Only A produces the correct answer.

95. A glide reflection involves

   A. A translation and dilation

   B. A reflection and dilation

   C. A translation and a reflection

   D. A reflection and a rotation

Answer: C.

A glide reflection involves a combined translation along and a reflection across a single specified line. The characteristic that defines a glide reflection as opposed to a simple combination of an arbitrary translation and arbitrary reflection is that the direction of translation is parallel with the line of reflection.

(Average) (Skill 10.5)

96. A point at (1, 2) on a Cartesian coordinate plane is translated two units to the left, reflected in the y-axis and then reflected in the x-axis. What is its final position?

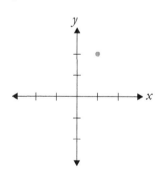

   A. (3, 2)

   B. (-1, 2)

   C. (-2, 1)

   D. (1, -2)

Answer: D.

After translation 2 units to the left, the point is at (-1, 2). After reflection in the y-axis, it is back in its original position (1, 2). After reflection in the x-axis it is at (1, -2).

Trigonometry and Calculus

(Average) (Skill 11.1)

97. Determine the measures of angles A and B.

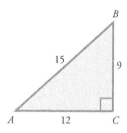

   A. $A = 30°, B = 60°$

   B. $A = 60°, B = 30°$

   C. $A = 53°, B = 37°$

   D. $A = 37°, B = 53°$

Answer: D.

It is the case that $\tan A = \frac{9}{12} = .75$ and $\tan^{-1} .75 = 37$ degrees. Since angle B is complementary to angle A, the measure of angle B is therefore 53 degrees.

(Average) (Skill 11.1)

98. For an acute angle x, sin x = 0.6. What is cot x?

   A. $\frac{5}{3}$

   B. 0.75

   C. 1.33

   D. 11

Answer: C.

Using the Pythagorean Identity, it is apparent that $\sin^2 x + \cos^2 x = 1$. Thus, $\cos x = \sqrt{1 - \frac{9}{25}} = \frac{4}{5}$ and $\cot x = \frac{\cos x}{\sin x} = \frac{4}{3}$.

(Easy) (Skill 11.3)

99. **Which of the following is a Pythagorean identity?**

    A. $\sin^2 \theta - \cos^2 \theta = 1$

    B. $\sin^2 \theta + \cos^2 \theta = 1$

    C. $\cos^2 \theta - \sin^2 \theta = 1$

    D. $\cos^2 \theta - \tan^2 \theta = 1$

Answer: B.

The Pythagorean identity $\sin^2 \theta + \cos^2 \theta = 1$ is derived from the definitions of the sine and cosine functions and Pythagorean Theorem of geometry.

(Average) (Skill 11.3)

100. **Which expression is not identical to $\sin x$?**

    A. $\sqrt{1 - \cos^2 x}$

    B. $\tan x \cos x$

    C. $\frac{1}{\csc x}$

    D. $\frac{1}{\sec x}$

Answer: D.

Using the basic definitions of the trigonometric functions and the Pythagorean identity, it can be seen that the first three options are all identical to $\sin x$. $\sec x = \frac{1}{\cos x}$ is not the same as $\sin x$.

(Average) (Skill 11.3)

101. **Which expression is equivalent to $1 - \sin^2 x$?**

    A. $1 - \cos^2 x$

    B. $1 + \cos^2 x$

    C. $\frac{1}{\sec x}$

    D. $\frac{1}{\sec^2 x}$

Answer: D.

Using the Pythagorean Identity, it is apparent that $\sin^2 x + \cos^2 x = 1$. Thus, $1 - \sin^2 x = \cos^2 x$, which by definition is equal to $\frac{1}{\sec^2 x}$.

(Rigorous) (Skill 11.3)

102. **The trigonometric expression $\frac{\tan \theta + \cot \theta}{\tan \theta}$ is identical to**

    A. $\sin^2 \theta$

    B. $\cos^2 \theta$

    C. $\sec^2 \theta$

    D. $\csc^2 \theta$

Answer: D.

$\frac{\tan \theta + \cot \theta}{\tan \theta} = 1 + \frac{\cot \theta}{\tan \theta} = 1 + \frac{1}{\tan^2 \theta} = 1 + \frac{\cos^2 \theta}{\sin^2 \theta} = \frac{\sin^2 \theta + \cos^2 \theta}{\sin^2 \theta} = \frac{1}{\sin^2 \theta} = \csc^2 \theta$

(Here we used the relationship $\cot \theta = \frac{1}{\tan \theta}$ and the Pythagorean indentity $\sin^2 \theta + \cos^2 \theta = 1$.)

(Rigorous) (Skill 11.3)

103. **Solve $2\cos x + 1 = 0$.**

    A. $\frac{2\pi}{3} + 2n\pi, \frac{4\pi}{3} + 2n\pi$ where n is an integer

    B. $\frac{2\pi}{3} + 2n\pi$ where n is an integer

    C. $\frac{2\pi}{3} + n\pi$ where n is an integer

    D. $\frac{\pi}{3} + 2n\pi$ where n is an integer

Answer: A.

Rearrange the equation to get $\cos x = \frac{-1}{2}$. Within the interval 0 to 2π, $\cos x = \frac{-1}{2}$ has two solutions $\frac{2\pi}{3}$ and $\frac{4\pi}{3}$. Since the cosine function is periodic, there are infinitely many solutions that can be written by adding $2n\pi$ to each of these two solutions.

(Rigorous) (Skill 11.5)

104. A boy tosses a ball at a velocity of 20m/s to his friend 20 m away. At what angle θ from the horizontal was the ball tossed given that the range of a projectile R $= \frac{1}{10}v^2 \sin 2\theta$ *m* where v is the initial velocity of the ball?

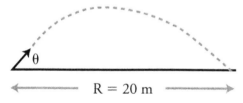

A. 20°

B. 15°

C. 30°

D. 25°

Answer: B.

Since the range of the ball is 20m, we can write

$$\frac{1}{10} 20^2 \sin 2\theta = 20$$
$$\rightarrow \sin 2\theta = \frac{200}{400} = \frac{1}{2}$$
$$\rightarrow 2\theta = \sin^{-1}\frac{1}{2} = 30°$$
$$\rightarrow \theta = 15°$$

(Easy) (Skill 12.1)

105. L'Hopital's rule provides a method to evaluate which of the following?

A. Limit of a function

B. Derivative of a function

C. Sum of an arithmetic series

D. Sum of a geometric series

Answer: A.

L'Hopital's rule is used to find the limit of a function by taking the derivatives of the numerator and denominator. Since the primary purpose of the rule is to find the limit, A is the correct answer.

(Average) (Skill 12.1)

106. Find the following limit: $\lim\limits_{x \to 2} \frac{x^2 - 4}{x - 2}$

A. 0

B. Infinity

C. 2

D. 4

Answer: D.

First, factor the numerator and cancel the common factor to get the limit.

$$\lim\limits_{x \to 2} \frac{x^2 - 4}{x - 2} = \lim\limits_{x \to 2} \frac{(x - 2)(x + 2)}{(x - 2)} =$$
$$\lim\limits_{x \to 2} (x + 2) = 4$$

(Rigorous) (Skill 12.1)

107. **Find the following limit:** $\lim\limits_{x\to 0} \frac{\sin 2x}{5x}$

  A. Infinity

  B. 0

  C. 0.4

  D. 1

Answer: C.

Since substituting $x = 0$ will give an undefined answer, we can use L'Hopital's rule and take derivatives of both the numerator and denominator to find the limit.

$$\lim\limits_{x\to 0} \frac{\sin 2x}{5x} = \lim\limits_{x\to 0} \frac{2\cos 2x}{5} = \frac{2}{5} = 0.4$$

(Rigorous) (Skill 12.1)

108. **Evaluate** $\lim\limits_{x\to 0} \frac{e^{3x} - 1}{2x}$.

  A. $-\frac{1}{2}$

  B. 0

  C. -1

  D. $\frac{3}{2}$

Answer: D.

Substituting $x = 0$ in the expression results in the indeterminate $\frac{0}{0}$. So we can use L'Hopital's rule and take derivatives of the numerator and denominator before substituting $x = 0$.

$$\lim\limits_{x\to 0} \frac{e^{3x} - 1}{2x} = \lim\limits_{x\to 0} \frac{3e^{3x}}{2} = \frac{3}{2}$$

(Rigorous) (Skill 12.3)

109. **The equation of the tangent line to the curve** $x^4 + x^2 + 1$ **at** $x = 1$ **is**

  A. $y = 6x + 3$

  B. $y = -6x + 3$

  C. $y = 6x - 3$

  D. $y = -6x - 3$

Answer: C.

The slope of the tangent line is the value of the derivative at $x = 1$.

$$\frac{d}{dx}(x^4 + x^2 + 1) = 4x^3 + 2x$$

At $x = 1$, the derivative and the slope of the tangent line is 6.

The tangent also touches the curve at the point $x = 1$ and $y = 1^4 + 1^2 + 1 = 3$.

Using this point, along with the slope, we can write the equation of the tangent line in the point-slope form as $(y - 3) = 6(x - 1)$

Rearranging the terms, $y - 3 = 6x - 6$ or $y = 6x - 3$.

(Rigorous) (Skill 12.3)

110. **Find the slope of the line tangent to** $y = 3x(\cos x)$ **at** $\left(\frac{\pi}{2}, \frac{\pi}{2}\right)$.

  A. $-\frac{3\pi}{2}$

  B. $\frac{3\pi}{2}$

  C. $\frac{\pi}{2}$

  D. $-\frac{\pi}{2}$

Answer: A.

To find the slope of the tangent line, find the derivative, and then evaluate it at $x = \frac{\pi}{2}$. $y' = 3x(-\sin x) + 3\cos x$. At the given value of x,

$$y' = 3\left(\frac{\pi}{2}\right)\left(-\sin\frac{\pi}{2}\right) + 3\cos x\frac{\pi}{2} = \frac{-3\pi}{2}.$$

(Rigorous) (Skill 12.3)

111. **Find the equation of the line tangent to** $y = 3x^2 - 5x$ **at** $(1, -2)$.

A. $y = x - 3$

B. $y = 1$

C. $y = x + 2$

D. $y = x$

Answer: A.

To find the slope of the tangent line, find the derivative, and then evaluate it at $x = 1$.

$y' = 6x - 5 = 6(1) - 5 = 1$. Then using point-slope form of the equation of a line, we get $y + 2 = 1(x - 1)$ or $y = x - 3$.

(Rigorous) (Skill 12.4)

112. **Find the first derivative of the function:** $f(x) = x^3 - 6x^2 + 5x + 4$

A. $3x^3 - 12x^2 + 5x$

B. $3x^2 - 12x^2 - 5$

C. $3x^2 - 12x^2 + 9$

D. $3x^2 - 12x^2 + 5$

Answer: D.

Use the Power Rule for polynomial differentiation: if $y = ax^n$, then $y' = nax^{n-1}$. Apply this rule to each term in the polynomial to yield the result in answer D.

(Rigorous) (Skill 12.5)

113. **Find the absolute maximum obtained by the function** $y = 2x^2 + 3x$ **on the interval** $x = 0$ **to** $x = 3$.

A. $-\frac{3}{4}$

B. $-\frac{4}{3}$

C. 0

D. 27

Answer: D.

Determine that $y' = 4x + 3$ and $y' = 0$ at $x = -\frac{3}{4}$. Therefore the critical point is at $x = -.75$. Since the critical point is not in the interval from $x = 0$ to $x = 3$, simply find the values of the function at the endpoints. The endpoints are $x = 0$, $y = 0$, and $x = 3$, $y = 27$. Therefore, 27 is the absolute maximum on the given interval.

(Average) (Skill 12.5)

114. **How does the function** $y = x^3 + x^2 + 4$ **behave from** $x = 1$ **to** $x = 3$?

A. Increasing, then decreasing

B. Increasing

C. Decreasing

D. Neither increasing nor decreasing

Answer: B.

To find critical points, take the derivative of the function and set it equal to 0, and solve for x.

$f'(x) = 3x^2 + 2x = x(3x + 2) = 0$

The critical points are at $x = 0$ and $x = -\frac{2}{3}$. Neither of these CPs is on the interval from $x = 1$ to $x = 3$. Testing the endpoints: at $x = 1$, $y = 6$, and at $x = 3$, $y = 38$. Since the derivative is positive for all values of x from $x = 1$ to $x = 3$, the curve is increasing on the entire interval.

(Rigorous) (Skill 12.6)

115. An open cylindrical container has a surface area of 5 square feet. What should be the radius r and height h of the container so that the volume is maximized?

   A. $r = 0.73, h = 0.73$

   B. $r = 1, h = 1$

   C. $r = 1, h = 0.5$

   D. $r = 0.67, h = 0.73$

Answer: A.

The surface area of the container is given by $\pi r^2 + 2\pi rh = 5$

The volume of the container $= \pi r^2 h$

In order to maximize the volume with respect to the radius r, express h in terms of r using the first equation and substitute in the expression for the volume.

$h = \dfrac{5 - \pi r^2}{2\pi r}$ and the volume

$V = \pi r^2 \dfrac{5 - \pi r^2}{2\pi r} = \dfrac{5r}{2} - \dfrac{\pi r^3}{2}$

Taking the derivative of the volume with respect to r and setting it to zero,

$\dfrac{dV}{dr} = \dfrac{5}{2} - \dfrac{3\pi r^2}{2} = 0$

$\rightarrow r^2 = \dfrac{5}{3\pi}$

$\rightarrow r = \sqrt{\dfrac{5}{3\pi}} = 0.73$

Substituting the value of r in the expression for h we get,

$h = \dfrac{5 - \pi r^2}{2\pi r} = \dfrac{5 - \dfrac{5}{3}}{2\pi \times 0.73} = \dfrac{10}{3 \times 2\pi \times 0.73}$
$= 0.73$

(Rigorous) (Skill 13.2)

116. Find the antiderivative for $4x^3 - 2x + 6 = y$

   A. $x^4 - x^2 + 6x + C$

   B. $x^4 - \dfrac{2}{3}x^3 + 6x + C$

   C. $12x^2 - 2 + C$

   D. $\dfrac{4}{3}x^4 - x^2 + 6x + C$

Answer: A.

Use the rule for polynomial integration: given ax^n, the antiderivative is $\dfrac{ax^{n+1}}{n+1}$. Apply this rule to each term in the polynomial to get the result in answer A.

(Rigorous) (Skill 13.2)

117. Find the antiderivative for the function $y = e^{3x}$.

   A. $3x(e^{3x}) + C$

   B. $3(e^{3x}) + C$

   C. $\dfrac{1}{3}(e^x) + C$

   D. $\dfrac{1}{3}(e^{3x}) + C$

Answer: D.

Use the rule for integration of functions of e ($\int e^x dx = e^x + C$) along with definition of a new variable $u = 3x$. The result is answer D.

(Rigorous) (Skill 13.2)

118. Evaluate: $\int_0^2 (x^2 + x - 1)dx$

   A. $\dfrac{11}{3}$

   B. $\dfrac{8}{3}$

   C. $-\dfrac{8}{3}$

   D. $-\dfrac{11}{3}$

Answer: B.

Use the fundamental theorem of calculus to find the definite integral: given a continuous function f on an interval $[a, b]$, then $\int_a^b f(x)dx = F(b) - F(a)$, where F is an antiderivative of f.

$\int_0^2 (x^2 + x - 1)dx = (\frac{x^3}{3} + \frac{x^2}{2} - x)$

Evaluate the expression at $x = 2$, at $x = 0$, and then subtract to get $\frac{8}{3} + \frac{4}{2} - 2 - 0 = \frac{8}{3}$.

(Average) (Skill 13.2)

119. Evaluate: $\int_1^2 (3x^2 + \frac{1}{x^2})dx$

A. 12.25

B. 7.5

C. 8.25

D. 5.5

Answer: B.

$\int_1^2 (3x^2 + \frac{1}{x^2})dx = 3 \cdot \frac{1}{3}x^3 - \frac{1}{x} \Big|_1^2 =$
$2^3 - \frac{1}{2} - (1 - 1) = 8 - 0.5 = 7.5$

(Average) (Skill 13.3)

120. Find the area under the function $y = x^2 + 4$ from $x = 3$ to $x = 6$.

A. 75

B. 21

C. 96

D. 57

Answer: A.

To find the area, set up the definite integral: $\int_3^6 (x^2 + 4)dx = (\frac{x^3}{3} + 4x)_3^6$. Evaluate the expression at $x = 6$ and $x = 3$ to get $(\frac{x^3}{3} + 4x)_3^6 = \frac{6^3}{3} + 4(6) - \left[\frac{3^3}{3} + 4(3)\right] = 72 + 24 - 9 - 12 = 75$. The correct answer is A.

(Average) (Skill 13.4)

121. If the velocity of a body is given by $v = 16 - t^2$, find the distance traveled from $t = 0$ until the body comes to a complete stop.

A. 16

B. 43

C. 48

D. 64

Answer: B.

Recall that the derivative of the distance function is the velocity function. Conversely, the integral of the velocity function is the distance function. To find the time needed for the body to come to a stop when $v = 0$, solve for t:

$v(t) = 16 - t^2 = 0$

$t = 4$

Thus, the body travels from time $t = 0$ to time $t = 4$. The distance function (excluding the constant of integration, which is unneeded here) is

$s(t) = \int v(t)\,dt = 16t - \frac{t^3}{3}$.

At $t = 4$,

$s(4) = 16(4) - \frac{4^3}{3} = \frac{128}{3} \approx 42.7$.

The body travels approximately 42.7 units.

(Rigorous) (Skill 13.4)

122. A ball is thrown up with an initial velocity of 15m/s. The acceleration due to gravity (about 10 m/s²) slows it down until it stops and falls back to the ground. At any time *t* after the ball is thrown, the velocity *v* and the distance traveled upwards *s* are given by

A. $v = 15 + 10t; s = 15t + 5t^2$

B. $v = 15 - 10t; s = 15t - 5t^2$

C. $v = 15 - 10t; s = 15t - 10t^2$

D. $v = 10t; s = 10t^2$

Answer: B.

Note that the acceleration *a* is negative since it acts in the direction opposite to the direction of motion and slows the ball down. Also recall that the velocity is the antiderivative of the acceleration and distance is the antiderivative of the velocity.

Hence velocity $v = \int a\, dt = \int -10\, dt = -10t + c$, where *c* is a constant that has to be determined. Since the initial velocity at time $t = 0$ is 15m/s, substituting $v = 15$ and $t = 0$ in the above equation we get $15 = 0 + c$.

Hence $c = 15$ and $v = -10t + 15 = 15 - 10t$.

The distance traveled $s = \int v\, dt = \int (15 - 10t)\, dt = 15t - 10\left(\frac{1}{2}t^2\right) + \text{constant}$.

Since the initial distance at $t = 0$ is $s = 0$, the constant in the above equation is also zero.

Hence $s = 15t - 5t^2$.

Statistics, Probability, and Discrete Mathematics

(Easy) (Skill 14.1)

123. What conclusion can be drawn from the graph below?

MLK Elementary School
Student Enrollment

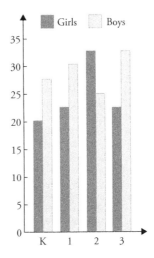

A. The number of students in first grade exceeds the number in second grade

B. There are more boys than girls in the entire school

C. There are more girls than boys in the first grade

D. Third grade has the largest number of students

Answer: B.

In Kindergarten, first grade, and third grade, there are more boys than girls. The number of extra girls in grade two is more than compensated by the extra boys in all the other grades put together.

(Easy) (Skill 14.1)

124. The pie chart below shows sales at an automobile dealership for the first four months of a year. What percentage of the vehicles were sold in April?

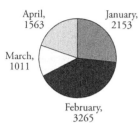

April, 1563   January, 2153
March, 1011
February, 3265

A. More than 50%

B. Less than 25%

C. Between 25% and 50%

D. None

Answer: B.

It is clear from the chart that the April segment covers less than a quarter of the pie.

(Easy) (Skill 14.1)

125. Which statement is true about George's budget?

A. George spends the greatest portion of his income on food

B. George spends twice as much on utilities as he does on his mortgage

C. George spends twice as much on utilities as he does on food

D. George spends the same amount on food and utilities as he does on mortgage

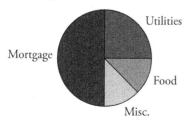

Utilities
Mortgage
Food
Misc.

Answer: C.

(Average) (Skill 14.1)

126. Which type of graph uses symbols to represent quantities?

A. Bar graph

B. Line graph

C. Pictograph

D. Circle graph

Answer: C.

A pictograph shows a comparison of quantities using symbols. Each symbol represents a number of items.

(Average) (Skill 14.2)

127. Linear least squares regression is performed on a data set and the correlation coefficient is found to be 0.98. This implies that the quality of fit is:

A. Poor

B. Fair

C. Good

D. Excellent

Answer: D.

The value of the correlation coefficient ranges from zero (for a poor fit) to one (for a perfect fit).

(Easy) (Skill 14.2)

128. The following stem and leaf plot shows rainfall data in inches over several consecutive days. What is the median value?

0	7
1	3 9
2	1 5 7 8
3	0 3 4 6 6 9
4	3 5 5 7 8
5	0 0 3 5
10	3

A. 3.6 in

B. 3.9 in

C. 4.3 in

D. 3.4 in

Answer: A.

Since there are 23 data points, the median or middle value is the 12th one.

(Easy) (Skill 14.3)

129. Compute the median for the following data set:

{12, 19, 13, 16, 17, 14}

A. 14.5

B. 15.17

C. 15

D. 16

Answer: C.

Arrange the data in ascending order: 12, 13, 14, 16, 17, 19. The median is the middle value in a list with an odd number of entries. When there is an even number of entries, the median is the mean of the two center entries. Here the average of 14 and 16 is 15.

(Rigorous) (Skill 14.3)

130. Half the students in a class scored 80% on an exam, and most of the rest scored 85%, except for one student who scored 10%. Which would be the best measure of central tendency for the test scores?

A. Mean

B. Median

C. Mode

D. Either the median or the mode because they are equal

Answer: B.

In this set of data, the median is the most representative measure of central tendency because the median is independent of extreme values. Because of the 10% outlier, the mean (average) would be disproportionately skewed. In this data set, it is true that the median and the mode (number which occurs most often) are the same, but the median remains the best choice because of its special properties.

(Rigorous) (Skill 14.3)

131. The probability density function for an exponential distribution is given by $f(x) = 2e^{-2x}; x \geq 0$. What is the median value for the variable x?

A. 0.35

B. 0.5

C. 2.0

D. 0.45

Answer: A.

The integral of the probability distribution function to the upper limit of the median value is equal to $\frac{1}{2}$.

If the median value is $x = a$,

$\int_0^a 2e^{-2x}dx = \frac{1}{2}$

$\rightarrow -[e^{-2x}]_0^a = \frac{1}{2}$

$\rightarrow 1 - e^{-2a} = \frac{1}{2}$

$\rightarrow e^{-2a} = \frac{1}{2}$

$\rightarrow -2a = \ln\left(\frac{1}{2}\right)$

$\rightarrow a = 0.35$

(Rigorous) (Skill 14.3)

132. Compute the standard deviation for the following set of temperatures:

(37, 38, 35, 37, 38, 40, 36, 39)

A. 37.5

B. 1.5

C. 0.5

D. 2.5

Answer: B.

First find the mean: $\frac{300}{8} = 37.5$. Then, using the formula for standard deviation yields

$$\sqrt{\frac{2(37.5 - 37)^2 + 2(37.5 - 38)^2 + (37.5 - 35)^2 + (37.5 - 40)^2 + (37.5 - 36)^2 + (37.5 - 39)^2}{8}}$$

This expression has a value of 1.5.

(Easy) (Skill 14.4)

133. Systematic random sampling involves

A. choosing items arbitrarily and in an unstructured manner

B. targeting a particular section of the population

C. the collection of a sample at defined intervals

D. proportional sampling from subgroups

Answer: C.

Systematic random sampling involves the collection of a sample at defined intervals (for instance, every tenth part to come off a manufacturing line). Here, it is assumed that the population is ordered randomly and there is no hidden pattern that may compromise the randomness of the sampling.

(Easy) (Skill 15.1)

134. A jar contains 3 red marbles, 5 white marbles, 1 green marble, and 15 blue marbles. If one marble is picked at random from the jar, what is the probability that it will be red?

A. $\frac{1}{3}$

B. $\frac{1}{8}$

C. $\frac{3}{8}$

D. $\frac{1}{24}$

Answer: B.

The total number of marbles is 24 and the number of red marbles is 3. Thus the probability of picking a red marble from the jar is $\frac{3}{24} = \frac{1}{8}$.

(Easy) (Skill 15.1)

135. If a horse will probably win three races out of ten, what are the odds that he will win?

A. 3:10

B. 7:10

C. 3:7

D. 7:3

Answer: C.

There are 3 chances that the horse will win to 7 chances that he will not.

(Average) (Skill 15.2)

136. A sack of candy has 3 peppermints, 2 butterscotch drops, and 3 cinnamon drops. One candy is drawn and replaced, then another candy is drawn; what is the probability that both will be butterscotch?

A. $\frac{1}{2}$

B. $\frac{1}{28}$

C. $\frac{1}{4}$

D. $\frac{1}{16}$

Answer: D.

With replacement, the probability of obtaining a butterscotch on the first draw is $\frac{2}{8}$ and the probability of drawing a butterscotch on the second draw is also $\frac{2}{8}$. Multiply and reduce to lowest terms.

(Rigorous) (Skill 15.2)

137. A die is rolled several times. What is the probability that a 3 will not appear before the third roll of the die?

A. $\frac{1}{3}$

B. $\frac{25}{216}$

C. $\frac{25}{36}$

D. $\frac{1}{216}$

Answer: B.

The probability that a 3 will not appear before the third roll is the same as the probability that the first two rolls will consist of numbers other than 3. Since the probability of any one roll resulting in a number other than 3 is $\frac{5}{6}$, the probability of the first two rolls resulting in a number other than 3 is $\left(\frac{5}{6}\right) \times \left(\frac{5}{6}\right) = \frac{25}{36}$. Then multiply the probability of rolling something other than a 3 twice with the probability of rolling a 3: $\frac{25}{36} \times \frac{1}{6} = \frac{25}{216}$

(Rigorous) (Skill 15.2)

138. If there are three people in a room, what is the probability that at least two of them will share a birthday? (Assume a year has 365 days.)

A. 0.67

B. 0.05

C. 0.008

D. 0.33

Answer: C.

The best way to approach this problem is to use the fact that the probability of an event plus the probability of the event not happening is unity. First, find the probability that no two people will share a birthday, and then subtract that value from 1. The probability that two of the people will not share a birthday is $\frac{364}{365}$ (since the second person's birthday can be one of the 364 days other than the birthday of the first person). The probability that the third person will also not share either of the first two birthdays is $\left(\frac{364}{365}\right)\left(\frac{363}{365}\right) = 0.992$. Therefore, the probability that at least two people will share a birthday is $1 - 0.992 = 0.008$.

(Rigorous) (Skill 15.3)

139. A circular disc of radius 1 ft is placed on a 6 ft by 6 ft square table. The center of the disc may be placed on any point on the table top. What is the probability that the entire disk will be on top of the table without any portion hanging over the edge?

A. $\frac{4}{9}$

B. $\frac{25}{36}$

C. $\frac{1}{2}$

D. $\frac{16}{25}$

Answer: A.

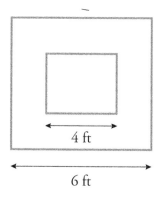

4 ft

6 ft

The disk will stay entirely on top of the table if the center is placed at least 1 ft away from each edge. Therefore the center must be within a square of side

4 ft in the middle of the table. Thus the probability of the disc lying entirely on the table top $= \frac{\text{area of 4 ft square}}{\text{area of 6 ft square}} = \frac{16}{36} = \frac{4}{9}$.

(Average) (Skill 16.1)

140. A school has 15 male teachers and 35 female teachers. In how many ways can they form a committee with 2 male teachers and 4 female teachers on it?

A. 525

B. 5,497,800

C. 88

D. 263,894,400

Answer: B.

The number of ways one can pick 2 male teachers out of $15 = {}^{15}_{2}C = \frac{15!}{13!2!} = \frac{14 \times 15}{2} = 105$

The number of ways one can pick 4 male teachers out of $35 = {}^{35}_{4}C = \frac{35!}{31!4!} = \frac{32 \times 33 \times 34 \times 35}{2 \times 3 \times 4} = 52360$

Hence, the total number of ways the committee can be chosen $= 105 \times 52360 = 5497800$

(Average) (Skill 16.2)

141. Which of the following is a recursive definition of the sequence {1, 2, 2, 4, 8, 32, ...}?

A. $N_i = 2N_{i-1}$

B. $N_i = 2N_{i-2}$

C. $N_i = N^2_{i-1}$

D. $N_i = N_{i-1}N_{i-2}$

Answer: D.

Test each answer, or look at the pattern of the numbers in the sequence. Note that each number (with the exception of the first two) is the product of the preceding two numbers. In recursive form using index i, the expression is $N_i = N_{i-1}N_{i-2}$ and the correct answer is D.

(Average) (Skill 16.2)

142. **What is the sum of the first 20 terms of the geometric sequence (2, 4, 8, 16, 32, …)?**

    A. 2,097,150

    B. 1,048,575

    C. 524,288

    D. 1,048,576

Answer: A.

For a geometric sequence a, ar, ar^2, … , ar^n, the sum of the first n terms is given by $\frac{a(r^n - 1)}{r - 1}$. In this case, $a = 2$ and $r = 2$. Thus, the sum of the first 20 terms of the sequence is $\frac{2(2^{20} - 1)}{2 - 1} = 2,097,150$.

(Rigorous) (Skill 16.2)

143. **Find the sum of the first one hundred terms in the progression.**

    (−6, −2, 2, …)

    A. 19,200

    B. 19,400

    C. −604

    D. 604

Answer: A.

Examine the pattern of the sequence. To find the 100th term, use the following expression:

$t100 = -6 + 99(4) = 390$

To find the sum of the first 100 terms, use

$$S = \frac{100}{2}(-6 + 390) = 19200$$

(Average) (Skill 16.2)

144. **{1, 4, 7, 10, . . .}**

    What is the 40th term in this sequence?

    A. 43

    B. 121

    C. 118

    D. 120

Answer: C.

Examine the pattern of the sequence. To find the 40th term, use the following expression:

$t40 = 1 + 39(3) = 118$

(Easy) (Skill 16.3)

145. **The scalar multiplication of the number 3 with the matrix $\begin{pmatrix} 2 & 1 \\ 3 & 5 \end{pmatrix}$ yields:**

    A. 33

    B. $\begin{pmatrix} 6 & 1 \\ 9 & 5 \end{pmatrix}$

    C. $\begin{pmatrix} 2 & 3 \\ 3 & 15 \end{pmatrix}$

    D. $\begin{pmatrix} 6 & 3 \\ 9 & 15 \end{pmatrix}$

Answer: D.

In scalar multiplication of a matrix by a number, each element of the matrix is multiplied by that number.

(Easy) (Skill 16.3)

146. Find the sum of the following matrices.

$$\begin{pmatrix} 6 & 3 \\ 9 & 15 \end{pmatrix} + \begin{pmatrix} 4 & 7 \\ 1 & 0 \end{pmatrix}$$

A. $\begin{pmatrix} 10 & 10 \\ 10 & 15 \end{pmatrix}$

B. $\begin{pmatrix} 13 & 7 \\ 9 & 16 \end{pmatrix}$

C. 45

D. $\begin{pmatrix} 20 \\ 25 \end{pmatrix}$

Answer: A.

Two matrices with the same dimensions are added by adding the corresponding elements. In this case, element 1, 1 (i.e. row 1, column 1) of the first matrix is added to element 1, 1 of the second matrix; element 2, 1 of the first matrix is added to element 2, 1 of the second matrix; and so on for all four elements.

(Average) (Skill 16.3)

147. The product of two matrices can be found only if:

A. The number of rows in the first matrix is equal to the number of rows in the second matrix

B. The number of columns in the first matrix is equal to the number of columns in the second matrix

C. The number of columns in the first matrix is equal to the number of rows in the second matrix

D. The number of rows in the first matrix is equal to the number of columns in the second matrix

Answer: C.

The number of columns in the first matrix must equal the number of rows in the second matrix because the process of multiplication involves multiplying the elements of every row of the first matrix with corresponding elements of every column of the second matrix.

(Rigorous) (Skill 16.3)

148. Evaluate the following matrix product

$$\begin{pmatrix} 2 & 1 & 3 \\ 2 & 2 & 4 \end{pmatrix} \begin{pmatrix} 6 & 5 \\ 2 & 1 \\ 2 & 7 \end{pmatrix}$$

A. $\begin{pmatrix} 20 & 32 & 24 \\ 24 & 40 & 48 \end{pmatrix}$

B. $\begin{pmatrix} 20 & 32 \\ 40 & 24 \\ 24 & 48 \end{pmatrix}$

C. 116

D. $\begin{pmatrix} 20 & 32 \\ 24 & 40 \end{pmatrix}$

Answer: D.

The product of a 2 × 3 matrix with a 3 × 2 matrix is a 2 × 2 matrix. This alone should be enough to identify the correct answer. Each term in the 2 × 2 matrix is calculated as described below.

Matrix 1, row 1 multiplied by matrix 2, column 1 yields entry 1, 1: $2 \times 6 + 1 \times 2 + 3 \times 2 = 12 + 2 + 6 = 20$.

Matrix 1, row 1 multiplied by matrix 2, column 2 yields entry 1, 2: $2 \times 5 + 1 \times 1 + 3 \times 7 = 10 + 1 + 21 = 32$.

Matrix 1, row 2 multiplied by matrix 2, column 1 yields entry 2, 1: $2 \times 6 + 2 \times 2 + 4 \times 2 = 12 + 4 + 8 = 24$.

Matrix 1, row 2 multiplied by matrix 2, column 2 yields entry 2, 2: $2 \times 5 + 2 \times$

$$1 + 4 \times 7 = 10 + 2 + 28 = 40.$$

(Average) (Skill 16.3)

149. Given a vector with horizontal component 5 and vertical component 6, determine the length of the vector.

    A. 61

    B. $\sqrt{61}$

    C. 30

    D. $\sqrt{30}$

Answer: B.

Using the Pythagorean Theorem, we get a length of $\sqrt{36 + 25} = \sqrt{61}$.

(Average) (Skill 16.4)

150. Determine the number of subsets of set K. $K = \{4, 5, 6, 7\}$

    A. 15

    B. 16

    C. 17

    D. 18

Answer: B.

A set of n objects has n^2 subsets. Therefore, here we have $4^2 = 16$ subsets. These subsets include four which each have 1 element only, six which each have 2 elements, four which each have 3 elements, plus the original set, and the empty set.

CPSIA information can be obtained
at www.ICGtesting.com
Printed in the USA
BVOW09s2337011217
501711BV00025B/1360/P